"Since the 2008 economic crisis, neo-liberal capitalism has intensified its onslaught on nature through accelerating resource extraction and privatizing the commons of nature. This book demonstrates exquisitely the havoc wrought by these infernal dynamics and charts possible terrains for thought and action that could lead to a more just and equitable society-nature relationship. A must read for all concerned with the dwindling rights of nature."

– Erik Swyngedouw, *University of Manchester, UK*

"This timely book offers an unprecedented synthesis of cutting-edge research and grassroots activism in pursuit of progressive environmentalism. An exemplar of radical praxis, it will be indispensable for scholars in a wide range of fields as well as activists and policymakers seeking greater conceptual clarity in their work."

– Robert Fletcher, *Wageningen University, The Netherlands*

"A much-needed and compelling account of how the alliance between critical scholarship and social struggles can radically reconfigure environmental policies worldwide. This book makes an outstanding contribution to research engaged in understanding, and supporting, alternatives to the neoliberal agenda."

– Stefania Barca, Center for Social Studies, *University of Coimbra, Portugal*

THE RIGHT TO NATURE

Since the 2008 financial crash the expansion of neoliberalism has had an enormous impact on nature–society relations around the world. In response, various environmental movements have emerged opposing the neoliberal restructuring of environmental policies using arguments that often bridge traditional divisions between the environmental and labour agendas.

The Right to Nature explores the differing experiences of a number of environmental-social movements and struggles from the point of view of both activists and academics. This collection attempts to both document the social-ecological impacts of neoliberal attempts to exploit non-human nature in the post-crisis context and to analyse the opposition of emerging environmental movements and their demands for a radically different production of nature based on social needs and environmental justice. It also provides a necessary space for the exchange of ideas and experiences between academics and activists and aims to motivate further academic-activist collaborations around alternative and counter-hegemonic re-thinking of environmental politics.

This book will be of great interest to students, scholars and activists interested in environmental policy, environmental justice, social and environmental movements, and radical alternatives to capitalism.

Elia Apostolopoulou is a Lecturer at the University of Cambridge, UK.

Jose A. Cortes-Vazquez is an InTalent Postdoctoral Researcher at the University of A Coruña, Spain.

Routledge Studies in Environmental Policy

For more information about this series, please visit: https://www.routledge.com/
Routledge-Studies-in-Environmental-Policy/book-series/RSEP

THE RIGHT TO NATURE

Social Movements, Environmental Justice and Neoliberal Natures

Edited by
Elia Apostolopoulou and
Jose A. Cortes-Vazquez

Routledge
Taylor & Francis Group

LONDON AND NEW YORK

First published 2019
by Routledge
2 Park Square, Milton Park, Abingdon, Oxon OX14 4RN

and by Routledge
52 Vanderbilt Avenue, New York, NY 10017

Routledge is an imprint of the Taylor & Francis Group, an informa business

British Library Cataloguing-in-Publication Data
A catalogue record for this book is available from the British Library

Library of Congress Cataloging-in-Publication Data
Names: Apostolopoulou, Elia, editor. | Cortes-Vazquez, Jose A., editor.
Title: The right to nature : social movements, environmental justice and neoliberal natures / edited by Elia Apostolopoulou and Jose A. Cortes-Vazquez.
Description: Abingdon, Oxon ; New York, NY : Routledge, 2019. | Series: Routledge studies in environmental policy | Includes bibliographical references and index.
Identifiers: LCCN 2018037538 (print) | LCCN 2018051162 (ebook) | ISBN 9780429427145 (eBook) | ISBN 9781138385351 (hbk) | ISBN 9781138385375 (pbk) | ISBN 9780429427145 (ebk)
Subjects: LCSH: Environmentalism—Case studies. | Social movements—Case studies. | Environmental justice—Case studies. | Conservation of natural resources—Social aspects—Case studies. | Neoliberalism—Case studies. | Economic policy—Environmental aspects—Case studies. | Environmental policy—Economic aspects—Case studies.
Classification: LCC GE195 (ebook) | LCC GE195 .R55 2019 (print) | DDC 363.7—dc23
LC record available at https://lccn.loc.gov/2018037538

ISBN: 978-1-138-38535-1 (hbk)
ISBN: 978-1-138-38537-5 (pbk)
ISBN: 978-0-429-42714-5 (ebk)

Typeset in Bembo
by Apex CoVantage, LLC

MIX
Paper from
responsible sources
FSC
www.fsc.org   FSC® C013056

Printed and bound in Great Britain by
TJ International Ltd, Padstow, Cornwall

CONTENTS

TABLES

FIGURES

BOXES

CONTRIBUTOR BIOGRAPHIES

Elia Apostolopoulou is a political ecologist and her main research interest is the investigation of nature–society relationships in capitalism. She is currently a lecturer in the Department of Geography, University of Cambridge. Elia's research is guided by radical geographical research on the neoliberalization of nature, on the historical-geographic conception of neoliberalism, on uneven development and the capitalist production of nature and space, as well as by Marxist political economy and especially the Marxian theory of value and rent. At present, her research mainly focuses on neoliberal conservation in post-crisis Europe with an emphasis on free market environmentalism, on the links between biodiversity offsetting and extended urbanization and on the exploration of environmental movements in the post-crisis era with an emphasis on the right to the city and how it can be linked to the right to nature.

Sam Beck is senior lecturer in the College of Human Ecology and director of the Urban Semester Program at Cornell University. His publications include *Manny Almeida's Ringside Lounge: The Cape Verdean Struggle for Their Neighborhood* (1992), *Toward Engaged Anthropology* (2013), ed. with Carl A. Maida, and *Public Anthropology in a Borderless World* (2015), ed. with Carl A. Maida.

Sandra Bell has worked for Friends of the Earth England, Wales and Northern Ireland for 18 years on a range of campaigns and issues ranging from supermarket power, sustainable livestock and pesticides to the Nature's Keepers project and the EU wide campaign to save the Nature Directives. She is currently working on the Bee Cause campaign, which worked with key allies to secure a National Pollinator Strategy in the UK, and, more recently, the UK's commitment to toughen restrictions on bee-harming pesticides.

Alfred Burballa-Noria is a PhD candidate at the University of Ulster at the Department of Criminology, Politics and Social Policy. His research interests include the fields of political ecology and urban politics, in particular the subject of megaprojects, which was the topic of his thesis. On a voluntary/activist basis he has contributed to the EJOLT (Environmental Justice Organizations, Liabilities and Justice) research project.

Charlotte Christiaens has a master's degree in Social and Cultural Anthropology. She has been working for CATAPA since 2007, first on a voluntary basis, and as a coordinator since 2011. She has done research on the social and ecological impact of open-pit mining on local communities in Latin America (in Bolivia, Peru, Guatemala and Colombia), and also in Greece. She also did research on fair trade artisanal small-scale mines in Peru.

Citizens' Coordinating Committee of Ierissos against Gold-copper Mining consider more relevant to apply a relational biographical note in place of a more traditional one. In order to jointly reflect upon the social challenges our community – and our world – faces, we find it enriching to pool together our individual resources and draw from our diverse experiences, viewpoints and educational backgrounds in social and environmental sciences. It is a feeling of being deeply rooted in both the practice of critical thinking, and the land we belong to, that inspires the dialogue we are engaged in, as community members of the SOS Halkidiki movement against the expansion of the extractive industry in Northeastern Halkidiki, Greece.

Jose A. Cortes-Vazquez is a social anthropologist currently employed as InTalent research fellow at the Department of Sociology and Communication Sciences, University of A Coruña, Spain. He has done research on the political and historical dimensions of nature–society relations and the critical examination of sustainability, participatory conservation policies and centre–periphery relations within the EU as these are performed in natural protected areas in Spain and Ireland. He has also contributed to the political ecology of environmental discourses and neorural movements in Spain. At present, he is engaged in a detailed examination of the neoliberalization of environmental governance in post-crisis Europe through the study of the roll-back of the state from nature conservation and the roll-out of new institutions and market mechanisms.

Ioana Florea is part of grassroots platforms such as The Common Front for Housing Rights (fcdl.ro), Political Art Gazette (artapolitica.ro) and Quantic Association in Bucharest. For the last ten years she has been involved in environmental and social justice education and actions. She also works in participatory research projects on social inequality, social history, urban transformations and social struggles. She is interested in collaborative learning, especially on emancipatory practices and processes in the region and elsewhere.

Mary Gearey is senior research fellow at the University of Brighton's School of Environment and Technology. Mary undertakes empirical qualitative fieldwork to explore the corresponding relationships between practices of community resilience and water resources policy, planning and management in the context of sustainable futures. Her current work focuses on the following areas: community responses to changing water environments; ecological infrastructure from a social–ecological systems resilience perspective; socio-political dimensions of integrated water resource management; and transition pathways towards sustainable water futures. Her work is critically engaged with understanding how developed economies organize and manage their freshwater resources with regards to transitioning towards sustainable futures in the context of climate change.

Mario Hernandez-Trejo is a doctoral researcher in Human Geography at the Geography Department, the University of Manchester. He completed a BA in Social Anthropology at the Universidad Autónoma Metropolitana (Mexico City), where he engaged in applied research projects to support local development and organization in rural communities from Oaxaca, Mexico. He holds an MA in Environment and Development at the University of Manchester. His current research interests are situated at the relationship between land rent, environmental change and the state space.

Mumta Ito is the founder of the international non-governmental organization (NGO) Nature's Rights and initiator of a European Citizens Initiative to put rights of nature on the EU legislative agenda. A former structured finance lawyer with top-ranking global law firm Clifford Chance, Mumta set up an NGO in the Caribbean to create a people's' movement to save an island of global ecological importance and bring about legislative change. She is an expert and advocate for rights of nature, advisor to the United Nations (UN) General Assembly as European Continental level facilitator of the UN Harmony with Nature Knowledge Network Expert Dialogues and convenor of the UK Environmental Law Association Wild Law group.

Les Levidow is a senior research fellow at the Open University, UK, where he has been studying agri-environmental-technology issues since the 1980s. He is co-author of two books: *Governing the Transatlantic Conflict over Agricultural Biotechnology: Contending Coalitions, Trade Liberalisation and Standard Setting* (Routledge, 2006) and *GM Food on Trial: Testing European Democracy* (Routledge, 2010). He is also editor of the journal *Science as Culture*.

Julyan Levy is an interdisciplinary ethnographer with a background in anthropology, political ecology and human geography. His current research interests include agroecological practices, the anthropology of community and human–cannabis relationships across scale.

Julia Loginova is a PhD candidate at the University of Melbourne in Australia. In her PhD thesis, Julia explores justice implications of climate change and expanding resource extraction activities in northern Russia. In particular, she is interested to understand the role of socio-environmental movements and local communities in "extracting" justice in cross-scale natural resource and climate change politics.

Lucy Mears has an MSc in Gender and International Relations, and has experience working on issues including sustainable development, global health in the context of human immunodeficiency virus (HIV)/acquired immune deficiency syndrome (AIDS), sex work and education. Her key research interests range from eco-feminism to gender and sexuality studies.

Massimiliano Montini is professor of European Union Law at the University of Siena (Italy), where he teaches EU Law and Sustainable Development Law, and is co-director of the Research Group R4S (Regulation for Sustainability). He is a life-member of Clare Hall College and a fellow of C-EENRG Research Centre at the University of Cambridge (UK). Moreover, he is a co-founder and current vice-chair of the Ecological Law and Governance Association (ELGA) and a member of several scientific networks, including: UN Knowledge Network "Harmony with Nature", the International Union for Conservation of Nature (IUCN) World Commission on Environmental Law, Avosetta, Nature's Rights, Girls Education Initiative of Ghana (GEIG), and Climate Strategies.

Leo Name holds a degree in Architecture and Urbanism from Federal University of Rio de Janeiro (Universidade Federal do Rio de Janeiro) (UFRJ) (Rio de Janeiro, Brazil) and master and doctoral degrees in Geography from the same university. From 2008 to 2013, he was lecturer in Geography at Pontical Catholic University of Rio de Janeiro (Pontifícia Universidade Católica do Rio de Janeiro) (PUC-Rio) (Rio de Janeiro, Brazil) and since 2014 he is lecturer in Architecture and Urbanism at Interdisciplinary Center of Territory, Architecture and Design, Federal University of Latin-American Integration.

Camila Nobrega Rabello Alves is a journalist and an academic researcher from Rio de Janeiro, Brazil. She has written for local and international media outlets in the last ten years, focusing on social-environmental debates and struggles from social movements in Latin America. She is currently a PhD Student at the Environmental Policy Research Centre, Institute of Political Science, at Free University of Berlin. Her supervisor is Dr Achim Brunnengräber.

James Ordner is an environmental sociologist and visiting professor at Humboldt State University in Arcata, California. Dr Ordner's research interests include community mobilization and natural resource protection, particularly local efforts to protect community assets from oil and gas energy project encroachment. His other research interests include federal public lands management and conservation, and the intersection of politics, cultural reproduction and environmental justice issues.

Tristan Partridge is a social anthropologist who works on environmental justice and indigenous political action. Through projects on land and water rights, energy, community organizing and climate change, his research examines the use and extraction of natural resources and the uneven distribution of related socio-environmental impacts. He received a PhD in Social Anthropology from the University of Edinburgh and has conducted fieldwork in Ecuador, the UK, India and the US. He is currently a research fellow at the Universitat Autònoma de Barcelona (ICTA Institute of Environmental Science and Technology) and the University of California, Santa Barbara.

Re:Common works to produce structural change both in finance and natural common management, in solidarity with those directly affected by an harmful and unjust development model, both in the global South and in Italy and Europe. In order to achieve its long-term goal Re:Common has a strong commitment to developing, promoting and practicing alternatives reclaiming both public finance and public interest natural commons management policies. Re:Common is a public, membership-based organization challenging the financialization of the natural commons in solidarity with affected communities both in the South and in the North and advocating for new and democratic public financial institutions at national and global level to promote the commons.

Hannibal Rhoades is currently communications and advocacy coordinator at The Gaia Foundation, UK, with a focus on extractivism. In this role, and as coordinator for Northern Europe for the Yes to Life, No to Mining Global Solidarity Network, Hal is working in solidarity with frontline communities around the world to resist unwanted mining projects and advance the case for going beyond extractivism. He is also a member of the London Mining Network's advisory committee and has worked as a journalist, covering stories about environmental and social justice on every continent.

Denisse Rodríguez is a PhD candidate at the School of Geography of the University of Melbourne, Australia. Under a political ecology approach, her research examines water-related concerns over extractivism in the Ecuadorian highlands, with a particular focus on emotional geographies of resource extraction, alternative development trajectories and socio-environmental mobilization.

Kate Symons is a fellow at the Centre of African Studies at the University of Edinburgh. Her research focuses on the political aspects of society and nature in developing country contexts, especially Mozambique and Kenya. Her research

interests include the neoliberalization of conservation and environmental governance, contestation and resistance to extractives-led development and conservation,
the governance of people and more-than-human nature in conservation spaces and
how nature conservation has contributed to the formation and ongoing production
of the Mozambican state.

Céline Veríssimo works at the Department of Architecture and Urbanism,
UNILA – Federal University of Latin American Integration, Brazil. Since 1996
to 2007, she worked as an architect, researcher and lecturer in Oslo, Tokyo, Kuala
Lumpur, London and Coimbra. She holds a PhD in Development Planning at the
Bartlett Development Planning Unit, UCL, and her research focuses on the political dimension of cities' challenges, environmental impacts and social inequalities,
taking the Outdoor Domestic Space as starting point, specifically the urban context
of Mozambique.

Noura Wahby is a PhD candidate in Development Studies at the University of
Cambridge, focusing on the role of the state in urban development. She completed
her Masters of Public Administration from the American University in Cairo
(AUC). Her doctoral research examines urban governance and infrastructural citizenship in Cairo, Egypt. She studies access to urban water systems in informal areas
and gated communities. Her research interests include urban issues in the Global
South, the public commons, urban contention, informality and governance.

Andy Whitmore has worked for more than 25 years in solidarity with indigenous peoples, particularly focused on the issue of indigenous issues and the extractive industries, where he has specialized in support around the issue of free, prior,
informed consent. Andy is currently coordinator for an EU funded project with
London Mining Network, called Stop Mad Mining, and working as a project
officer in the Responsible Finance team at Forest Peoples Programme.

Amanda K. Winter is a postdoctoral research fellow at the University of Nottingham, working on the interdisciplinary Leverhulme project Sustaining Urban
Habitats. Her current work involves a comparative case study of Nottingham and
Shanghai's environmental policy-making from a multilevel urban governance
perspective. She has a PhD from Central European University's Department of
Environmental Sciences and Policy, where her research focused on the politics
of Copenhagen and Vancouver's green city policies. Amanda has research interests in urban sustainability and governance, (urban) political ecology, and human
geography.

Friedrich Wulf started out professionally as a field biologist for a nature conservation centre and volunteer for Friends of the Earth Germany, but turned "political"
20 years ago. He has worked as a nature conservation officer ever since, albeit for

different NGOs (first BirdLife and then FoE Germany). Since 2008, he works for Pro Natura – Friends of the Earth Switzerland – on international policies and their implementation and is steering group member of the Friends of the Earth Europe Biodiversity Campaign, which has jointly developed the "Rights to Nature" approach that he now helps promote.

ACKNOWLEDGEMENTS

The authors would like to acknowledge the financial support of both Elsevier and the journal *Geoforum* for sponsoring the organisation of the conference "Rights to Nature: Tracing Alternative Political Ecologies against the Neoliberal Environmental Agenda" (Cambridge, June 2016). This work has also been supported with two Marie Curie Intra-European Fellowships (IEF) grants from the European Commission (Marie Curie IEF grant numbers: PIEF-GA-2013–623409, acronym PAENCE; and PIEF-GA-2013–622631, acronym CESINE) and the British Academy/Leverhulme research project "Tracing Alternative Political Ecologies against the Neoliberal Environmental Agenda through the Study of Environmental Movements" (Ref. SG161266). The work of Jose A. Cortes-Vazquez has also been supported with one InTalent UDC-Inditex grant from the Universidade da Coruña (Spain) and the work of Elia Apostolopoulou from a Carson Fellowship (Rachel Carson Center for Environment and Society, Ludwig-Maximilians-Universität München, Germany). We would like to also thank all the people, scholars, activists and members of the public who participated in the Conference we organized in Cambridge in June 2016 and also those who responded to our call for contributions to this book after the completion of the Conference. Without them this book wouldn't be possible. The contributing authors, rather than the editors, are responsible for the ideas, opinions and information included in their respective chapters of this volume.

INTRODUCTION

Neoliberalism and environmental movements across the world after the 2008 financial crash: defending the right to nature

Elia Apostolopoulou and Jose A. Cortes-Vazquez

In the last three decades, neoliberal policies and ideologies have brought about fundamental changes to nature–society relationships across the globe, deepening existing environmental conflicts and creating profound new injustices. The neo-liberalization of nature (Heynen et al., 2007; Castree 2008a, 2008b), itself a crisis-inducing process of market-disciplinary regulatory restructuring (Peck et al., 2012), has intensified particularly in the era following the 2008 global financial crash, proving that nature remains the main source of wealth along with labour power (Marx, 1973 [1857], 1990) and women bodies (Federici, 2014 [1988]), and plays a key role in capital accumulation (O'Connor, 1998; Smith, 2010).

Even though responses to the economic crisis have been uneven (Harvey, 2011), neoliberalism[1] proved to still dominate the agendas of governments and international organizations across the globe. The "dead but still dominant" (Smith, 2008[2]) neoliberal regime has been particularly evident in the rescue or "bailout" packages from the European Union (EU) and the International Monetary Fund (IMF) for southern European economies. If we try to summarize the key developments since 2008 we could say that these involve extensive deregulations and market-friendly reregulations of environmental and planning legislation, privatizations of public property, land and natural resources in both urban and rural areas, a quantitative and qualitiative expansion of the commodification of nature and a profound and prolonged fiscal austerity expressed, inter alia, in major cuts in public spending (Apostolopoulou et al., 2014; Cahill, 2011; McCarthy, 2012; Harvey, 2011; Peck et al., 2012). In the post-2008 era, various forms of "green" (Fairhead et al., 2012) and "un-green" grabbing (Apostolopoulou and Adams, 2015) have been spreading across the world, including fracking; mining; land grabbing; loss of green public spaces, places and natural ecosystems due to large infrastructure, urban redevelopment and gentrification projects; the privatization of water, energy and public nature assets; the further commodification of protected natures; the increasing implementation of market-based instruments, such as payments for ecosystem services; and carbon and biodiversity offsetting. In most of these cases, natural ecosystems are being symbolically and materially expropriated from local communities under the neoliberal ideological justification that more economic development and growth is the only way to overcome economic recession.

In parallel, several places around the world are becoming the locus of resistance against the unequal distribution of the costs and benefits of neoliberal policies, and their increasing social-environmental and spatial injustices. At the date of writing, the Environmental Justice Atlas, a collaborative map of socio-environmental conflicts around the world, had already documented 2.472 of such cases, including struggles around nuclear energy, mining, waste and water management, and biodiversity conservation, among others (Temper et al., 2018). Not surprisingly, these are distributed unevenly across the world with southern European and Balkan countries being one (but of course not the only) hotspots of conflicts,[3] reinforcing the argument that uneven development "is the concrete pattern and process of the production of nature under capitalism" (Smith, 2010, p. 8; see also Harvey, 2005b, 2010). Importantly, uneven geographical development contributes to social and spatial injustices (Soja, 2010) and acting against such injustices requires building networks of solidarity (Hadjimichalis, 2011). Indeed, alongside environmental conflicts, new social, environmental and political movements have been emerging with the purpose to articulate a critical narrative to neoliberalism and to produce and defend alternative futures, sometimes at the price of risking their own lives (see www.globalwitness.org/en/blog/new-data-reveals-197-land-and-environmental-defenders-murdered-2017/). In some of these cases local struggles have proved their capacity to directly question capitalist rationality (Temper et al., 2018).

Despite the fact that resistance against neoliberal capitalism has been experienced vividly in recent years, both in the academic and activist fields, we observe four key paradoxes that impede the advance of critical scholarship and its explicit link to radical practice.

First, discussions on the environmental contradictions of capitalism have remained divided between different research areas and movements: struggles against the impacts of infrastructure mega-projects and the operations of extractive industries, the privatisation of natural resources, the commodification of water and land grabbing, or against market environmentalism, environmental offsetting and other forms of "neoliberal conservation" (Igoe and Brockington, 2007), are often inadequately connected, creating, inter alia, a gap between urban and rural areas, between the "city" and the "countryside" and, ultimately, between society and nature. This gap is of key importance in the current era: despite the fact that in several places across the globe rural and urban struggles for socio-environmental justice have intensified and even though research on extended or generalized (Lefebvre, 1970) urbanization has been rapidly emerging in the post-2008 era (see, for example, Angelo and Wachsmuth, 2015; Brenner and Schmid, 2015) critical academic research is rarely exploring the links between the post-2008 deepening of the economic exploitation of places within the limits of traditional "cities" and places beyond those limits. Brenner and Schmid (2015, p. 178) aptly describe the importance of these interconnections; as they put it: "from Nigeria, South Africa, India and China to Brazil, Mexico and northern Canada, new political strategies are being constructed by peasants, workers, indigenous peoples and other displaced populations to oppose the infrastructuralization and enclosure of their everyday social spaces and the destruction of their established forms of livelihood". Politics of anti-gentrification movements and resistance to corporate mega-projects in dense city cores "can be connected, both analytically and politically, to mobilizations against land enclosure, large-scale infrastructures (dams, highways, pipelines, industrial corridors, mines) and displacement in seemingly 'remote' regions" (ibid.). In this, we would add that what further connects these struggles is that they all oppose the capitalist treating of nature as a mere material condition of capital accumulation and the impacts of this to their everyday lives, from subsistence issues to issues of quality of life.

Second, critical and radical scholars analysizing nature–society relationships under capitalism and environmental activists have not engaged with each other as thoroughly as needed. A systematic exchange of theoretical analyses, practical experiences, and ideas about successful political strategies and radical agendas and demands is urgent. The latter becomes even more crucial if we consider that the voice of many environmental movements, particularly when they are linked to precarious communities, have been often ignored or simply used to support academic arguments. Environmental struggles often hinge on the uneven distribution of ecological impacts and benefits (Guha and Martinez-Alier, 1997) as well as profound injustices related to class, race and gender, and, thus, the recognition of existing power assymetries and structural injustices is a prerequisite to fight against social invisibilizations (see Martin et al., 2015) and economic, social and cultural unevenness. Yet, their superficial incorporation in academic analyses have disregarded their fundamental role for understanding human–environment relations and imagining non-capitalist forms of nature production (see Demaria and Kothari, 2017). To put it simply, we cannot continue to claim that we are conducting radical or even anti-capitalistic research without actually engaging with the people and communities who are on the ground fighting against the various consequences of the capitalist production of nature.

Third, and relatedly, efforts by critical scholars working on environmental issues to explicitly address the class aspects of environmental degradation and of environmental movements and struggles against it have fell short, impeding an in-depth and sustained dialogue with activists, environmental movements and particularly with the labour movement about the impacts of the economic and ecological crisis and potential alternatives to the neoliberal agenda (see Barca, in press; Harvey, 2014; Burkett, 1999). The limits of ecology (Foster, 2002) or environmentalism without class are obvious not only in the inability to formulate a 21st-century revolutionary red-green agenda but also in the increasing hegemony of "post-political" apocalyptic framings of environmental problems reinforced by the discussion evolving around the "Anthropocene". As long as discussions in the public domain are dominated either by pessimist projections about a fatal ecological crisis or by technomanagerial narratives, as the one described in the *Ecomodernist Manifesto*,[4] it would seem easier to imagine the world ending in an environmental disaster (see Klein, 2007 about "disaster capitalism") than to collectively challenge and ultimately end the neoliberal, and capitalist, order (Swyngedouw, 2010) and imagine a non-exploitative relationship between humans and non-human nature.

Fourth, comparative studies between different places, countries and continents remain extremely limited, impeding a meaningful comparison of specific, "actually existing" neoliberalizations. In particular, we notice a significant gap between political ecology studies with a focus on countries in the global North, which tends to be underrepresented and are usually centred on urban struggles, and the global South, where most attention is paid among political ecologists, with a predominant focus on rural issues. While different histories and political traditions justify a more balanced focus (Ferguson, 2010), it is because of the potential of cross-fertilization that we feel that more exchanges are needed. Furthermore, we consider such exchanges crucial not because we believe that it is possible to "extract some composite picture of a typical neoliberal state' from its 'unstable and volatile historical geography" – this would rather be a "fool's errand" as David Harvey (2005a, p. 70) argues – but because we are confident that such a systematic comparison is necessary in order to formulate the theories and methods that would enable us to know "our enemy better, in general, and in its many guises" (Peet, 2013, p. 3). This, in turn, has the potential to make it possible to offer a radical critique of nature–society relationships under capitalism that would be explicitly and directly linked both to theory and praxis.

This book is a first step to redress these gaps at the core of the critical opposition to the neoliberalization of nature and environmental policies. It is the result of a collective attempt to map out and bring closer the diversity of voices, actions and approaches that are currently leading different forms of opposition to the nature–society conflicts that neoliberal policies and ideologies are generating. It includes the experience of many activist groups fighting against the ecological damage and livelihood losses of extractive industries, the evictions and expropriations by big infrastructure projects and the violence and coercions of the state to impose corporate interests. It also includes the views and voices of many different academics. Some of them speak from the direct experience of participating in protests and activist movements. Others adopt the more distanced perspective of a researcher interested in the alternative framings that these movements mobilize against the "There Is No Alternative" (TINA) ideology of neoliberal capitalism.

However, the book is something more than a collection of different texts, views and perspectives. It is a proposal for an exchange of ideas and a sustained dialogue between different experiences around questions of key importance for both radical theory and practice, such as: What is the role of non-human nature for capitalist production and capital accumulation and how environmental protection fits into the wider context of nature's exploitation in capitalism? Can capitalism shift towards a model of "green economy" and will this really end nature's exploitation?

How can alternative paths towards a non-exploitative and non-alienating relation-ship between society and nature be traced and which are the key steps in that direction?

In recent decades, critical social scientists have contributed significantly in addressing the above questions. The work of Neil Smith on the production of nature and the work of David Harvey on the historical-geographical materialistic understanding of nature–society relationships are now considered classical contri-butions to these debates and constitute an inspiration for this book along with many other important contributions from scholars working on the intersections between radical geographical and social sciences scholarship on nature–society relationships, environmental justice and critical political ecology. For us the ultimate question in this debate is what kind of society and thus what kind of nature we want to pro-duce, by whom and for whom. We strongly believe that this issue, either implicitly or explicitly, lies at the core of any academic–activist dialogue on environmental conflicts, social movements and neoliberalism both in this book and beyond it. But asking how we want to produce nature is not enough. We should also try to find answers to this pressing question and doing so is necessary for beginning again to encourage a revolutionary imaginary for social and environmental change (Smith, 2006) as politically possible.

From the Right to the City to the Right to Nature: fifty years of ecological and class conflicts

The rationale – and title – of this book finds inspiration in "the Right to the City" thesis, elaborated mostly by Henri Lefebvre (1968, 1996) and David Harvey (2008, 2012). Lefebvre advanced this thesis in 1968 to argue in favour of the co-production of the urban public space and against its privatization and commoditization that lead to profound class inequalities. David Harvey, by building on Lefebvre's analysis, has offered insightful analyses of the urgency of the right to the city to confront the consequences of capitalist urbanization and its class effects. This discussion is more than relevant in the current era. The restructuring of environmental and develop-ment policies after the 2008 financial crash has involved a total disregard for the economic, social, cultural, spatial and ecological consequences of land use change, leading to an unequal distribution of environmental costs and benefits, disrupting the social, economic and cultural ties between (and within) communities and par-ticular places, restricting public access to natural landscapes and green spaces, and exposing communities to displacement, exploitation or/and dispossession from the areas they live and work.

The exploitation of non-human nature has not of course started after the 2008 global economic crisis. However, the intensity of governmental attacks against both the working class and non-human nature since 2008 has been remarkable and widespread. Indeed, governmental responses to the crisis repudiated pre- and post- crisis analyses, arguing that "hard" neoliberalism belongs to the past. Over-all, what we increasingly see is the emergence of contradictory and reactionary public policies that try to respond to the increasing environmental contradictions of capitalism by deepening uneven development and the conceptual and material alienation between society and nature. Crucially, these developments entail the loss of rights for the majority of the affected communities. This, along with the governmental suppression of environmental struggles, the further shrinking of the "welfare" state and the increasing role of non-elected and unaccountable institutions, expose that the consensus-driven neoliberal rhetoric has been increasingly lapsing into undemocratic and even authoritarian governance (Apostolopoulou et al., 2014) in an era of harsh global capitalist crisis. The severity of the latter in countries like Greece or Spain (the countries of the two editors of this book) shows not only the consequences of the crisis but also its limits: domination without hegemony (Gramsci, 1971) rapidly enters into a crisis that threatens its very existence (see Thomas, 2009), creating the need for radical alternatives.

We feel that a key step towards the above direction would be to directly question capitalism's dystopian vision for nature–society relationships in the era of the *Capitalocene* (Moore, 2017). This will require from all of us to give a battle both within neoliberal academia and outside it, along with social and environmental movements. As the experiences that this book discusses show us, there is actually an enormous potential for a new emancipatory politics that would encompass a "right to nature" as a key element of struggles for the "right to the city".

But what could a "right to nature" possibly mean? We would define it as the right to influence and command the processes by which nature–society relationships are made, remade and disrupted by generalized urbanization and economic development (Apostolopoulou and Adams, in press), and consider it not only as a key element of struggles for the right to the city but also as a key element of anti-capitalistic struggles beyond the city. Politically, some may argue that this is a challenging concept. In the Marxist tradition, environmental and urban struggles are usually considered as being about issues of reproduction rather than production, and therefore not about class, and thus dismissed as devoid of revolutionary potential or significance (see Harvey, 2012). However, many communities fighting the creation of new urban enclaves, large infrastructure projects, speculative developments, environmental offsetting, mining and fracking, consider opposition to ecosystem degradation and biodiversity loss a key part of their struggles, which seek to defend not only the "right to the city" but also the "right to nature". This suggests that the right to influence and command the processes by which nature–society relationships are made, transformed and disrupted, is increasingly becoming a key element of struggles against capitalism everywhere (Brenner and Schmid, 2015). Moreover, and relatedly, environmental struggles, as the various chapters in this book show, have the potential (and in many cases they have realized this potential in practice) to disrupt the reproduction of the relations that are essential for the production and exchange of commodities and for the realization of surplus value and profits. In this sense, such struggles have the potential to become anti-capitalistic struggles.

David Harvey (2008, p. 23) argues that "the right to the city is far more than the individual liberty to access urban resources: it is a right to change ourselves by changing the city". And he further points out that this is a "common rather than an individual right since this transformation inevitably depends upon the exercise of a collective power to reshape the processes of urbanization". We would argue that this is also the case for the right to nature, which, in most cases, is also our right to a specific way of living, feeling, seeing and breathing. Claiming our right to nature will require to put ourselves against analyses that see it as part of a caring liberalism open to philantropists, industries and sections of capital that are keen to establish an "environmental-friendly" profile and thus against ecology or environmentalism "without class".

The right to nature, defined as above, and the right to the production of nature, namely to a different production of nature based on social needs, openly calls us to question not only neoliberal rationality and economic growth but also the capitalist mode of production. In this fight, radical scholars should meet with people and groups participating in anti-fracking and anti-mining movements, housing and anti-offsetting struggles (and more generally resistance to neoliberal conservation), movements against land grabbing, the expropriation of green spaces in both urban and rural areas, and the privatization of natural resources and public assets, including forests and water and struggles against gentrification, regeneration, urban redevelopment, large infrastructure projects and the dismantling of traditional forms of using natural resources. The right to nature, as both a working slogan and political ideal (see Harvey, 2008 about the right to the city), can be a step towards unifying these struggles because it refocuses the discussion on who commands the production of nature and whose interests this production serves. The right to nature ultimately calls us to fight for a radically different, socially and ecologically just, production of nature, for every ecosystem and place, and every piece of land. Besides all these do not belong to capitalists or landowners but, as Woody Guthrie wrote in 1945, it is our land and it was made for all of us.

Steps towards a closer academic–activist dialogue: a book overview

The seeds of this publication, which we see as a set of first steps towards closer academic–activist collaborations in the field of environmental struggles against neoliberal policies, are in the variety of voices that were present at a conference that we organised in June 2016 at the University of Cambridge entitled: "Rights to nature. Tracing alternative political ecologies against the neoliberal environmental agenda"[5]. This conference aimed to facilitate an open dialogue between scholars, activists and members of political and social movements in the Left in order to initiate a collective discussion on the content and form of a new radical political agenda for nature–society relationships. The reason to call this conference was that we felt that so far this dialogue had been deficient. We considered urgent to create a space where a sustained and critical communication between these different communities would be made possible. The reach and significance of this initiative lies in the number of people who responded positively to our call and participated at the conference. Since then, many new voices of activists and scholars have jointed this dialogue and are now also part of this book.

The varieties of cases, views and experiences presented at the conference were enormous. A selection of them are presented in this book and include cases in Colombia, Greece, Ireland, Mozambique, Mexico, USA, Ecuador, Russia, Romania, Madagascar, UK, Canada, Egypt and Brazil. Despite such diversity, they all have two things in common: a promise that more just nature–society relationships are possible, and specific suggestions of how to achieve this aim. We have grouped these writtings in different subject sections, which we hope will assist the reader to navigate the broad diversity of themes.

Part 1, on extractivism and environmental justice movements, starts with an introduction by Christiaens, Mears, Whitmore and Rhoades on how new mining initiatives in Colombia have been met with local opposition. As members of the activist groups CATAPA, The Gaia Foundation and the London Mining Network, they describe the complex knowledge framings with regards the value of nature that these local communities articulate, which contrast with the reductive market-based framings defended by the extractive industries. In the following chapter, Ordner explores the potential for community-based coalitions to protect natural resources from risky energy projects as exemplified by landowner and concerned citizen opposition to the KXL pipeline in Nebraska. Ordner argues that in a time of rising petro-politics and corporate authoritarianism based on an ideology of energy dominance, connecting community resource protection and greater environmental concerns through citizen coalitions can offer a hopeful way towards achieving social and environmental justice.

In Chapter 3, Rodríguez and Loginova analyse the struggles of two socio-environmental movements: the water guardians of Kimsakocha in Ecuador and the Pechora River saviours in Russia. They explore how the socio-environmental movements have navigated through power asymmetries in the quest of spaces to demand meaningful participation in decision-making and secure their own aspirations for development. In Chapter 4, Christianou and Vasileiou speak about their own experience of fighting against the construction of a gold mine in Halkidiki and present a clear example of the kind of neoliberal corporate attack on people's livelihood and the coercive and repressive role of the state in defence of corporate interests that are nowadays commonplace in neoliberal environmental experiences.

Symons (Chapter 5) uses the case of Anadarko and the Afungi communities to explore how Mozambique's ostensible commitment to rights and its encouragement of "a good business environment" has provided opportunities for those fighting for community rights to use certain strategies and tactics to great effect, while, at the same time, entrenching certain aspects of neoliberal development. Symons argues that the case of Anadarko demonstrates the power of a politicized approach from civil society activists that emphasizes the relationship between global capitalist accumulation and environmental dispossession suffered by poor and marginalized communities. Finally, comparing anti-mining movements in Romania and Colombia, Florea and Rhoades (Chapter 6) debate about the complexity and risks of their actions in the context of the environmental justice movement. Among others, some of these risks are connected to what they refer to as "the distant gaze". While conflicts usually occur at specific sites, opposition and contestation can reach actors in sometimes very distanced locations. In such cases, the risk of distortion is rather high. They propose a number of methods to counteract such negative outcomes.

In Part 2, on urban environmental conflicts, Wahby (Chapter 7) further develops the argument outlined by Florea and Rhoades about the complexity of local action, the divisions that can be created in different environmental movements within local communities, and the challenge of using concepts and discourses that advance actual environmental justice. Wahby describes how localized grassroots forms of contention against state damage and negligence in Egypt are undermined by a particular definition of nature put forth by the new bourgeois classes and co-opted civil society movements. In Chapter 8, Veríssimo and Name focus on community actions in the city of Dondo, in Mozambique, and explore the practice of edible landscaping at the outdoor domestic spaces as a means of a silent popular resistance against marginalization, and household/community empowerment. They argue that through these practices production strategies are reorganized to assure livelihoods, food sovereignty and environmental quality in a process of spatial resistance.

Moving into the topic of megaprojects, Alves describes in Chapter 9 the conflicts generated by the construction of new infrastructure in Rio de Janeiro before the 2014 World Cup and 2016 Olympic games. Alves argues that lack of access to information impedes the development of counter-narratives that contest and problematize the official state and corporate propaganda that depicts megaprojects as instruments of development and ignores their social and environmental impacts. In Chapter 10, Beck takes us to Williamsburg, in Brooklyn, to describe population dynamics during the dramatic changes brought about by gentrification and displacement that materialized from the 1990s until today. By empasizing the class aspects of gentrification and the importance of contesting the private ownership of property under capitalism, Beck sees the symbolic, cultural, space as a viable arena of resistance to counter the hegemonic power of neoliberalism.

Chapter 11, by Burballa Noria, takes up the challenge of testing different activist movements and demands within an expanded environmental justice academic framework. Burballa Noria by examining how environmental justice claims are expressed and framed in conflicts over the development of infrastructure megaprojects in Europe contributes to identifying the similarities between different struggles and thus the potential for collaborations between environmental struggles occurring across the globe.

In Part 3, Hernandez-Trejo (Chapter 12) and Levidow (Chapter 13), each in their own respective chapters, further elaborate on the academic debate around the economic valuation of nature. Hernandez-Trejo analyses the idealistic assumptions and developments of Thünen's model of efficient land use in environmental policy, specifically, in the spatial targeting of payments for ecosystem services and the role of such models in redefining the political aspect of environmental issues. Levidow, on the other hand, describes how the 'natural capital' metaphor has taken root in the financialization of conservation. He argues that natural capital accounting (NCA) does not create new value but rather facilitates the business aim of rent-seeking, for example, stable, exclusive or privileged access to the conditions of production, ultimately depoliticizing the power relations around natural resources allocation and legitimizing company stewardship as a substitute for state responsibility.

In Chapter 14, members of Re:Common transfer us from the academic debates on the economic valuation of nature to activist action against it. Re:Common by looking into the implementation of offsetting by the mining company Rio Tinto in Madagascar, explain the new forms of eviction and dispossession that lie at the core of offsetting projects. Through their analysis they challenge the wider shift towards the economic valuation of nature and they explore the way that it's used to undermine environmental justice demands.

In Chapter 15, Bell and Wulf, from Friends of the Earth, highlight the limitations of valuing nature in economic terms and advocate for a new rights-based agenda. Ito, from the NGO Nature's Rights, and Montini, from the University of Siena, Italy, elaborate on this new rights-based approach (Chapter 16). They contend that recognizing nature's own rights can subvert the existing property paradigm and establish a duty of care towards nature embedding the reality of our relationship with nature in law and offerring a powerful counter-balance to corporate rights. Finally, on Chapter 17, Lohmann argues that every history of natures is a history of rights, and vice versa. He warns that emerging political movements for "rights of nature" aimed at countering what he considers evolving capitalist movements for "rights to nature" need to be aware that such contrasting regimes of rights/natures are constantly in play, and are being used by all sides.

In the final part, Partridge (Chapter 18), by focusing on a case in the Global South, the indigenous community of San Isidro in Ecuador's Cotopaxi province, shows us how different resources held in common can become the basis of both physical and social forms of infrastructure vital to the realization of a range of social and political goals. Partridge invites us to see San Isidro's community-operated irrigation system as both an expression of collaborative potential and an illustration of how a network of communities seized emergent political opportunities – where different elements of "the commons" are the basis for an emergent political space that fosters collaboration.

In Chapters 19 and 20, Winter and Gearey respectively discuss different cases of community resistance in the Global North, namely in Canada and the UK. In particular, Winter explores two cases of camping in tents on public land in Vancouver. She approaches them as acts of resistance to state-corporate power and to the commodification and privatization of land under neoliberalism and as having the potential to contribute to the creation of new spaces of solidarity and new ideas towards an environmentally and socially just urbanization. On the other hand, Gearey, by drawing on empirical research conducted in the River Adur valley in West Sussex (UK), invites us to appreciate the radical interventions, actions and performances of community elders. Gearey argues that community elders have managed to create new "gerontocracies of affect" and understands these radical actions as necessary acts towards the "right to nature" and social-environmental justice. Finally, in the last chapter of the book, Levy (Chapter 21) explores the spaces created by two low-impact communities in the UK, Diggerville and Woodville, and argues that these communities not only exemplify the realities of economic degrowth, but they also embody postcapitalist relationships by relying less on monetary economics and by providing tantalizing examples of an alternative to capitalism social organization.

Despite the great diversity of cases, it seems that there are also many common-alities between the social movements and environmental conflicts discussed in this book. For this reason, it is our belief that fruitful cross-fertilization can occur only if such different experiences engage with one another more closely and systemati-cally. Although such exchange must materialize outside the confined space of this book or the boundaries of academia, in the field of day-to-day political and social struggle against the capitalist production of nature, we dedicate the afterword of this book to highlight a number of lessons that could be learned from the variety of cases presented, and the future directions that they point out. The closing ideas of this book are, thus, an attempt to contribute to the enormous debate on social movements, environmentsal justice and neoliberal natures, and they are based on those lessons and directions that we considered more important while reading the different contributions of activists and scholars in this book. We hope every reader will engage critically and creatively with these experiences and enrich, in one way or another, discussions around such crucial issues.

Notes

1 Neoliberalism can be understood as a political-economic project that emerged during the 1970s initially in the US and the UK, and later also in continental Europe and then around the globe, with the key aim to re-establish, renew and expand the conditions for capital accumulation (Harvey, 2005a, p. 19). Neoliberalism is thus in many respects a counter-revolutionary project (Harvey, 2016; see also Duménil and Lévy, 2004) that inten-sifies social inequality: its key expressions include new configurations of income distribu-tion, an organized political assault on organized labour and anti-corporate reforms with the explicit goal to disempower labour, bubbles in the asset market, as well as extensive deregulations, market-friendly reregulations and privatizations.
2 See www.berghahnjournals.com/view/journals/focaal/2008/51/focaal510113.xml
3 For more information, visit: https://ejatlas.org/
4 See www.ecomodernism.org
5 More information on the conference, the programme and full videos of the presentations can be found on the conference website: https://conservationandtransformation.com/conference-rights-to-nature/

References

Angelo, H. and Wachsmuth, D. (2015) Urbanizing Urban Political Ecology: A Critique of Methodological Citycism. *International Journal of Urban and Regional Research* 39, 16–27.

Apostolopoulou, E. and Adams, W.M. (2015) Neoliberal Capitalism and Conservation in the Post-crisis Era: The Dialectics of "Green" and "Un-green" Grabbing in Greece and the UK. *Antipode* 47, 15–35.

Apostolopoulou, E., and Adams, W.M. (in press) Cutting Nature to Fit: Urbanization, Neo-liberalism and Biodiversity Offsetting in England. *Geoforum*.

Apostolopoulou, E., Bormpoudakis, D., Paloniemi, R., Cent, J., Grodzińska-Jurczak, M., Pietrzyk-Kaszyńska, A. and Pantis, J.D. (2014) Governance Rescaling and the Neoliberalization of Nature: The Case of Biodiversity Conservation in Four EU Countries. *International Journal of Sustainable Development & World Ecology* 21, 481–494.

Barca, S. (in press) Labour and the Ecological Crisis: The Eco-modernist Dilemma in Western Marxism(s) (1970s-2000s). *Geoforum*.

Brenner, N. and Schmid, C. (2015). Towards a New Epistemology of the Urban? *City* 19, 151–182.

Burkett, P. (1999) *Marx and Nature: A Red-Green Perspective*. New York: St Martin's Press.

Cahill, D. (2011) Beyond Neoliberalism? Crisis and the Prospects for Progressive Alternatives. *New Political Science* 33, 479–492.

Castree, N. (2008a) Neoliberalizing Nature: The Logics of Deregulation and Reregulation. *Environment and Planning A* 40: 131–152.

Castree, N. (2008b) Neoliberalizing Nature: Processes, Effects and Evaluations. *Environment and Planning A* 40, 153–173.

Demaria, F. and Kothari, A. (2017) The Post-Development Dictionary Agenda: Paths to the Pluriverse. *Third World Quarterly* 28, 2588–2599.

Duménil, G. and Lévy, D. (2004) *Capital Resurgent: Roots of the Neoliberal Revolution*. Cambridge, MA: Harvard University Press.

Fairhead, J., Leach, M. and Scoones, I. (2012) Green Grabbing: A New Appropriation of Nature? *The Journal of Peasant Studies* 39, 237–261.

Federici, S. (2014 [1988]) *Caliban and the Witch. Women, the Body, and Capital Accumulation*. Brooklyn, NY: Autonomedia.

Ferguson, J. (2010) The Uses of Neoliberalism. *Antipode* 41, 166–184.

Foster, J.B. (2002) *Ecology against Capitalism*. New York: Monthly Review Press.

Gramsci A. (1971) *Selections from the Prison Notebooks*. Hoare, Q. and Nowell-Smith, G. (eds and trans). New York: International Publishers.

Guha, R. and Martinez-Alier, J. (1997) *Varieties of Environmentalism. Essays North and South*. London: Earthscan.

Hadjimichalis, C. (2011) Uneven Geographical Development and Socio-spatial Justice and Solidarity: European Regions after the 2009 Financial Crisis. *European Urban and Regional Studies* 18, 254–274.

Harvey, D. (2005a) *A Brief History of Neoliberalism*. Oxford: Oxford University Press.

Harvey, D. (2005b) *Spaces of Neoliberalization: Towards a Theory of Uneven Geographical Development* (Vol. 8) Stuttgart, Germany: Franz Steiner Verlag.

Harvey, D. (2008) The Right to the City. *New Left Review* 53, 23–40.

Harvey, D. (2010) *The Enigma of Capital*. London: Profile Books.

Harvey, D. (2011) Crises, Geographic Disruptions and the Uneven Development of Political Responses. *Economic Geography* 87, 1–22.

Harvey, D. (2012) *Rebel Cities: From the Right to the City to the Urban Revolution*. London and New York: Verso Books.

Harvey, D. (2014) *Seventeen Contradictions and the End of Capitalism*. London: Profile Books.

Harvey, D. (2016) Neoliberalism is a Political Project. *Jacobin*. Available at: www.jacobinmag. com/2016/07/david-harvey-neoliberalism-capitalism-labor-crisis-resistance/

Heynen, N., J. McCarthy, S., Prudham and Robbins, P. (eds) (2007) *Neoliberal Environments. False Promises and Unnatural Consequences*. London and New York: Routledge.

Igoe, J. and Brockington, D. (2007) Neoliberal Conservation: A Brief Introduction. *Conservation and Society* 5, 432–449.

Klein, N. (2007) *The Shock Doctrine*. New York: Metropolitan Books.

Lefebvre, H. (1968) *Le Droit À La Ville*. Paris: Anthropos.

Lefebvre, H. (1970) *La révolution urbaine* (Vol. 216). Paris: Gallimard.

Lefebvre, H. (1996) *Writings on Cities* (Vol. 63(2)). Oxford: Blackwell.

Martin, A., Akol, A. and Gross-Camp, N. (2015) Towards an Explicit Justice Framing of the Social Impacts of Conservation. *Conservation and Society* 13, 166–178.

Marx K. (1973 [1857]) *Grundrisse*. London: Penguin.

Marx, K. (1990) *Capital: A Critique of Political Economy* (Vol. I). Ben Fowkes (trans.). London: Penguin Classics.

McCarthy, J. (2012) The Financial Crisis and Environmental Governance "After" Neoliberalism. *Tijdschrift voor economische en sociale geografie* 103, 180–195.

Moore, J. (2017) The Capitalocene, Part I: On the Nature and Origins of our Ecological Crisis. *Journal of Peasant Studies* 44(3), 594–630.

O'Connor, J. (1998) *Natural Causes. Essays on Ecological Marxism*. New York and London: Guilford Press.

Peck, J., Theodore, N. and Brenner, N. (2012) Neoliberalism Resurgent? Market Rule after the Great Recession. *South Atlantic Quarterly* 111, 265–288.

Peet, R. (2013) Comparative Policy Analysis: Introduction. *Human Geography* 6, 1–10.

Smith, N. (2006) Nature as Accumulation Strategy. In L. Panitch and C. Leys (eds), *Socialist Register 2007: Coming to Terms with Nature*. London: Merlin. Pp 16–36.

Smith, N. (2010) *Uneven Development* (3rd edn). New York: Verso.

Soja, E. (2010) *Seeking Spatial Justice*. Minneapolis, University of Minnesota Press.

Swyngedouw, E. (2010) Impossible Sustainability and the Post-political Condition. In M. Cerreta, M. Concillio and G. Monno (eds), *Making Strategies in Spatial Planning*. Netherlands: Springer. Pp. 185–205.

Temper, L., Demaria, F., Scheidel, A., Del Bene, D. and Martinez-Alier, J. (2018) The Global Environmental Justice Atlas (EJAtlas): Ecological Distribution Conflicts as Forces for Sustainability. *Sustainability Science* 13, 573–584.

Thomas, P.D. (2009) *The Gramscian Moment: Philosophy, Hegemony and Marxism*. Leiden: Brill.

PART I

Extractivism and environmental justice movements

1

SELF-DETERMINATION AS RESISTANCE

Re-asserting control over natural resources in Colombia

Charlotte Christiaens, Lucy Mears, Andy Whitmore and Hannibal Rhoades

Introduction

CATAPA (Comité Académico Técnico de Asesoramiento a Problemas Ambi-entales), The Gaia Foundation and London Mining Network (LMN) support global grassroots movements struggling against the social and ecological impacts of extractive industries. Local communities have long suffered the loss of con-trol over their lands and natural resources at the hands of State-based and mul-tinational companies – a loss that often entails a radical shift from sustainable to unsustainable and destructive land and water use. This chapter focuses on three cases in Colombia: La Colosa, Cerrejón and Yaigojé Apaporis. In each case, local and indigenous communities are mobilizing to exercise and expand their rights to self-determination and to protect clean water, healthy soils and living ecosystems required for livelihoods and life itself to thrive.

Despite Colombia's reputation as the country with the longest and most pro-ductive history of gold exploitation in Latin America, during the years of its brutal internal conflict, most companies were reluctant to invest in the country due to security issues (Global Business Report, 2011). However, an ease in the conflict in recent years, as well as the privatization of much of Columbia's industry (Pombo and Ramírez, 2003), have exposed the country to increased foreign interest in extractivism, what Zaitch and Gutiérrez Gómez call *a new gold fever* (Zaitch and Gutiérrez Gómez, 2015). Exports have increased, boosting the Colombian econ-omy, but to the detriment of its biodiverse landscape (Rudas Lleras and Cabrera Leal, 2015). The most exported products are oil, coal, gold and coffee (Observatory of Economic Complexity, 2016). During the administration of former President Alvaro Uribe Vélez, large areas of land were parcelled out to multinational min-ing companies (Colombia Solidarity Campaign, 2013), and, in 2007, the Ministry of Mines and Energy announced that a huge gold deposit had been found in Cajamarca (Tolima, Colombia) (Colombia Solidarity Campaign, 2013).

Local communities in Colombia are generally excluded from policy-making that will determine how their lands and natural resources will be used. Negotiations between mining companies and the Colombian government happen behind closed doors. Policy-making processes are formalized without any access or information being given to local communities. The three cases used in this article are emblematic cases, showing how local communities are ignored and how they are struggling together with local and international NGOs to claim their rights.

First Colombian case: Cerrejón

The Colombian government has been promoting an expansion of privatized, large-scale, open-pit coal mining for export in the belief that this will bring about "development", both nationally and in the vicinity of the mines. It will allegedly do this through increased revenue, employment and by advancing industrialization (EJOLT, 2015a, 2015b). The government aims to double coal exports by 2021, with about 90% of Cerrejón's hard coal being shipped abroad to fuel power plants, mainly in Europe and the United States (Coal Action Network, 2016; Heinrich Boell Stiftung and Friends of the Earth, 2015).

The Cerrejón coal mine, a vast opencast mine in the La Guajira province, is meant to satisfy this dream. It was Colombia's first large-scale coal mining operation, with a primary focus on coal for export, and is now the largest open-pit coal mine in South America (Balch, 2013). The initial contract was signed in 1975, between the State-owned Carbocol, and a subsidiary of US Exxon, known as Intercor. The mine began operating in 1985. Carbocol's rights were sold to global mining multinationals BHP Billiton, Anglo-American and Glencore in 2000, followed by a buyout of Exxon's 50% share in 2002, which left them as the sole owners (Coal Action Network, 2016). The mine's annual production in 2014 was 34.4 million tons, with a total accumulated production of 508.8 million tons, and the whole mining complex extending to more than 69,000 hectares (Coal Action Network, 2016; Betancur and Villa, 2016).

The mine has been hugely contested at the local level, as it has impoverished the surrounding soils and contaminated or dried up water sources. This has had devastating impacts on the local economy of farming and livestock keeping (Heinrich Boell Stiftung and Friends of the Earth, 2015). La Guajira has a 64% poverty rate, which is the highest in Colombia (EJOLT, 2015). This contradicts the government's thesis on the regional developmental benefits of such mining.

The impact on the land rights of the affected communities, particularly on the ancestral territory of the indigenous Wayúu people, has been severe. The mine is in a region where 42–45% of the population are indigenous people and 7.5% are Afro-Colombian communities (Heinrich Boell Stiftung and Friends of the Earth, 2015). The advance of the mine has had a determining – and restricting – effect on the territory of the region's ancestral inhabitants, the indigenous Wayúu people. It is in the middle of their land, and the train track delivering coal to the coast divides their territory (Coal Action Network, 2016). The Wayúu people have had little in the way of security over their land as their territory only began to be titled as 'reserve land' from the mid-1980s, with 21 reserves carved arbitrarily out of Wayúu ancestral territory, and – most importantly – the coal-rich areas excluded from that demarcation (Betancur and Villa, 2016).

At least five indigenous communities and a number of Afro-descendant communities have disappeared with the dispersing of their inhabitants (Coal Action Network, 2016). In terms of direct land conflict, there have been violent forced evictions of communities, including fairly recent examples involving the primarily Afro-descendent community of Tabaco in 2001, and even this year at Roche (Solly, 2016). There have also been social and cultural impacts due to labour migration associated with the mine.

The struggle of the Wayúu and Afro-Colombian communities has been one for self-determined development, and for their environment, notably to have their right to free, prior, informed consent – as recognized by the Constitutional Court – respected. Food sovereignty has been impacted by land loss and environmental pollution. The area is very dry, but the coal mine uses up to 17 million litres of water daily, despite people being faced with a scarcity of water (Heinrich Boell Stiftung and Friends of the Earth, 2015). This has led to a deterioration of flora and fauna. Air pollution has led to an increase in respiratory diseases. A 2015 decision by the Inter-American Commission of Human Rights directed the Colombian government to take immediate precautionary measures to ensure the lives and personal safety of the Wayuu people in La Guajira (Mines and Communities, 2016).

Local indigenous and environmental groups have increasingly linked up to fight for the rights of affected communities around many of the issues listed above. They have even managed to form a "roundtable" with the local mining union, who have their own concerns, including health and safety and working conditions. Although they do not always agree – given many local communities want the company to leave their land – it is a commendable model of how local groups with concerns about large mega-projects can create broad alliances to advance joint agendas. A noteworthy example of local action is the resistance to the company's decision in 2012 to begin a diversion project of the Ranchería River, in order to reach the 500 million tons of coal under it. Because of the concerted protest, including direct action of indigenous Wayúu women stopping coal trains, Cerrejón decided to suspend the project.

However, in 2014 they announced another diversion project on a tributary of the Ranchería called the Arroyo Bruno. Peaceful protests, such as the *Marcha de Mantas Rojas*, have been protesting against the diversion, but at the time of writing it appears that Cerrejón is just starting to divert the river (London Mining Network, 2016).

The recent protests in La Guajira were matched by actions of international solidarity. For example, LMN member group, Colombia Solidarity Campaign, organized a vigil outside the Colombian Embassy in London. Such solidarity work was happening in the UK before LMN came into existence, but since its inception in 2007, LMN has been offering various forms of support to affected communities.

Being based in London, where all of the three controlling companies have some form of presence, we have been able to make direct interventions with the company at the request of the communities. We have been most effective when ensuring that the voice of community leaders is heard directly by the companies, and that has meant frequent support for representatives to come to London to attend company annual general meetings, and to take part in associated press and advocacy opportunities. Those who have visited frequently attest to how effective such interventions can be, although the positive effects at the local level are often short-lived.

What is taking place in La Guajira is a conflict over lifestyles and control of territory and the local economy; it is a battle of the local land-based communities to determine their development for themselves. In this struggle they are frequently supported by international human rights norms and international solidarity, but face an uphill struggle against powerful vested interests, in both the company and the State, as well as entrenched ideas of what constitutes "development". As is blatantly clear it is also a struggle for both the local environment, and – given coal's impact as a fossil fuel – a struggle for the global environment. This may not be the major concern of those affected communities, but their victories may just help save our planet.

Second Colombian case: La Colosa

Further south in Cajamarca, Tolima, another local community is challenging the mining industry. Cajamarca is a city close to the capital of Bogotá, with a population of almost 24,000 inhabitants. A total of 80% of its area is a forest reserve. It has many strategic river sources, essential to the neighbouring areas, which are used by farmers, inhabitants and companies. Due to the numerous water resources and its ideal climate, the area is seen as the agricultural heart of Colombia (McNeish, 2016).

In 2007, concessions over Cajamarca were granted to AngloGold Ashanti (AGA), a South-African mining company, which is the third biggest gold mining company in the world (Zaitch and Gutiérrez Gómez, 2015). Due to the increasing internal conflicts in various countries in Africa as a result of AngloGold Ashanti's mining projects (Prosansky, 2007; Colombia Solidarity Campaign, 2011), AGA had long been looking overseas for other mining sites. Cajamarca proved to be a fruitful option for the company. Having spent time test drilling in Colombia since 1999, the preparation of the field was planned to start as early as 2017 (Colombia Solidarity Campaign, 2011), with the first gold production scheduled for 2020 (AngloGold Ashanti, 2012). This project, named La Colosa, poses a huge threat to the highly complex ecosystems and to the agriculture upon which inhabitants rely in Cajamarca.

The impacts of the project in Cajamarca are two-fold. First, the project poses a threat to the environment. This comes in the form of water usage, waste rock and toxic waste. The mining process requires a huge amount of water, specifically, the transportation of ore via pipelines, which could cause drought, resulting in decreased crop production, thus creating a food shortage for animals and humans

(Colombia Solidarity Campaign, 2011). It is estimated that La Colosa will consume more water per year than the total water consumption of all of the households in Tolima (Colombia Solidarity Campaign, 2013). Further, the waste rock produced by the process takes up a vast amount of space and remains after projects are abandoned. Toxic waste is impossible to recycle and requires impounding with tailing dams. Since the waste cannot be cleaned or filtered, it is kept in containers, at high risk of breaking, leaking and heavily polluting the ground and water, causing the destruction of animals' habitat and potentially resulting in their deaths (Colombia Solidarity Campaign, 2011).

Second, the project poses a threat to the inhabitants of the area. Health problems are rife as a result of exposure to toxic waste and to mined precious metals. Exposure to cyanide (which can leak into the air in the form of clouds) can cause problems ranging from headaches or heart problems to death (Hesperian Health Guides, 2012). Exposure to mercury can lead to neurological and behavioural disorders, miscarriage and birth defects among other serious problems (World Health Organization, 2016). Exposure to other minerals released during the mining process can cause problems ranging from cancer and dementia, and at the correct level of toxicity, death. In terms of social and economic damage, mining projects increase living costs due to the steep rise in rent (Colombia Solidarity Campaign, 2013), and such economic problems can lead to criminal activity, including prostitution and drug dealing.

One of the starkest examples of a threat to human rights and to democracy in this case is the corruption of the Colombian government. The government often backs companies and industries in their fight against local protesters, and AGA uses its financial resources to influence the decisions of local politicians and decision makers (Colombia Solidarity Campaign, 2013). Freedom of speech is also heavily censored through intimidation and threats in order to protect foreign investors (Colombia Solidarity Campaign, 2013). Over the past few years, a number of local protesters have been killed in Cajamarca (Colombia Solidarity Campaign, 2013). These actions illustrate the Colombian State's concerted failure to protect and promote the rights of its citizens, a duty required of the State as sovereign.

CATAPA supports local resistance committees in a number of ways. One of the most recent examples of this was CATAPA's contribution to the planning of a referendum, or Popular consultation in Cajamarca, which was given the green light by the city council of Ibagué. Thus, on 26 March 2017, local inhabitants were asked to vote on whether they supported La Colosa mining project. CATAPA facilitated the exchange of best practices and lessons from Peru and Bolivia with the local residents organizing the consultation. The aim of this referendum was to return collective power back to communities in order to allow for greater self-determination of the local people. The notion of returning power and rights to the local level corresponds with the concept of sovereignty. Local people should have a say in the fate of their lands and water resources, because it is they, and their children who live on that land. Empowering local communities by sharing "lessons learned" from other local affected communities is very efficient.

The referendum resulted in 98% of citizens voting against the project. Despite this clear call for self-determination, and the fact that Colombian law states that the results of this democratic instrument must be respected by national authorities, the outcome's validity has been contested by various stakeholders, including the Ministry of Mining. At the time of writing, the project's fate remains unclear.

More and more communities in Latin America have demanded the right to "self-determination" in regard to their territories and water supplies, as well as the property and land rights over their environment and traditional livelihood. Lessons have been learnt from such cases and consumers in the Global North have started to raise their collective voice to ensure better social and ecological conditions during the manufacturing of their products. This requires a radical paradigm shift in terms of the role of the consumer, from passive user to active agent in a global supply chain. Together with local youth movements, CATAPA is also applying for funding to register the water sources in the neighbourhood. Once water sources are officially registered, mining companies cannot simply claim the land upon which they lie. This will simplify the right to claim access to clean water for local communities.

Third Colombian case: Yaigojé Apaporis, a pioneering success

Comprising one million hectares of virgin rainforest in the northwestern Colombian Amazon, Yaigojé Apaporis is a hotspot for biodiversity, including endangered mammals such as the giant anteater, jaguar, manatee and pink river dolphin (PNN, n.d.). The region is also the ancestral home of the Makuna, Tanimuka, Letuama, Barasano, Cabiyari, Yahuna and Yujup-Maku indigenous peoples (Gomez Soto, 2015). These peoples share the Yuruparí spiritual tradition, which is rooted in a deep connection to territory and manifests in cultural and spiritual values that are coherent with what is described in the Global North as conservation (UNESCO, 2011). This cosmology underpins the governance systems and everyday economic activities of indigenous communities living in Yaigojé, compelling them to act as the region's guardians.

In 1988, this protective role was strengthened when, with the assistance of Colombian NGO Gaia Amazonas, the indigenous peoples of Yaigojé successfully encouraged the Colombian government to establish the Yaigojé Apaporis Resguardo over their traditional territory (TIG, n.d.). The creation of the *resguardo*, or "reserve", explicitly recognizes the rights of the indigenous peoples of Yaigojé Apaporis to land and self-determination. In recent years, however, the ability of Yaigojé's peoples to determine their own relationship with their territory has come under grave threat from a Canadian-owned mining project. The people of Yaigoijé's struggle against this project represents a struggle for self-determination and power not just between the mining company, State and indigenous peoples, but between two ways of knowing, interacting with and valuing nature.

Under Colombian law, a *resguardo* grants its inhabitants collective ownership of and rights to the soil, but the subsoil remains in the control of the State (Article 332) (Colombian Constitution 1991), leaving it vulnerable to prospecting. With companies seeking to exploit this loophole and the Colombian government declaring mining an "engine of growth", the Colombian Amazon has seen an increase in mining interest since the mid-2000s (Globe 24/7). In the late-2000s, representatives of Canadian mining company Cosigo Resources began visiting the *Malocas* (traditional riverside houses) of indigenous leaders in Yaigojé Apaporis. These leaders allege that officials offered them money in return for their support for the company to mine gold at a major sacred natural site, known as Yuisi/Yuika or La Libertad, that plays a central role in the cosmology and origin stories of Yaigojé's indigenous peoples (Rhoades, 2015).

The advances of Cosigo Resources were rejected by local leaders, who deemed the company's plans to extract at a sacred site unconscionable (Gomez Soto, 2015). To the people of Yaigojé, as a sacred site in the Yurupari tradition, Yuisi is a vital place, inextricably tied to their stories of origin, identities and ability to care for the territory and the planet as a whole (UNESCO, 2011). "Yuisi is the crib of our way of thinking, of life and power. Everything is born here in thought: nature, the crops, trees, fruits, everything that exists, exists before in thought" (Unnamed Elder cited in Rhoades, 2015).

Given that negotiation with Cosigo was out of the question, the Asociación de Capitanes Indígenas del Yaigojé Apaporis (ACIYA), an indigenous organization formed of representatives from the different peoples living along the Apaporis River, began organizing to protect their territory from mining. At the forefront of their strategies was a plan to expand their rights to self-determination to the subsoil.

Supported by NGO ally Gaia Amazonas, and advised that achieving national park status would extend protection to the subsoil, ACIYA formally requested that the Colombian National Parks Department create a national park over their *resguardo* and traditional territory (Gomez Soto, 2015).

> The best way to shield the territory was to call upon the state. In other words: Western disease is cured by Western medicine. If all mining licenses are given by the state, it is necessary to call on the state to defend the territory.
>
> (Gerardo Macuna, a representative of ACIYA)

ACIYA's efforts to add a third layer of protection for their territory were initially successful and in October 2009, Yaigojé Apaporis became Colombia's 55th national protected area (PNN, n.d.). But celebrations were short lived. Just two days after the area was awarded national park status, Cosigo Resources was granted a 2,000-hectare exploration and exploitation concession for the Yuisi area, catalysing a five-year legal struggle (Environmental Justice Atlas, 2008).

Recognizing that the establishment of a national park would mean the end of its mining ambitions, Cosigo Resources pursued the case doggedly through the courts. The company was initially buoyed by support from indigenous organization ACITAVA, from the region of Yaigojé Apaporis, lying in Vaupés State. Just months after Yaigojé was declared a national park, ACITAVA launched a legal challenge to Yaigojé's status at the Colombian Constitutional Court. This asserted that they had not been fully or adequately consulted in the process of creating the national park and it therefore violated their right to Free Prior and Informed Consent. However, during a public hearing in January 2014, involving Constitutional Court judges and 160 inhabitants from along the Apaporis River (Wilton, 2014), ACITAVA admitted its legal strategy was encouraged, organized and paid for by Cosigo Resources. In what would prove the critical turning point in the case, the indigenous members of ACITAVA who had initially supported the challenge made a public apology, said they had been misled and declared their support for the creation of the national park (Gomez Soto, 2015). More than a year later, in October 2015, the Colombian Constitutional Court formally recognized Yaigojé Apaporis's national park status, ending Cosigo's hopes of mining in the region as a whole (Rhoades, 2015). The company is now seeking damages as part of a $16 billion investor dispute settlement brought against the Colombian government under the Colombia-USA Free Trade Agreement (IAReporter, 2016).

At the heart of ACIYA's ultimately successful struggle lies a pioneering effort to go beyond the limited protections and self-determination afforded by Colombia's *resguardo* system. The arrival of Cosigo in Yaigojé exposed the fact that the protection conferred upon a territory by a *resguardo* and the self-determination it grants, stops at the soil "as deep as the manioc's root". This is an alien concept for the peoples of Yaigojé, whose shared conception of territory extends vertically, down into the earth and up into the sky, as well as horizontally across the land and water. ACIYA is now engaging with the Colombian National Parks Department to develop a collaborative-management plan that centres indigenous knowledge and extends indigenous peoples' self-determination and control over natural wealth beneath the soil, to include minerals.

Since the original proclamation of Yaigojé's national park status, a group of 27 young leaders from nine communities in Yaigojé Apaporis have become engaged in a process of endogenous cultural research, documenting the traditional knowledge of their elders and communities and mapping their territory (see: https://vimeo.com/116700866). This process is supported by Gaia Amazonas, and builds on decades of experience working alongside The Gaia Foundation (UK) to secure the land rights and governance systems of indigenous communities. The young leaders' research will form the basis for the collaborative management plan, which itself stems from a constitution that directly recognizes the authority of indigenous peoples and their knowledge in the future management of the Yaigojé Apaporis National Park:

> The indigenous traditional authorities have been managing the environmental elements in the territory, guaranteeing the continuation of life based in the principles that each ethnic group holds . . . The integral management of the territory will be done based on the traditional knowledge and the regulations given to each ethnic group since the beginning of the world.
>
> *(Constitution of Yaigoijé Apaporis National Park, agreed by ACIYA and the Colombian National Parks Department cited in Gomez Soto, 2015)*

By pursuing a proactive resistance strategy founded on self-determination and indigenous conceptions of sacred territory, ACIYA has done more than stop a mine; it has planted the seeds for an exciting new chapter in indigenous-led conservation. News of this innovative approach is now spreading, as young leaders engaged in the research process travel to other areas within Colombia and beyond. The story of what has been achieved in Yaigojé is also being spread through the efforts of the global Yes to Life, No to Mining Network. This network of mining-affected communities and their allies exists, in part, to promote examples of successful resistance and share lessons that may help other communities involved in preventative mining struggles (see: www.yestolifenotomining.org).

Conclusion

The growth in mining in Colombia in recent decades, supported by the extractivist policies of successive governments, has sparked anti-mining struggles across the nation. These struggles often manifest as movements for self-determination and the democratization of decision-making concerning the sources of natural wealth – clean water, healthy soils and ecosystems – that support sustainable livelihoods and human health.

The cases of Cerrejón, La Colosa and Yaigoje Apaporis each demonstrate the different ways in which diverse communities are attempting to re-assert control over this natural wealth and the places in which they live. The diversity of tactics employed in each case – from localized popular consultations to international solidarity campaigns – demonstrate the creative and well-networked nature of these efforts to combat projects, whose impacts are increasingly understood in their global context. As the threats have changed, so have the resistance tactics. At a deeper level, these struggles for self-determination reflect a push back against the corporate and State capture, not only of resources, but also of the meanings of nature and development that determine how those resources are used.

Viewed from the extractivist perspective, mining may be an "engine of growth" and, vis-à-vis, materialist development. But the communities who have lost livelihoods, sources of clean water and even relatives and friends to mining operations rarely feel the benefits of this questionable development. Nor do they necessarily define development in such narrow economic terms as gross domestic product (GDP) growth and foreign direct investment, which continue to be dominant development metrics, the benefits of which are vulnerable to capture by local and global elites. Likewise, the dominant understanding of nature as a potential resource to be exploited, which underpins the operations of the extractive industries, is not often one shared by frontline communities, whose physical, cultural and spiritual relationship to place is integral to their livelihoods and well-being.

Struggles for self-determination and democratization within conflicts involving the extractive industries represent a radical attempt to re-organize power over who values, and decides what to do with, resources, and to what end. As in the case of

Yaigoje Apaporis, they are also often an attempt to protect and revive the knowledge, ways of life and value systems that enable communities to live well in their own places, have truly sustainable relationships with the ecosystems that sustain them and negotiate the meaning of development for themselves. The struggle of communities in the Global South shares many similarities with the growing collection of voices in Europe seeking to reclaim the commons. Consumerism has bred individualistic values in European citizens; it is key for us to return to a collective way of thinking in the defence of our commons. Lessons can be learned from local communities in the South.

At a time of converging global social and ecological crises, precipitated in part by the globalization of unsustainable models of economic development, finding alternative models of development and new ways to live well with nature have never been more essential. This is why CATAPA, London Mining Network and The Gaia Foundation are supporting frontline communities and indigenous peoples struggling to realize their rights to self-determination, Free Prior and Informed Consent and democratic participation.

References

AngloGold Ashanti (2005) *Report to Society.* Available at: www.anglogold.com/NR/rdon lyres/E69E5630-9189-4F8E-9C52-B5F74DD50632/0/AngloGold_report05.pdf.

AngloGold Ashanti (2012) *2012 Project Profile La Colosa, Colombia*, 1–4. Available at: www.aga-reports.com/12/download/AGA-OP12-col-lacolosa.pdf.

Balch, O. (2013) Cerrejón Mine in Colombia: Can it Address its Human Rights Risks? *The Guardian.* Available at: www.theguardian.com/sustainable-business/cerrejon-mine-colombia-human-rights.

Betancur, A.C. and Villa, W. (2016) Mining and Indigenous Peoples in Colombia. *IWGIA.* Available at: www.iwgia.org/publications/search-pubs?publication_id=739.

Cerrejón (2016) *Our Company.* Available at: www.cerrejon.com/site/english/our-company.aspx.

Coal Action Network (2016) *Ditch Coal: The Global Impacts of the UK's Addiction to Coal.* Available at: http://coalaction.org.uk/ditchcoal/.

Colombia Solidarity Campaign (2011) *La Colosa: The Quest for El Dorado in Cajamarca, Colombia*, 1–34. Available at: www.colombiasolidarity.org.uk/attachments/article/548/La%20Colosa%20Report%204%20June%202011.pdf.

Colombia Solidarity Campaign (2013) *La Colosa: A Death Foretold.* London: BM Colombia Solidarity Campaign.

Colombian Constitution (1991) Available at: www.constituteproject.org/constitution/Colombia_2013.pdf?lang=en.

Environmental Justice Atlas (2008) *Yaigojé, Apaporis minas de oro, Colombia/Gold mining in Yaigoje paporis, Colombia.* Available at: http://ejatlas.org/conflict/Yaigojé-apaporis.

EJOLT (Environmental Justice Organisations, Liabilities and Trade) (2015a) *PPT Case: Glencore and El Cerrejón mine, Colombia.* Available at: https://ejatlas.org/conflict/el-cerrejon-mine-colombia.

EJOLT (Environmental Justice Organisations, Liabilities and Trade) (2015b) *Refocusing Resistance for Climate Justice: COPing in, COPing Out and Beyond Paris.* Eds Temper, L. and Gilbertson, T. Available at: www.ejolt.org/2015/09/refocusing-resistance-climate-justice-coping-coping-beyond-paris/.

Global Business Report (2011) Mining in Colombia. Exploring the Last Andean Frontier. *Engineering and Mining Journal* 12, 80–118.

Globe 24/7, *Mining in Colombia – An Engine of Growth.* Available at: www.globe24-7.com/7983/.

Gomez Soto, M. (2015) *The Unfolding Voice of Gaia.* MA thesis, Schumacher College.

Heinrich Boell Stiftung and Friends of the Earth (2015) *Coal Atlas: Facts and Figures on a Fossil Fuel.* Available at: www.boell.de/en/2015/11/05/coal-atlas-facts-and-figures-fossil-fuel?utm_campaign=ds_coal_atlas.

Hesperian Health Guides (2012) *Mining and Health.* Available at: http://hesperian.org/wp-content/uploads/pdf/en_cgeh_2012/en_cgeh_2012_21.pdf.

IAReporter (2016) *Canadian Mining Companies to Sue Colombia for 16.5 Billion Dollars.* Available at: www.yestolifenotomining.org/usa_canadian_mining_companies_to_sue_colombia_for_16-5billion/.

London Mining Network (2016) *Cerrejon Coal: The Marcha de Mantas Rojas.* Available at: http://londonminingnetwork.org/2016/08/cerrejon-coal-the-marcha-de-mantas-rojas/.

McNeish, J.A. (2016) Extracting Justice? Colombia's Commitment to Mining and Energy as a Foundation for Peace. *The International Journal of Human Rights*, 1–17.

Mines and Communities (2016) *Colombia's Largest Indigenous Group is Dying.* Available at: www.minesandcommunities.org/article.php?a=13489.

Observatory of Economic Complexity (OEC) (2016) *Colombia.* Available at: http://atlas.media.mit.edu/en/profile/country/col/.

PNN (n.d.) Yaigoije Apaporis National Park Profile. Available at: www.parquesnacionales.gov.co/portal/en/national-parks/yaigoje-apaporis-apaporis-natural-park/.

Pombo, C. and Ramírez, M. (2003) *Privatization in Colombia: A Plant Performance Analysis.* IDB Working Paper No. 166. Available at: https://ssrn.com/abstract=1814715 or http://dx.doi.org/10.2139/ssrn.1814715.

Prosansky, B. (2007) Mining Gold in a Conflict Zone: The Context, Ramifications, Lessons of AngloGold Ashanti's Activities in the Democratic Republic of the Congo. *Northwestern Journal of International Human Rights* 5 (2), 236–274.

Rhoades, H. (2015) *Indigenous Peoples of Yaigojé Apaporis Victorious as Court Ousts Canadian Mining Company.* Available at: https://intercontinentalcry.org/indigenous-peoples-of-yaigoje-apaporis-victorious-as-court-ousts-canadian-mining-company/.

Rudas Lleras, G. and Cabrera Leal, M. (2015) *Colombia and China: Social and Environmental Impact of Trade and Foreign Direct Investment. Discussion Paper, Global Economic Governance Initiative.* Boston University, 1–43. Available at: www.bu.edu/pardeeschool/files/2014/12/Colombia1.pdf.

Solly, R. (2016) *A Struggle Between a Tethered Donkey and a Tiger.* London Mining Network. Available at: http://londonminingnetwork.org/2016/08/cerrejon-coal-a-struggle-between-a-tethered-donkey-and-a-tiger/.

TIG (n.d.) Apaporis: Un territorio Donde los Indígenas Eligen la Figura de Área Protegida. Available at: www.territorioindigenaygobernanza.com/col_14.html.

UNESCO (United Nations Educational, Scientific and Cultural Organization) (2011) *Traditional Knowledge of the Jaguar Shamans of Yuruparí.* Available at: www.unesco.org/culture/ich/en/RL/traditional-knowledge-of-the-jaguar-shamans-of-yurupari-00574.

Wilton, F. (2014) *Judges Travel to the Amazon for Public Hearing on Yaigojé Apaporis and Gold Mining.* Available at: https://iccaconsortium.wordpress.com/2014/02/18/judges-travel-to-the-amazon-for-public-hearing-on-yaigoje-apaporis-and-gold-mining/.

World Health Organization (2016) *Mercury and Health.* Available at: www.who.int/mediacentre/factsheets/fs361/en/.

Zaitch, D. and Gutiérrez Gómez, L. (2015) Mining as State-Corporate Crime: The Case of AngloGold Ashanti in Colombia. In Gregg Barak (ed.), *The Routledge International Handbook of the Crimes of the Powerful.* New York: Routledge. Pp. 386–397.

Further reading

Global Campaign to Dismantle Corporate Power (2014) *Testimony of the Case in the Permanent Peoples Tribunal Hearing – Corporate Human Rights Violations and Peoples Access to Justice*. Geneva, 23 June. Available at: http://justice5continents.net/fc/viewtopic.php?t=1069&vplay=1.

Chomsky, A., Leech, G. and Striffler, S. (2007) *The People Behind Colombian Coal: Mining, Multinationals and Human Rights*. Bogota: Casa Editorial Pisando Callos.

Moore Foundation (2011) Co-Management of the Yaigoije Apaporis National Park. *Gaia Amazonas Grant History*. Available at: www.moore.org/grant-detail?grantId=GBMF2048.

The Gaia Foundation (2015) *Traditional Knowledge at the Heart of Protecting the Amazon*. Available at: https://vimeo.com/116700866.

UNCTAD (United Nations Conference on Trade and Development) (2016) *Cosigo Resources and Others vs Colombia*. Available at: http://investmentpolicyhub.unctad.org/ISDS/Details/726.

Uriana, G. (2008) Impactos Ambientales de la Extracción de Recursos Naturales y el Rol de La Mujer Wayuu Frente a los Cambios Climáticos en el Departamento de la Guajira, Colombia. In Ulloa, Astrid, Elsa Matilde Escobar, Luz Marina Donato y Pía Escobar, Editoras Ulloa et al. *Mujeres Indígenas y Cambio Climático*. Fundación Natura Colombia, UNODC and UNAL, Bogotá. Pp. 117–122.

2

PETRO-POLITICS AND LOCAL NATURAL RESOURCE PROTECTION

Grassroots opposition to the keystone XL pipeline in Nebraska

James Ordner

Introduction

After the global economic downturn in 2008, the structure of contemporary neo-liberalism entered a precarious phase of transformation that prompted a variety of economic responses from Western nations. In Europe, several countries enacted austerity and privatization measures to reduce the public deficit and economically stabilize the Eurozone. In the United States, the Obama Administration bailed out Wall Street banks as unemployment rates rose sharply across the country and thousands of people lost their homes. While the public sector and labour rights were impacted by economic austerity measures in Europe due to the financial collapse (see also Apostolopoulou et al., 2014 and Apostolopoulou and Adams, 2015 for an analysis of post-crisis environmental mobilizations in Europe), community safety and vital natural resource stocks were being threatened through a significant expansion of shale fracking operations in the United States.

In the wake of the economic downturn, oil and gas companies introduced several major pipeline projects and ramped up shale oil production in the United States using hydraulic fracturing technology. The shale fracking boom lasted throughout the Obama Administration, producing a glut of oil that dropped the price of crude to $37.04 a barrel in 2015 due to overproduction. During this time fracking operations contributed to local drinking water contamination, flaring pollution (carbon monoxide, nitrogen oxides), fresh water use competition between community and industry use and earthquakes in the heavily industrialized oil and gas state of Oklahoma. As the economic contours of neoliberalism adapt to the tensions created between capitalism's petroleum-dependent growth imperative and the real limits of vital natural resources, new forms of federal and state-level petro-politics have emerged in the US intent on disenfranchising community management of natural resources, criminalizing protests against energy projects and putting the monetary interests of oil and gas corporations before constituent's community needs and safety concerns.

This chapter explores the shift towards petro-politics in the United States through a discussion of several factors that paved the way for what can be described as a takeover of several federal government agencies by oil and gas industry representatives, and the potential for community-based coalitions formed to protect natural resources from risky energy projects as exemplified by landowner and concerned citizen opposition to the KXL pipeline in Nebraska.

I begin by discussing three key political factors that have contributed to tensions between communities and State political representation in relation to the protection of local natural resources and the expansion of oil and gas development: 1) Obama's "all of the above" energy policy, 2) the Citizens United campaign finance decision and 3) several administrative appointments and energy policy decisions enacted by the Trump Administration. To illustrate how local communities can mobilize to protect natural resources and challenge political leadership, I examine the case of the anti-Keystone XL pipeline (KXL) fight that occurred in rural Nebraska from 2010 to 2015. My analysis of the pipeline opposition movement in Nebraska is based on four years of research, including a content analysis of 528 individual testimonies from four KXL environmental review hearings held in Nebraska, in-depth interviews with key opposition members, and extensive field work in Nebraska. I examine the grievances that drove the opposition movement, how they framed those grievances and the resource mobilization strategies employed by the social movement organization Bold Nebraska to build and maintain an enduring grassroots movement in rural Nebraska.

Petro-politics and civil society

Neoliberalism is a difficult term to define. The basic founding ideology of neoliberalism is based on the "assumption that individual freedoms are guaranteed by freedom of the market and of trade" in the pursuit of capital accumulation (Harvey, 2005, p. 7). As a mode of capitalism, the political and economic contours of neoliberalism have evolved over time, adapting to advances in technology, transportation and politics. The economic impacts of neoliberalism are well known: privatization of public services, de-industrialization and automation, the outsourcing of manufacturing, globalization and expanded international trade and a general shift from material production to finance (Monbiot, 2016). In terms of the social and cultural outcomes of neoliberalism, we find a widening gap in earnings and wealth, the erosion of civil society, loss of social security and, most recently, a rise in nationalist and populist political sentiments due to economic insecurity, scarcity, fear of the other and widespread disenchantment with political leadership. After the 2008 economic crisis, neoliberalism began to take more authoritarian forms in Western democracies, illustrated by strict austerity policies across Europe and widespread economic insecurity in the US. The 2008 financial collapse shook the world economy and opened a space for the rise of corporate authoritarianism in the name of preserving the neoliberal programme from its self-destructive tendencies.

"All of the above" energy

Following the 2008 financial crisis, Barack Obama's Administration continued the Bush Administration's neoliberal economic agenda by bailing out the banks. Rather than cutting into social welfare programmes, the US turned to its untapped natural gas supplies via hydraulic fracturing technology to stimulate the economy. The Obama Administration's "all of the above" energy strategy represents an important policy that set the stage for the U.S. shale fracking revolution (Steffy, 2014). Obama's fracking policy was essentially a neoliberal solution to energy demands against the backdrop of the 2008 financial crisis, although the demands of economic growth – dependent on fossil fuels – likely made the decision to open up shale plays across the nation necessary. Relaxed fracking regulations certainly pleased the oil and gas industry and their shareholders.

The natural gas revolution, marketed to the public as a clean energy alternative, ultimately represents an experiment in testing the relationship between energy/economic demands and the needs of community safety and the protection of community assets, such as clean water. The safety and environmental risks associated with fracking, deep-sea drilling and tar sands extraction, all of which are considered "extreme energy" sources, are well documented (Ridlington et al., 2016). In relation to fracking, there have been numerous cases of drinking water contamination, competition for fresh water use between communities and fracking operations, and earthquakes related to fracking have occurred in fracking-heavy areas, particularly Oklahoma (Conca, 2016; Environmental Protection Agency, 2016; Rubright, 2016; Stockton, 2015). Barack Obama's "all of the above" strategy for energy production represents the neoliberal-lite style that he also employed in other policy arenas. He did ultimately reject the KXL pipeline due to environmental concerns, signed on to the Paris Climate Agreement and encouraged renewable energy development, yet the fracking revolution that Obama enabled also destroyed the natural environment and put communities at risk (Kelly, 2013; Ball, 2014).

Another important development that changed the political landscape in favour of oil and gas industry interests, particularly at the state level, was the Citizens United legal decision. On 21 January 2010 the Supreme Court ruled five to four that "political spending is protected under the First Amendment, meaning corporations and unions could spend unlimited amounts of money on political activities, as long as it was done independently of a party or candidate" (Levy, 2015). The Citizens United decision transformed the relationship between corporate campaign finance, political leadership and citizen representation.

The idea that corporations are due the same political rights as citizens is very controversial, and the Citizens United decision completely politicized campaign finance in favour of big business interests, particularly at the state level.

Citizens United and the oil and gas industry

One of the biggest benefactors of the Citizens United decision has been the oil and gas industry. Koch Industries, one of the most influential oil and gas organizations, contributed more than $9,000,000 to Republican candidates in 2016 (Center for Responsive Politics, 2017), and plan on spending a staggering 300 to 400 million on the 2018 mid-term elections (Beavers, 2017). Campaign contributions from oil and gas lobby groups, political action committees (PACS) and organizations offered to State level representatives is concerning because state political leaders have more power to shape legislation that directly impact State laws and regulations focused on energy production and infrastructure. Dissatisfaction with Washington, D.C. political leaders is nothing new in the US, but when State and local political leaders work against their constituents' health and safety concerns because of *quid pro quo* relationships with the oil and gas industry, political disenchantment can quickly erode public trust and create a leadership vacuum easily seized upon by political opportunists with good or ill intentions.

As a result of the 2008 financial collapse, combined with Obama's "all of the above energy" strategy and the Citizens United campaign financing law, we are now beginning to see the emergence of an emboldened petro-politics and corporate neoliberalism that threaten civil society and democratic institutions. Several thinkers have discussed the recent structural transformation of the classical neoliberal project and the danger it poses to democracy (Gamble et al., 2017; Lydon, 2017).

With the election of Donald Trump to the White House we have witnessed a drastic reversal of environmental protections, direct threats to citizens' right to protest energy projects and the installation of some of the most anti-environmental individuals to top posts in the federal government. The election of Trump, in many ways, represented a silent coup of several federal agencies by the oil and gas industry and corporate interests (Hand, 2017; Roberts, 2017b). The president of the oil and gas trade group Western Energy, for example, opined that "not in our wildest dreams, never did we expect to get everything" due to the election of Trump (Tabuchi and Lipton, 2017). With the appointment of Scott Pruitt to the Environmental Protection Agency, Rex Tillerson head of the State Department and Ryan Zinke as Interior Secretary, the Trump Whitehouse has installed people determined to transform America into an "energy dominant" power by opening up protected federal lands to oil and gas drilling and expanding fracking operations. The public safety implications and environmental consequences of radically deregulating the oil and gas energy, coupled with the vast amount of money funnelled into politics by industry lobbyists, could be devastating. Oil and gas oligarchs are capitalizing on the failures of neoliberalism by reshaping the economic and natural landscapes to encourage petroleum profiteering, while also curtailing of civil society protections in the name of economic necessity. This is a recipe for authoritarian capitalism (see also Apostolopoulou et al., 2014) driven by petro-politics.

In addition to the infiltration of the federal government by oil and gas industry lobbyists, we are also seeing the balkanization of State politics in terms of control of public lands, protest rights, and hostility towards community control of vital natural resources. Several States have put forth legislation to make it illegal for citizens to protest energy projects (Chen, 2017). States that depend on the oil and gas industry, such as Texas, have attempted to limit local control of natural resources when citizens mobilize to protect vital community assets (Phillips, 2015). Many of these States are deeply Republican, and there is a clear contradiction between the classical conservative values of limited government regulation/intervention and legal sanctions against a community's right to protect citizen health and safety. In 2014, for example, residents in Denton, Texas passed a moratorium (by 59%) on fracking in their community, citing safety concerns about water contamination, only to have Republican State legislators quickly pass a State law barring local communities from halting risky energy projects (Roth, 2016).

One of the first tasks of Interior Department Secretary Brian Zinke was to review the protected status of several national monuments and federally owned lands in western states. Zinke claims that deregulating federal lands and turning over control to States will boost oil and gas development in rural areas, create jobs and stimulate the overall economy (Volcovici, 2017). The concern is that States can ill afford to manage federal lands at the State level and cannot guarantee that deregulated land would not be sold to private interests in the future.

It is interesting that the attitudes towards public lands maintained by the Trump Administration closely mirror the radical populist ideology promoted by the Bundy militia that took over the Mauler Wildlife Refuge in Oregon in 2016. In January 2016, a group of about 50 armed men led by Amon Bundy occupied the Mauler Wildlife Refuge in Oregon to make a political statement against the federal ownership of land (Fuller, 2016). The Bundy's anti-government rhetoric disregarded federal claims to public land, demanding the government open federally owned land for ranching, mining and logging. While the Bundy's mobilization effort failed, the strong anti-public lands sentiments embraced by the Bundy's are reflected in policy decisions now being made by Trump Administration officials.

The Bundy militia connection, and the group's anti-government ideology, is also important for another reason. Politics in the US has always engendered partisanship, but the degree of resentment and bitterness we see in partisan politics today has reached a toxic level that is dividing the country. Conspiracy theories, political demonization, fake news, and social media applications that cause ideological tunnel-vision have worked to radicalize segments of the population. Many discussions examining the tensions between liberals and conservatives focus on ideological differences, but the rural/urban dichotomy is much more salient here. The Bundy takeover of the Malheur Wildlife Refuge captures the stark divergence of rural populism, which focuses on the plight of white rural males, and multicultural urbanism that tends to promote progressivism: two visions of the American experience defined by geography, non-human nature and the built environment.

So what potential solutions can overcome the divisive politics that pervades our society today? There are no simple answers to this question, but one area for coalition building to fight political authoritarianism and mitigate the impacts of climate change can be found in people's connection with the land they live on and around: *their community*.

The environmental cause and natural resource protection represents a threat to the oil industry because the realities of limited natural resources, and conserving those resources, is in many ways an extra-cultural problem that works to transcend partisan identity politics. Where culture fails us and identity politics result in exclusion, citizens can begin building coalitions by recognizing common cause beyond NIMBY (not-in-my-backyard) and short-term economic thinking. The successful mobilization of a determined group of landowners against the Keystone XL pipeline in rural Nebraska provides such a template for inclusive environmental civil engagement in the age of petro-politics.

Coalition building through natural resource protection

Neoliberal policies that in the past encouraged privatization and the dismantling of government regulation are now transforming into petro-political forms that increasingly threaten democracy and civil society. The growing tension between the aggressive expansion of oil and gas transportation infrastructure and the natural landscape surrounding communities is becoming a new front in the struggle to protect community assets and mitigate climate change through citizen mobilization.

Landowner opposition to the Keystone XL (KXL) pipeline in rural Nebraska provides a model for fighting risky energy projects and holding political power to account. Here I want to focus on landowners' grievances and examine some of the creative resource mobilization strategies Bold Nebraska employed to successfully organize and maintain a diverse coalition of political and cultural interests against the pipeline.

In 2008, the Canadian pipeline construction company TransCanada applied to the State Department for a permit granting permission to construct the KXL pipeline. The 1,179-mile-long, 36" diameter pipeline would cross six states in the US (Montana, South Dakota, Nebraska, Kansas, Oklahoma and Texas) and transport an estimated 850,000 barrels of diluted bitumen (dilbit for short) per day to refineries located on the Texas Gulf Coast and Louisiana. Facing rapidly growing anti-pipeline sentiment, President Obama delayed a permit decision while awaiting a supplemental Environmental Impact Statement, which he requested in response to citizens' concerns about potential leaks in the ecologically sensitive Sandhills and Ogallala Aquifer in Nebraska.

While the KXL debate became highly politicized at the national level, the primary battleground for the pipeline controversy was undoubtedly the state of Nebraska. Almost every delay in the permitting process or reconsideration of the pipeline's route was a result of persistent resistance within rural communities located along the pipeline's path in Nebraska, where about 100 landowners and several hundred concerned citizens organized a sustained mobilization campaign through the social movement organization Bold Nebraska to protect the Ogallala Aquifer.

Perceptions of injustice

Social movement scholars have long recognized the fundamental role perceptions of injustice and grievances play in motivating collective action (Gamson et al., 1982). When an individual or community feels that an injustice has been committed against them, it provides a rationale and justification for political engagement and collective mobilization. Injustice is a broad and somewhat malleable concept that can be perceived in a variety of ways. For example, community opposition to energy project proposals can be driven by political and government agency corruption, exclusion from the review process or unfulfilled promises made by energy companies, among other possible causes. In the case of the KXL debate in Nebraska, several key injustices drove landowner opposition to the pipeline, primarily concerns about toxic chemical leaks into the agriculturally vital Ogallala Aquifer. Landowners and concerned citizens demanded TransCanada either move the pipeline out of the Sandhills and off the aquifer or abandon the project altogether. While some of the injustices experienced by landowners were specific to the KXL debate in Nebraska, political corruption and concern for local natural resources, like clean water, are common oppositional frames appearing across many community opposition movements fighting energy projects (McAdam, Doug and Boudet, 2012; Sherman, 2011).

Besides potential contamination of the Ogallala Aquifer, there were two perceived injustices related to petro–politics and corporate authoritarianism that drove landowner opposition to the pipeline: 1) state political influence by TransCanada, and 2) threats of eminent domain and bullying of landowners. Looking at the public comment testimonies, we find that many landowners felt betrayed by their political representatives, complaining that Nebraskan legislators directly colluded with the oil and gas industry to get the project approved. There were several references to TransCanada's effort to influence state politicians and shape the outcome of the review process in Nebraska. In fact, TransCanada worked very hard to develop relationships with state politicians, county level officials and local Chambers of Commerce in order to promote the economic benefits of the project. TransCanada secured approval from political representatives and community business leaders before they confronted landowners with easement offers.

With pipeline support secured from political leaders and business interests, landowners were left disadvantaged if they decided to fight the pipeline. Unfortunately, the environmental review process as it stands tends to treat citizen input concerning energy projects as secondary. After spending millions of dollars to conduct an environmental review for approving the pipeline, coupled with state political leaders' quid pro quo agreements with oil and gas interests, the deck was stacked against Nebraska citizens fighting for their community's safety. Lobbying local and state officials for pipeline support worked to isolate landowners and create a sense of powerlessness within communities. Nebraskan politicians' failure to listen to citizen concerns bolstered the opposition mobilization campaign, and due to a lack of political leadership landowners began organizing to fight the project.

Two final injustices commonly identified in opposition testimonies included TransCanada's eminent domain threats and bully tactics employed by the company's land agents. The eminent domain issue (forced taking of private land) was a very important issue for many landowners, and in relation to perceptions of injustice, the threat of property condemnation by a foreign company represented a direct threat to farmer and rancher livelihoods. Property rights are considered sacred to farmers and ranchers, and TransCanada had no legal right to impose eminent domain on landowners without a State Department building permit.

Mobilizing resources: the Bold Nebraska model

Now we can turn to a discussion of the resource mobilization strategies used by Bold Nebraska (the social movement organization leading the anti-KXL fight) to form political coalitions to protect local natural resources. Bold Nebraska addressed citizen grievances through the use of a variety of resources, from economic to cultural assets. In most cases, successful social movement organizations (SMOs) mobilization campaigns require a wide range of resources to sustain a mobilization campaign. SMO resources can be either fungible or proprietary. Fungible resources, like money, are context independent and easily exchangeable between individuals, while proprietary resources, such as office space, are mostly context dependent (Edwards and McCarthy, 2004). Table 2.1 identifies the various types of resources utilized by Bold Nebraska for mobilizing rural landowners.

The first row of Table 2.1 contains examples of material resources, such as money, supplies and employees. The most obvious resource necessary for any mobilization attempt is financial support. Financial support translates to freedom of

TABLE 2.1 Bold Nebraska resource mobilization strategies

General resources	Sub-types	Examples
Material	Money, supplies, Employment	Donations, office space, and equipment, Bold employees, interns
Human	Generalized labour Specialized labour Leadership	Sign-making, Energy barn, Legal work, Lawsuits, Artists (PR) Charismatic/Inspirational
Social-organizational	Infrastructures, Social networks, Formal organizations	Meeting spaces, Protest spaces Allied with progressive organizations
Moral	Legitimacy, Solidarity Celebrity support	National protests, Sierra Club, 350.Org, Willie Nelson and Neil Young concert
Cultural	Repertoires of contention, Internet, Literature, Media	Nebraska cultural knowledge Bold Website, Reports, Videos

Source: James Ordner.

movement, and the more money a SMO has at its disposal, the more freedom it has to mobilize people. Bold Nebraska was very successful in soliciting donations on their website and organizing fundraising events. For example, on Bold's website you could donate money or purchase T-shirts, postcards and an anti-pipeline themed music CD. The Harvest of Hope concert held in Neligh on 27 September 2014 that showcased Willie Nelson and Neil Young raised approximately $125,000 dollars for Bold. With a steady flow of funds and material support, Bold was able to open an office in Lincoln, procure office equipment and hire staff members and interns.

In the second row of Table 2.1 are listed three types of human resources available for SMO mobilization campaigns: *generalized, specialized*, and *leadership*. In relation to Bold's mobilization campaign, generalized labour refers to unpaid volunteer labour at gatherings and events like billboard-making sessions and a renewable energy barn-raising, which took several months to complete. Unlike generalized labour, which almost anyone can do, specialized labour requires a particular skill set or experience working in a particular profession. The barn-raising event required both generalized and specialized labour. The barn project, which exemplifies Bold's effort to host events that resonated with rural Nebraskans' cultural values, required a range of specialized construction work, from laying the foundation to installing the wind turbine and solar panels that provides electricity for the barn.

Early in the KXL fight, the leader of Bold Nebraska Jane Kleeb and prominent Nebraska lawyer David Domina formed the Nebraska Easement Action Team (NEAT) to collectively represent landowners against TransCanada's eminent domain threats. The legal work NEAT undertook was also a form of specialized labour. More than any other action taken by landowners in Nebraska, the lawsuits brought by landowners ultimately killed the project. This fact cannot be understated in the context of community natural resource protection and petro-politics: traditional mass protests are very important for networking and building solidarity, but legal action is a much more effective method of stopping pipelines.

In addition to specialized legal counsel, Bold hired a graphic art designer (JKDC) to develop organization paraphernalia and movement imagery that resonated with rural Nebraskans. These art projects, such as event posters and T-shirts, were professionally designed and produced, and the style of the artwork is eye-catching in its simplicity. Leadership roles within social movements are also a key human resource for SMOs. Some people have that rare combination of charisma and passion that intersect with historical circumstances to produce important social movement leaders. The charismatic Jane Kleeb was the definitive leader of pipeline resistance in Nebraska. Without the leadership experience and tenacious commitment of Kleeb, the opposition movement to KXL in Nebraska may have never grown into a formidable mobilization campaign.

The third row of Table 2.1 concerns social-organizational resources, such as infrastructural assets and social networking with other organizations opposed to the pipeline. Some of Bold's infrastructural assets included public libraries made available for Bold/NEAT information sessions and public spaces open to collective protest, such as in front of the White House or the state capital in Lincoln, Nebraska. Bold also networked with other state and national environmental organizations opposed to the pipeline, including 350.org, Sierra Club, National Wildlife Federation, and the Natural Resources Defense Council. These social networks and alliances directly relate to the next row of resource assets, which involve the moral dimension of mobilization campaigns.

A movement has little chance of gaining momentum if is not perceived as legitimate, or if the frames, narratives and messaging used by SMO leaders do not resonate with the movement's target population. At the national level, the KXL fight mobilized people across the country to various degrees, coalescing in mass protests in Washington, D.C. on several occasions. The pipeline fight was certainly perceived as legitimate within the broader environmental movement in the US, as it has become a central cultural symbol for the movement's fight to curb global carbon dioxide emissions and begin shifting towards a renewable energy economy. Solidarity with well-established national organizations is important for garnering outside resources and moral support for a cause, but these organizational ties were not very important for mobilizing landowners on the ground in Nebraska. It was Bold's uniquely tailored messaging strategy – which mostly focused on the aquifer and private property rights – that resonated with traditionally conservative landowners. The more environmentally driven messaging of national environmental groups was not strongly reflected in the attitudes of many people living in rural communities along the route. Bold's close alliance with the Nebraska Farmers Union, however, helped establish Bold's legitimacy among farmers and ranchers. This suggests there were two levels of organizational legitimacy at work in the KXL debate in Nebraska, one operating at the local level grounded in agricultural values (that is, Bold's relationship with landowners through Nebraska Farmer's Union) and another operating at the national level based on solidarity (that is, Bold's relationship with nationally recognized organizations).

The last type of resources available to SMOs involves media and cultural assets. From the beginning of Bold's establishment in 2010, the organization maintained a website that acted as an information and motivational hub for people interested in learning about landowner resistance against the pipeline in Nebraska. Bold's website is professional looking and easy to navigate. Visitors can get the latest updates on the KXL fight, learn where the next action will take place and donate money. In addition to the website, Bold also maintains Flickr, YouTube, Twitter, Facebook and Google Plus accounts for archiving and distributing information, and they have also developed a "web-based interactive map and mobile App that will help promote small, local businesses who are working to keep Nebraska a great place to live and visit" (Bold, 2014).

For a SMO to be effective in their mobilization campaign, they must use mobilization strategies and tactics that reflect the cultural values of their constituency. This is where the notion of *repertoires of contention* comes into play. Repertoires of contention are essentially strategies for mobilization, although the term "repertoires" suggests the existence of a standardized set of potential mobilization tactics to choose from (McAdam et al. 2011). The range of tactics and strategies available for mobilization are virtually unlimited in terms of creative possibilities. The symbolic and cultural values embodied in acts of protest depend on the creative and imaginative capacities of SMO leaders and organization members.

Conclusion

Bold's mobilization efforts in rural Nebraska tapped into the cultural values and experience of rural landowners. The organization employed several recognizable repertoires of contention with a bit of rural Nebraska flavour added to make their campaign events relate to people living along the route. The creative projects and events organized by Bold reflected rural cultural values such as trial rides, several crop art projects and the Harvest of Hope Concert headlining Willie Nelson and Neil Young. Bold Nebraska successfully utilized all five types of resource assets to help facilitate mobilization efforts in rural Nebraska. The organization's staff (all natives of Nebraska) were knowledgeable about Nebraska's most pressing cultural and environmental issues and worked with landowners all along the proposed route to devise creative forms of protest.

Although the Trump Administration revived the KXL project, Bold Nebraska has vowed to keep fighting the pipeline in Nebraska, along with other communities fighting unwanted energy projects in other states. Bold Nebraska's grassroots organizational model has expanded to form the Bold Alliance, a network of state-based organizations located in Louisiana, Iowa, Oklahoma and Nebraska (Duggan, 2016), while many other communities, such as the Standing Rock mobilization in North Dakota, have organized broad alliances to fight oil and gas energy projects (Roberts 2017a).

With more communities threatened by risky energy projects, it is important to remember that environmental concerns represent the most powerful source of political opposition to neoliberalism (McCarthy and Prudham, 2004). Many people are frustrated and unhappy with the impacts of neoliberal policies on civil society, democratic institutions and environmental protection. Fighting risky energy projects to protect local natural resources represents a fruitful political space for overcoming the limits of long-standing cultural divisions. Making the cognitive connection between local concerns, like access to clean water, and global climate change can be difficult. In a time of rising petro-politics and corporate authoritarianism based on an ideology of energy dominance, the Bold Nebraska model for connecting community resource protection and greater environmental concerns through citizen coalitions offers a hopeful way towards achieving social and environmental justice.

References

Apostolopoulou, E. and Adams, W. (2015) 'Neoliberal Capitalism and Conservation in the Post-crisis Era: The Dialectics of "Green" and "Un-green" Grabbing in Greece and the UK.' *Antipode* 47, 15–35.

Apostolopoulou, E. et al. (2014) 'Governance Rescaling and the Neoliberalization of Nature: The Case of Biodiversity Conservation in Four EU Countries.' *International Journal of Sustainable Development & World Ecology* 21, 481–494.

Ball, J. (2014) *Obama's Meaningless "All of the Above" Energy Strategy is Infuriating Both Environmentalists and Fossil Fuelers.* Available at: https://newrepublic.com/article/116397/obamas-energy-policy-all-above-meaningless. [Accessed 16 July 2017.]

Beavers, O. (2017) *Koch Brothers to Spend $400 Million on Republican Candidates in 2018.* Available at: http://thehill.com/blogs/blog-briefing-room/news/339399-koch-brothers-to-spend-400-million-on-republican-candidates-in. [Accessed 25 May 2017.]

Bold Nebraska (2014) *We Mobilize Unlikely Alliances to Protect the Land and Water.* Available at: http://boldnebraska.org/about/. [Accessed 25 June 2017.]

Center for Responsive Politics (2017) *Oil and Gas Top Contributors, 2015–2016.* Open Secrets.org. Available at: www.opensecrets.org/industries/indus.php?ind=E01. [Accessed 4 May 2017.]

Chen, M. (2017) *America's Freedom to Protest is Under Attack.* Available at: www.thenation.com/article/americas-freedom-protest-attack/. [Accessed 6 June 2017.]

Conca, J. (2016) *Thanks to Fracking, Earthquake Hazards in Parts of Oklahoma Now Comparable to California.* Available at: www.forbes.com/sites/jamesconca/2016/09/07/the-connection-between-earthquakes-and-fracking/#13a8bfb6d68e. [Accessed 7 September 2016.]

Dugan, J. (2016) *Bold Nebraska Leader to Run Umbrella Group, Bold Alliance, with Chapters in Three Other States.* Omaha Herald. Available at: www.omaha.com/news/nebraska/bold-nebraska-leader-to-run-umbrella-group-bold-alliance-with/article_e05ee2a2-e551-51d2-a430-498d6d7a204c.html. [Accessed 3 June 2016.]

Duggen, J. (2017) *Bold Nebraska Leader to Run Umbrella Group, Bold Alliance, with Chapters in Three Other States.* Available at: www.omaha.com/news/nebraska/bold-nebraska-leader-to-run-umbrella-group-bold-alliance-with/article_e05ee2a2-e551-51d2-a430-498d6d7a204c.html. [Accessed 8 May 2017.]

Edwards, R. and McCarthy, J. (2014) Resources and Social Movement Mobilization. In D. Snow and S. Soule (eds), *The Blackwell Companion to Social Movements.* London: Blackwell. Pp. 116–152.

Environmental Protection Agency (2016) *Hydraulic Fracturing for Oil and Gas: Impacts from the Hydraulic Fracturing Water Cycle on drinking water resources in the United States.* Available at: https://cfpub.epa.gov/ncea/hfstudy/recordisplay.cfm?deid=332990. [Accessed 15 December 2016.]

Fuller, J. (2016) *The Long Fight between the Bundys and the Federal Government, from 1989 to Today.* Available at: www.washingtonpost.com/news/the-fix/wp/2014/04/15/everything-you-need-to-know-about-the-long-fight-between-cliven-bundy-and-the-federal-government/?utm_term=.7c3bff15f240. [Accessed 16 July 2017.]

Gamble, J., Mason, P., Covert B., Darity, W. and Barnes, P. (2017) *What Will Kill Neoliberalism?* Available at: www.thenation.com/article/what-will-kill-neoliberalism/. [Accessed 4 May 2017.]

Gamson, W., et al. (1982) *Encounters with Unjust Authority.* Illinois: Dorsey Press.

Gamson, W. and Myer, D. (1996) Framing Political Opportunity. In D. McAdam, J. McCarthy and M. Zald (eds), *Comparative Perspectives on Social Movements.* New York: Cambridge University Press, pp. 275–290.

Hand, C. (2017) *New Database Shows Trump is Filling the Government with Fossil Fuel Lobbyists.* Available at: https://thinkprogress.org/dirty-deputies-fill-trump-administration-9e78a260e62b. [Accessed 26 June 2017.]

Harvey, D. (2005) *A Brief History of Neoliberalism.* New York: Oxford University Press.

Jones, D. (2014) *Masters of the Universe: Hayek, Friedman, and the Birth of Neoliberal Politics.* New Jersey: Princeton University Press.

Kelly, S. (2013) *A Closer Look at Obama's "All of the Above" Energy Policy.* Available at: www.ecowatch.com/a-closer-look-at-obamas-all-of-the-above-energy-policy-1881713052.html. [Accessed 16 Jul 2017.]

Levy, G. (2015) *How Citizens United Has Changed Politics in 5 Years: The Controversial Supreme Court Ruling Has Remade How Campaigns are Run in the U.S.* Available at: www.usnews.com/news/articles/2015/01/21/5-years-later-citizens-united-has-remade-us-politics. [Accessed 21 January 2015.]

Lydon, C. (2017) *Noam Chomsky – Neoliberalism is Destroying our Democracy.* Available at: www.thenation.com/article/noam-chomsky-neoliberalism-destroying-democracy/. [Accessed 2 June 2017.]

McAdam, D. and Boudet, H. (2012) *Putting Social Movements in Their Place: Explaining Opposition to Energy Projects in the United States, 2000–2005.* New York: Cambridge University Press.

McAdam, D., McCarthy, J. and Sidney, T. (2011) *Dynamics of Contention.* New York: Cambridge University Press.

McCarthy, J. and Prudham, S. (2004) Neoliberal Nature and the Nature of Neoliberalism. *Geoforum* 35, 275–283.

Monbiot, G. (2016) *Neoliberalism – The Ideology at the Root of All our Problems.* Available at: www.theguardian.com/books/2016/apr/15/neoliberalism-ideology-problem-george-monbiot. [Accessed 16 July 2017.]

Phillips, A. (2015) *Texas Governor Signs Bill that Makes Local Fracking Bans Illegal.* Available at: https://thinkprogress.org/texas-governor-signs-bill-that-makes-local-fracking-bans-illegal-bccd73b6046. [Accessed 16 July 2017.]

Ridlington, E., Norman, K. and Richardson, R. (2016) *Fracking by the Numbers: The Damage to our Water, Land and Climate from a Decade of Dirty Drilling.* Available at: www.environmentamerica.org/reports/ame/fracking-numbers-0. [Accessed 4 April 2016.]

Roberts, D. (2017a) *Blue America Reaches Out to the World, Ignoring Trump: States and Cities are Forming a Kind of Parallel National Government around Climate Change.* Available at: www.vox.com/energy-and-environment/2017/6/30/15892040/blue-america-trump?utm_campaign=vox.social&utm_medium=social&utm_source=twitter&utm_content=1498850010. [Accessed 1 July 2017.]

Roberts, D. (2017b) *Donald Trump is Handing the Federal Government over to Fossil Fuel Interests.* Available at: www.vox.com/energy-and-environment/2017/6/13/15681498/trump-government-fossil-fuels. [Accessed 14 June 2017.]

Roth, Z. (2016) *What Happened in Denton: The War on Local Democracy.* Available at: www.nbcnews.com/news/us-news/what-happened-denton-war-local-democracy-n620926. [Accessed 2 August 2016.]

Rubright, S. (2016) *34 States Have Active Oil & Gas Activity in U.S. Based on 2016 Analysis.* Available at: www.fractracker.org/2017/03/34-states-active-drilling-2016/. [Accessed 23 March 2017.]

Sherman, D. (2011) Critical Mechanisms for Critical Masses: Exploring Opposition to Variation in Low-level Radioactive Waste Sight Proposals. *Mobilization* 16, 721–743.

Steffy, L. (2014) *Obama's "All-of-the-Above" Energy Push Becomes a Strategy of One.* Available at: www.forbes.com/sites/lorensteffy/2014/01/29/obamas-all-the-above-energy-push-becomes-a-strategy-of-one/#53d4b1735172. [Accessed 16 July 2017.]

Stockton, N. (2015) *Fracking's Problems Go Deeper than Water Pollution.* Available at: www.wired.com/2015/06/frackings-problems-go-deeper-water-pollution/. [Accessed 18 May 2015.]

Tabuchi, H. and Lipton, E. (2017) *How Rollbacks at Scott Pruitt's E.P.A. are a Boon to Oil and Gas.* Available at: www.nytimes.com/2017/05/20/business/energy-environment/devon-energy.html. [Accessed 20 May 2017.]

Volcovici, V. (2017) *Interior Head Says Public Lands Can Make U.S. a "Dominant" Oil Power.* Available at: www.reuters.com/article/us-usa-interior-zinke-idUSKBN19A1KG. [Accessed 19 June 2017.]

3

NAVIGATING STATE-LED EXTRACTIVISM IN ECUADOR AND RUSSIA

Fluid identities and agendas of socio-environmental movements

Denisse Rodríguez and Julia Loginova

Introduction

The discourse of ecologically responsible and sustainable resource extraction has been one of the promises of the contemporary neoliberal environmental agenda, and has shaped the development trajectory of many countries seeking to legitimise intensive resource extraction, often at the expense of environmental and social justice. Resource extraction-driven development results in conflicts over control of and access to natural resources, such as land and water. In particular, mining projects are notable for significantly altering rural livelihoods and the underlying social and cultural fabric of surrounding communities (Gilberthorpe and Hilson, 2014).

Rural communities, concerned about the socio-economic and environmental implications of large-scale resource extraction, often feel compelled to mobilize, giving rise to socio-environmental movements. A political ecology approach allows an understanding of mobilization around environmental issues as encompassing the defence of endangered livelihoods and territories that are usually contested or repressed by both powerful states and private actors (Bebbington et al., 2008; Leff, 2015; Martínez-Alier, 2002). We use this approach to analyse the struggles of two socio-environmental movements: the water guardians of Kimsakocha in Ecuador and the Pechora River saviours in Russia. The first movement contests an impending gold mining project in Ecuador, where large-scale metal extraction is promoted by the government as an engine for development. The movement in Russia opposes negligent crude oil extraction and the ongoing expansion of the industry, which is central to the government's geopolitical and development agenda.

The experiences of the water guardians of Kimsakocha and the Pechora River saviours exhibit similar patterns that offer grounds for comparison. Both movements emerged from rural communities potentially or already affected by large-scale resource extraction projects. They defend the ecosystems that sustain local livelihoods: the *páramo* (Andean wetlands ecosystem) of Kimsakocha and the Pechora River and its valley. Further, the movements find themselves directly contesting their governments, as in Ecuador and Russia major decisions over whether or not to extract resources, and under what terms, are strongly influenced by the state. Both governments have also adopted a fair and sustainable resource extraction agenda. Despite the rhetoric of good governance, uneven power structures become evident when the state apparatus favours extraction through privileges in licensing, taxation and subsidies, as well as influencing corporate decision-makers. Moreover, to ensure a social licence to operate, governments intervene in emerging conflicts and grievances. Their approaches can range from oppression to complex appeasement to tame dissent and to limit participation.

The aim of this chapter is to explore how the socio-environmental movements have navigated through power asymmetries in the quest of spaces to demand meaningful participation in decision-making and secure their own aspirations for development. We ask how the water guardians of Kimsakocha and the Pechora River saviours have adapted to the changing political environment resulting from the promotion of resource extraction as an imperative for development by the Ecuadorian and Russian governments. Fieldwork, conducted in Ecuador in 2016 and in Russia in 2015, revealed that the movements address a wide portfolio of strategies and transit through multiple identities, successively and in parallel. Their collective identities and agendas are not fixed; rather they are flexible and adapt according to the communities' perceptions of the multiple implications of extractivism, as well as the opportunities and constraints of the political environment. We argue that an understanding of the movements' identities and agendas through the metaphor of "fluidity" better accounts for the reactive and strategic adaptation that allows them to navigate myriad processes and actors in an ever-changing context.

The next section introduces the socio-economic and political context in which the water guardians of Kimsakocha and the Pechora River saviours emerged. Then, we compare how both movements have adapted in response to the shifting context that followed the promotion of resource extraction. For analytical purposes, we focus on three domains: networking and building alliances, moving across scales of political and popular support and adapting to legal frameworks. Next, we discuss how fluid identities and agendas enabled that adaptation. The chapter concludes by reflecting on opportunities for promoting transformations.

The struggles over the environment and local livelihoods in Ecuador and Russia

Extractivism and the water guardians of Kimsakocha

The 2008 Constitution of Ecuador was considered a milestone for social and environmental justice, since it advocated for a displacement of the neoliberal agenda and the adoption of a post-neoliberal, post-development or even an "alternative" to development regime (Acosta, 2010; Gudynas, 2011). It proposed *Buen Vivir* (collective well-being) as a development model based on harmonious coexistence with nature and recognized the Rights of Nature (Articles 71–74). At present, the socio-environmental movements that supported this development regime have a contentious relationship with the government given the path subsequently followed under the leadership of former president Rafael Correa. The state assumed the role of promoter of development and has been sponsoring mining ventures. First, metal mining has been declared an area of strategic development and, therefore, of national interest. Legally, this allows the state to control strategic non-renewable resources in indigenous and community territories without consent. Second, legal frameworks have been modified to authorize mining exploitation in protected areas. Third, tax incentives and exemptions have been offered to multinational companies to attract mining investments. Overall, the discourse of fair mining for development has been adopted to legitimize extractivism, framing it as a transitional stage or a means towards *Buen Vivir* (Escobar, 2010, p. 22).

The breach of the national agreement for a new development model triggered a strong response from civil society. Socio-environmental movements emerged especially from people potentially affected by extractivist projects. Such is the case of the resistance against the Loma Larga gold project, owned by the Canadian company INV Metals.

The mine is located within the Macizo El Cajas Biosphere Reserve, in the *páramo* of Kimsakocha (see Figure 3.1), which supplies drinking water and irrigation community systems. Since 2003, the community water users of the Tarqui-Victoria del Portete system have mobilized as the water guardians of Kimsakocha. More than being an anti-mining movement, the participants define themselves as a pro-life, pro-community and pro-nature movement (Rodríguez, 2016). Their main concerns are the threats imposed to the *páramo* as a strategic ecosystem and to their livelihoods as farmers, mostly dedicated to dairy production. The movement has appealed to the right to resist (Article 96, 2008 Constitution), mainly through civil disobedience and public protests. They contested the deepening of extractivism under Correa's rule and his government's tendency to repress and criminalise social protest (Gudynas, 2009; Ospina, 2015; PADH, 2012). Since 2012, environmental rights' defenders, including three community leaders of Kimsakocha, have been accused and condemned for acts of rebellion, terrorism or sabotage when participating in public protests.

Hydrocarbon extraction and the Pechora River saviours

Since the 2000s, under the presidency of Vladimir Putin, strategic policy to integrate Russia into the global capitalist economy has been centred on large-scale extraction and export of hydrocarbons. The government has supported state-owned, transnational and national private energy companies to access the reserves in Siberia and the Arctic. Increasingly overlapping with territories of traditional land use and protected areas, oil extraction has generated social and environmental impacts that currently co-exist with pressing issues of cultural loss and lack of

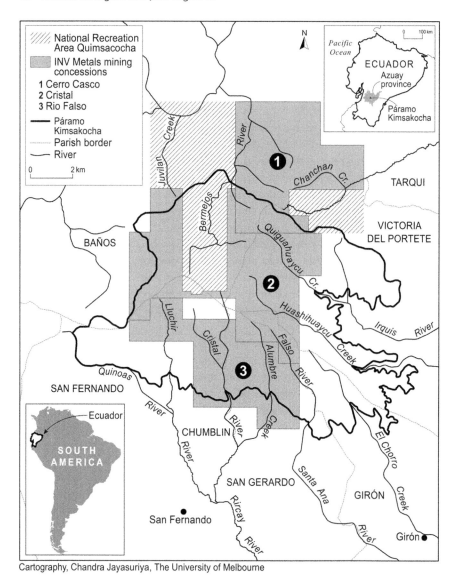

Cartography, Chandra Jayasuriya, The University of Melbourne

FIGURE 3.1   Water sources of the *páramo* of Kimsakocha and mining concessions

Source: Community mapping developed by Nataly Torres (2015), Paola Maldonado and FIAN.

development in rural areas. The socio-environmental movement of the Pechora River saviours was established as the Save Pechora Committee (SPC) in 1989 by rural and urban residents of the *Pripechor'e* area in the Komi Republic, a region west to the northern Ural Mountains (see Figure 3.2). Residents have been in the front line, defending rivers and forests from irresponsible oil extraction and transportation, resulting in water, land and air pollution. They also contest the expansion

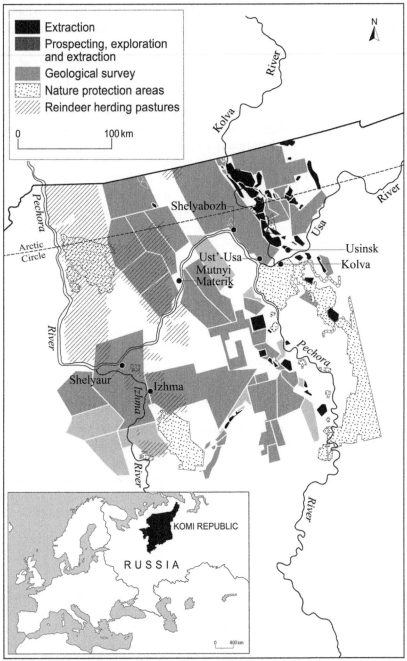

Cartography, Chandra Jayasuriya, The University of Melbourne

FIGURE 3.2 The Pechora River valley, oil extraction concessions and reindeer herding pastures

Source: Rosgeolfund (2018) and community mapping.

of the oil industry in protected areas and ancestral lands, threatening traditional livelihood activities of Komi and Komi-Izhma people, including reindeer herding, fishing, hunting and gathering.

The legal right to organize collective actions in Russia is a by-product of Gorbachev's policy of *glasnost* (openness and freedom of expression) in the late 1980s. The 1993 Russian Constitution granted rights for collective actions, including protests (articles 29, 30, 31) and the federal laws defined the regime for legitimate collective actions, including a requirement for non-governmental organisations (NGOs) to register with the Ministry of Justice. Social movements in Russia are often regarded as hard to sustain, due to financial constraints, a deficit of information, and censorship (Alexander and Grävingholt, 2002). In 2006, the government seriously restricted the right to association and challenged the privacy of social movements (Federal Law #18-FZ; Kamhi, 2006). Since 2012, the pressure on civil society has been particularly strong, resulting in increased restrictions on the sources of funding and the political agenda of NGOs (Federal Law #121-FZ; Gilbert, 2016). Many civil society groups had to cease their activities or have been fined for not declaring their political status.

In summary, the political transformations that took place in Ecuador and Russia, the way in which actors frame resource extraction, the increased legal restrictions to the movement's sphere of action and consequent fear and self-censorship, reflect the asymmetrical power relations that characterize the interaction between the movements and the governments.

Navigating state-led extractivism in Ecuador and Russia

In order to find spaces for action and navigate asymmetrical power relations, socio-environmental movements engage simultaneously in evolving social, political and legal arenas. We compare the experiences of the water guardians of Kimsakocha and the Pechora River saviours aiming to show how a diversity of roles have emerged from the strategic and reactive responses to everyday struggles when coping with a shifting environment through alliance-building, achieving popular and political support and engaging with legal frameworks.

Networking and building alliances

In Ecuador, since their emergence from water users' associations, the water guardians of Kimsakocha have been affiliated with various peasant and indigenous organizations. At a local level, water users are organized through the Union of Community Water Systems of Azuay (UNAGUA). This Union is related at a provincial level to the Federation of Indigenous and Peasant Organizations of Azuay (FOA). Regionally, it is linked to the Confederation of Peoples of Kichwa Nationality (ECUARUNARI) and, at the national level, to the Confederation of Indigenous Peoples of Ecuador (CONAIE). Furthermore, their role of water guardians has broadened through the adoption of a holistic vision of defending the hydrologic system – not only the water sources for community water systems. This created affinities with urban, environmental and youth movements, most prominently *Yasunidos* that demands the protection of *Macizo El Cajas* as a whole. In addition, the framing of environmental defence not only as a local, but as a national struggle, has favoured networking with national social movements as *Asamblea de los Pueblos del Sur* and international ones from Central America and Peru, NGOs (Acción Ecológica, Fundación Savia Roja and Food First Information and Action Network (FIAN)) and foreign experts (Miningwatch Canada and university researchers).

In Russia, the Pechora River saviours partnered with Greenpeace Russia following the dramatic Usinsk oil spill in 1994. Recently, the SPC has engaged with the protection of the Arctic's fragile environment and indigenous livelihoods internationally, as the global interest in the Arctic and its energy resources grow, for example, through the Greenpeace International campaign on restricting Arctic oil extraction. The incessant oil pollution in the region continually attracts foreign and domestic scholars, offering advice on future actions. The SPC maintains close connections with ethnic movements and associations of indigenous peoples, including the Komi-Izhma people Movement 'Izvatas', the Committee of the Finno-Ugric Peoples, the Russian Association of Indigenous Peoples of the North (RAIPON) and environmental movements like Silver Taiga, Ecologists of Komi, International Socio-ecological Union, and the Network of the Russian rivers.

The engagement with various movements and organizations, through personal relationships, alliance building and networking, has allowed not only the opposition to mining and oil extraction projects, but also to address broader issues of the development models imposed by the Ecuadorian and Russian governments.

Political and popular support

In the Ecuadorian case, engagement with politicians is viewed with suspicion by the community. The common reaction towards the movement's leaders approaching authorities to get their political support was explained by one of the interviewees: "You know, countryside people always distrust politicians" (personal communication, February 2016, Victoria del Portete). Notwithstanding, it is at the political level where the water defenders of Kimsakocha have achieved two main successes. The first in 2008, when the Constitutional Assembly – adopting the claims of indigenous and social movements to regulate mining activity – issued the Mining Mandate that declared the extinction of mining concessions granted within natural protected areas or affecting water sources (Constitutional Mandate no. 6, Article 3). In January 2017, the second achievement was the declaration of the city of Cuenca and the Cajas National Park as free from metal mining. This was accomplished after several months of lobbying for a Cantonal Council debate on the mining threat. In pursuing them, the movement has assumed an active political role and has consolidated ties with allies at different scales, from the national indigenous movement, to different decentralized governments at provincial, cantonal and parish level. Unfortunately, their successes have not been enforced.

In Russia, the SPC continually press for changes in regulations and practices by securing close connections with the regional and local environmental government offices. The movement has successfully promoted several regulatory initiatives, for example, in the area of oil spills monitoring and replacement of outdated oil pipelines, which has achieved support at the national level after Greenpeace Russia and the SPC made a claim. The commitment to support traditional livelihoods of Komi-Izhma people, fighting for their recognition as "indigenous small-numbered peoples of the North, Siberia and the Far East", according to Russian legislation, brought the SPC wider popular support from rallies and protests in villages of *Pripechor'e*. The movement also runs the only newspaper in the region dedicated to environmental issues and maintains a website (www.savepechora.ru) with updates on important accidents, meetings and protests. To sum up, seeking the support of authorities has proven fruitful for both movements, however, there has been a limited enforcement of the commitments achieved. Under these circumstances, empowerment and enhancing the participation of community members has been decisive, as shown in the Russian case.

Engaging with legal frameworks

The water guardians of Kimsakocha have defined themselves as defenders of the collective, human and environmental rights set forth in the new Constitution. They supported the demands of illegality made to the Constitutional Court by CONAIE over the 2009 Mining Law, claiming that it breached the 2008 Mining Mandate and the right to free, prior and informed consent, and over the 2014 Water Law, for breaching the rights of community water managers. In addition, numerous international demands have been made to the Inter-American Commission of Human Rights. Also asserting constitutional rights, in 2012 UNAGUA presented a proposal for a referendum to ask the population of Girón canton if they agree that mining activities be carried out in the *páramo* and water sources of Kimsakocha. After delays in the process, in 2015 the National Electoral Council (CNE) delivered the forms for the collection of signatures, followed by their submission in July. The next step was the validation of signatures, which according to leader Jhonny Tapia was challenging and led to fear and demotivation given the frustrating experience of *Yasunidos*. In 2014, they proposed a referendum for preventing the exploitation of the Yasuni ITT oilfields but 40% of their signatures were invalidated (personal communication, August 2016, Girón). The water guardians "survived" the validation process but the deadlines for implementing the referendum have not been respected by CNE.

In their actions, the Pechora River saviours feel a constant need to adapt to evolving legal frameworks, bridging the Russian constitutional principles and their interpretation by government officials. A recent example is the Foreign Agent Law, enacted in 2012, which requires NGOs to register as foreign agents if they receive foreign grants and engage in politics. In response to this legislation, the SPC has opted to be independent from the state and work as an informal movement rather than as a registered NGO. As Pierk and Tysiachniouk (2016, p. 1003) explain, this was a strategic choice and as a result "no allegations of being a foreign agent can be brought by the state". There also have been apparent attempts to neutralize the critical voices of the SPC, for example, through the Komi regional government support of the short-lived NGO Zelennaya Respublika (Green Republic), which not only promoted the sustainability of the oil extraction industry in the "Eco-Republic of Komi", but also portrayed the actions of the SPC as undermining the stability of the state. Moreover, the regional political leadership continues to favour resource extraction projects. Following the arrest of the former Komi Governor in 2015, a newly elected Governor has been promoting gold extraction in the Yugyd Va National Park (included in the UNESCO World Heritage List of "Virgin Komi Forests") and also merged the Ministry of Natural Resources and Environmental Protection into the Ministry of Industry, Transport and Energy. The reactive response by the SPC was to demand an environmental referendum in 2017, and besides resolving issues of controversial gold extraction and Ministerial conflict of interests, they insist on a ban on the use of oil pipelines commissioned prior to 2000. Despite operating within constitutional and legal frameworks, the bureaucratic procedure to register the referendum initiative has been overwhelming. For example, the signatures have been hard to validate, and the government office has not met the deadlines. A leader of the SPC summarizes the common experiences: "the laws and legislation are on our side, the bureaucrats are not" (personal communication, June 2015, Usinsk).

The two movements have adopted an active role in seizing the opportunities offered by evolving legal frameworks in Ecuador and Russia. However, their efforts have been neutralized by different government institutions, suggesting that navigating government processes requires not only taming legislation, but strategizing and engaging with bureaucrats that follow the rules of the game delineated to secure state-led extractivism.

Fluid identities and agendas of socio-environmental movements

Collective action is a process rather than an end-point (Bebbington et al., 2008; Escobar and Alvarez, 1992). In this process, the construction of collective identity is fundamental. It constitutes "an interactive and shared definition produced by several individuals and concerned with the orientations of action and the fields of opportunities and constraints in which the action takes place" (Melucci, 1985, p. 342). Identity is not fixed, but continuously constructed and shaped through the process of organisation and strategic actions by social movements (Foweraker, 1995; Leff, 2015). Therefore, identities and agendas are intertwined. We propose that the analogy of "fluidity" is useful to describe the process of constant reshaping and moulding of identities and agendas embedded in everyday practice of social movements. It has potential to explain their flexibility to change, to adapt to the immediate situation and to operate through coexisting multiple identities and agendas.

According to Sheller (2000, p. 1), metaphors of "flow", "ubiquitous" and "liquidity" are already being used in the literature on social movements. She suggests that "fluid" imageries can explain the relational mechanisms of interaction between movements and their changing context, as reflected in their engagement with institutions and communities and the scope of their actions.

Although the distinct historical and geographical context cannot be ignored, the experiences of the water guardians of Kimsakocha and the saviours of the Pechora River exhibit three patterns of our understanding of fluidity. First, we observe that taking advantage of fluid identities and agendas, these movements mobilized resources to influence their social and political environment, but also to adapt to the ever-changing context. Thus, fluidity is produced by the continuous interaction between movements and context, and reflects the processes of "movements-in-action and contexts-in-process" (Sheller, 2000, p. 3). Second, both movements emerged within communities concerned with the multiple impacts of resource extraction and other overlapping socio-economic and cultural processes. Also, their commitment to social and environmental justice requires flexibility to address the myriad concerns of the communities. Therefore, fluidity of identities and agendas is rooted in the nature of the movements' origin and simultaneously it constitutes a strategic choice. And, finally, the experiences of the movements in Ecuador and Russia show that operating at different scales is crucial. On the one hand, local struggles are linked with globalized processes of capital accumulation through state-led extractivism. On the other hand, legal and institutional opportunities and constraints are present at different government levels. In this sense, fluidity enables a flexible engagement with the increasingly blurred boundaries between the local and the global as well as the interaction with multiple political actors and networking and alliance-building across scales. Through two examples we explain how the water guardians of Kimsakocha and the Pechora River saviours have put their identities and agendas in motion exhibiting these three patterns of fluidity.

The water guardians of Kimsakocha and the Pechora River saviours have defined themselves as rights defenders, which has allowed them to respond to changes in the social and political context, to defend community livelihoods and also to raise their concerns across different levels of government. First, the adoption of this identity resulted from the need to find alternative ways to protest when open resistance is restricted. Novel frameworks offered opportunities to demand environmental and social justice. Accordingly, both movements appealed to referendum proposals to demand popular participation in environmental decision-making. Second, the defence of rights also allows to address the multiple concerns of the communities from which the movements emerged. Both movements have become custodians of livelihoods and defenders of the communities' rights, expanding their range of action to respond to emergent issues affecting the local population, beside the threats of mining and oil extraction. For example, in Ecuador, the water guardians have defended the local communities in recent struggles affecting dairy farmers, including an attempt at land grabbing of community territory in the *páramo*. Likewise, the Pechora River saviours are committed to support the recognition of Komi as indigenous people, which would guarantee them access to territories of traditional land use. Third, the defence of rights has empowered both movements to address their concerns about the impacts of mining and oil extraction on livelihoods at the local level, at the national level to contest development models affecting the rights of indigenous and peasant people and at the international level to resist neoliberal policies concealed through discourses of sustainable resource-extraction.

When adapting to asymmetrical power relations, assuming the identity of community representatives has been critical for the water guardians of Kimsakocha and the Pechora River saviours in their encounters with bureaucrats at different spheres and levels of government. First of all, the arrival of extraction projects theoretically opens space for local participation and negotiation, however, as analysed experiences show, the strategic importance of such projects has tended to silence critical voices. For this reason, representing communities in decision-making has become a priority for both movements. Second, the role of mediators has been decisive for addressing important issues of local participation in decision-making. For instance, the water guardians of Kimsakocha, acting as community water managers, have participated in debates over legal frameworks around water management, integrating their concerns over the threats that mining exploitation imposes to water sources. In Russia, the Pechora River saviours have initiated public discussions of oil-extraction based development and its persistent impacts, representing rural people in the monitoring of environmental impacts and negotiation of compensations. The enactment of these multiple roles is possible because of community trust in the movements' goals, knowledge and skills. And, finally, the movements have crossed scales when channelling their influence on decision-making to areas in which opportunities for success have been found, ranging from local councils to provincial and national governments.

Our empirical work shows that fluidity is acknowledged as a vital approach to resist and sustain the actions of movements over time. Leader Carlos Pérez refers to the water guardians of Kimsakocha as "a community movement, [which is] not a schematic and rigid structure, but instead a totally open-ended, flexible and far-reaching structure without scheme, rather, it is visionary" (personal communication, June 2016, Cuenca). And, the Pechora River saviours believe that as a movement they are ubiquitous, pervasive in their resistance with all-encompassing strategies to sustain their livelihoods and culture.

Concluding remarks: promoting change from the local level

Fluid identities and agendas of social movements are a strategic choice derived from the commitment to account for the plural concerns of the communities in which they emerged, but also are a reactive response to the "contexts-in-process". Fluid identities and agendas become another resource to mobilize in order to address multiple issues derived from development trajectories, interact with multiple actors and move across scales to support the claims of socio-environmental movements.

The journey experienced in these long-lasting struggles for social and environmental justice reveals that resistance is not only sustained over time by strategies based on direct contestation and protest, but also by finding innovative approaches for promoting transformations. In the search for alternative ecologies against the neoliberal agenda, local practices have been modified and learning processes have been set in motion.

In the Ecuadorian case, small-scale agroecology projects are encouraging the tightening of the bonds between people and land, as well as self-sufficiency outside the market. Communities are visiting the *páramo* to reconnect the population with their "sources of life" and to embrace the role of environmental guardians. And, among other plans, a community tourism project is envisaged to revive the spiritual and scenic attributes of the landscape. For the SPC, the motivation for their struggle is maintaining the identity of *Pripechor'e*, the authentic place of culture and traditions in the midst of oil wells and pipelines. The collective awareness emerging from their first-hand experience of environmental disasters has spurred reconnection to the river, the land, traditional livelihoods, culture and language. Perhaps the next stage will be to welcome the opportunities that community tourism and small-scale agriculture could offer, which may last beyond the lifetime of an oil well.

Acknowledgements

This research was supported by the Australian Government Research Training Program Scholarship and the Melbourne Research Scholarship Program of the University of Melbourne. We are grateful to Professor Simon Batterbury and Dr Paula Satizábal for their insightful comments. We also thank cartographer Chandra Jayasuriya for her contribution.

References

Acosta, A. (2010) *El Buen Vivir en el camino del post-desarrollo Una lectura desde la Constitución de Montecristi*, Policy paper, vol. 9, FES-ILDIS, Quito.

Alexander, J. and Grävingholt, J (2002) Evaluating Democratic Progress inside Russia: The Komi Republic and the Republic of Bashkortostan. *Democratization* 9(4), 77–105.

Bebbington, A., Abramovay, R. and Chiriboga, M. (2008) Social Movements and the Dynamics of Rural Territorial Development in Latin America. *World Development* 36(12), 2874–2887.

Escobar, A. (2010) Latin America at a Crossroads. *Cultural Studies* 24(1), 1–65.

Escobar, A. and Alvarez, S.E. (1992) *The Making of Social Movements in Latin America: Identity, Strategy, and Democracy.* Boulder: Westview Press.

Foweraker, J. (1995) *Theorizing Social Movements.* Boulder: Pluto Press.

Gilbert, L. (2016) Crowding Out Civil Society: State Management of Social Organisations in Putin's Russia. *Europe-Asia Studies* 68(9), 1553–1578.

Gilberthorpe, E. and Hilson, G. (2014) *Natural Resource Extraction and Indigenous Livelihoods: Development Challenges in an Era of Globalization.* Farnham: Ashgate.

Gudynas, E. (2009) Diez tesis urgentes sobre el nuevo extractivismo. Contextos y demandas bajo el progresismo sudamericano actual. *Extractivismo, política y sociedad,* CAAP/CLAES, Quito, 187–225.

Gudynas, E. (2011) Más allá del nuevo extractivismo: transiciones sostenibles y alternativas al desarrollo. In F. Wanderley (comp.), *El Desarrollo en cuestión. Reflexiones desde América Latina*. La Paz: Oxfam, CIDES- UMSA. Pp. 379–410.

Kamhi, A. (2006) The Russian NGO Law: Potential Conflicts with International, National, and Foreign Legislation. *International Journal of Not-for-Profit Law* 9(1), 34–57.

Leff, E. (2015) The Power-full Distribution of Knowledge in Political Ecology: A View from the South. In J. McCarthy, G. Bridge and T.A. Perreault (eds), *Routledge Handbook of Political Ecology*. Oxon: Routledge. Pp. 64–75.

Martínez-Alier, J. (2002) *The Environmentalism of the Poor – A Study of Ecological Conflicts and Valuation*. Cheltenham: Edward Elgar.

Melucci, A. (1985) Getting Involved: Identity and Mobilization in Social Movements. In H. Kriesi, S. Tarrow and B. Klandermans (eds), *International Social Movement Research: From Structure to Action-Comparing Social Movements Across Cultures*. London: JAI Press. Pp. 329–348.

Ospina, P. (2015) Movilización y organización social en la revolución ciudadana. *Alternativas* 4, 1–15.

Pierk, S. and Tysiachniouk, M. (2016) Structures of Mobilization and Resistance: Confronting the Oil and Gas Industries in Russia. *The Extractive Industries and Society* 3(4), 997–1009.

Programa Andino de Derechos Humanos (PADH) (2012) *Informe sobre derechos humanos Ecuador 2012*. Quito: UASB.

Rodríguez, D. (2016) Experiencias comunitarias de gobernanza ambiental: el caso Kimsakocha. In P. Andrade (ed.), *La gobernanza ambiental en Ecuador: historia, presente y desafíos*. Quito: UASB, CEN. Pp.133–148.

Rosgeolfund (2018) *Digital maps of the state of the subsoil and the subsoil use for hydrocarbon resources*. http://www.rfgf.ru/2-9-1.htm [Accessed 18 September 2018.]

Sheller, M. (2000) *The Mechanisms of Mobility and Liquidity: Re-thinking the Movement in Social Movements*, Department of Sociology, Lancaster University, Lancaster. www.lancaster.ac.uk/fass/resources/sociology-online-papers/papers/sheller-mechanisms-of-mobility-and-liquidity.pdf [Accessed 13 July 2017.]

Torres, N. (2015) *El derecho a la alimentación y las implicaciones de la minería a gran escala en Quimsacocha*. Quito: FIAN.

4

BEYOND WINNING AND LOSING

The rise of the social movement against mega-mining projects in Northern Greece

Citizens' Coordinating Committee of Ierissos against gold-copper mining

By way of introduction

This chapter evolved from a joint contemplative process. Any social movement is experienced through a diversity of viewpoints, encompassing differing perspectives in an ongoing dialogue. Being aware that multiple narratives are possible and indeed necessary in a social dialogue, what follows is but our own momentary reflection around complex issues that form the bedrock of a social movement we are immersed in. We invite you to weave your own reflections into ours, as we take you into journey into our world.[1]

Small-scale mining activity in northeastern Halkidiki has been going on for many decades, as have the struggles against its destructive consequences. During the years of economic crisis and "memoranda of understanding" the mineral-rich field of northeastern Halkidiki was transformed into a field of neoliberal politics, repression and simultaneously the space of a dynamic social movement. The proposed large-scale mining project, the logic of "investments at any cost" and the total absence of informed public consent brought about an ominous certainty to local communities that their homeland was being transformed into a sacrifice zone. Slowly, and through much effort, a mass social movement was born. Faced with the logic of imposed decisions, local communities responded with scientific documentation, a legal struggle, wide dissemination of information, local assemblies, actions, protests, and resistance – throwing public debate around silenced issues wide-open. The state mechanism's response was based on a campaign of violent repression, propaganda, intimidation and, finally, prosecution. This social struggle is far from over, if one presumes that such struggles can be definitively won or lost. Whatever the outcome, what surely remains is the awareness that in a world where corporate profits dictate lives, wielding power through manipulation of the political sphere, local societies have no choice but to respond by taking matters into their own hands.

BOX 4.1   BREAKING THE TAILINGS DAM
OF SILENCE

Sometimes it takes giving an interview to hear your own voice.

It happened to me yesterday, sitting on a boulder by the side of a flowing river in the nearby forest of Kakavos. As I slowly surrendered to the investigative reporter's grueling questions, I experienced something that's even more frightening than the large-scale mining project about to go ahead in the forest around us. Something higher than the 143-meter-high tailings dam designed to be constructed just behind the curve of the river.

The danger of becoming deaf to my very own voice. The construction of an inner tailings dam of accumulated toxic perceptions, beliefs and attitudes.

Many months of systematic, systemic intimidation and attempted silencing of a community's voice has a side effect that's not written on the packaging. You slowly dip into a despair of being heard (forget about being understood) as you internalize the blame placed on you. You begin to feel like nothing but a nuisance to progress, an inconvenient hindrance. We know who you are. We'll single you out, hold you accountable for each word you say, keep you under surveillance, ridicule you in public, persecute you in courts, tear gas you and fence you out. If you could just go away, be silent, stop questioning, stop expressing differing opinions – then we could get on with the project at hand. Keep your opinions to yourself. It's then the very feeling of desperation that finally deafens you to your own voice.

But this investigative reporter was listening. I was no longer experiencing the camera and microphone as tools of surveillance. Through human contact, I felt I was speaking to the world's listening ear. As I attuned to my voice, as the river near my feet gently, consistently nudged me to encourage a flow of expression within myself, I could no longer distinguish whose voice it was – mine, my community's, the forest's? Who was speaking, and did it really matter? Was the dialogue happening – no longer silenced – more important than each separate viewpoint? Could this be what a living ecosystem could teach us if we could but respect the real value of its processes?

The dam broke. The questioning flowed.

Where is water and oxygen born, if not in a forest? Are resources merely a consumable quantity – to be bought and sold, – or a source of life – calling us into sustainable relationship? What if – here in Europe – we the colonizers are becoming the colonized? What exactly is the mining-project issue in Halkidiki, and more importantly, as seen from whose point of view?

My day in the forest – witnessing its destruction, remembering the value of the wild (seen and unseen) surrounding me and the river, called me back to my senses, back to common sense.

"What does the river mean, for you?", the investigative journalist quietly asked. Silence. Sensing. Senses. Common sense. The commons. This is the water that connects, I heard inside. Flow, free of dams. "Connection." I quietly answered.

Sometimes, controlling our own wild nature is the best way to ensure that nothing changes. Sometimes, surrendering to intimidation eerily turns into compliance. It may well be that a dam failure of our inner landscape of toxic perceptions, beliefs and attitudes may be the only way through this very real crisis we are all facing – each in our own local backyard of threatened environments. Hearing our own voice of common sense might then become a compass in avoiding the insanity of destroying the very source of our own lives, our land-bases.

There must be a better way. Is it already here, if only we paid attention, if only we encouraged less silencing? I wonder.

Welcome to the Greek El Dorado

Halkidiki is a peninsula in Northern Greece, with a very diverse, biologically important natural landscape, combining complex terrestrial and marine ecosystems. Today, in several regions of Northern Greece, Eldorado Gold Corporation – a Canadian mining company based in Vancouver – has several mining projects in the works, at various stages of exploration, permitting approval and implementation. In Halkidiki, Eldorado Gold has already begun executing its large-scale mining project which destroys forest ecosystems to prepare an open-pit gold mine. Eldorado Gold plans to extract 360 million tons of ore from Halkidiki, ten times the amount that has been extracted in the last 2500 years, in 100 times less time. An open pit of 705 metres diameter and 220 metres depth will be created in the middle of the ancient forest ecosystem of Skouries, on the largest aquifer of the region. For the Skouries open-pit mine, the processing plant and two tailings dams – 400,000 square metres of devastation are replacing a forest ecosystem. Eldorado Gold plans to extract 24,000 tons per day from Skouries, using six tons of explosives. As it becomes obvious from reading the relevant environmental impact assessement study the region's character will change direction, from one of agriculture and tourism to one of heavy industry.

The Skouries open-pit gold mine is situated on top of the region's main aquifer and Eldorado's Gold mining project requires drainage and massive amounts of fresh water use. Mining activities will produce ore dust of up to 4,324 tons per hour, with high concentrations of heavy metals, polluting the ecosystem and putting its ability to sustain life at risk. People's livelihood in the surrounding communities relies heavily on small scale tourism, agriculture, beekeeping, fishery and forestry – a local economy totally dependent on the ecosystem's well-being.

Investment: market versus agora

Is it all for sale? The economic crisis has been an opportunity for the entrenchment of neoliberal values and practices as well as for questioning their real costs. We seem to be living within a structurally questionable ethos – as if the whole of the earth existed solely for human profit and consumption – instead of living within an ethos of symbiosis. We seem to be caught in a web of contradictions, where, on the one hand, a corporation's duty by law is to put shareholder profit above all else, and, on the other, it is deemed legitimate for corporate interests to dictate and impose the direction that society will follow – as we are witnessing in the plethora of global trade agreements currently on the table.

An extractivist mindset applies to the way we approach so-called "natural resources" both outwardly and inwardly. Mindlessly mining minerals mirrors mindlessly living in denial of a deadly pattern of wasteful, toxic consumption, settling for a both social and natural toxic environment and calling it "sustainable development", engaging in non-reciprocal relations as if it were only a "natural process". Under the threat of economic crisis and widespread unemployment, the extraction of natural wealth was marketed as an investment deemed necessary for public interest.[2] However, natural resources are not wealth just because they exist, or because financial markets define them as such. When extraction leads to the destruction of a region's livelihood for generations to come, creating an El Dorado out of Halkidiki is tantamount to the degradation of both natural and social cohesion.

In a very typical manner – practiced worldwide – the region's villages experienced corporate hiring tactics that wreaked havoc upon social cohesion. Ripping apart families and whole villages into clearly delineated "for or against" camps or company "workers" and "non-workers" and pitting one against the other in conflictual relation seemed to be the corporate sense of social responsibility.

> Perhaps the public support Eldorado refers to is that which the company has paid for. Eldorado has ramped up its hiring of local people, even if they don't really have work to do, so that they'll have an interest in the project's approval. Eldorado has also taken advantage of the economic crisis to put increasing pressure on Greek authorities, as evidenced by the "fast track" designation granted under "austerity" policies to allow the company to get its permits without meaningful public participation. [excerpt from *Gold and Democracy Don't Mix – Eldorado Gold Faces Determined Opposition in Greece,* Mining Watch Canada, May 2013, http://miningwatch.ca/blog/2013/5/2/gold-and-democracy-don-t-mix-eldorado-gold-faces-determined-opposition-greece]
>
> On Apr. 9, a Facebook page dedicated to the company received more than 10,000 "likes", many of them originating in Moscow, eliciting accusations from social media aficionados that the company has resorted to "buying" a good reputation. According to statistics from the research company Media Services SA, Hellas Gold has given itself a virtual makeover. Between January and March 2013, the company paid over 630,000 euros for adverts,

more than the company spent for all of 2012, shelling out roughly 370,000 euros in March alone. One of the most popular advertisements uses images of the "workers" along with their names, implying that these are legitimate defenders of a plan resisted by hooded vandals. Against a 24 percent dip in the advertising market in Greece, it is clear the company is going against the trend of the business community to stabilise its position in Greece. [excerpt from *Greeks Fight Canadian Gold-Diggers*, A. Fotiadis, Inter Press Service, April 2013, www.ipsnews.net/2013/04/greeks-fight-canadian-gold-diggers]

Reinventing the agora in the age of market-driven polity

The need to strip our lives from the prevailing stories[3] around economic well-being and the primacy of material wealth that we are entrenched in often comes from a feeling of imminent threat, the ground being removed under our feet. This experience can be an unsettling wake-up call. Faced with the reality of a mega-mining extraction project jolted the very basic stories that society had become accustomed not to question.

> Naomi Klein: Because I am working on a book and a film[4] on climate change, that's why I've been following the extractive side of the shock doctrine in Greece, which has gotten a lot less attention. Understandably, people are focused on having their pensions cut, and the layoffs – and those definitely are more immediate. Although in the case of the [Skouries] goldmine, there is an immediate threat to safety, to livelihood, and to economy, and so people are extremely vocal about that. [excerpt from *Is Greece in shock?*, article by Lynn Edmonds in EnetEnglish, April 2013, www.crisismirror.org/library/articles/is-greece-in-shock-naomi-klein-tells-enetenglish-how-the-shock-doctrine-relates-to-greece]

Before long, as individuals turn to one another in questioning dialogue, trepidation turns into outrage. From a deeper-felt sense of place – rooted in both past and future – and the certainty that as individuals we are responsible, local communities woke up to a deep and driving desire to empower ourselves and actively engage in forming our own future.

> At the heart of the protests is a demand that the government open itself up to alternative visions of the country's future, which would allow for the adoption of an economic strategy that promotes – rather than inhibits – the protection and healing of the environment and society. [excerpt from *Protesters against Gold Mining in Greece Demand Alternatives to Austerity*, article by Felicity Le Quesne in the online news provider The International, August 2013, http://soshalkidiki.gr/?p=7806]

The need for engagement arose on several levels: with scientists, universities and technical institutions, state agencies, ever-widening circles of society (local to international), the blaring silence of the entrenched mainstream corporate media and consensus reality issues (jobs, investment, resource extraction, "there is no alternative" mentality). It was a lived, organic process of social organization over time that gave rise to an evolving social movement rather than planned, hierarchically organized activism. In diametrical opposition to the "market-driven" worldview of the agora – as local communities responded with social investment in a struggle – a different agora emerged within a community of resistance, one closer to its essential meaning as a "space of coming together to exchange".

> The Skouries campaign has become a symbolic issue for people all over Greece. At the café in Ierissos, I chatted about these developments with the anti-gold-mine campaigners. Thanasis the carpenter had a neat way of putting it: "When the politicians go out, solidarity comes in." As we talked, I got a sense of how the very things that a conservative like Samaras might brandish as Greek values – community, friendship, self-reliance – were now valuable weapons. The café is a centre of village life where teenagers lounge and flirt, or play with their phones, where people drop in to exchange greetings or gossip. And now, of course, it is where "terrorists" come to plot. [excerpt from *Shock Therapy and the Gold Mine*, article by Daniel Trilling in the *New Statesman*, June 2013, www.newstates man.com/austerity-and-its-discontents/2013/06/shock-therapy-and-gold-mine]

In resisting the inevitability and wisdom of accepting Eldorado's expansion of mining projects in Halkidiki and Northern Greece at face value, local communities joining the struggle began to question the real costs of the extractivist mindset. In doing so, an alternative process of *social autopoiesis* was experienced. By recognizing previously devalued human resources and pooling them together in a public social context through numerous actions as members of various collectives within the context of the struggle, communities became aware of an abundance of social wealth. In the context of an evolving social movement, engaging ever-widening circles of solidarity in Greece and beyond,[5] an alternative form of social investment emerged as a lived practice – one involving personal expense, relational skills, physical integrity and freedom from imprisonment.

BOX 4.2 SOCIETY – BEFORE AND AFTER

Until recently, Halkidiki's local communities were not significantly different than the rest of the societies of the western capitalist world – both on an individual level and on the level of community organizations and local governance. The ruling philosophy was the promotion of individual interests and welfare.

We had been socialized within a model where it was more important for a human to watch television than to gather with others, engage in dialogue and be concerned with issues which are relevant to one's life. We had become disoriented and had lost touch with the essence, with how important it is to function as a local community. All together. We lived within a virtual reality, turning our back on the achievements and wisdom of our ancestors, demolishing whatever had been built to support a healthy society.

. . . We ended up dependent on others, multinationals, big business owners, politicians. We had forgotten that the human being and local communities produce food, create culture and cultivate the spirit. A model of life which brought the human being to second place and consumerism was dominant was imposed on us. A model of life which impels us to consider mining activities as development and a natural life to live with their impacts. A model which ignores the essence of life and the components which support it, and focuses on useless materials which do not contribute to survival, but only enhance a sense of strength of the rich and powerful.

. . . We hadn't become aware of the strength of companionship and solidarity until the threat of the destruction of our homeland – hence our very own life – by mining activities paid us a visit. And in an authoritarian and violent way want to impose themselves on us.

It was then that we understood that we were in danger of losing valuable resources. Water, the forest, the air, health and in the end the very future of the human being. In the past we considered these as given and insignificant.

It was then that we understood that one person – whether mayor or politician – cannot save all of us. Let alone one who creates, supports and permits the source of the problem. We cannot expect that this one person can be at the same time the solution to our problem.

We understood that if we do not take initiatives as a local community we will not be able to face the danger and the big economic and political interests in the background. All for our homeland and our homeland for us.

This awareness gave us strength, we united collectively, into one group. Each, with one's own thought and action became a ring in a chain which will protect our homeland and our lives. We learned to share, to care, to stand by one another. And all this took deep root in us. It's not only the need to rally against a shared danger. We came close to each other and we created together. We built the village's nursery school with our own hands, we organized a ten-day event for our children during the New Year holidays and with every occasion we organized and participated in all the local celebrations and commemoration events. We felt the need to be together both in the pleasant and in the difficult moments of our lives. We became aware that we are part of a whole, social and natural.

Source: Excerpts of reflections on the experience of the social movement

BOX 4.3 WOMEN'S OPEN LETTER

An OPEN LETTER from women who are struggling against the destruction of Halkidiki in Northern Greece, the expansion of the existing mining activities and gold mining.

We are the great-grandmothers who experienced the occupation during WWII and decided – never again fascism. We are the grandmothers who experienced civil war and declared – never again war.

We are the mothers who saw our children becoming immigrants and declared – never again racism. We are the daughters who experienced the dictatorship and declared – never again authoritarian regimes.

We are the granddaughters who have never before experienced occupation, civil war, immigration or dictatorship and are now experiencing all of them simultaneously. We are the great granddaughters who dream, who hope, who demand a better future.

Until recently, we had never felt the burning sensation of tear gas chemicals, we knew not what antacid lotion is, we knew not what riot and special police forces mean. Until recently we believed that the Greek Police exists in order to protect citizens. We believed that the Greek State is there to promote the interests of citizens and ensure their rights.

They attacked us with tear gas and chemicals, they chased after us, they beat us, they arrested us, they interrogated us, they invaded our homes and schools. They accused us of not respecting the laws.

They called us uneducated, uninformed and disobedient women, liars and even terrorists! We endured through all this. Besides, we brought our children into this world with untold pain and we are raising them with incredible effort. We will not be intimidated by terrorizing practices.

But now they attack our grandsons, sons, fathers, and brothers. They grab them in the middle of the night, in front of our children's horrified eyes. They lock them up in jail – as if they were common criminals- with fabricated charges.

They claim they are defending legality!

By adopting actions which violate laws and human rights? They claim they are promoting investments, at all costs, for the benefit of the people! By exercising violence and terror on the people?

They claim that decisions of the judicial system must be respected! By biasing them in advance and ignoring them when they disagree? They claim that they are defending democracy!

By challenging the presumption of innocence, one of democracy's fundamental principles? WE CALL ON WOMEN of all Greece, of all the world to stand by our cause. In solidarity with a struggle to defend dignity. A struggle to protect the future of our children, the environment and human rights.

A struggle for life, where the lives of our children are above corporate profits. We appeal to all of you! We ask for your support and solidarity, in any form of expression! We denounce the manufacturing of guilt and the criminalization of social struggles. We condemn police violence, state repression and procedural arbitrariness. We denounce methods of "trial and conviction by television".

We demand the release of our fathers, our sons, our brothers. We demand immediate, fair, impartial and transparent justice.

In any other case, they will find us standing opposed. Us, the great grandmothers, grandmothers, mothers, daughters, granddaughters and great granddaughters. All of us!

Source: Excerpts of reflections on the experience of the social movement

---

BOX 4.4   SINGING TO SAVE THE LAND

And so the time has come for us to join together once again. All of us who dream of a better world. All of us who believe in solidarity and common struggles.

In our longtime struggle against catastrophic mining activities we have met with so many people, collectives, and social movements. Each with their own problems and struggles. Each with their own ideology and viewpoint. We have realized, however, that – in its essence – the problem is a common one. A brutal exploitation of people and nature, by few whose only interest lies in money and power.

Our struggle is a struggle for survival. We are contesting the right of existence and self determination. We are struggling for a healthy natural and social environment. We refuse to be a cog in a machine which manufactures money for few and destruction for the rest. We are here so that there may be a tomorrow for the children of all of nature's species.

"There is no other way", they tell us. "It is we who pave the way", we answer. With struggles, words, music, images.

On the 27th of September, we take another step on the road we've begun to journey. Together with fellow travelers all those who have stood near us, all those who will add their voice to ours from afar. "Because we, my fellow human, don't sing to distinguish ourselves from the people. We sing to join people together."

Source: Press Release, September 2014 – Big Concert in Ierissos against Gold Mining – We sing, my fellow human, to save the land

Democracy and justice

Democracy – as a term – sounds benign and is used extensively by almost everyone. It seems though that it does not have the same meaning for everyone.

> Eldorado Gold Corp. has many supporters in Greece. The Government of the country (which would protect the "investment" at all costs), the police (to which the company is particularly generous offering financial and logistical assistance), intertwined media (whose shareholders happen to be shareholders of the company), magistrates (whose relatives are associated with the company), ministers (who have held positions in companies which are shareholders of Eldorado Gold), ambassadors (who intervene and promote the company's investments). Eldorado Gold Corp. however, has many people opposing its tactics and activities. Thousands of people, collectives, political bodies, organizations, both in Greece and abroad, stand in solidarity with our struggle for life and nature. Hundreds of demonstrations,[6] activities, informative events, resolutions of support. [excerpt from *Resolution Delivered to Canadian Embassy of Greece: Open Letter to Canadian Citizens*, Committees of the Struggle Against Gold Mining of Chalkidiki and Thessaloniki of Ierissos, 2013, http://soshalkidiki.gr/?p=7774]

People of Halkidiki thought that democracy is to participate in a sincere public consultation and dialogue about proposed plans that greatly affect the local communities, as is stated by the Aarhus Convention. Instead, local communities were excluded from the decision-making process, despite the fact that their arguments were based on strong scientific grounds. The multinational mining company on the other hand was recognized by the government as a peer social partner and interlocutor.

> Halkidiki may be seen as an operational exercise, where the state refines the policy of enforcing the predatory exploitation of natural resources and the selling off of public property. It is an experimental laboratory, where the government and the social movements of resistance collide and measure their power. The state is crossing the limits of society's tolerance at all levels: through financial scandals, environmental destruction, corruption, arbitrariness, lawlessness, repression, propaganda, bullying, selling off public wealth and circumventing political, constitutional and human rights. Where will it stop? In Greece, the issue of environmental protection is deeply political. Our attitude as a society towards the natural environment incorporates our philosophy on life. How much are we willing to sacrifice in order to pay back financial debt and enjoy the "goods" of consumerism? How artificial are ultimatums such as "either economic prosperity or environmental protection"? How much democracy is left in Greece? For an increasing part of

the Greek population, such questions now matter more than ever. [excerpt from *A Canadian Company, the Police in Greece and Democracy in the Country that Invented It*, article by Nick Meynen in the Environmental Justice Organizations, Liabilities and Trade, June 2013, www.ejolt.org/2013/06/a-canadian-company-the-police-in-greece-and-democracy-in-the-country-that-invented-it]

How democratic, or even logical, is it to allow a corporation – whose only goal is the maximization of profit – to participate, affect and even impose its will, on vital decision-making and social processes – leaving the *demos* out of the partnership equation?

People of Halkidiki thought that democracy is to be heard even when a decision has already been made. Ever since the state decided in the summer of 2011 to approve the large-scale mining project of Eldorado Gold – excluding local communities from the dialogue – no further protest or dispute was allowed. Instead, the doctrine "investments at any cost" dictated that the social movement against mining should be confronted by a campaign of violent repression,[7] propaganda, intimidation and, finally, prosecution. In its reports, Amnesty International repeatedly called for investigations,[8] while more than 450 members of the social movement currently face legal prosecution.

> The social movement against gold mining in Halkidiki struggles not only against the destruction of the environment and predatory exploitation of common resources. It also struggles against all that which puts profit for the few above life of the many. And in this struggle none will be left alone. [excerpt from the press release of the Coordinating Committee of Ierissos, *Local Community Prosecuted for Resisting Eldorado Gold's Skouries Mining Project in Halkidiki*, May 2016, http://soshalkidiki.gr/?p=11934]

People of Halkidiki thought that democracy is to follow a set of rules that protect human rights, the environment and public interest.

> Canadian Eldorado Gold's Skouries mining project in Halkidiki, Greece has been advancing without the required by law construction permits for over a year, despite numerous objections filed with the authorities. A new scandalous bill is to be passed by the Summer Chamber of Parliament by the end of the week, which – if passed – signifies the end of the strict environmental protection laws of forests which has existed by law to date in Greece. [excerpt from *Illegal Construction Works at the Skouries Mining Project in Halkidiki, Greece to be Legalized by a Scandalous New Bill of Parliament*, Coordinating Committee of Ierissos, July 2014, http://soshalkidiki.gr/?p=9603]

Although such legislative frameworks exist to a degree, people became aware of a huge gap[9] between what is on paper (the constitution, EU directives, state law, political statements) and what is experienced in daily life. The laws seem to be clearly skewed – and in some cases overtly written – in favour of the interests of corporate entities and powerful economic lobbies. Thus, what is legal – based on existing law – is not necessarily legitimate and needs to be contested.

> The historian of the future – if one exists – will be impressed to observe the current spectacle. The project to avert catastrophe is being undertaken by the so-called "primitive societies": the indigenous inhabitants of Canada, the indigenous peoples of South America and so on across the world. We see this struggle for the salvation and protection of the environment taking place today in Greece as well, where residents of Skouries in Halkidiki are heroically resisting the predatory disposition of Eldorado Gold and the police support provided by the Greek state. The richest and most powerful societies, like the U.S. and Canada, are so enthusiastically leading us to the cliff. [Noam Chomsky, from an interview to C.I. Polychroniou and Anastasia Giamali – article (in Greek) in *Avgi*, December 2013, www.avgi.gr/article/1458668/ noam-tsomski-kapoioi-sti-germania-theloun-tin-ellada-se-sklabia]

Although one may wonder whether democracy has ever been about elected governments being obliged to implement the programme on which they are elected, what seems certain is that under economic crisis and "memoranda of understanding" Greece is being reduced to a debt colony within the EU partnership. The widening gap between rich and poor, the corrupting power of money,[10] the absence of concern for the common good – all reflect a colonial mindset, both in the non-reciprocal way we relate to one another and to the natural communities our lives and livelihoods are embedded in. What European colonialism has long practiced on other continents seems to be coming home. Is the social cohesion of developed Western Europe to be protected by turning homelands such as ours into sacrifice zones?

Reflections: next, what?

This social struggle is far from over, if one presumes that such struggles can be definitively won or lost. Whatever the outcome, what surely remains is the awareness that in a world where corporate profits dictate lives – wielding power through manipulation of the political sphere – local societies have no choice but to respond by taking matters into their own hands. And this is both difficult and complex as it requires both social change and breaking free from norms that, although dysfunctional, conform to our comfort zones.

Local society is changing itself through this struggle. It is questioning and critically challenging the political, economic and legal system that gives birth to problems such as those created by Eldorado Gold in Halkidiki. In becoming aware that unrestrained capitalism and the system's need for perpetual economic growth are based on enormous cost that people and places of the planet pay, local society is being forced to reevaluate and prioritize its needs. It is realizing that it is not weak, that it possesses important and useful skills and mainly that society – as a living organism – is much more than the sum of its members.

However, more important than all may be that a long-term, persistent struggle for a "no" creates the need for a "yes" to emerge. Within an environment of suffocating pressure and imposition, society matures to demand the space and time for a dialogue around the way we imagine a tomorrow. For what we need to demolish and what we need to build. For what we will refuse and what we will lay claim to.

Beyond winning and losing, it is crucial for a society to metabolize a totality of experiences – both positive and negative – in order to keep alive the vision of a life of reciprocity within nature, of social relationships that are based on synergy and solidarity, of a world without sacrifice zones.

Notes

1 Two different strands were woven together in our presentation at the conference "Rights to Nature" (Cambridge, 2016) – one represented by an ongoing photo narrative, and another by our spoken words. Juxtaposing a stream of reflections with an image stream of an evolving social struggle, our presentation mirrored the process we underwent as we awoke to thinking critically about the complex issues involved. For a video recording of the full presentation, please visit the conference website: https://conservationandtrans formation.com/conference-rights-to-nature/

2 As the voice of the communities' resistance began to break through media silence, light was shed on its wider socio-political context through investigative reports, for example: *Golden Times – Casandra's Treasure* (Small Planet Production documentary for ERT, Greece's public broadcaster), *Greece Sees Gold Boom, but at a Price* (https://www.nytimes. com/2013/01/14/world/europe/seeking-revenue-greece-approves-new-mines-but-environmentalists-balk.html) and *Questioning Greek Growth* (*The New York Times*), *The Heavy Price of Greek Gold* (*The Independent*/Ecologist Film Unit).

3 Examples of some of the prevailing stories can be found in the following articles: *Ecology vs Economy: Dirty gold dig split Greeks in Chalkidiki*, Russia Today (2013); *As Greece sinks, gold mine seen as savior to some -- curse to others*, Fox News (2013); *Greek dilemma: Are new jobs created by gold mine worth the ecological risk?*, The Christian Science Monitor (2014).

4 The voice of the struggle against the extractive project in Halkidiki is included in Naomi Klein's book *This Changes Everything* (2014), as well as in Avi Lewis's documentary film (2015) by the same title. In the autumn of 2015, special film screenings were hosted in Ierissos and Megali Panagia for the communities struggling against gold mining in Halkidiki and at Syntagma Square in Athens in front of the Greek Parliament at Syntagma Square in Athens, as part of the events organized across Europe for the film. Video: Avi Lewis and Naomi klein in discussion with the audience following the screening in Ierissos.

5 Link to solidarity messages and resolutions from individuals and groups within the international community.

6 See, for example: *15,000 march on Canadian consulate in Greece in opposition to gold mines*, The Council of Canadians (2013).

7 *Riot police storm the village of Ierissos once again*, Coordinating Committee of Ierissos (2013); *Greek police chase anti-mining demonstrators at the Skouries forest, beating them up*, Environmental Justice Organisations, Liabilities and Trade (2013); *Protest in Skouries, Halkidiki, Greece: A just struggle will not be stifled by riot police chemicals*, Coordinating Committee of Ierissos (2014).

8 Amnesty International Reports: (1-OCT 2012) Don't beat protesters EU countries warned; (2-OCT 2012) Europe: Policing demonstrations in the European Union; (3-MAR 2013) Greece: Need for investigation of police conduct towards residents of town objecting gold mining operations; (4-APR 2014) Greece: A law unto themselves: A culture of abuse and impunity in the Greek police

9 For more depth, see: http://soshalkidiki.gr/?p=7794, *Environment minister defoliates Greece's forests of vital legal protection*, WWF Greece (2014); *Parliamentary questions: Hellas Gold SA is damaging the ecosystem of Chalkidiki*, European Parliament (2014); *Selective legality in Skouries, Halkidiki, Greece*, Coordinating Committee of Ierissos (2014); *Hellas Gold (Eldorado Gold) Technical Study returned*, Coordinating Committee of Ierissos (2016).

10 *Special Report: Greece's triangle of power*, Reuters (2012); *Another govt serving the mining giants rather than its own people*, Papua New Guinea Mine Watch (2013); *A new page in Greek-Canadian relations*, Capital (2013).

5

LAND RIGHTS AND JUSTICE IN NEOLIBERAL MOZAMBIQUE

The case of Afungi community relocations

Kate Symons

People should know Mozambique is different now! Now what we have are the locals disrupting things!

(Email correspondence between author and civil society activist, July 2015)

Introduction

Land exploitation has reached unprecedented levels globally, with land occupied by communities often targeted for redevelopment by companies in the agricultural commodities, extractives and tourism sectors (Hall, 2013; White et al., 2012). Mozambique is increasingly the target of large-scale land acquisitions for industrial, gas, coal and agricultural uses. Deals have often involved land currently occupied by communities on insecure and customary tenures, communities that are increasingly asserting their rights against such development. Land grabs, even in the face of protest, are reported across many regions. These include displacements for biofuels in southern and eastern Africa (Molony and Smith, 2010), relocations to make way for biodiversity conservation in southern Africa (Benjaminsen and Bryceson, 2012; Büscher and Ramutsindela, 2016), protests against mining across Latin America (Bebbington and Bebbington, 2011; Burchardt and Dietz, 2014; North and Grinspun 2016) and land grabs for tourism redevelopment in Greece (Hadjimichalis, 2014). These changes prompt debates over rights and justice: who has the right to the land, who can benefit from resources, and how, and by whom such decisions are made.

This chapter focuses on one such case: how communities and civil society are contesting land use changes by the US oil and gas company Anadarko. Anadarko was granted permission by the Mozambican state in 2012 to build a gas processing plant on the Afungi Peninsula in Cabo Delgado province in the north of the country. In June 2015, a coalition of civil society activists, communities and their legal representatives challenged the planned relocation of 1500 existing residents of the site, citing that they considered Anadarko's land rights to be illegal. This campaign achieved several important concessions on behalf of the communities scheduled for relocation, especially financial compensation. The campaign has been celebrated by civil society activists as a clear victory leading to a new era of political accountability whereby community needs and rights would hold a central place in Mozambique's resource politics, and where this could be secured through particular right-based strategies of engagement and protest. However, even though the Afungi communities have been able to assert certain legal rights (in this case, a right to compensation and a right to be consulted), they have not been able to prevent their relocation. Nor has this case led to a broader assertion of land rights by the Mozambican state (defined as secure tenure and ownership over ancestral land, or land that has been occupied according to traditional or customary rights), and violent land disputes in Mozambique are escalating.

This chapter uses the case of Anadarko and the Afungi communities to explore how Mozambique's ostensible commitment to rights and its encouragement of foreign business investment has provided opportunities for those fighting for community rights to use certain strategies and tactics to great effect, while at the same time, entrenching certain aspects of neoliberal development. Contestation of land deals is often theorized as a simplistic "expulsion and resistance" dynamic, between "local communities" on the one hand, and large corporate and state interests on the other (Borras and Franco, 2013; Ferguson, 2005, 2006; Hall, 2011). This implies that victory only means successfully resisting relocation. Yet in articulating a positive politics around community rights to compensation, consultation and due process, civil society activists and communities in the Afungi Peninsula have made themselves visible and secured numerous concessions, while also failing to negotiate their ability to remain in place. I consider whether, and in what ways, the Anadarko case constitutes a *victory* for the Afungi communities, and discuss the wider lessons that can be drawn from this case. I draw on field work in Mozambique in 2013 and 2014 with civil society activists and policy makers involved in land acquisitions, along with analysis of policy reports, legal documents, reports by civil society organizations and records of community meetings. The chapter is structured around four sections: following this introduction, I explain the background to land rights contestation in Mozambique's resources boom, and the controversies caused by Anadarko's proposals. I then discuss Anadarko's attempts at engagement with communities, and how these were radically shaped by the civil society coalition, culminating in the legal challenge of 2015. I then explore what this victory really means in the light of Mozambique's extractives scramble.

Land grabs in Mozambique's resources boom

Mozambique is undergoing a period of intensified natural resource exploitation and export, with state and private actors preoccupied with the development potential of natural resource exploitation. Across the country, mega-projects in a variety of sectors are changing the country's topography. Projects range from the controversial ProSavana soy farming project in Nacala Province, which uses Brazilian-style intensive farming techniques (including mono-cropping and use of agro-chemicals), to the coal fields of Tete province, and newly discovered natural gas sources in Cabo Delgado's coastal waters (the subject of this chapter). These schemes have led to a sustained growth rate over recent years, 7% per year from 2008 to 2015 (World Bank 2013, 2014, n.d.). Under President Filipe Nyusi (elected in 2015), Mozambique may be entering a new era of political responsibility characterized by sustainable long-term economic prospects, a reduction in the need for international aid and a break with the corrupt politics of the President Guebuza era (Vines *et al.*, 2015, although for a contrasting view see Macuane *et al.*, 2017). For a country that remains near the very bottom of the Human Development Index, the resources boom could indeed be extremely significant, if conducted fairly and for the national interest.

However, the resources boom has been intensely contested. Its critics observe a government and a private sector pursuing an extractives agenda regardless of social or ecological outcomes, while often serving personal and private, rather than national interests (CIP, 2014; Hanlon, 2016; Kirshner and Power, 2015; Santos et al., 2015). The boom has meant that many communities have lost access to their land in the name of wider national economic development. Approximately 2.5 million hectares of land were transferred away from traditional and subsistence-based uses to major international corporations from 2004 to 2009 (Manuel and César, 2014; Twomey, 2014), and while more recent figures are not available, it is notable that this figure does not even include the 35 million hectares required by Prosavana, the soy project mentioned previously, or the area required by Anadarko in Cabo Deglado. These changes have often caused conflict with communities. For example, in Tete province, farming and herding communities have been forcibly moved from the 60 million hectare site now occupied by Brazilian coal giant Vale (and its British and Australian partners), while Manuel and César (2014), report over 50 more sites where community land rights and access to livelihoods conflict with planned or existing extractive and industrial uses.

This major land transfer has taken place despite strong legal protections for customary and informal land use. This is land use defined by the Mozambican government as "the occupation of land by individual persons and by local communities, in accordance with customary norms and practices, as long as these do not contradict the Constitution". Law no. 19/97 of 1 October further states that its purpose is "to ensure the rights of the Mozambican people over the land and other natural resources, and to promote investment in sustainable and equitable use of these resources". This same legislation states that all land is owned by the state, and land rights are granted to companies, collectives, organisations or individuals under a DUAT (Direito de Uso e Aproveitamento da Terra) (right to use and benefit from the land) (Article 10, Mozambique Land Act, No. 19/97). Informal rights where communities have occupied the land for more than ten years are also protected. However, in 2014, the Mining Law was revised to establish that economic activities, especially gas and mining, take priority over informal land rights (Article 12 and Article 2, Law no. 20, 18 August 2014). This is intended to act as an incentive to the extractives industry, with similarly favourable revisions for minerals and precious gem extraction (Bloomberg Business News, 17 December 2014; EY, October 2014). Nevertheless, community rights are still protected under current legislation, and holders of mining permissions are required to consult communities and to provide financial compensation for relocation (whether through the restoration of living standards elsewhere, or through the chance to benefit from the proposed operations) (Mozambican Resettlement Decree of 2012). These signals from the Mozambican government are ambiguous: although the law clearly protects informal land rights and places obligations on developers, recent history has been of escalating conflicts between communities and projects in which DUATS have been awarded to private interests, while community rights are ignored (Salcedo-La Viña, 2015).

It is precisely this gap between legal commitment and practice that civil society activists exploited in the Anadarko case. In 2002, about 20 organisations, ranging from large NGOS, like Action Aid, to small Mozambican civil society groups, formed the Civil Society Platform for Extractive Industries and Natural Resources (CSPEINR) to improve the representation of local communities in the decision-making process around extractives. The secretariat of the platform rotates around its members every two years, and from 2013 to 2015 it was held by Centro Terra Viva (CTV), a small Maputo-based civil society organization. CTV comprises approximately 20 staff engaged in community advocacy, legal training and education around environmental issues, with a focus on biodiversity conservation, land use and the extractives sector. Alda Salomão, an environmental lawyer, is CTV's legal adviser and heads its Environmental Policy and Legislation Programme, and has been a very land rights active campaigner in Mozambique for several years. In 2012, Salomão, fellow activists and communities began campaigning against the proposed community relocations. I now turn to discuss the case of Anadarko and the Afungi communities in more detail.

Contesting the world's second-largest liquefied natural gas (LNG) plant

The Afungi Peninsula is located approximately 2000 miles north of Mozambique's capital city Maputo in the province of Cabo Delgado, near to the Tanzanian border. Cabo Delgado is the home constituency of President Nyusi, a Frelimo (Mozambique's ruling party) stronghold with nearly 80% of the vote in 2015. In 2012, Anadarko and partners discovered 100 trillion cubic feet of natural gas in the region's coastal waters, reported as "enough fuel to build the world's second-largest LNG plant" (Bloomberg Business, 14 June 2013). The proposals for the plant, which at the time of writing have not yet been constructed, include onshore and offshore extraction and processing infrastructure, along with facilities to keep the gas at very low temperatures for safe storage and transportation, and support buildings including worker accommodation, offices and an airport and airstrip, all on a 7000-acre site secured by a large exclusion area. For the Afungi Peninsula to be remade as this hyper-modern, globally connected gas export zone, it must first be cleared of its existing residents. These include about 1500 people spread over three villages, namely Quitupo, Maganja and Senga, alongside several hundred more people who live outside of the zone proposed for the plant, but whose livelihoods depend on it (Salcedo-La Viña, 2015). Although the region is changing fast, many of these villagers live traditionally, focusing on cashew nut production and fishing. These communities are deeply concerned about the impact of the gas plant on their livelihoods (Aljazeera, 2014).

Community concerns can be understood as falling into two broad categories. Importantly, these cannot be reduced to resistance to relocation. The first category centres on the distribution of benefits from the plant. As the mining and extractives sector was able to secure a sympathetic tax agreement under the 2014 Mining Law revision, any immediate benefits to local people depend on being able to secure jobs at the plant or provide services to gas workers, rather than any taxation and public spending. However, communities are unlikely to meet the demands for highly skilled gas workers. Moreover, experiences in other sites in Mozambique and Africa more widely indicate that local communities tend to be prevented from getting anywhere near the sites, and end up providing informal and low-skilled services such as sex work, rather than finding opportunities to engage in resource production at any significant scale (Ferguson, 2006; Kirshner and Power, 2015; Human Rights Watch, 2013). For the Afungi communities, this is compounded by the threats to existing livelihoods from the destruction of cashew trees and the loss of access to fishing grounds. In essence, they consider that they are unlikely to gain from employment at the site, even as their existing source of livelihood is removed. These concerns can be understood as being about distributive justice, defined as being concerned with the distribution of goods or value across a society, and the mechanisms necessary to determine fairness or equity across different social groups (Capeheart and Milovanovic, 2007; Lamont, 2017). This includes communities' calls for rights to protect their livelihoods and to ensure they gain from the proposed plan, rather than see gains simply accrued by state and Anadarko actors.

The second category of community objections concerns the methods by which Anadarko gained its land rights, including its consultation with the local community. Throughout its early stages, agreements around the plant were very secretive. An informant considered that Anadarko was encouraged by a handful of government officials to bypass the official process:

> I understand the government gave these concessions, but the government was just two or three guys, not really representing the well-being of the whole country, saying: "Yeah, I'll give you leases, whatever". . . . So no democracy. So people in Mozambique say: "Well the government gave Anadarko all

this land". Well that wasn't really the government, that was just two or three individuals in high power that can give these concessions.

(Interview with donor, Maputo, 24 April 2014)

Several other informants confirmed that it has been common practice in Mozambique for government officials and companies to collude in expediting decisions on land allocations for extractive projects, reflecting the Mozambican elite's power and privilege in relation to foreign corporate investors (Fairbairn, 2013). This can be understood as being about procedural justice, that is, the process by which Anadarko and the Mozambican government worked together to secure the DUAT for the plant. Procedural justice requires a process "that is recognised as being fair, where stakeholders can participate in the process and where their values and preferences are recognised" (Larcom and van Gevelt, 2017; Schlosberg, 2009). This was, according to my interviews, not the approach initially taken by Anadarko.

Distributive and procedural justice were both key to the civil society campaign. The campaign prioritized the training of community paralegals through local associations, and established community committees for each of the three affected villages, training members on how to make the most of the consultation that Anadarko was obliged to perform to call for recognition of their rights to compensation and more comprehensive consultation. At several points these committees were successful in shifting Anadarko's interaction with the communities from a superficial to a meaningful process, for example, halting the licensing process in 2013 and 2014 by refusing to grant community consent, effectively bringing Anadarko's project to a temporary stop and threatening their desire to do business in Mozambique (Salcedo-La Viña, 2015). The campaign also made regular use of media publicity, thereby publicly questioning Anadarko's claims to corporate social responsibility. Such activities called the Mozambican state and Anadarko to account over their professed commitment to the rule of law and to good business practice.

In June 2015, CTV and a team of national senior jurists, composed of Judge Retired Counselor, João Carlos Trindade and lawyers Lucinda Cruz and André Cristiano José, contested to the Mozambican government that Anadarko's DUAT was illegal (CTV Bulletin, 2015). The case raised several serious claims made by community activists, including that Anadarko had not gained community consent for relocation; that communities did not understand why they had to be resettled and what would happen to their livelihoods, that compensation had not been offered, that an Environmental Impact Assessment had not been satisfactorily undertaken and that engagement with communities had not been the kind of genuine and substantive engagement required by the 2012 Resettlement Decree (Salcedo-La Viña, 2015; CTV Bulletin, 2015). CTV also reported the ongoing police intimidation of activists, community members and paralegals, and the arrest and subsequent release of Salomão under charges of promoting civil disobedience (reported to me during an interview with a CTV officer in October 2013 and again in email correspondence in June 2015). These allegations clearly run counter to Anadarko's public commitments to be conducting a responsible, comprehensive and transparent resettlement process.

Although the Mozambican government concluded that Anadarko's DUAT was awarded legally, the civil society campaign brought notable benefits for the Afungi communities, and prompted a significant change in approach by Anadarko and the Mozambican government. Anadarko greatly increased its public consultation activity, from the sporadic efforts throughout 2013 and 2014 to a series of extensive consultation meetings, along with setting out how it intends to employ local people and use local services (Mozambique Gas Development Project website, 2018). The Anadarko Chief Operating Office Al Walker met publicly with President Nyusi to reaffirm a joint commitment to good business practice and reject the questionable shortcuts the company had taken earlier (Mozambique Gas Development Project press release, 13 July 2015). Most significantly, a large compensation package for the Afungi communities was announced, including US$180 million in community payouts; US$90 million to compensate for the loss of cashew trees and other assets; US$90 million to fund the construction of homes, schools, hospitals and access roads in the new town, and commitment to benefits such as training for local people (Mozambique Gas Development Project, 2015). While this figure is small compared to the US$212 billion estimated worth of the project, it is nonetheless a significant concession from Anadarko.

While the civil society campaign secured a large financial settlement for the Afungi communities along with public acknowledgement of their rights, it has not prevented their eventual relocation. There are therefore two important questions for activists to consider when drawing lessons from the case of Anadarko in Mozambique. First, what made the campaign successful? What strategies and tactics were open to activists and communities, and how are these modes of engagement related to broader trends in land rights activism in different situations? Second, we must also explore the nature of the victory. In successfully leveraging the law to claim their rights to compensation and consultation, communities have ultimately negotiated away their land rights and the legality of Anadarko's DUAT has been confirmed. What, then, constitutes success in a situation where the communities will still be relocated? In the next section, I consider what this case means for land rights campaigners against neoliberal economic development more widely.

Community activism for a neoliberal era

Anadarko's proposals and wider contemporary policy developments in Mozambique are identifiably neoliberal: they exemplify the production of wealth from the privatization of common resources, the production of new regulations by the state that promote the needs of the private sector (re-regulation), and the creation of new spaces, whereby some people and natures are connected to global capital networks, and others are dispossessed (Harvey, 2005; Moore, 2015). A variety of forms of power and control are necessary to dominate, coerce and encourage people to go along with these neoliberal reforms. These include authoritarian tactics, such as arrest, eviction, detention and intimidation by state agents like police, and softer methods like consultation, designed to persuade activists and communities that given proposals are in their own or the broader national "best interest" (see Apostolopoulou et al., 2014 and Hönke, 2013 for discussions of different uses of consent and coercion in neoliberalizing contexts). By the same token, opposition to neoliberalism can also take many forms, ranging from directly contesting dispossession by refusing eviction in land disputes, to subverting the original intention of neoliberal reforms in day-to-day practices (Butler and Athanasiou, 2013; Ferguson, 2010). In understanding what makes the Afungi case relevant to activists, it is important to consider how neoliberalization processes open new strategies and discourses for different actors to achieve particular ends, and how these may be mobilized to protect citizen's land rights. Neoliberal processes, even as they reinforce certain pathways of uneven development, can also provide new ways for marginalized groups to articulate and press their claims.

The first observation for activists is that the civil society coalition's successful interruption of Anadarko's proposals was achieved through giving the community access to legal advice, and training community members themselves to act as paralegals, able to assert their own rights in line with existing Mozambican law. This gave Afungi communities legal representation, and prevented the government from conducting questionable legal fixes (as it attempted to do at the outset of the scheme). Giving poor communities voice and power forced the Mozambican state to recognize their rights, and put pressure on authorities to act in accordance with the law. The campaign was contingent on an existing progressive land law in Mozambique: rather than agitate for legislation to protect communities in the first instance, CTV activists were able to ask that existing rights be enforced, an approach that the organization intends to use in other cases in Mozambique as part of a wider campaign to encourage the government to better incorporate rural and urban poor in redevelopment decisions. In this sense, the campaign was primarily targeted at the enforcement of the existing legislation, cementing the state as a player that should be central in activists' minds when considering their strategies. Activists can thus achieve significant results where legal regimes that protect informal community rights are in place, leveraging these regimes to put pressure on authorities and companies.

The campaign also indirectly challenged Anadarko's reputation and its public commitment to corporate social responsibility, and led the company to question its involvement in Mozambique. At several stages in 2013 and 2014, there were media rumours that the company was intending to pull out of the country over difficulties in doing business, to the obvious detriment of the state and the company that both desired to gain benefits from exploiting the large and potentially lucrative gas find (AllAfrica, 2013). The activities of CTV, other civil society organisations and the communities thereby invoked global liberal norms in order to threaten Anadarko's reputation. They exploited Anadarko's and the Mozambican government's ostensible commitment to legal process and the establishment of stable business conditions, encouraged under the "trade not aid" investment and development regime (that is, the dominant idea in international development that poor countries' route out of poverty lies in international trade rather than aid). This suggests that corporate reputation, and broader visions of trade-led development provide key leveraging points.

However, it is also significant that the Afungi communities are still due to be relocated. Despite the significant concessions awarded to them, it is notable that the renewed effort on community consultation has not tabled the possibility of remaining in place. For Anadarko and the state, the relocation is taken for granted and the consultation material focuses on issues such as compensation and restoration of livelihoods elsewhere. Some activists therefore continue to highlight problems with the consultation approach and compensation scheme. The CESPINR recently reported that the compensation figure has not been fairly allocated, and that the project's promises regarding local employment and benefits are unrealistic (Mimbire and Nhamirre, 2015). There is still ongoing, low-level harassment of activists, and community activists are still presented as being "against development", painted as enemies of the national public good (interview with CTV officer, June 2015). There are, therefore, ongoing personal risks to activists protesting against the impacts of Mozambique's resources boom. And the financial settlements have been met with such "collective euphoria" by local residents that they are, in the view of local activists, blindly signing away land rights without taking into account the constraints imposed by the contracts (CTV Bulletin, 2018, p. 8). In this sense, the victory of 2015 has been superseded by ongoing contestation, and reassertions of power by the state and private interests in pursuit of neoliberal economic development.

The ongoing situation in Afungi compares to others in Mozambique. Of the 20 Mozambican cases of activism against extractive projects currently recorded on the Environmental Justice Mapping Database,[1] only one is reported to be a clear success – the Pande and Temene Gas Field in central Mozambique, where activists were successful in preventing the scheme from being registered as part of the Clean Development Mechanism (CDM), on the grounds that this would be an incorrect application of CDM investment rules. The Pande case is thereby also an example of environmental and civil society organizations leveraging the application of existing regulations, akin to the Anadarko case. However, all other 19 Mozambican cases currently active have not been reported as successes due to the fact that, regardless of any concessions gained for communities, the contested projects have not been permanently halted. An increased focus on community rights and corporate reputation has not translated to a permanent cessation of any of these projects, so far.

In light of this wider context, activists must therefore also question what they mean when they claim that there is a new era of community assertiveness in Mozambique. CTV and the Afungi communities have adopted a pragmatic approach to defining success. Specifically, success does not necessarily mean halting the relocations. Indeed, as some communities have reported, they do not necessarily *want* the proposals halted. Rather, they seek both procedural and distributive justice in the context of Mozambique's economic development: compensation for loss of land and livelihood, and recognition of their rights in the decision-making process. This involves reclaiming ideas of national development, and putting forward a wider vision of fairness and development in the interests of the public good. The broader success enjoyed by CTV and the civil society coalition has therefore been to establish pathways to make citizens' rights visible, bringing the dispossession often suffered by poor communities into the foreground.

Conclusion

Extractive capitalist projects in Mozambique are leading to escalating political contestation, especially concerning land rights and the resettlement of local communities. The rise in civil society activism, centred on rights-based discourses, represents an important emerging trend that is bringing community rights onto the development agenda. The case of Anadarko in Cabo Delgado has demonstrated the power of a politicized approach from civil society activists that emphasizes the relationship between expanded capitalist accumulation at a global scale and environmental dispossession suffered by poor and marginalized communities. By giving legal representation to communities, citizens have been empowered to seek greater procedural and distributive justice from a scheme that was initially imposed unfairly and secretively.

CTV activists demonstrated a creative approach, using Mozambique's existing progressive land laws along with media and community awareness as leverage to ensure that the rights of Afungi communities were respected. In particular, they were successful in mobilizing and empowering communities to speak on their own behalf using community paralegals to conduct training. This strategy secured notable successes, including temporarily halting the project, greater consultation for affected communities and securing commitment to a large financial package to compensate for livelihood losses (although it is significant that this redress package is still being questioned by some communities and activists). All these concessions were specified by Mozambican law, demonstrating the effectiveness of a rights-based approach in situations where the necessary legislation exists but is not being implemented. In this sense, CTV's approach has been highly effective in a neoliberal era where the production of stable business environments and "trade not aid" development discourses dominate, and where land deals involve transnational actors like Anadarko that can be influenced by threatening their public reputation.

I started this chapter with a quotation from a CTV activist celebrating the beginning of a new political era in Mozambique, where communities are newly empowered in ensuring their rights are respected within the context of the resources boom. Undoubtedly, communities and activists were able to take a major step in securing substantive gains for the Afungi residents. And, in this sense, the Afungi citizens have fought to make themselves visible as a means of counteracting predatory extractive processes. However, this was achieved through making communities present within a wider neoliberal system, rather than shutting down the proposals from the "outside" or from "below". James Ferguson asks us to dispense with the simplistic notion of civil society activists engaged in warfare against a neoliberal state on behalf of working people, and consider the new and contested political terrains that activists engage on:

> The image of civil society as a zone of trench warfare between working people and the capitalist state served the left well enough at one moment in history . . . But invoking such topographies today can only obscure the real political issues, which unfold on very different ground.
>
> *(Ferguson, 2006, p. 109)*

Navigating these new topographies involves compromise and pragmatism. In Mozambique, those opposing land grabs have increasingly chosen to adopt the very same political discourse and strategies that the extractives companies used to pursue and legitimize their agendas, and to seek gains for communities within this framework. Communities and activists have not necessarily disputed the broader economic development goals and projects pursued in Mozambique; rather, they are using the law to state that they are due their fair share of gains. While this position has, so far, provided some success, it has also legitimized a wider set of development norms that underpin Anadarko's claims to exploit the land, namely the principles of private property that underpin notions of distributive justice, and notions of legal process and the rule of law that sit behind procedural justice. This case thus puts the notion of "victory" at the centre of the debate: as I have noted, Anadarko's plans, as with many other mega-projects in Mozambique, have not been halted. As land acquisitions in Mozambique intensify, activists and community victories may find that concentrating their attention on ensuring both procedural and distributive justice for relocated communities provides productive political terrain, even as such activities endorse wider capitalist development dynamics.

Note

1 The database is a teaching, networking and advocacy resource that collates cases of activism and protests against damaging projects, especially the extractives industry, from across the world. It can be viewed at https://ejatlas.org

References

Aljazeera (2014) Mozambique Fishermen Decry Gas Drilling. 22 January. Available at: www.aljazeera.com/indepth/features/2014/01/mozambique-fishermen-decry-gas-drilling-201411414032481195.html. [Accessed 24 July 2014.]

AllAfrica (2013) Mozambique: Distrust Surfaces at Public Meeting on LNG Plant. 17 September. Available at: http://allafrica.com/stories/201309171474.html [Accessed 22 September 2017.]

AllAfrica.com (2015) Mozambique: Prime Minister Receives Anadarko Vice Chairperson. 22 May. Available at: http://allafrica.com/stories/201505230299.html [Accessed 24 July 2015.]

Apostolopoulou, E., Bormpoudakis, D., Paloniemi, R., Cent, J., Grodzińska-Jurczak, M., Pietrzyk-Kaszyńska, A. and Pantis, J.D. (2014) Governance Rescaling and the Neoliberalization of Nature: The Case of Biodiversity Conservation in Four EU Countries. *International Journal of Sustainable Development & World Ecology* 21(6), 481–494.

Bebbington, A. and Humphreys Bebbington, D. (2011). An Andean Avatar: Post-neoliberal and Neoliberal Strategies for Securing the Unobtainable. *New Political Economy*, 16(1), 131–145.

Benjaminsen, T.A. and Bryceson, I. (2012) Conservation, Green/blue Grabbing and Accumulation by Dispossession in Tanzania. *Journal of Peasant Studies* 39(2), 335–355.

Bloomberg Business News (2013) Oil Hunted in Mozambique After World's Largest Gas Finds. 14 June. Available at: www.bloomberg.com/news/articles/2013-06-14/oil-hunted-in-mozambique-after-world-s-largest-gas-discoveries [Accessed 25 June 2017.]

Bloomberg Business News (2014) Mozambique Publishes Law Enabling Eni, Anadarko Gas Investments. 17 December. Available at www.bloomberg.com/news/articles/2014-12-17/mozambique-publishes-law-enabling-eni-anadarko-gas-investments [Accessed 22 September 2017.]

Borras Jr, S.M. and Franco, J.C. (2013) Global Land Grabbing and Political Reactions '"from Below"'. *Third World Quarterly* 34(9), 1723–1747.

Brenner, N., Peck, J. and Theodore, N. (2010b) Variegated Neoliberalization: Geographies, Modalities, Pathways. *Global Networks* 10(2), 182–222.

Burchardt, H.J. and Dietz, K. (2014) (Neo-) extractivism – A New Challenge for Development Theory from Latin America. *Third World Quarterly* 35(3), 468–486.

Büscher, B. and Ramutsindela, M. (2016) Green Violence: Rhino Poaching and the War to Save Southern Africa's Peace Parks. *African Affairs* 115(458), 1–22.

Butler, J. and Athanasiou, A. (2013) *Dispossession: The Performative in the Political*. Cambridge: Polity Press.

Capeheart, L. and Milovanovic, D. (2007) *Social Justice: Theories, Issues, and Movements*. New Brunswick: Rutgers University Press.

Castree, N. (2008b) Neoliberalising Nature: Processes, Effects, and Evaluations. *Environment and Planning A* 40(1), 153–173.

Centro de Integridade Publica Mocambique (CIP) (2014) Good Governance, Transparency and Integrity Newsletter. Edition No 03/2014. Petroleum Legislation, Round Two: No Consultation and No Transparency, Again? Maputo. Available at www.cip.org.mz/cipdoc%5C294_spinformacao_2014_03_en.pdf [Accessed 1 November 2015.]

Centro Terra Viva Bulletin (2015) *Publicação de Informação Ambiental Boletim Informativo Nº 2, Agosto 2015*. August. Available at: www.ctv.org.mz/boletim/Boletim%20Informa tivo%20-%20Terra%20Viva%20-%2002.pdf

Centro Terra Viva Bulletin (2018) *Publicação de Informação Ambiental Boletim Informativo Nº 1. Março 2018*. March. Available at: www.ctv.org.mz/boletim/boletim%20Informativo%20-%201%20edicao.pdf

EY Global Tax Alert. (2014) Mozambique Introduces New Tax Regime and Incentives for the Mining Industry. 20 October. Available at: www.ey.com/gl/en/services/tax/international-tax/alert--mozambique-introduces-new-tax-regime-and-incentives-for-the-mining-industry [Accessed 12 July 2017.]

Fairbairn, M. (2013) Indirect Dispossession: Domestic Power Imbalances and Foreign Access to Land in Mozambique. *Development and Change* 44(2), 335–356.

Ferguson, J. (2005). Seeing Like an Oil Company: Space, Security, and Global Capital in Neoliberal Africa. *American Anthropologist,* 107(3), pp.377–382.

Ferguson, J. (2006). *Global Shadows: Africa in the Neoliberal World Order*. Durham, NC: Duke University Press.

Ferguson, J. (2010). The Uses of Neoliberalism. *Antipode* 41(s1), 166–184.

Government of Mozambique, Mining Law (2003) Decree 28/2003 of 17 June.

Government of Mozambique. Land Act. Law No. 19/97 of 1 October.

Government of Mozambique (2012) Mozambican Resettlement Decree. Available at www.acismoz.com/lib/services/translations/Regulamento%20de%20Reassentamento%20August%20as%20published%20JO.pdf [Accessed 28 June 2017.]

Government of Mozambique, Petroleum Law Decree 21/2014 of 18th August.

Hadjimichalis, C. (2014) Crisis and Land Dispossession in Greece as Part of the Global "Land Fever." *City: Analysis of Urban Trends, Culture, Theory, Policy, Action* 18(4–5), 502–508.

Hall, R. (2011) Land Grabbing in Southern Africa: The Many Faces of the Investor Rush. *Review of African Political Economy* 38(128), 193–214.

Hall, D. (2013) Primitive Accumulation, Accumulation by Dispossession and the Global Land Grab. *Third World Quarterly* 34(9), 1582–1604.

Hanlon, J. (2016). 9 June 2016. Mozambique: Hoping 'Something Will Turn Up'. AllAfrica. com. Available at http://allafrica.com/stories/201606131636.html

Harvey, D. (2005) *A Brief History of Neoliberalism.* Oxford: Oxford University Press.

Hönke, J. (2013) *Transnational Companies and Security Governance. Hybrid Practices in a Postcolonial World.* Boston, MA and London: Routledge.

Human Rights Watch (2013) "What is a House without Food?" Mozambique's Coal Mining Boom and Resettlements. 23 May.

Kirshner, J., and Power, M. (2015) Mining and Extractive Urbanism: Postdevelopment in a Mozambican Boomtown. *Geoforum* 61, 67–78.

Lamont, J. (ed.) (2017) *Distributive Justice.* Oxon and New York: Routledge.

Larcom, S., and van Gevelt, T. (2017) Regulating the Water–Energy–Food Nexus: Interdependencies, Transaction Costs and Procedural Justice. *Environmental Science & Policy* 72, 55–64.

Macuane, J.J., Buur, L. and Monjane, C.M. (2017) Power, Conflict and Natural Resources: The Mozambican Crisis Revisited. *African Affairs* 117(468), 1 July 2018 .1–24.

Manuel, L. and F. César (2014) *Ocupação da terra por empreendimentos económicos no país: Relatório da avaliação preliminar das áreas com potencial de conflitos de interesse. Relatório de Investigação* No 5. Maputo, CTV.

Mimbire, F. and Nhamirre, B. (2015) Public Consultations LNG Project: Without Transparency, Misinformed Community, Apathetic Government. Centro de Integridade Publica Mocambique Report (September). Maputo.

Molony, T. and Smith, J. (2010) Biofuels, Food Security, and Africa. *African Affairs* 109(436), 489–498.

Moore, J.W. (2015) Ecology, Capital, and the Nature of our Times: Accumulation & Crisis in the Capitalist World-ecology. *Journal of World-Systems Research* 17 (1), 107–146.

Mozambique Gas Development Project (2015) Moving Forward in Mozambique. Press release, Maputo, Mozambique 13 July. Available at: www.mzlng.com/content/docu ments/MZLNG/LNG/Development/APC_Nyusi_and_Walker7-13-15.pdf [Accessed 13 July 13 2017.]

Mozambique Gas Development Project website (2018) Local Stories. Available at: www. mzlng.com/Responsibility/National-Content/Local-Stories/

North, L.L. and Grinspun, R. (2016) Neo-extractivism and the New Latin American Developmentalism: the Missing Piece of Rural Transformation. *Third World Quarterly*, 37(8), 1–22.

Salcedo-La Viña, Celine (2015) Q&A with Alda Salomao: Natural Gas Project Threatens Community Land in Mozambique. Available at www.wri.org/blog/2015/03/qa-alda-salomao-natural-gas-project-threatens-community-land-mozambique

Santos, A.A., Roffarello, L.M. and Filipe, M. (2015) *African Economic Outlook, Mozambique Country Note, ADB and UNDP.* Available at: www.africaneconomicoutlook.org/filead min/uploads/aeo/2015/CN_data/CN_Long_EN/Mozambique_GB_2015.pdf

Schlosberg, D. (2009) *Defining Environmental Justice: Theories, Movements, and Nature.* Oxford: Oxford University Press.

Twomey, H. (2014) *Displacement and Dispossession through Land Grabbing in Mozambique*. Refugee Studies Centre, Oxford Department of International Development, University of Oxford, Working Paper 101.

Vines, A., Thompson, H., Jensen, S.K. and Azevedo-Harman, E. (2015) *Mozambique to 2018: Managers, Mediators and Magnates*. Chatham House Report, June.

White, B., Borras Jr, S.M., Hall, R., Scoones, I. and Wolford, W. (2012) The New Enclosures: Critical Perspectives on Corporate Land Deals. *The Journal of Peasant Studies* 39 (3–4), 619–647.

World Bank (2013) *Africa Development Indicators 2012–13*. Washington, D.C.: World Bank.

World Bank (2014) Generating Sustainable Wealth from Mozambique's Natural Resource Boom. Policy note. World Bank Mozambique, Maputo.

World Bank (n.d.) *Country Overview, Mozambique*. Available at: www.worldbank.org/en/country/mozambique/overview [Accessed 10 March 2015.]

6

POSSIBILITIES AND PITFALLS OF ENVIRONMENTAL JUSTICE ACTION

Learning from Roşia Montană and Yaigojé Apaporis anti-mining struggles

Ioana Florea and Hannibal Rhoades

Introduction

In the last two decades, one of the major environmental conflicts unfolding in Romania has been related to open-pit gold extraction using cyanide, in the Apuseni Mountains. Ioana Florea was involved in several awareness campaigns and protest events opposing open-pit exploitation, as part of Quantic Association – a Bucharest-based platform for social and environmental justice actions, and critical education.

In another long-running anti-mining struggle, indigenous communities in the North Western Colombian Amazon successfully resisted a Canadian multinational's attempts to extract gold from their traditional territories. Hannibal Rhoades has reported on this struggle and supported the indigenous-led campaign to prevent mining in his role at The Gaia Foundation, an organization that works alongside local and indigenous communities and social movements to achieve environmental justice and restore a respectful relationship with the Earth.

After meeting at the *Rights to Nature* conference in June 2016, Hannibal and Ioana started discussing the complexities of environmental justice action, their field observations, the reflective processes involved in their work and in their teams. This paper is the result of that conversation. It represents a work-in-progress – an ongoing questioning about the possibilities of action for social and environmental justice in the global context of the neoliberal grab on human and non-human nature.

Roşia Montană and the protests against open-pit gold mining in Romania

The environmental conflict in the Apuseni Mountains started in the late 1990s, when the formerly state-owned Roşia Montană conventional mining company was privatized and Canadian company Gabriel Resources bought most of its shares. Soon after, Gabriel Resources established a new entirely private company named Roşia Montană Gold Corporation (RMGC), for the purpose of developing a massive gold and silver mining project. In 1999–2000, the national authorities gave the company a concession for a large state-owned property, covering several mountains with a long history of conventional mining. RMGC embarked on the elaborate process of authorizing the mining project and the open-pit extraction method: the plan involved the use of 12,000 tons of cyanide per extraction year, the excavation of 500 million tons of rock from four mountains, resulting in a 400 metres deep / 8 kilometres diameter crater, and a deposit-lake with 215 million cubic metres of waste waters laced with cyanide (Grupul pentru Salvarea Roşiei Montane din ASE, 2010).

The mountain village of Roşia Montană was the closest to the planned mining project and, for reasons of strategic access, RMGC's operation centre. In 1999, the local population became aware of the imminent evictions and relocation required by the mine's development. Resistance to the mine started soon after, with Alburnus Maior Association established by September 2000, representing 300 families in Roşia Montană and 100 families in the neighbouring settlement Bucium, resisting relocations and, according to their mission, "opposing the use of cyanide technologies and the large-scale open-pit extraction of gold"[1]. As the Canadian company intensified its aggressive intrusion in the Apuseni Mountains (buying almost 800 houses in eight years and demolishing most of them, digging new truck-roads into the mountains, claiming access to the land of an ancient cemetery and so forth) and its aggressive lobbying (sponsored trips for state representatives, sponsored research conferences and mass-media campaigns and so on), resistance and unrest continued to grow. It expanded beyond the local residents' circles (although they remained central to the mobilization), involving diverse groups of supporters, opinion leaders, researchers and journalists. The heated discussions and protests reached Romania's big cities – mostly Cluj-Napoca, Bucharest and Timişoara.

In 2007, Romania's Environmental Ministry blocked the authorization process for the mining project, only for it to be re-opened in 2010. The aggressive RMGC lobby split public opinion between mining supporters (mostly advocating jobs and mining royalties) and mining opponents (mostly pointing to irreversible pollution and irreversible destruction of culturally significant territories). Local and national resistance to the extraction project peaked in late-summer 2013, when the Romanian government proposed to grant RMGC the special statute of a "national interest project" and forwarded a legislative project towards the Romanian Parliament allowing extractive corporations to by-pass environmental regulations. Weekly street protests followed in response, gathering more than 10,000 people in several cities; the state authorities employed thousands of riot police agents against the protesters and to protect corporate operations.

In this confrontational context and throughout its decade of intense history, the main discourses and actions of the resistance movement opposing mining were built around the idea of protecting local private property against a foreign corporate grab, opposing the ancient/inherited property rights of the worthy locals to the corrupt interests of the unworthy foreigners. This framing, centred on local private property, is aligned[2] with the post-socialist Romanian context, marked by ubiquitous privatization and (media instrumented) denigration of the commons. It's also aligned to generalized suspicion of "foreigners" – a culturally charged suspicion that has often distracted people from the actual economic interests at stake. This frame alignment led to compromises with the dominant system: for example, promoting Roşia Montană as a valuable – thus worth saving – touristic and cultural destination, instead of most prominently promoting equal rights to clean water/healthy environments/green jobs, or instead of challenging the externalization of social and environmental mining-costs.[3] This alignment also led to nationalism and far-right claims penetrating the dominant discourse of the main environmental movement in Romania.

Although leftist groups and claims were present in the movement from the beginning, they were slowly marginalized in the Save Roşia Montană campaign, with people suffering aggression at the hands of right-wing co-protestors during movement events. Nevertheless, some of these groups continued to be involved in the movement. With limited resources, they kept making claims based on ideas such as common resources, equal rights to nature, cross-border solidarity, and environmental justice. They also kept discussing what we discuss here – how can alternative framings of the environmental movement be built, in the global context of neoliberalism interconnected with rising nationalism and hate speech?

These discussions are still relevant today. After Roşia Montană Gold Corporation was finally denied exploitation permits in early 2014, in July 2015 Gabriel Resources registered a complaint against the Romanian state, at the International Centre for Settlement of Investment Disputes (World Bank), claiming four billion dollars in compensation. The trans-Atlantic trade agreements under negotiation between the EU, Canada and the US could alter the result of the trial, as well as of similar future trials.[4] In addition, avoiding public scrutiny, smaller open-pit gold mines are being planned in the Apuseni Mountains by other companies trying to authorize exploitations involving the use of cyanide.[5]

Expanding indigenous self-determination in response to gold mining in Yaigojé Apaporis, Colombia

In the late 2000s, indigenous leaders from the Yaigojé Apaporis region in the northwestern Colombian Amazon first reported that representatives of Canadian mining company Cosigo Resources (CR) were visiting their Malocas (traditional riverside houses). The leaders allege that the visiting officials offered them money in return for their support for the company to mine gold at a sacred natural site, known as Yuisi/Yuika or La Libertad, that plays a central role in the cosmology and origin stories of Yaigojé's indigenous peoples.[6] The advances of Cosigo Resources, aimed at securing access to a 2000 hectare area for gold exploration, were rejected by local indigenous leaders, who deemed the company's plans to extract at a sacred site unconscionable (Gomez Soto, 2015, p. 39).

In response to Cosigo Resources' interest in mining at Yuisi, the Asociación de Capitanes Indígenas del Yaigojé Apaporis (ACIYA), a pre-existing indigenous organization formed of representatives from the different peoples living along the Apaporis River in Amazonas State, began organizing a preventative resistance process to protect their territory from mining. This process involved visible mobilizations, endogenous research methodologies and networking at local, regional and international levels, bringing together indigenous peoples from the Makuna, Tanimuka, Letuama, Barasano, Cabiyari, Yahuna and Yujup-Maku indigenous communities (p 38), Colombian and international environmental justice organizations, lawyers and scientists.

At the forefront of ACIYA's strategies was a plan to expand indigenous communities' rights of self-determination to the subsoil. Under Colombian law, an indigenous resguardo, of the kind recognized in Yaigojé Apaporis in 1988, grants its inhabitants collective ownership of and rights to the soil, but the subsoil remains in the control of the state (Article 332), leaving it vulnerable to prospecting and exploitation.

Supported by national-level NGO ally Gaia Amazonas, and advised that achieving national park status would extend protection to the subsoil, ACIYA formally requested that the Colombian National Parks Department create a national park over their resguardo and traditional territory (p. 40). ACIYA's efforts to add another layer of protection for their territory were initially successful, and in October 2009 Yaigojé Apaporis became Colombia's 55th national protected area.

Just two days after Yaigojé was awarded national park status, however, Cosigo Resources was granted a 2000 hectare exploration and exploitation concession for the Yuisi area, catalysing a five-year legal struggle for the area's future.[7]

Recognizing that the establishment of a national park would mean the end of its mining ambitions, Cosigo Resources doggedly pursued its pro-mining case through the Colombian courts. The company was initially buoyed by support from indigenous organization ACITAVA, from the region of Yaigojé Apaporis lying in Vaupés State. Just months after Yaigojé was declared a national park, ACITAVA launched a legal challenge to Yaigojé's park status at the Colombian Constitutional Court. This asserted that they had not been fully or adequately consulted in the process of creating the national park and it therefore violated their right to Free Prior and Informed Consent. The legal challenge was accompanied by a media campaign and demonstrations denouncing the national park as an assault on the autonomy of the indigenous peoples represented by ACITAVA, who share the Yaigojé Apaporis Resguardo.

However, during a public hearing in January 2014, involving Constitutional Court judges and 160 inhabitants from along the Apaporis River,[8] ACITAVA admitted its legal strategy was encouraged, organized and paid for by Cosigo Resources. In what would prove the critical turning point in the case, the indigenous members of ACITAVA who had initially supported the challenge made a public apology, said they had been misled and declared their support for the creation of the national park (ibid.). More than a year later, in October 2015, the Colombian Constitutional

Court formally recognized the validity of Yaigojé Apaporis's national park status, as declared in 2009, ending Cosigo's hopes of mining in the region.

The struggle to prevent mining in Yaigojé Apaporis has most dominantly been framed in terms of indigenous self-determination over the sacred territory. Where indigenous peoples and others invoke this framing, indigenous self-determination is usually understood to guarantee the enduring conservation of critical ecosystems and their protection against incoming destructive threats like mining. Making alternative lifeways and ethics more visible, prioritizing and empowering indigenous valuations and governance of nature as collectively managed and sacred has a radical potential to challenge the neoliberal framing of nature as a collection of resources awaiting privatization, exploitation and commodification. However, the temporary struggle in which ACIYA and ACITAVA were opposed to each other over the creation of the Yaigojé Apaporis National Park reveals the potential vulnerability of this framing to both conflicting claims and cooptation by neoliberal actors.

In sponsoring ACITAVA's initial rejection of the Yaigojé Apaporis National Park on grounds of self-determination, Cosigo Resources used this framing and the platform it creates for indigenous participation, to its advantage. Although the company was ultimately unsuccessful, the conflict it was able to spark between the two indigenous organizations indicates the potential complexities and risks involved in indigenous struggles for land and water that are represented using this framing, even if it accurately reflects reality. The temporary conflict between ACIYA and ACTITAVA also sheds light on the paradox of "keeping while giving" in the struggle to stop Cosigo Resources. In order to expand protection against mining through the creation of a national park, the indigenous peoples of Yaigojé Apaporis had to engage with the Colombian State, specifically in the form of the Colombian National Parks Department. It was this concession of self-determination ACITAVA initially rejected, albeit under the influence of Cosigo Resources. Since that time, however, ACIYA has worked with the Colombian National Parks Department to develop a collaborative-management plan that genuinely extends indigenous peoples' self-determination, is grounded in indigenous knowledge and challenges exclusionary and neoliberal conservation approaches.

Since the original proclamation of Yaigojé's national park status, a group of 27 young leaders from nine communities in Yaigojé Apaporis, including representatives from ACIYA and ACITAVA-affiliated communities, have become engaged in a process of endogenous cultural research, documenting the traditional knowledge of their elders and communities and mapping their territory.[9] The young leaders' research will form the basis for the collaborative management plan, which itself stems from a constitution that directly recognizes the authority of indigenous peoples and their knowledge in the future management of the Yaigojé Apaporis National Park: "The integral management of the territory will be done based on the traditional knowledge and the regulations given to each ethnic group since the beginning of the world" (Constitution of Yaigojé Apaporis National Park, agreed by ACIYA and the Colombian National Parks Department, cited on p. 125).

As in the case of Rosia Montana, highly secretive supra-national trade law, and in particular investor–state dispute settlements, continue to pose a threat to environmental justice victories like that in Yaigojé Apaporis. Cosigo Resources is now seeking damages as part of a $16 billion investor–state dispute settlement brought against the Colombian government under the Colombia–USA Free Trade Agreement. The potential for proceedings such as these to induce political and regulatory "chill" in governmental decision-making concerning extractive projects and entrench neoliberal norms of deregulation is a massive concern now and for the future.

Challenges in solidarity building

We live and work in London, respectively Bucharest, quite far from the front-line communities involved in the environmental struggles we are observing, and in quite different contexts. What could be the problems with this "distant gaze"?

Any struggle to achieve social and environment justice or to revive cultural and governance practice that are eco-literate involves complex social, political and historical dynamics. One main danger is that the discourses and framings surrounding a struggle are accepted uncritically as reality, without an in-depth assessment of the situation on the ground to understand who holds the power to influence such public discourses, to own and distribute land and so on.

More distant agents for social and environmental justice are often sheltered from the violent state and paramilitary repression, defamation and incarceration faced by communities struggling for social and ecological justice, as well as the wider political context in which a struggle is occurring. This sheltered position, if unchallenged, may lead an organization or individual to follow up inappropriate advocacy and campaigning strategies at national and international level that are potentially damaging to a community's own efforts, their safety and their own wishes. This is especially dangerous in cases where communities appear to be split over the future of a destructive project, putting them at risk of devastating inter-communal violence or suppression by self-interested local elites.

The unawareness of the wishes and ambitions of local communities that can be a result of the distant gaze can also lead to usury narrative theft by non-frontline agents and the transfer of power away from a community in a struggle. In the past, international NGOs and other support groups have been guilty of "adopting" struggles and using their participants to build their own narratives and campaigns, which do not necessarily reflect the narratives and understandings built by front-line communities through more horizontal means. These distant actors may thus become the arbiters of acceptable reality in a struggle, using their power and expertise to dominate a discourse and influence the "right" and "wrong" reasons for resistance.

Bearers of the distant gaze may also be guilty of proposing and influencing communities to adopt "alternative" livelihoods, and economic and political campaigns that pander to the dominant neoliberal model for development – the very model that has incentivized the projects front-line communities are rejecting. In struggles over land rights, it is also not unheard of for distant actors to be framed as the proponents of "green colonialism" by extractivist states. By today's dominant economic and developmental logic, attempts to secure land in the hands of land-based local and indigenous communities, which often involves removing it from the neoliberal economic domain, is regarded as a land-grab made against the wider citizenry of a nation. The controversy emerging from such accusations may turn public opinion against the struggle of a front-line community.

How can the dangers of the distant gaze be overcome?

This is the critical question for organizations working to provide solidarity and support to front-line communities. Despite the pitfalls of the distant gaze, local, national and international networking and solidarity play a crucial role in supporting front-line communities. There are many methods for disassembling the distant gaze. The practice of active listening, dialogue and frequent direct contact between front-line communities and distant allies is one crucial aspect. Where possible, before any action is taken, horizontal exchange and dialogue between communities and potential allies should be organised, so that supporting organisations can better understand the complexities and dangers of any struggle, and communities' key reasons for resisting. This information should be used to inform future engagements.

Local partner NGOs or community-based organizations may also be crucial information points, enabling overseas supporters to negotiate the local and national political context, advising how international/outside action can genuinely support a struggle. For example, The Gaia Foundation collaborates with local and national organisations through long-term "affectionate alliances" based on trust that provide the organization with critical information and enable it to support more sensitively.

As far as possible, supporting groups should aim to create platforms for the voices of affected peoples to be heard, rather than speaking on their behalf. These platforms may be created online, through the media or in the form of exchanges and events, and will help front-line communities reach new audiences with their own messages. The Gaia Foundation and allies such as the London Mining Network have consistently worked to build platforms such as these over decades, working with local and indigenous communities. These groups, and others like them, also provide capacity building trainings, for example, in participatory video, that empower community members to communicate their own struggles and avoid narrative theft. Most importantly, however, organizations and individuals must be encouraged to develop a reflective practice that makes visible and acknowledges the power dynamics present in any struggle for social and environmental justice, the danger of distance and the importance of staying true to those at the forefront of that struggle, who will reap the rewards of a victory, or suffer most badly from a defeat, to avoid replicating colonial power-dynamics.

How to establish initial contacts with front-line groups? How to support them from a distance?

Working directly alongside and in support of existing networks of peoples' organizations and aligned NGOs can help ameliorate the dangers created by the distant gaze and enable organic connections to emerge between front-line groups and their supporters. As can working in a process-led way that centres the concerns and strengths of each community.

The Gaia Foundation, for example, works with partner organizations in countries across sub-Saharan Africa, the Amazon basin and historically in Eurasia also. In some cases, staff members from these partner organizations are themselves members of the communities supported, acting as animators of the connection. In all cases partners are embedded in national and regional social movements that are closely connected to communities opposing destructive "development" projects. These partner groups are most often the bridges for initial contact.

It is alongside these partners that Gaia undertakes long-term processes to revive local and indigenous knowledge, governance systems and intergenerational learning flows, using participatory "talking tools" such as eco-cultural maps and calendars.[10] These processes are led by communities with initial facilitation support, the aim being to establish self-sustaining processes for revival and the development of communities' own life plans for the future.

Gaia also supports these communities to oppose unwanted "developments" such as mines and industrial agricultural plantations, and secure land rights and specific protections for sacred sites. In some cases, the knowledge revival processes we have begun in one community have had a magnetic effect, drawing in neighbouring communities who are interested to learn about and initiate these processes themselves.

Gaia itself is also a member of international networks that bring community-based and national and international groups into direct contact with one another. One example is the Yes to Life, No to Mining Global Solidarity Network, a network of and for communities rejecting mining and their supporters. This network has responded to numerous direct calls for reactive solidarity, in the form of letter writing, petition campaigns, peer-to-peer community exchanges and direct actions, from community groups.

Challenges in building emancipatory discourses

What are some examples of resistance processes that have not fallen into exclusive discourses and/or neoliberal approaches?

The local resistance in Roşia Montană, the lasting and growing opposition to RMGC, and, later, the multi-city protest events generated a lot of debate and led to the involvement of diverse groups. It was an unprecedented networking process in "third millennium" Romania: students and researchers met with the locals; one journalist from Cluj-Napoca moved to live in Roşia Montană in order to closely investigate the actions of RMGC; diverse artists and creative groups tackled the issue in their works (music, theatre, graffiti and so forth) reaching new audiences; Romanians abroad, foreign journalists and environmentalists became interested in the topic and brought it to even further audiences; people from different cities met in Roşia Montană and in protest events, whereas locals travelled to different cities to meet protestors from around the country.

This intense mobilization profited mostly those who were already aligned to the dominant system, in terms of neoliberal conservation agendas or nationalistic agendas, and those who were already organized – such as NGOs, football hooligans, church groups and political organizations – although not necessarily in harmony with one another. But this intense mobilization also brought new vitality, new people, new ideas and more organizing experience to the groups oriented towards social and environmental justice.

One example is the "Căşi sociale ACUM" (Social Houses NOW) movement for social and environmental justice in Cluj-Napoca, claiming social housing rights for the people working and living on the city's landfills, due to the cumulative effects of racist (anti-Roma) and classist local policies (Dohotaru et al., 2016). Most of those involved in this mobilization were also involved in the protests against RMGC; people evicted from the city to the landfills were also joining Save Roşia Montană protests and solidarity events. This movement combines claims to social housing rights with claims to policies against racism, and policies for environmental justice: the right to clean water and air, the right to a healthy environment for all, the just recognition and remuneration of the vital recycling work performed by the people living on the landfills, and the ecological reorganization of the waste management system in Cluj-Napoca.[11]

Another example is the h.arta group of artists and art educators from Timişoara. They have been actively involved in social and environmental justice actions since 2001: building open community gardens in public spaces in their neighbourhoods, organizing exhibitions and collective books on women's solidarity and intersectional approaches, using critical educational methods while working in several schools, criticizing the consumerist society and the military-industrial complex.[12]

h.arta's involvement in the protests against RMGC in 2013 brought them more visibility in the online media and more connections to social and environmental groups in Timişoara and Bucharest, including Quantic Association; these enriched connections led to further collective works on social and environmental justice.[13] Moreover, the involvement of h.arta group in the anti-mining protests represented a learning process on environmental issues; in this learning process, the art educators at h.arta group developed a new school curriculum on social and environmental justice, now being implemented in their schools in Timişoara. Moreover, taking part in Save Roşia Montană protests and solidarity events strengthened the Quantic Association team and connected it to other groups in Bucharest, Cluj-Napoca, Timişoara and abroad.

How can we address these issues and build more inclusive, unified environmental and social justice mobilizations?

Quantic's work is mostly about self and peer-to-peer education and information sharing on both social and environmental justice, with kids, young people, youth workers and groups affected by injustice. Issues of social and environmental justice are tackled together, as strongly interconnected. Because this is still a marginal approach (not only in Romania), the Quantic team focuses on translating, producing, debating and sharing informational materials. Its collaborators also contribute to and generate (online and face-to-face) contexts in which such materials can be accessed and discussed. Some collaborators are teachers, willing to discuss issues of social and environmental justice with their pupils; some collaborators work with students; others work with art or new media; and others organize public events and conferences. On every occasion, the topics addressed and the materials disseminated follow several directions: discussing the unequal distribution of social and environmental costs of the diverse interconnected industries fuelling capitalism (from extractive industries, to industrial agriculture, military and so forth), as well as confronting the historical processes leading to unjust and disproportionate corporate profits; discussing the interconnectedness of all persons and species in the current economic and social system; illustrating existing resistance efforts and more just proposals for social organizing.

Although Quantic members were involved in Save Roşia Montană campaign since 2006, only in the last few years have we created occasions for these kinds of debates: our social and environmental justice discourse is also a work-in-progress and a learning process. In addition, Quantic also works to build connections with other groups, exchanging information and mutual support, and finding common directions for action: supporting the actions of the Common Front for Housing Rights in Cluj-Napoca and Bucharest and investigating together the corporate alliances corrupting the authorities; sharing information with social and environmental justice groups in France, Germany, Portugal and UK (and others, as facilitated by our social networks); collaborating and learning together with young people activated by the Roşia Montană protests; collaborating with independent artists in exhibitions and theatre plays dealing with environmental and social (in)justice; organizing international youth and youth workers exchanges in places marked by social and environmental conflicts (including in Roşia Montană), with participants from those regions, analysing together both the international and local contexts of those conflicts and the possibilities for action.

The Association is cautious in its collaborations, searching for like-minded groups and avoiding giving support and legitimacy to groups with other views – despite their involvement in the same movement. For this reason, Quantic's interaction with many of the groups involved in the anti-cyanide-mining campaign in Romania, with a patriotic/nationalistic approach or with a neoliberal conservationist approach, was very limited.

Tactical choices

Environmental mobilizations are often interlinked with a neoliberal logic because they have to negotiate with a neoliberal system. What are the spaces we can use/that need to be created locally and internationally to address these issues?

Quantic's experience mostly comes from working with micro-social solidarities. From this standpoint, the association sees that meeting spaces allowing recurrent horizontal debates and knowledge exchanges could play a vital role in struggles for environmental justice. Such spaces are scarce. They are also hard to access for some people (for example, those with histories of migration and dispossession) and hard to keep in the face of neoliberal advancement. In the system's "peripheries", small rural property, family houses opened for small-scale regional tourism and indigenous protected land could represent such tactical spaces – as forms of autonomy against big capital, opposing different forms of land grabbing from the system's "core", corporate colonization and exploitation. But they (easily) become problematic and neoliberal-friendly, when opposing the movement or settling of other groups, when facilitating inequalities and even turning themselves into forms of exploitation – of "others" who don't have "traditional ways" or "local property" (as in the case of the Apuseni Mountains).

Tactical spaces could also develop as resistance camps and recurrent protests events, school classes[14] and university halls, local support groups, written texts and online platforms, cooperative bars[15] and art spaces,[16] community gardens[17], hang-out places, NGO or union offices – each with their own challenges of facilitating access and keeping their character. All kinds of spaces can be reclaimed and used, but they must be permanently negotiated and reflected upon, in order to remain inclusive and as resistant as possible to the neoliberal logic.

How can environmental mobilisation discourses and practices stay inclusive? What concepts of social solidarity could be strategic for these forms of mobilization?

Keeping environmental justice processes inclusive involves constant reflective practice within movements. One important step towards inclusivity seems to be the effort to find the intersections between movements of indigenous and non-indigenous peoples. It is possible to see a lot of hope here and some inspiring examples, but also a lot of fragility.

The alliance of indigenous and non-indigenous peoples in Cerrejon, Colombia, where indigenous Wayuu communities and mine workers have found common ground to unite for environmental and social justice, provides an example of both the possibilities and the difficulties of this kind of intersectional action. Big victories have been won by intersectional alliances like these, which are able to transcend long-running historical oppositions for a time. In Cerrejon, for example, the unified resistance of Wayuu communities and worker's union SINTRACARBON has so far prevented Cerrejon Coal's plan to divert 26 kilometres of the region's major river – the Rio Rancheria.[18]

Relations in intersectional movements can also become strained easily, as seen in other cases. Ultimately, the histories that have brought these societal groups into the same places and into conflict with one another before will not disappear as a result of a single contained victory. Perhaps, though, as the analysis and historical understandings underlying these alliances gets deeper – going beyond a single project or set of circumstances to understand a common pattern of injustice and therefore a deeper common cause – these intersections and alliances could become stronger and more enduring forces for environmental justice. There are many things in the way of coming to that understanding, many centuries of violence, devastation and an inclination to scapegoat the "other", whoever that may be. But these intersectional alliances, however fragile and complex, at least open spaces to begin to develop a shared and more constellational understanding of injustices.

Within the remits of this discussion, we have tackled the inclusivity of inter-human concepts of social and environmental justice. One other potential pathway for exploration, through decolonization, is to expand the focus of justice to encompass non-anthropocentric, inter-species definitions and practices. This approach is particularly coherent with many indigenous struggles for environmental justice that do not recognize strict culture–nature binaries. Exploring inter-species justice may yield new analyses that re-situate struggles for social and environmental justice in more coherent understandings of the entangled ecological realities of the Earth system, and the cosmologies and knowledge practices of marginalized land-based peoples. This is a promising approach for finding common ground for justice, expanding the boundaries of community, while acknowledging the multiplicity of experiences, including of oppression, within the respective community.

Conclusion

The anti-mining movements in Roşia Montană and Yaigojé Apaporis entail local conflicts, transnational complexities, challenges and intensive collective learning for the groups involved at different levels of these movements. Although successful until now in blocking the mining projects concerned, and in generating new alliances and potential for environmental actions, these two parallel struggles are under threat by investor–state dispute settlements under the power of international trade laws and agreements – a developing phenomenon.

Thus, the involvement of both authors in anti-mining struggles and this collaborative paper are marked by an ongoing questioning of the possibilities of action for social and environmental justice. One key conclusion is that the extent of these possibilities, arising as they do in unique-yet-interconnected, and rapidly changing contexts, cannot be fully known.

The social and environmental justice discourses of each of the authors' teams are a work-in-progress and a learning process. These learnings don't yield concrete, fixed answers, but rather directions to travel in and promising practices that may help create more inclusive and intersectional forms of justice. These practices include establishing frequent direct contact between front-line communities and "distant" allies; contact that involves actively listening to communities' key reasons for resisting, their hopes, goals and perceptions of the complexities and dangers of any environmental struggle. Those scarce meeting spaces that allow recurrent horizontal debates and knowledge exchanges are crucial. In developing or reclaiming such spaces, it is important to acknowledge that they are hard to access for some people and hard to keep in the face of neoliberal advancement; thus, it is also important to practice continuous "reality-checks" on them.

Another significant conclusion is that organizations, activist groups and individuals must develop a reflective practice that makes visible and acknowledges the power dynamics present in any struggle for social and environmental justice, the danger of "distance" and the importance of "staying true" to those at the forefront of that struggle, to avoid replicating (colonial) power-dynamics. With this comes caution in developing collaborations, searching for like-minded groups and avoiding giving support and legitimacy to groups with approaches that entrench neoliberal patterns of exploitation and inequality, despite their involvement in the same movement.

In-depth research carried out according to participatory principles is one important step towards highlighting promising pathways towards more inclusive and intersectional forms of environmental justice. This includes researching the complexities of involved and affected groups, inter-species interactions, the intersections between movements of indigenous and non-indigenous peoples, the histories underlying common patterns of injustice – and therefore a deeper common cause. Understanding these intersections would make alliances stronger and more enduring forces for environmental justice.

Notes

1 www.rosiamontana.org/node/1899
2 For further discussions on "frame alignment" in social movements see Snow et al. (1986).
3 For further discussions on social movements' alignment to the dominant system in market-oriented Romania see Florea (2015).
4 https://stop-ttip.org/what-is-the-problem-ttip-ceta/faqs/
5 http://miningwatch.ro/en/categorie/certej_baita_craciunesti/
6 https://intercontinentalcry.org/indigenous-peoples-of-yaigoje-apaporis-victorious-as-court-ousts-canadian-mining-company/
7 https://ejatlas.org/conflict/yaigoje-apaporis
8 www.youtube.com/watch?v=QjVLNfjO8cQ
9 https://vimeo.com/116700866
10 https://vimeo.com/9831187
11 www.facebook.com/CasiSocialeACUM/
12 www.hartagroup.ro
13 For example, collective papers in Gazeta de Artă Politică, www.artapolitica.ro

14 For example, http://laurentiuridichie.blogspot.ro/2013/12/bradul-de-craciun.html
15 For example, www.facebook.com/macazcoop/
16 For example, www.youtube.com/watch?v=-sRrGOWPNCg
17 For example, http://asociatia-komunitas.ro/projects/gradina-136/
18 http://londonminingnetwork.org/2014/06/cerrejon-coal-colombia-an-abusive-mar
riage-full-of-machismo/

References

Dohotaru, A., Harbula, H. and Vincze, E. (eds) (2016) *Pata*. Cluj-Napoca: Editura Fundației
pentru Studii Europene.
Florea, I. (2015) The Ups and Downs of a Symbolic City: The Architectural Heritage Pro-
tection Movement in Bucharest. In K. Jacobsson (ed.), *Urban Grassroots Movements in
Central and Eastern Europe*. Farnham: Ashgate. Pp. 55–78.
Gomez Soto, M. (2015) *The Unfolding Voice of Gaia*. MA thesis, Schumacher College.
Grupul pentru Salvarea Roșiei Montane din ASE (2010) 24 argumente "contra" proiectului
Roșia Montană. Niciun argument "pentru". Observatorul Urban București. Available
at: www.observatorulurban.ro/24-argumente-contra-proiectului-roia-montana.html.
[Accessed January 2017.]
Snow, D. et al. (1986) Frame Alignment Processes, Micromobilization, and Movement Par-
ticipation. *American Sociological Review* 51: 464–481.

PART II

Green struggles against capitalist urbanization and infrastructure construction

7

EGYPTIAN ENVIRONMENTALISM AND URBAN GRASSROOTS MOBILIZATION

Noura Wahby

Introduction

In February 2015, a group of mostly upper-class women gathered to protest a viral social media video that shows the killing of a street dog in one of Cairo's low-income areas, and treatment of wildlife in general. The women laid siege to a famous square in the quaint Zamalek neighbourhood, next to the exclusive Gezira Club. Everything seemed to run smoothly, until a veiled woman in humble clothes carrying her sickly child approached and began reprimanding the women. She accused them of caring more about the rights of animals than the rights of Cairo's poor, invoking her dilemma of treating her son's unknown disease (Omara and Ghoneim, 2015). Aggressively, the woman was shunned and attacked by the protesters for her lack of understanding surrounding animal rights. She was then arrested by police officers and held with other women accused of prostitution. Meanwhile, the protest continued, and the women left after they felt their voices were sufficiently heard by the media at hand.

A few months later, residents of a low-income class neighbourhood in Giza, part of the Greater Cairo region, took to the streets in September to protest repeated water shortages in the governorate (Abdel Azim, 2015). They cut off a nearby highway in order to capture the attention of authorities, to bring to light the chronic water shortages they had experienced over the past year (ibid.). This was not the first time this sort of protest had taken place. Similar scenes had played out due to lack of running water during the peak summer months of 2015, where citizens were expected to fend for themselves without a clear state solution (Ezz and Arafat, 2015). Motorists picked fights with the protestors and the police scrambled to regain control, promising a resolution. Yet, the authorities responded to the Giza protestors as they have always done – blaming other neighbourhoods for illegally diverting water, providing water tanks for a week and returning to a state of negligence[1].

These two examples offer a glimpse of a highly fragmented environmental scene in Egypt, characterized by class and regional divisions. This scene bears great resemblance to other cases in the developing world such as Delhi (Baviskar, 2003), as well in developed nations where a "sustainability fix" has dominated state policies and marginalised grassroots groups (Béal, 2011, p. 410.). In both cases, the role of the Egyptian state in regulating the environment, class relations and contention, is central. The significance of this role needs to be understood within a wider system of "purposeful negligence" by the state, self-help systems of the grassroots and the co-optation of civil society.

This chapter thus focuses on the interplay between state institutions and environmental movements in shaping Egyptian "environmentalism". The term is defined as the conceptual, procedural and political meanings and actions delineating society–Nature relationships (Choucri, 2001). This discussion will thus shed light on urban governance issues and accompanying contention in the built environment. It examines the melange of civil society groups, urban elites and the marginalized poor in informal areas around Cairo. It will also illustrate the current domination by certain forms of largely middle-class environmentalism, and efforts by the urban poor and their 'Non-Movements' (Bayat, 2013), which have thus far gone unrecognized.

As such, the chapter argues that localized grassroots forms of contention against state damage and negligence of the surrounding environment are undermined by a particular definition of Nature put forth by the new bourgeois classes and co-opted civil society movements. Several cases of grassroots contention will be looked at, and especially water protests in Cairo.

First, the chapter examines the historical development of the relationship between the Egyptian state and the environment. This will lead to a discussion on the role of the state in organizing, managing and implementing environmental policies, as well as the role of donor agencies. The following section will touch upon the difference between middle-class environmentalism and how the poor have claimed their rights to the built environment within cities. The third section will delve further, describing different forms of contention within the Cairene context, and how the poor's environmental activism has been undermined by the state. This will culminate in the concluding remarks to retackle the main question of the state's interest in maintaining a fragmented natural landscape.

Nature and state: a historical look

Many clichés surround Egypt's relationship with its environment, the Nile being the central focus for several historians. This includes Herodotus, who dubbed the country "The gift of the Nile" (Mikhail, 2011, p. 1.), a coinage that has transferred into everyday spoken Arabic and is professed proudly by those living on the riverbanks. The blue river, separating the swathes of desert land on either side, made agriculture the defining feature of the Egyptian economy throughout history. While recent industrialization and service-provision policies, as well as urbanization, have led to sharp decline in the country's agricultural sector, it still contributes to at least 14% of the Gross Domestic Product (GDP) (Kheir-El-Din and El-Laithy, 2008).

Traditionally, Egypt's ruling elites and consecutive colonial powers exploited the country's "commercial agriculture" to their benefit, with land-owning families exerting large political influence for centuries (Mikhail, 2014; Fahmy, 1997). Yet it was only under Ottoman control from the mid-19th century that a change in the relationship between state, citizen and Nature actually took place. With the increasing incorporation of Egypt into trade markets, the centralized government began to invest in large projects to service the needs of global capitalism. Before the 1850s, peasants were left to perform limited maintenance and interventions on their surrounding environment, mostly through improving embankments, irrigation strategies and local infrastructure (Mikhail, 2011, 2014). These were decentralized processes, where rural communities worked on local issues and had autonomy over their natural environment (Mikhail, 2014).

Nonetheless, as Egypt's contribution to international trade grew in size, so did the needs of the Ottoman empire for greater infrastructural investment. This includes areas such as grains storage facilities, and the linking of major cities to the River Nile (ibid.). A major change to Egypt's agriculture took place when large numbers of peasants were recruited across the countryside and forced into labour in the 'grands projects' under Ottoman leaders (Fahmy, 1997), as well as in later years under British rule. In this process, peasants who had historically worked on the land were separated from their natural resources and forced into new forms of labour relations away from their fields. These new labour relations and forcible removal of peasants from their land, dominated by state control and regulation, has become "a primary site of contestation over . . . political and economic power" (Mikhail, 2014, p. 25).

While large-scale infrastructure projects served the needs of the developmental state, recent decades have seen a pattern of investment in grand infrastructure projects as a strategy for authoritarian regimes to solicit public support. As aptly put by Mikhail, every 50 years there is a project announced by different governments "regardless of their purported political bent, whether khedival, colonial, socialist, nationalist, neoliberal, or otherwise" (p. 24) to create a "New Egypt". These include the Suez Canal – 1850s and recent 2016 expansion – the Aswan Dam (1890s, 1950s and 1960s), the Toshka Scheme[2] (2000s) and the recent New Administrative Capital[3] (announced 2016).

In the process of manipulating Nature and changing the landscapes of the seas, river and desert, ordinary Egyptians played no role in imagining Nature's future, despite ultimately being its builders. Instead the state remains the sole actor entrusted with the transformation of Nature. Since the 19th century, the state has created institutions, enacted laws and manipulated regulations to this end, as the following section will discuss.

Harnessing and pacifying Nature from the 1970s

Although various institutions traditionally managed Egypt's natural resources, it was only in the 1970s that a real discussion on an overarching environmental policy occurred (Sowers, 2013). These ideas were brought forth by the local scientist community as they began to participate in several global conferences, such as the Stockholm Conference of 1972. They used Egypt's international convention ratifications as leverage to launch a national dialogue on environmental policy (Gomaa, 1997). This led to the institutionalization of the question of the environment and concretized political interests, as will shortly be described.

A first step was to establish the Egyptian Environmental Affairs Agency (EEAA) in 1982 by Presidential decree no. 631 of the same year (ibid.). The agency went through several institutional reforms, the first in 1985 and another in 1991 (Sowers, 2013). The latter expanded its mandate over more environmental resources, but also removed provincial technical offices from its organization (Gomaa, 1997), following a governmental pattern of provincial marginalization. Yet, both these reforms enshrined the agency's limited role to simply coordinate between ministries, albeit for "land protection, afforestation and park development" where they had authoritative powers (p. 8). Even with the establishment of a Ministry of State for Environmental Affairs, the control of Nature remained fragmented across state sectors, as institutions competed for resources (Egyptian Environmental Affairs Agency, 2016).

This became particularly clear within a wide societal discussion on the Environmental Law No.4 of 1994. In an unprecedented display of the inner workings of state policy-making, parliamentary debates on the law illuminated competing ministerial interests, which worked to delay the law (Sowers, 2013). In particular, ministries concerned with industry and petrochemicals advocated for the lowest possible environmentalist standards, in order to satisfy their customers, while the military establishment and industries continued to maintain its para-legal status (protecting its operations from civilian oversight) (ibid.). Eventually, the law was passed and revised once more in 2009, while a National Environmental Action Plan (NEAP) was created as early as 1992, with significant contributions by the World Bank (Gomaa, 1997, p. 36). The main issues targeted were air and water pollution, land degradation and solid waste management, as well as natural heritage protection (p. 39).

The directives of foreign institutions played a large role in determining the state's authority over the environment. The governments of the 1990s and early 2000s were engrossed in a dual mission – on the one hand, they catered to multinationals in an effort to increase Foreign Direct Investment (FDI). On the other, the state also wanted to promote its environmental profile to increase its cut of global environmental aid. The first objective in particular resulted in a plethora of public ventures with foreign companies, as part of the privatization drive of the 1990s. This resulted in creating spaces of investment, such as Free Industrial Zones, providing tax exemptions and public land leases (ElMusa and Sowers, 2009). These implicitly meant a relaxation of environmental standards.

Several cases of de-prioritizing environmental regulations can be found across various sectors. The most flagrant of these is along the Red Sea Coast, where investment in tourist resort development skyrocketed during the Mubarak era (Sowers, 2013). Marine and local heritage activists in the affected areas fought long battles against international hoteliers and local real estate giants to preserve Bedouin life-styles and underwater life endangered by the exploitative tourism industry (ibid.). The same holds true for the Delta fisheries industry. Exploitative strategies pro-moted by USAID advocated for the creation of fish farms in the Northern Delta, and these have left local fishermen unable to access the privatized commons (Bush and Sabri, 2000).

These examples and many more cases illustrate how the Egyptian state has employed a purposefully unequal management of resource allocation "and the increasing privatization of historically collective assets", thus prioritising FDI and global capital ventures (ibid.)

On the other hand, international interventions contributed to pressuring the Egyptian state towards fuller environmental regulation for some positive results. The first of these was the direct establishment of a technical office within the EEAA to develop concrete policies in line with international standards (Gomaa, 1997). Similarly, donors pressured the government to pass the Environmental Law of 1994, with promises of appetizing environmental aid packages for "environmental main-streaming" (Sowers, 2013). In reality, aid agencies actually funded a narrow range of projects and mostly relating to water and sanitation infrastructure, due to their visibility and tangible impact on communities (Hicks et al. cited in Sowers, 2013).

Quickly, Egypt began to rank as one of the highest recipients of environmental aid in the 1980s and 1990s. It was numbered in the 1990s as the seventh high-est recipient among developing countries with an approximate $3.2billion share (Sowers, 2013, p. 30; Barnes, 2014). This became apparent in the increased level of institutional reporting by state agencies, for instance. Environmental reporting per governorate and per sector have been regularly published by the government from the late 1990s onwards, providing essential statistics that had not been previously available (EEAA website). These also include assessment reports on the current state of the environment, coinciding, for example, with the 2005 Egypt Human Development Report that termed environmental deterioration as "limiting Egypt's development prospects" (Sowers, 2013, p. 7.). This was especially true in predomi-nantly urban governorates, and the case of Cairo as a significant example will be explored as follows.

The urban built environment

As previously described, a fragmented scene of environmental mobilization exists across the country, and particularly in the case of urban contexts such as Cairo. Cai-ro's built environment has been on the receiving end of uneven state investments, which have resulted in the dominate growth of informal areas and gated com-munities. This has contributed to the isolation of grassroots mobilizations within an unequal city. As such, there is very little recognition of their attempts to regain control over the built environment through individualized self-help systems. This will be further discussed, but it is important to first understand the urban make-up of the city.

In 1997, Cairo had a countable number of 100 informal 'slum' areas (Bayat, 1997), but an exponential growth led to about 1105 *ashwaiyat*[4] (slums) areas as recorded in 2011 (Cities Alliance, 2008). These areas have been stigmatized by the state as representative of a negative urbanization process that has engulfed the capital. Yet informal areas have been the only form of major housing growth in Egypt's urban cities (Sims, 2010). In most areas, inhabitants are marginalized citizens who have not been able to afford housing within the traditional city centres, ranging from informal workers to low-ranking bureaucrats and refugees. Meanwhile, the state has invested in reclaiming the surrounding desert circling the city and establishing new suburbs to absorb gated elite aspirations and the new middle classes (ibid.).

The result is a fragmented and unequal urban landscape composed of a dilapidated urban core, enmeshed informal communities, old residential areas and sparkling suburbs on the peripheries. The material imagery of this fragmentation corresponds to the state of environmental efforts by a polarized citizenry, which will be discussed in the following section.

Environmental movements– co-opted contention

The above discussion suggests that the state has always been able to determine society–Nature relationships through creating a rigid framework of acceptable interventions. In reality, however, as noted by Bell in early 2000, the state remains incapable of "monopoliz(ing) the environmental agenda" (p. 25). Environmental questions and interventions are thus highly contested by several groups.

As early as the 1980s, environmental groups formed part of civil society, numbering about 62 by early 1990–85% of which were based in Cairo (Gomaa, 1997). They were inspired by the work of the Green Party, which aimed to increase public consciousness over issues such as different types of pollution, and more significantly poverty "as the worst form of pollution" (p. 19). However, this group of early environmental civil society groups was mostly formed by older and conservative academics who avoided confrontation with the state (ibid.).

Along with availability of new data, the aid influx in Egypt changed the shape of environmental groups and created a "technical society". This is an exclusive sphere where academics, scientists and activists turned into "consultants" for projects funded by donors. These consultants were in high demand and for these individuals, it was a financially preferable vocation as opposed to working for the state or local non-governmental organizations (NGOs) (Gomaa, 1997). These "consultants' formed an important part of environmental movements.

Similarly, scientific societies and research institutes also increased in number, especially as environmental aid required the assistance of local expertise (ibid.). These culminated into what Sowers terms "managerial networks" that have attempted to dominate the implementation and narrative of environmental issues within the country (2013, p. 11.). This included the establishment of a multitude of consulting firms that benefit from relationships with the state and enjoy donor trust (Gomaa, 1997). In some cases, these firms even form transnational connections with foreign consultancies, such as Chemonics Egypt (Sowers, 2013).

Today, most local environmental NGOs work on single issues and within specific locales. These include, for instance, the Association for the Protection of the Environment (APE) that has adopted the cause of solid waste management communities and recycling policies (Gomaa, 1997). Admirably, the appointment of the first Minister for Urban Renewal and Informal Settlements was an NGO leader involved in solid waste management projects, although the Ministry was prematurely dissolved for political reasons. Another well-known organization is the Hurgada Environment Protection and Conservation Association (HEPCA), which aims at protecting marine biodiversity and local Bedouin communities surrounding the Red Sea (Sowers, 2013).

Another example is the Association for Health and Environment Development (AHED), which focuses on the health consequences from interventions in the environment. They adopted the unique approach to partner with grassroots communities to address pollution resulting from private investment, such as Lake El Manzalah fisheries and lead poisoning in Cairo (Gomaa, 1997). At the other end of the spectrum lies Environmental Quality International (EQI), which focused on a regional approach. This consulting firm was established as early as 1981, and continues to provide consulting services across the Middle East and Africa to a plethora of international donors.

It is important to note that Egypt's environmental expert networks and other civil society groups are characterized by their middle-class, elitist nature. Most in fact lack "linkages to broader constituencies" (Sowers, 2013, p. 37). They share this feature with most civil society groups, social institutions and movements in the country (Abdelrahman, 2002). In fact, some scholars have promulgated a theory that "those who are the least likely to be exposed to environmental hazards are the most concerned with the environment" (Gomaa, 1997, p. 5). This ties in with the fact that most NGOs are situated in Cairo among groups with higher socio-economic status and access to political institutions (ibid.; Abdelrahman, 2002).

Egypt is no exception in this regard. Scholars of South Asia in general have recorded the emergence of a "bourgeois environmentalism" (Baviskar, 2003, p. 90.) where elite groups work with the state to create "legible natural terrain" and apolitical subjects (Scott, 1998, p. 18). This means that elite urban classes are able to force their imaginaries of "clean" cities unto environmental policies to shape a dominant way of life (ibid). A multitude of such cases can be seen where governments strive to have "world class cities" and are thus unchecked in pursuing slum demolitions, environmental degradation by approved industries and making space for real estate capital (Arabindoo, 2011; Roy, 2005).

The elitism of Egypt's environmental activists sometimes translates into a discourse that claims that "the public does not care about environmental problems" (Sowers, 2013, p. 5.). An early ambitious study undertaken by Hopkins et al. (2001) aimed specifically to dispel these claims by targeting poor areas in Cairo and the countryside to question what "local people" understand about their environment.

The results indicated that in fact residents were fully aware of the changes to their environment, even if it was not articulated using the discursive narrative of environmentalists (Hopkins et al., 2001, p. 6.). The study also revealed the existence of local organizations and movements battling for local environmental issues that have not been widely publicized (ibid).

Very little scholarship has emerged on such local movements of the long decades before the 2011 Revolution, which featured forms of fragmented mass mobilization around multiple issues (Abdelrahman, 2015). Even less have looked at actions around Nature and the built environment. One such case appeared in Damietta, a city in the north Nile Delta, where the Canadian firm Agrium planned a large fertilizer factory near a popular domestic tourist location (Sowers, 2013). Protests erupted as residents began to understand the environmental implications of the factory on their surroundings and sources of income (ibid.). Yet the state remained reluctant to cancel the agreement, as it was wary of its international standing and the signal this would send to potential investors, rather than prioritizing citizens' demands (ibid.).

The local community thus fought against both the state and a multinational enterprise over several years. It was only through prolonged community strategies that they were able to turn their local problems into an issue of public interest. A significant success factor was the soliciting of local economic and political elites, and appealing to a "stratified citizenry" or different categories of citizens – politicians, local media and similar Delta communities. An organized popular committee coordinated efforts and maintained a "legitimate" discourse, keeping away from national politics and focusing on environmental consequences in an attempt to remain mainstream (ElMusa and Sowers, 2009).

Another instance of grassroots mobilization, which had started in the late 1980s, targeted lead smelters in Northern Cairo (Tewfik, 1997), with the NGO AHED as a strong supporter. Local residents organized themselves once more into citizen committees and used several strategies to make themselves heard by the state. These included complaints, petitions, media appearances, reliance on scientific data and the avoidance of foreign donors to remain within a nationalistic framing (ibid.). Recently, NGOs working with agricultural communities, such as the Egyptian Land Centre, have adopted similar approaches to encourage poor farmers to establish organic organizations, such as independent unions and associations, in order to combat land confiscations and arrests by utilities police (Land Centre for Human Rights, 2016). Similarly, a successful campaign by local environmental groups in Alexandria lead to changes allowing public access to historical heritage (Bell, 2000).

Nonetheless, similar narratives on grassroots mobilization in the urban centres are missing. It is here that organic movements within cities remain neglected by the state and have come to intervene directly in their built environment with escalating confrontations. The following section will discuss these grassroots efforts in urban Cairo.

Urban water movements – regaining autonomy through self-help

Environmental problems facing the urban fabric are quite different based on place-making within the city. Some overarching problems facing Cairo however include air pollution and water shortages. For the latter, its strongest manifestation is the "black cloud", which has been blamed on everything from the poor burning garbage, to rice husk burning in the Northern Delta (Hopkins et al., 2001), encroachment on agricultural land and the pollution of the Nile. In most of these cases, there is a constant "blame game" among the classes, with the media mostly pointing to the poor's activities as the cause of environmental degradation (ibid.).

Another recent significant problem is the issue of water shortages. Water, like most infrastructural utilities, continues to be monopolized by the Egyptian state, where state-owned Water Companies provide accessibility, pricing and maintenance for all residents of cities and villages (AbuZeid et al., 2014). Egypt has 2612 water treatment plants across the country, but these have struggle to keep up with water supply demands and have lead to pronounced shortages (ibid.). Over the past few years, electricity and water shortages have been particularly acute in Cairo, especially in summer (Ezz and Arafat, 2015), and even in elite settlements (Esterman, 2014). The Water Company manages these crises by simply warning residents through media outlets and supplying water trucks for grieved districts, usually at a price.[5]

Informal areas seem to see the worst end of these shortages (Ibrahim, 2012). Depending on the legal battles surrounding land tenure, residents may or may not have access to piped water. In many cases, however, the local administration and water company willingly formalize citizens' water systems, as it means more paying customers – while residents use utility bills as proof of tenure for their legal woes (Séjourné, 2012). This was made clear in 2006 when the Governor of Cairo announced "utilities for all" as a "temporary measure" (Sims 2010), regardless of the legality of tenure.

Nonetheless, the confrontation between the poor and the "commodified commons" continues. In many informal areas, communities installed their own infrastructural systems (Bremer and Bhuiyan, 2014) as the state refused recognition of these areas and maintained an "absent presence" as a practice of governance[6] (Denyer Willis 2016). Communities went through several processes of self-help systems accumulating in communities organizing to tap into mainframe pipes and create their own piped networks, providing access to more than 500 households in some cases (Bremer and Bhuiyan, 2014). Similarly, in the Giza governorate neighbourhoods that were built on agricultural land, residents came together to install deep underground water pumps to access groundwater.[7] Community organization, maintenance and financial investment dominated these grassroots projects, and added to the social cohesion of mostly fragmented areas of marginalized citizens.

These types of projects are often unaccounted for in scholarship on informal areas in Middle Eastern cities. As opposed to the more contentious Latin American and South Asian traditions on informality and slums, Arab informality has been looked at through the lens of "quiet encroachment" as coined by Bayat. This is a survival mechanism by which residents avoid political confrontations with the state and remain in search for basic survival in larger cities (Bayat, 2013). Recently, this incremental build-up of mundane activities has been termed "Non-Movements", where the urban poor move beyond simple encroaching, and their collective actions coalesce into extra-legal norms (ibid).

Through these Non-Movements, the urban poor attempt to make claims on the state in their struggle for citizenship (ibid.). But it is also clear that through these self-help strategies, they are reasserting their autonomy over their immediate natural environment. As previously described, this relationship was broken by the state in the 19th century as it centralized interventions and regulations (Mikhail, 2014). Yet through these unnoticeable systems, grassroots communities are imposing their own connection to Nature. Even in cases where the state intervenes to install its own official piping, community systems continue to serve as a main source of water during chronic shortages.[8]

As such, it seems that this form of contention is ever present in urban communities and takes shape in different ways. These include organic organizations installing infrastructure, popular committees defending neighbourhoods against vandalism during the 2011 Revolution and continued community social work, such as independent trade unions of workers, and local groups concerned with certain environmental causes (Abdelrahman, 2015). Despite their continued existence, they have not formed a uniform "movement" that could embody multiple demands and form a collective front against the state.

In fact, especially in the case of water shortages, these communities have actually come out in protest with a direct confrontation with the state. These could be individualized responses such as writing to local administrators, refusing to pay water bills and resisting formalization procedures, and even chasing water collectors out of neighbourhoods.[9] Of the collective responses, the most flagrant was the Giza case where different communities, such as Saft El-Laban and Talat Tawabek, burned tyres on highways for hours, protested in front of municipalities and appeared in the media to report their case (Abdel Azim, 2015).

In one sense, this demonstrates a deviation from Non-Movement definitions, as these mobilizations could be seen as having "evolved to a point where they undertook contentious action" (Abdelrahman, 2015, p. 66.). While environmentalists focused on debating cleanliness and solid waste management, the protests on water, air quality surrounding urban industries and poisonous tanneries were localized as communities took matters into their own hands (Tewfik, 1997). By protesting "for their environment" and reasserting their autonomy over their connection to Nature, these citizens are in fact making citizenship claims away from the political channels suffocated by the state (Abdelrahman, 2015).

On the other hand, although these citizens assert themselves in the public sphere, they remain reliant on the state's recognition in order to gain access to the monopolized commons. The same criticism has been made against self-help systems, where some have described them fuelling the state's neoliberal concepts of self-interest (Ben Néfissa, 2009). This means the poor are forced into paying for their own subsistence rather than having the opportunity to embrace their basic rights to public services. Yet, it remains clear that individualized activities within these contexts has coalesced into the collective form when communities are threatened or opportunities arise for improvement (Bayat, 2013). As the state gradually eases towards the privatization of infrastructure and utilities, it remains to be seen whether these movements will in fact come together to counter the danger, or remain entrenched in a fragmented scene.

Concluding remarks

With the threat of further privatization of the commons in Egypt (Ahmed, 2016), it is useful to look at regional examples of environmental contention for partial reassurance. These include the 2013 Gezi Park protests in Istanbul that countered the establishment of a shopping mall on the park (Yoruk and Yuksel, 2014), and the 2015 Beirut garbage protests, which forced a corrupt privatized solid waste management system into assessment (Atallah, 2015).

As this chapter has shown, however, the state continues to dominate the unequal management of all natural resources within Egypt, and maintains the severing of direct citizen–Nature relationships. This continues the evolution from the mid-19th century turnabout in centralizing and the institutionalization of an overarching regulatory regime over Nature, influenced by donor relations, private interests and managerial networks (Barnes, 2014; Sowers, 2013). At the same time, fragmented environmental mobilizations veering from "bourgeoisie environmentalism" to the Non-Movements of the poor, have removed the possibility of a collective mobilization for a common Nature.

The self-help systems and collective contention of the urban poor, on the other hand, have provided a different reading. They demonstrate a claim by the marginalized to directly intervene in their natural surroundings, bypassing the role of the state. It thus remains to be seen whether these struggles morph from 'quiet encroachment' and enable opportunities for concrete collective action for citizenship (Abdelrahman, 2015), especially in the face of recently increased state repression. This is the case with the aforementioned Damietta success story, which has since taken a turn for the worst. In 2015, the military regime approved the public venture with Canadian funding and imposed its implementation, even killing a protestor during continued demonstrations (Sowers, 2013).

Hence, for now, the state will continue to dominate the natural landscape and even play the mediator between classes fighting to define their relationship with Nature. For instance, in our first anecdote, although the marginalized woman was ejected from the animal rights protest, she was invited to meet the prime minister who recognized her struggle and provided free medical services for her son (Omara and Ghoneim., 2015). The state emerged as the saviour of the poor against elitist structures in this case, glossing over the negligence of its social contract with marginalized citizens.

Acknowledgements

The author would like to thank Dr Maha Abdelrahman for insightful comments on earlier drafts of this chapter. Any errors that remain are my sole responsibility. Fieldwork associated with the chapter was carried out in Cairo during 2015, as part of a larger PhD project.

Notes

1 Personal communication, Faysal Residents, 2015 Cairo.
2 The Toshka- New Valley- scheme was started in 1997 with the aim of diverting water from the Nile in the south of Egypt to the Western Desert.
3 Announced in 2015, the state proposed a megaproject to construct a new administrative capital, 45km outside of present-day Cairo. It has since been plagued with delays and developer uncertainty, but site construction has been underway since 2016.
4 Egyptian negative colloquialism for informal areas, literally meaning "random".
5 Personal communication, Faysal Residents, 2015 Cairo
6 Many scholars have discussed the role of the state in refraining from its role as the provider of services in informal areas. It is simultaneously able to maintain a presence in paralegal negotiations taking place at the local level, while remaining absent in formal governance paradigms. Denyer Willis (2016) describes this in Brazil, and Arias (2006) in Colombia.
7 Personal communication, Faysal Residents, 2015 Cairo
8 Personal communication, Faysal Residents, 2015, Cairo
9 Personal communication, Faysal Residents, 2015 Cairo

References

Abdel Azim, A. (2015) Water Shortage Affecting AlHaram and Faisal. *Sada El Balad*.18 August. Available at: www.el-balad.com/853517. (In Arabic.) [Accessed 6 August 2015.]
Abdelrahman, M. (2002) The Politics of "Uncivil" Society in Egypt. *Review of African Political Economy* 29 (91), 21–35.
Abdelrahman, M. (2015) *Egypt's Long Revolution – Protest Movements and Uprisings*. London: Routledge.
AbuZeid, K., Elrawady, M., CEDARE. (2014) "2030 Strategic Vision for Treated Wastewater Reuse in Egypt", Water Resources Mangement Program- CEDARE.
Ahmed, W. (2016) What Official Statements on Utility Privatization are Not Saying. *Mada Masr*. 8 December. Available at: www.madamasr.com/en/2016/12/08/feature/economy/what-official-statements-on-utility-privatization-are-not-saying/. [Accessed 20 December 2016.]
Arabindoo, P. (2011) Rhetoric of the "Slum": Rethinking Urban Poverty. *City* 15 (6), 636–646.
Atallah, S. (2015) Garbage Crisis Exposes Arrogance and Conflict among the Political Elite of Lebanon. *Jaddaliyya*. 7 September. Available at: www.jadaliyya.com/pages/index/22583/garbage-crisis-exposes-arrogance-and-conflict-amon. [Accessed 20 December 2016.]
Barnes, J. (2014) *Cultivating the Nile – The Everyday Politics of Water in Egypt*. Durham, NC: Duke University Press.
Baviskar, A. (2003) Between Violence and Desire: Space, Power, and Identity in the Making of Metropolitan Delhi. *International Social Science Journal* 55, 89–98.
Bayat, A (1997) *Cairo's Poor*. Middle East Report 202 Spring 2–12.

Bayat, A. (2013) *Life as Politics – How Ordinary People Change the Middle East.* Cairo: American University in Cairo Press.

Béal, V (2011) Urban Governance, Sustainability and Environmental Movements: Post-democracy in French and British Cities. *European Urban and Regional Studies* 19 (4), 404–419.

Bell, J. (2000) Egyptian Environmental Activists' Uphill Battle. *Middle East Report* 216 (3), 24–25.

Ben Néfissa, S. (2009) Cairo's City Government: The Crisis of Local Administration and the Refusal of Urban Citizenship. In D. Singerman (ed.), *Cairo Contested: Governance, Urban Space, and Global Modernity.* Cairo: The American University in Cairo Press.

Bremer, J. and Bhuiyan, S.H (2014) Community-led Infrastructure Development in Informal Areas in Urban Egypt: A Case Study. *Habitat International* 44, 258–267.

Bush, R. and Sabri, A. (2000) Mining for Fish-Privatization of the "Commons" Along Egypt's Northern Coastline. *Middle East Report* 216 (3), 20–45.

Choucri, N. (2001) Environmentalism. In J. Krieger (ed.), *The Oxford Companion to Politics of the World.* Oxford: Oxford University Press. Pp. 253–255.

Cities Alliance (2008) *Up Close Experiences of Six Cities.* Washington, D.C.: The Cities Alliance.

Denyer-Willis, G (2016) City of Clones: Facsimiles and Governance in Sao Paulo, Brazil. *Current Sociology*, 1–13.

Egyptian Environmental Affairs Agency (2016) *Environmental Reports Directory.* Available at: www.eeaa.gov.eg/en-us/mediacenter/reports/reportssearch.aspx [Accessed 20 December 2016.]

ElMusa, S. and Sowers, J. (2009) Damietta Mobilizes for its Environment. *Middle East Report* 216 (3), 24–25.

Esterman, I. (2014) Water Shortage Shrivels Dreams of the Good Life in New Cairo. *Mada Masr*, 4 September. Available at: www.madamasr.com/sections/environment/water-shortage-shrivels-dreams-good-life-new-cairo. [Accessed 6 August 2015.]

Ezz, M. and Arafat, N. (2015) "We Woke Up in a Desert" – the Water Crisis Taking Hold across Egypt. *The Guardian*, 4 August. Available at: www.theguardian.com/world/2015/aug/04/egypt-water-crisis-intensifies-scarcity. [Accessed 6 August 2015.]

Fahmy, K. (1997) *All the Pasha's Men.* Cambridge: Cambridge University Press.

Gomaa, S. (1997) *Environmental Policy Making in Egypt.* Florida: The University Press of Florida.

Hopkins, N., Mehanna, S. and el-Haggar, S. (2001) *People and Pollution: Cultural Constructions and Social Action in Egypt.* Cairo: The American University in Cairo Press.

Ibrahim, E. (2012) Egypt's Poor Suffer Most from On-going Water Crisis. *Al-Ahram Online*, 16 August. Available at: http://english.ahram.org.eg/WriterArticles/News ContentP/1/50155/Egypt/Egypts-poor-suffer-most-from-ongoing-water-crisis.aspx. [Accessed 6 August 2015.]

Kheir-El-Din, H. and El-Laithy, H. (2008) Agricultural Productivity Growth, Employment and Poverty in Egypt. Egyptian Centre for Economic Studies, Working Paper No. 129.

Land Centre for Human Rights (2016) *Report on Workshop for the Campaign to Stop Arrests of those incapable of Paying for Water Consumption.* [In Arabic.]

Mikhail, A. (2011) *Nature and Empire in Ottoman Egypt: An Environmental history.* Cambridge: Cambridge University Press.

Mikhail, A (2014) Labour and Environment in Egypt since 1500. *International Labor and Working-Class History* 85 (spring 2014), 10–32.

Omara, M. and Ghoneim, M. (2015) Asmaa's Story – kicked out by "Dog Protestors" and Received by Mehleb with Free Treatment for her Son. In Arabic.] *ElWatan News*, 2 March. Available at: www.elwatannews.com/news/details/675360. [Accessed 20 December 2016.]

Roy, A (2005) Urban Informality: Toward an Epistemology of Planning. *Journal of the American Planning Association* 71 (2), 147–158.

Scott, J. (1998) *Seeing like at a State. How Certain Schemes to Improve the Human Condition Have Failed*. New Haven: Yale University Press.

Séjourné, M. (2012) Inhabitants' Daily Practices to obtain Legal Status for their Homes and Security of Tenure. In Ababsa M. (ed.), *Popular Housing and Urban Land Tenure in the Middle East – Case Studies from Egypt, Syria, Jordan, Lebanon, and Turkey*. Cairo: American University in Cairo Press. Pp. 91–110.

Sims, D. (2010) *Understanding Cairo: The Logic of a City Out of Control*. Cairo: The American University in Cairo Press.

Sowers, J.L. (2013) *Environmental Politics in Egypt – Activists, Experts and the State*. New York: Routledge Studies in Middle Eastern Politics.

Tewfik, I. (1997) Community Participation and Environmental Change – Mobilization in a Cairo Neighborhood. *Middle East Report* 202 (spring), 26–27.

Yoruk, E. and Yuksel, M. (2014) Class and Politics in Turkey's Gezi Protests. *New Left Review* 89 (September–October), 103–123.

8

LANDSCAPE AND OUTDOOR DOMESTIC SPACE TOWARDS FOOD SOVEREIGNTY AND ENVIRONMENTAL REGENERATION

Approaches from Mozambique and Latin America

Céline Veríssimo and Leo Name

Introduction

It has been nearly seven decades that access to adequate food and housing have been acknowledged as human rights (UN, 1948). Yet, on the one hand, it is estimated that the world still has one billion people living in inadequate housing conditions in urban areas (UN, 2005). On the other hand, according to data from the Food and Agriculture Organization of the United Nations (FAO), about 795 million people are famished, which is equivalent to 10.9% of the world population (FAO, FIDA and PMA, 2015).

Since the 1960s, food production has been sufficient for the entire planet (FAO, 2015). However, monocultures increasingly advance over territories, not to guarantee food to human populations, but to bring profits and million-dollar patents to multinationals – at the expense of biodiversity and human health due to the indiscriminate use of agrochemicals, bio piracy and appropriation of local knowledge (Porto-Gonçalves, 2006).

In this context, the idea of food security has emerged to define an ideal and just situation in which "all people have at any time physical, social and economic access to sufficient, safe and nutritious food that meets their daily energy needs and food preferences to lead an active and healthy life" (World Food Summit, 1996). Social movements, however, see this definition as having important limitations – it restrains the fight against malnutrition, as it does not address impacts from large transnational food corporations and their agro-industrial capitalist organization.

The Via Campesina – an international entity composed of 164 peasant organizations, most of them located in Latin America and the Caribbean – stands for a different concept based on autonomy: *food sovereignty*. This is a set of principles and actions aimed at guaranteeing each nation or community "to maintain and develop their own capacity to produce the people's basic foods, respecting the productive and cultural diversity", "to practice the sustainable management of natural resources and to preserve biological diversity" and "to freely use and protect the genetically diverse resources, including seeds, developed by these same communities throughout history" (Via Campesina, 1996; Dominguez, 2015; Rosset, 2008).

It is important to clarify that the food security approach is usually adopted by intellectuals from the Global North and global multilateral agencies, whereas the discourse of food sovereignty was drafted by peasant social movements of the Global South. Equally important is to emphasize that the claim for the right to food is supported by a spatial understanding of food sovereignty, given that the application and reproduction of the right to food take place on a territorial basis. As Carlos Walter Porto-Gonçalves (2017, p. 39), a Brazilian geographer, points out, "we must bring space into history and let it speak", avoiding distorted provincialism as universality and recognizing new places of enunciation.

In this chapter, we focus on the city of Dondo, Mozambique. According to our previous research in Dondo (Veríssimo, 2010), ongoing pressure from both capitalist production and urban life has gradually led to a shift from itinerant to sedentary lifestyles, changing: (a) family size (causing the spatial fragmentation of traditionally extended families); (b) modes of production (family businesses, commerce and specialized services); (c) the use of domestic space (leading to the integration of agro-based and business productive activities for food security, income, a comfortable microclimate and social support networks); and (d) community organization (supporting dynamic networks linking neighbourhood communities in the "bairros", the natural environment and the *cement* city). It also led to a rescaled "dualistic" city – the expansion of spontaneously ruralized and green neighbourhoods has been taking place along with the consolidation and stagnation of the existing formal city.

Facing the degradation of their resource base, pressing environmental problems, unemployment and inadequate salaries, households have transformed their use of domestic space and reorganized production strategies for securing their livelihoods. In this context, the outdoor space that traditionally encloses the house and has domestic and social functions, which we have termed the Outdoor Domestic Space (ODS), becomes strategically green and productive in terms of food, income, shade, cool and clean air, and social networking, in order not only to adapt to environmental problems, resources degradation and climate change, but also to replicate the natural conditions that are required for livelihoods to be secured. For decades, women of varying backgrounds and places have been cultivating urban food gardens, either in the ODS or in other open spaces in cities across Mozambique (Sheldon, 1999). Drawing on the tradition of spatial resistance and the resilience of the population due to an enduring pre-capitalist subsistence economy and knowledge of ecological processes, the ODS is beginning to shape a new ruralized form of urbanization.

Existing practices in Dondo contradict the negative assumptions associated with spontaneous urban expansion, showing that ODS is not only vital for thermal comfort, food sovereignty and securing livelihoods but also tends to reverse environmental problems related to the lack of infrastructures and improves the environmental quality of the neighbourhood. Biophysical characteristics and benefits such as shade, greenery, lower air temperatures and improved air quality are inherent to ODS that, in addition to providing food locally, also creates a pleasant domestic and neighbourhood microclimate. Furthermore, the successful coexistence of commerce and specialized services in the ODS not only increases household incomes and promotes entrepreneurship but also facilitates the social inclusion of more vulnerable groups through neighbourhood and business networking. In addition, ODS contributes to the creation of greater self-esteem and a sense of identity. Non agro-based forms of production also benefit the natural environment in peri-urban areas by reducing the need to consume natural resources and improving life systems in those areas. All the above have the potential to become even more significant if optimized and maximized.

Furthermore, we argue that the Outdoor Domestic Space (Veríssimo, 2013) contributes to the food sovereignty of residents, provides a pleasant micro-climate and promotes environmental regeneration in vulnerable or degraded areas. For that reason, ODS is considered of fundamental importance in both architecture and landscaping for ensuring human rights – the right to housing, to food and to a healthy environment. We also believe that landscape, understood in its spontaneously produced nature beyond its aesthetic dimensions, articulates various phenomena and levels of analysis and has broad socio-ecological implications, that have been widely remained neglected and unexplored.

Landscape, livelihoods and edible . . . landscaping?

Landscape is not just what we see. It also refers to the many processes that constantly shape and transform space, whether geobiophysical, at different time scales and spatial contexts, or processes conducted by different social groups that appropriate what nature provides – harmoniously or destructively. However, we must not forget that the past discussion about different landscape types was, to a large extent, supported by what was deemed to be the European civilizational status and the practice of "wild" people in "inhospitable" places, especially those related to grazing, cultivation and consortium of plants meant for food. Crucially, the growth of agro-industrial capitalist organization based on large landowners and monocultures for exportation came hand in hand with the generalization of urbanization and industrialization processes. These processes were, on the one hand, understood as "progress" and, on the other hand, they were always accompanied by the destruction of landscapes and cultures – more interventionist disciplines, such as landscaping, probably arose from this contradiction.

Landscape praxis validates geographic theorizing about the landscape as simultaneously an idea or a way of seeing and as the result of the practices and processes that shape what must be seen. It also validates landscape as a product of continuous work and creation in time: this can refer to nature in the form of a countryside field or nature in the garden form (Cauquelin, 2000; Pires do Rio and Name, 2013). However, contemporary landscaping design concepts and practices (Cesar and Cidade, 2003; Farah et al., 2010; Martignoni, 2008) usually imply that the rational design of landscapes is capable of ubiquitously transforming habits, practices and societies, as they have rarely valued other aspects of nature other than the aesthetic ones. Only more recently, valuing approaches that take into consideration environmental comfort, green infrastructures design, ecological connectivity and the use of native species have emerged (Chacel, 2004; Benedict and McMahon, 2006; Demantova, 2011). Especially in the Global South, little practical attention is given to the use of plant species that can serve as food (Nahum, 2007; Name, 2016; Name and Moassab, 2014). On the contrary, it is in less "hungry" places, such as Europe, the United States of America and Australia (without underestimating that in those places there are huge class differences regarding access to food), that the debate on the so-called "edible landscaping" has been more frequent, preaching the autonomous production of domestic or community edible gardens, on buildings' rooftops or public spaces (Braga and Zamith, 2014; Sánchez-Torija, 2013), besides the edible forests − projects with heterogeneous tree clusters aimed at re-creating ecosystem interaction and consortia between plants for food (Pereira da Costa, 2012; Poe et al., 2013). The US publishing market has launched dozens of colourful manuals on edible landscaping (cf. Creasy, 2010; Bennett and Bittner, 2013; Nardozzi, 2015), which inform people about the aesthetic aspects of food plants and encourage them to introduce them in their gardens. In addition to this editorial boom, urban social movements, academics and professionals have been preaching for the autonomous production of edible crops in family and community food gardens. Probably by being influenced by debates about free seed exchange, tactical urbanism and guerrilla gardening, they also defend the use of food plants on rooftops, gardens, parks, sidewalks and public spaces, on a permanent or provisional basis (Sanchez-Torija, 2013; Braga and Zamith, 2014). Based on the principles of agroecology or permaculture, edible forests are also proposed, that is, projects with heterogeneous groups that aim to recreate ecosystem interaction and consortia among plants for food for humans (Pereira da Costa, 2012). Finally, there is a proliferation of urban and architectural design strategies to accommodate vertical and horizontal food gardens (Philips, 2013).

In the case of Latin America, the discussion on non-conventional food plants, or PANCs (Kinupp and Lorenzi, 2014), has strengthened in recent years and was made popular by activists, especially in Brazil. Simultaneously, the discussion on the production of food by design has been strongly influenced by urban agriculture, agroecology, and permaculture principles conducted by landscape architects and agronomists concerned with the recovery of degraded areas whereas, on the other hand, transition and peasants' movements traditionally have a social and environmental focus − the right for food and food justice.

The most significant debate in our case study region is the debate on domestic and community food gardens, understood as a pre-Colombian heritage and as a survival strategy similar to Mozambique's Outdoor Domestic Space. These are generally small, present in rural, peri-urban and urban areas, including *favelas* and traditional communities' settlements (indigenous and afro-descendent *quilombolas*, for example). Micro-landscapes, normally managed by women, are projects that are not based on formal technical knowledge, but respect agroforestry principles (Name, 2016) and can also provide shade and decrease temperatures (Niñez, 1987; Gillespie et al., 1993; Lok, 1998; Winklerprins, 2002; Mariaca, 2012). This is the point where landscape, landscaping and Outdoor Domestic Space intersect, with a view to food production and food sovereignty.

Outdoor domestic space: a historical legacy of spatial resistance

Historically, the people of Mozambique have faced oppression and social spatial segregation and have responded in a way that has reinforced rather than dismantled their traditional values. Since pre-colonial times, the population's strategy for escaping from environmental and foreign political disruption has been to reinterpret and reinvent tradition, based on the principles of resilience, resistance and self-reliance. The spatial resistance and resilience have been expressed through the development of decentralized human settlements. This has involved the appropriation of land for domestic space and the self-organization of neighbourhoods, both strategies that have been designed to protect the population from successive adversities. Following a tradition of popular spatial insurgency and the post-independence urban boom, the Mozambican city has gained more substance and autonomy to enable it to create the conditions for urban survival and improved welfare in times of hardship. The future of Mozambique's urbanization would benefit from acknowledging and reinforcing local practices developed by people living in informal neighbourhoods. These practices have proved to be more advanced than neo-colonial planning approaches as a means of effectively meeting the real needs of the population and helping them deal with urban challenges. The existing ODS practices observed in Dondo are considered crucial to the emergence of an alternative urban development paradigm based on a self-organized urban space. ODS is shaping a ruralized urban form that challenges the imported post-modern urbanism and top-down approaches that instead of improving urban life, exacerbate social inequality, spatial segregation and urban poverty. This chapter suggests that through awareness, recognition and collaborative processes the spontaneous urban expansion arising from spatial resistance and self-reliance can contribute not only to a legitimate and just form of urban development but also to positive environmental change by supporting non-alienating relationships not only between humans but also between humans and non-human nature.

In our case study in Mozambique, the Outdoor Domestic Space is where the daily activities of the family take place, involving strong social and productive as well as reproductive functions. The ODS is adapted to integrate both family agriculture and business, creating a green and ruralized urban growth pattern (see Figure 8.1).

As stated earlier, facing the degradation of their natural resource base, environmental problems and unemployment, residents of informal suburban neighbourhoods in Mozambique have transformed the use of domestic space and reorganized production strategies to ensure their livelihoods. Resulting from a historical legacy

FIGURE 8.1   Food garden at the Outdoor Domestic Space in Dondo neighbourhood, Mozambique

Author: Veríssimo, 2010.

of external oppression and spatial resistance, the ODS is strategically ecological and productive in terms of food, income, shade and fresh air, in addition to social interaction, not only to facilitate adaptation in relation to environmental problems, resource degradation, climate change and political economy change, but particularly to reproduce the natural conditions necessary for livelihoods that are traditionally linked to nature – "subsistence strategies are organized and developed in a way that allows people to face economic adversity without losing cohesion and family identity" (da Costa, 2002, p. 267). The ODS is a response to scarcity and adversity based on ancestral knowledge with a strong dialectical relation with nature, which ensures that the "biocultural memory" (Toledo and Barrera-Bassols, 2008) continues.

Despite the fact that most food production is derived from rural farms the national average area of family cultivated land was 1.66 hectares in 2002. Evidence from the field demonstrates that urban households in Dondo neighbourhoods depend on urban food gardens in the ODS as an important complementary source of food. In fact, urban food gardens are commonly seen in open spaces throughout the neighbourhoods of Dondo cultivated by households that have a small ODS (Veríssimo, 2010). As a response to scarcity and adversity from changing political economy, this has ensured that close ecological knowledge continues uninterrupted.

Given the limited public delivery of services, urban environmental maintenance is collectively managed, and infrastructures and services improvised by the communities in a spontaneous manner to help keep the urban system in balance. Detached from the neoliberal state, most urban households rely on informal activities provided by their ODS: domestic food gardens for subsistence and income, when a surplus allows for this, improvised stalls and grocers for selling basic goods and the typical services a city offers (carpenter, barbershop, tailor, mechanic and so forth).

The Outdoor Domestic Space has been spontaneously adapted and refined to resist historical oppression and adversity from external pressure and natural hazards, in a silent revolt to establish collective security. ODS is resilient because it is able to

adapt domestic space to new (agro and non-agro) productive functions as a strategy to secure livelihoods (food and income) and produce a comfortable and clean
domestic micro-climate in the neighbourhoods (shade and fresh air) (see Figures 1
and 2). Based on the principles of diversity and flexibility, intensive mixed cropping
is combined with livestock, services and commerce in the ODS, adapting domestic
food production to climate change and changing political and economic reforms,
coping with scarce resources while also generating income. The blurred boundaries
between the extended kinship relations that occur beyond the household level in
the ODS on a neighbourhood community level expand into the city, anticipating
the hidden potential of ODS for collective organization.

Even if the concept of ODS presented here originates from the observation of
Mozambican decentralized dynamics, as a social system that is autonomous and considerably disconnected from both the state and the market, we believe that it is useful
concept also for other contexts. After all, in many places the socio-environmentally
vulnerable populations make subsistence production in the open spaces of their
houses and their neighbourhoods spontaneously. Such self-managed horticultural
landscapes (see Figures 2 and 3), for example among rural, afro-descendent *quilom-
bola* or indigenous Latin American populations, besides guaranteeing access and a
certain autonomy in relation to food consumption, can be important for identity
emancipation, preservation of native agricultural knowledges and dietary regimes.
Strategies like the Outdoor Domestic Space are a tool for resisting the pressure of
agroindustrial and extractivist systems in the countryside and land regularization and
real estate speculation in the city (Name, 2016; Veríssimo and Name, 2017).

FIGURE 8.2 Family livelihoods and food sovereignty at the Outdoor Domestic Space
in Dondo neighbourhoods, Mozambique

Author: Veríssimo, 2010.

For that reason, relating the ODSs to edible landscapes and landscape design to food sovereignty offers an opportunity to move towards the notions of the so-called *buen vivir* (Acosta, 2016), and pay attention to the benefits of herbs cultivated and used by afro Latin religions (Camargo, 2014) and to other potentially beneficial spatial practices in open spaces next to dwellings by afro Latin or indigenous populations (Moassab, 2016).

Furthermore, landscape planning based on ecological aspects, especially in peripheral urban areas, can provide a healthy and viable environment in the long term: by increasing the capacity of gene flow exchange between species, it can also enhance landscape's recreational role and contribute to environmental regeneration processes (Bolund and Hunhammar, 1999; Veríssimo, 2013), affecting positively the entire population.

Final remarks

Cultivation of plants for food can be a form of resistance: social movements by adopting landscaping practices that deviate from the usual production of merely beautiful landscapes or intensively productive foodscapes produce food, and may generate income and comfortable micro-climates.

Indeed, different social groups and people in Latin America develop most domestic and social activities in the Outdoor Domestic Space and in urban open spaces as a form of resistance against marginalization. Edible landscaping, as presented here by drawing on experiences from Mozambique, is crucial for community survival and prosperity. Landscapes are transformed and reorganized to assure livelihoods, food sovereignty and environmental quality in a process of spatial resistance. The diversified nature of ODS, which includes location, dispersion, isolation, concentration, interrelation, as well as private and public dimensions, preserves a symbiotic human relationship with nature, which is fundamental to ensuring food sovereignty, the resource base for subsistence and the regeneration of natural life.

The practice of edible landscaping at Outdoor Domestic Spaces is not only a means of popular resistance, but also a means of household-community empowerment. Even though it is a set of actions practiced by non-landscape architects, landscape architects can incorporate these actions into their practices in technical assistance programmes in order to reverse the lack of knowledge about edible plant species, but also to expand the possibilities for equal access to food. Landscape architects have much to learn from food knowledges that are ignored from the technical-instrumental rationality and disregarded by professional practices and architecture/urban NGOs. The convergence between landscaping, architecture and geography towards achieving environmental and food justice is not only desirable but also necessary and can initiate and support social processes that generate more socially and environmentally just human habitats.

Finally, edible landscaping and the outdoor domestic space have a strong potential to contribute to struggles against hunger by supporting autonomous and self-organized forms of access to food and food availability for all. Crucially, if implemented in a wider scale, they can also be a response to the failure of the "green revolution" and a form of resistance to the predatory actions of agroindustrial and extractivist capitalism.

References

Acosta, A. (2013) *O bem viver*. São Paulo: Elefante.
Benedict, M. and McMahon, E.T. (2006) *Green Infrastructure*. Washington, D.C.: Island Press.
Bennett, L. and Bittner, S. (2013) *The beautiful edible garden*. Berkeley: Ten Speed Press.
Bolund, P. and Hunhammar, S. (1999) Ecosystem Services in Urban Areas. *Ecological Economics* (29), 293–301.
Braga, C.B. and Zamith, H. (2014) O jardim é uma arma de construção maciça! In H. Pires et al. (ed.), *Jardins – Jardineiros – Jardinagem*. Braga: Universidade do Minho. Pp. 158–173.
Camargo, M.T.L.A. (2014) *As plantas medicinais e o sagrado*. São Paulo: Ícone.
Cauquelin, A. (2000) *L'invention du paysage*. Paris: Quadrige/PUF.
Cesar, L.P.M. and Cidade, L.C.F. (2003) Ideologia, visões de mundo e práticas socioambientais no paisagismo. *Sociedade e Estado* 18(1–2), 115–136.
Chacel, F. (2004) *Paisagismo e ecogênese*. Rio de Janeiro: Artliber.
Creasy, R. (2010) *Edible landscaping*. Sierra Club Books.
Da Costa, A.B. (2002) *Famílias na periferia de Maputo: estratégias de sobrevivência e reprodução social*. Tese – Doutorado em Estudos Africanos. Lisbon: Instituto Superior de Ciências do Trabalho e da Empresa.
Demantova, G.C. (2011) *Redes técnicas e serviços ambientais*. São Paulo: Annablume.
Dominguez, D. (2015) La Soberanía alimentaria como enfoque crítico y orientación alternativa del sistema agroalimentario global. *Pensamiento Americano* (8) 15, 146–175.
Duncan, J. (1990) *The City as Text*. Cambridge and New York: The Cambridge University Press.
Food and Agriculture Organization of the United Nations (FAO) (2011) *La seguridad alimentaria: información para la toma de decisiones*. Roma: FAO.
Food and Agriculture Organization of the United Nations (FAO), FIDA and PMA (2015) *El estado de la inseguridad alimentaria en el mundo*. Roma: FAO.
Farah, I., Schelee, M.B. and Tardin, R. (ed.) (2010) *Arquitetura paisagística contemporânea no Brasil*. São Paulo: Editora Senac São Paulo.
Gillespie, A.R., Knudson, D.M. and Geilfus, F. (1993) The Structure of Four Home Gardens in the Petén, Guatemala. *Agroforestry Systems* 24, 157–170.
Kinupp, V.F. and Lorenzi, H. (2014) *Plantas alimentícias não convencionais (PANC) no Brasil*. São Paulo: Instituto Plantarum.
Lok, R. (ed.) (1998) *Huertos caseros tradicionales de América Central*. Turrialba: Centro Agronómico Tropical de Investigación y Enseñanza.
Mariaca, R.M. (ed.) (2012) *El huerto familiar del sureste de México*. Chiapas and Tabasco: Secretaría de Recursos Naturales y Protección Ambiental del Estado de Tabasco/Ecosur.
Martignoni, J. (2008) *Latinscapes*. Barcelona: Gustavo Gili.
Moassab, A. (2016) O patrimônio arquitetônico no século 21. Para além da preservação uníssona e do fetiche do objeto. *Arquitextos* (17), N. 198.07.
Nahum, N.N. (2007) *Paisagismo produtivo na proteção e recuperação de vales urbanos*. Dissertação – Mestrado em Urbanismo. Pontifícia Universidade Católica de Campinas. Campinas.
Name, L. and Moassab, A. (2014) *Por um ensino de paisagismo crítico e emancipatório na América Latina: um debate sobre tipos e paisagens dominantes e subalternos*. In: Encontro Nacional de Ensino de Paisagismo em Escolas de Arquitetura e Urbanismo no Brasil, 12. Anais … Vitória.

Nardozzi, C. (2015) *Foodscaping*. Minneapolis: Cool Springs Press.

Niñez, V. (1987) Household Gardens: Theoretical and Policy Considerations. *Agricultural Systems* (23), 167–186.

UN (1948) *Declaração Universal dos Direitos Humanos*. Paris. Available at: www.dudh.org.br/wp-content/uploads/2014/12/dudh.pdf. [Accessed 25 May 2016.]

UN (2005) *Press Briefing by Special Rapporteur Right to Adequate Housing*. Available at: www.un.org. [Accessed 13 September 2012.]

Pereira da Costa, M.P. (2012) *Florestas urbanas comestíveis: uma rede que podemos cultivar*. Dissertation – Master in Landscape Architecture. Universidade do Porto. Porto.

Philips, A. (2013) Designing urban agriculture. New Jersey: Wiley.

Pires do Rio, G.A. and Name, L. (2013) O novo plano diretor do Rio de Janeiro e a reinvenção da paisagem como patrimônio. In *Encontro da Associação Nacional de Pós-Graduação e Pesquisa em Planejamento Urbano e Regional, 15*. Anais . . . Recife: ANPUR.

Poe, M.R., McLain, R.J., Emery, M. and Hurley, P.T. (2013) Urban Forest Justice and the Rights to Wild Foods, Medicines, and Materials in the City. *Human Ecology* 41, 409–422.

Porto-Gonçalves, C.W. (2006) *A globalização da natureza e a natureza da globalização*. São Paulo: Record.

Porto-Gonçalvez, C.W. (2017) De saberes e de territórios: diversidade e emancipação a partir da experiência latino-americana. In V.C. Cruz and D.A. de Oliveira (eds), *Geografia e giro descolonial*. Rio de janeiro: Letra Capital. Pp. 37–51.

Rosset, P. (2008) Food Sovereignty and the Contemporary Food Crisis. *Development* 51 (4). 460–463.

Sánchez-Torija, J.G. (2013) Instalaciones hortícolas. Embelleciendo la ciudad. *Arte y Ciudad* 3, 539–556.

Sheldon, Kathleen E. (1999) Machambas in the City: Urban Women and Agricultural Work in Mozambique. *Lusotopie*, 121–140.

Toledo, V.M. and Barrera-Bassols, N. (2008) *La memoria biocultural*. Barcelona: Icaria Editorial.

Veríssimo, C. (2013) A importância do espaço doméstico exterior para um modelo de ecodesenvolvimento de cidades médias. O caso do Dondo, Moçambique. *Revista Crítica de Ciências Sociais* 100, 177–212.

Veríssimo, C. and Name, L. (2017) Paisagem, paisagismo comestível e espaço exterior doméstico voltados à soberania alimentar: notas iniciais. In *Encuentro de Geógrafos de America Latina, 16*. Memórias . . . La Paz: EGAL. Pp. 1–14.

Vía Campesina (1996) *Soberanía alimentaria, un futuro sin hambre*. Available at: www.nyeleni.org/spip.php?article38. [Accessed 25 May 2016.]

Winklerprins, A.M.G.A. (2002) House-lot Gardens in Santarém, Pará, Brazil: Linking Rural with Urban. *Urban Ecosystems* 6, 43–66.

World Food Summit. (1996) Rome Declaration on World Food Security.

9

ACCESS TO INFORMATION AND THE CONSTRUCTION OF SUSTAINABILITY DISCOURSE

The case of the Bus Rapid Transit Transolímpica, in Rio de Janeiro

Camila Nobrega Rabello Alves

Introduction[1]

The total budget for the Rio de Janeiro 2016 Olympic Games was about R\$ 39 billion (about US\$ 12 billion), according to the Olympic Public Authority,[2] a public body that unites the Federal Government of Brazil, the State of Rio de Janeiro and the municipality, to take care of the plan and infrastructure works of the mega-event. The biggest part of this amount was for projects in only one area of the city, the Western Zone, mainly in the neighbourhoods of Barra da Tijuca and Recreio. This is where most of the Olympic Games happened – an area identified in the last years as the main focus of property speculation and gentrification in the city.

The Bus Rapid Corridor (BRT) Transolímpica was one of the key mobility infrastructure projects for the Olympic Games, which would connect nine neighbourhoods of Rio de Janeiro. It costed R\$ 1.6 billion.[3] The construction work generated several social and environmental impacts, similar to the impacts of other mega-events in different cities worldwide. Indeed, some argue that the case of Rio de Janeiro is a key example of how sports mega-events function as mechanisms for the implementation of neoliberal modes of urban governance (Gaffney, 2015) by mainly focusing on private accumulation regimes that position the city into circuits of global capital,[4] through increasing global visibility and growing opportunities to extract surplus value from such events.

Less understood, however, is the issue of public access to information and the issue of wider communication dynamics. Both issues play a central role within the wider context of mega-events, where opportunities for private capital accummulation multiply (especially during the preparation of the Olympic Games) in the midst of an economic crisis to the detriment of the rights of the population. The main goal of this chapter is to analyse the evidence on violations with regards to access to information in the context of BRT construction works and to examine the discourses on the sustainability of the Olympic Games (Dossier Mega-Events and Human Rights, 2015, p. 192) in order to understand power asymmetries related to information and hegemonic sustainability discourses. This analysis is based on data collected on public transparency and access to information.[5] The empirical study started in 2015, one year before the Olympic Games took place in Rio de Janeiro, with the aim to investigate the transparency of different public bodies in the case of BRT Transolímpica[6] by following an interdisciplinary approach that has roots in political ecology and discourse analysis. Emphasis is given to data concerning access to information and to the consequences of lack of access from a human rights perspective. The chapter argues that access to information and communication are key issues in the social−environmental conflicts occurring in the case study area.

Methodology

In early 2013, construction works went through a process of environmental licensing that was questioned by the Public Prosecution Agency of Rio de Janeiro. Since 2012, the Popular World Cup and Olympics Committee of Rio de Janeiro pointed out the lack of public debate and information about those affected by the games. Assessments and urban works in communities of the districts of Curicica and Jacarepaguá, which would be in the pathway of the roadworks, were interrupted without residents having access to official information. Removals started with the works well advanced and the route still unknown for the region's residents (Dossier of Violations, 2015). The construction of the BRT Transolímpica affected about 1300 people and relevant evidence has been mainly presented by social movements, the Public Prosecution and academic scholars.

I was part of research conducted in the city of Rio de Janeiro from February 2015 to June 2015, under the coordination of the NGO Article 19.[7] The goal was to analyse the transparency of public institutions in relation to the works of the BRT Transolímpica, in the Western Zone of Rio de Janeiro, based on the Information Access Law − LAI (Law number 12,527/2011). The objective of our research was to contribute to an evaluation of the level of access to information from the perspective of an ordinary citizen.

The analysis on the enforcement of the Information Access Law was divided into two parts. The first part focused on the information divulged on the websites of different institutions. The second part looked at Passive Transparency, which, according to the Information Access Law, means information that is not necessarily available but can be requested by any citizen. To test this, 54 information requests were sent to the three levels of government (municipal, state and federal) concerning the level of response from the government to specific questions asked by citizens. The request proceedings were closely observed in each case. Finally, a consultation was performed in June 2015 with residents of areas affected by removals related to the construction work. It is important to point out that we sent these requests as citizens and not as members of the organization that was conducting the research.

Results

As mentioned above the analysis was divided into two parts. The first one hinges on the idea of Active Transparency, an operational concept that emerged from the application of the Law of Access to Information in countries like Brazil and Chile[8] It concerns information considered of high-level interest for the population, which, according to the law, should be available in official websites. Nevertheless, when searching for such information on the websites of 51 different public bodies (including municipal, state and federal governments) it was found out that basic information required by the law was absent (Article 19, 2015, p. 19).

At the municipal level, during the preparation for the Olympic Games different websites were created based on the principles of data transparency. During the study some of them were analysed, such as "Carioca Transparency" (in relation to the inhabitants of the city of Rio de Janeiro, usually called "cariocas"), "Olympic Transparency", "Mobility Transparency" and "Rio Transparent", [9] and it was shown that there was a major fragmentation regarding access to information. Moreover, even in these more specific websites, it was still not possible to find information about the communities that would be affected by the BRT Transolímpic or about environmental impacts, among other basic information.

The other option available was a telephone number displayed on the website Carioca Transparency, which any citizen could call asking for information, based on the Law of Access to Information. One of the researchers tried to call this number to register an official information request and described a two and half hour wait on the phone (ibid., p. 15). The results of the study, therefore, suggest a serious lack of access to information, and obstruction and disrespect to the federal law by governmental institutions.

The second part of the analysis of the study "Rio 2016: Violations to the Access to Information in the Case of BRT Transolímpica" was based on the idea of Passive Transparency. According to the Law, besides publishing information of public interest on official websites, public bodies should attend to information requests that were directly sent by any citizen. In the case of federal demands, there is a website where it is possible to create a profile and send an online request.[10] However, there was no such option for public bodies in the State of Rio de Janeiro and the municipality. In both cases, it was necessary to print out a form, follow instructions defined in the law and send the form to each institution.

Our information requests were based on information that could not be found during the first phase of Active Transparency. In total, 54 information requests were sent to 12 different public bodies. From that, 39 had to be delivered in person. The others were registered on the federal website. Each request had a specific protocol that we followed.

Three months after sending the Information Requests, less than 8% were adequately answered (ibid., p. 19). As the response rate was very low, in many cases there was a need to send an appeal at superior levels of government to access the information. In the majority of cases, this was unsuccessful. Some examples of findings are described below:

- The Municipal Housing Office (SMH, in Portuguese initials) was asked to give the details of the eviction plan for affected communities. The request was sent mentioning some communities, such as Vila Autódromo and Vila União de Curicica, but asking for a general list of all places affected by the BRT Transolímpica. Despite being notoriously known as responsible for marking houses for the removal of families in certain areas, the SMH answered that it did not have any information.
- The State Environmental Institute (INEA), which is responsible for environmental licensing in the State of Rio de Janeiro, was asked to give specific documents about the Transolímpica. The answer came more than two months later and there was no guidance about the organization of information inside the documents. The public body invited the author of the request to come into their office and gave them more than 4000 pages of documents. After more than two weeks analysing the documents, and with some initial findings, the institution denied access to some of the copies that were promised at the beginning (ibid., p. 42, e. 43). Without any warning, the documents disappeared one day from the place where the author was accessing them. According to the employees, it was requested with urgency by another section of the public body. Among the documents analysed, there was information on the degradation of one of the biggest urban forests in the world, localized in the Western Zone of Rio de Janeiro – Parque Estadual da Pedra Branca. Different documents pointed at judicial organs that questioned the legitimacy of the environmental licensing and also referred to inhabitants who had asked for information about what would happen with their houses.
- In the case of state and municipal institutions, terms were never mentioned, in opposition to what is stated in the Law. More than ten protocols were ignored and, even if we insisted on knowing more about them, we never received any kind of answer.
- In some cases, protocols were identified as "inexistent" when someone tried to follow the results online, by telephone and in person.
- One of the few answers received was in relation to the waste generated by the construction work in the area of the Parque Estadual da Pedra Branca, a State Park. The Municipal Secretary of Construction Work answered that 350,000 cubic metres would be generated.

BRT Transolímpica: a perspective from affected communities

> We were caught by surprise, when the municipal administration marked our homes. We were desperate. I questioned myself: "Where am I going? What is happening?" There was no information.
>
> (Member of the community Vila União de Curicica, whose identity was preserved, Article 19, 2015, p. 17)

In June 2015, a consultation with inhabitants from affected communities provided us with many testimonies. According to the inhabitants of the communities Vila Autódromo and Vila União de Curicica, there was a huge lack of information about the Transolímpica project. During the consultation, the participants told the researchers that "information' was one of the central problems they were facing (ibid.). They did not know how many people would be evicted, or when, and they felt left out of decision-making processes. As a woman who lives in the community of Vila União de Curicica pointed out: "even worse than lack of information is the manipulation of information". Another person at the consultation said: "They entered our houses, put a number on it and gave no kind of information, creating a division inside the community. The goal was to quit our rights."

Local residents further reported that representatives of the government have visited their areas many times, measuring their houses and taking pictures without responding to the questions that the residents were asking them. At the same time, both communities reported many visits from traditional media representatives who nonetheless never included the perspective of the community. In the same month with the consultation, June 2015, an action from the municipality to execute evictions in the community ended with six wounded people. All of them stopped in front of the tractors, trying to stop the eviction: "We never know when they will arrive. We are always prepared and sometimes we have to spend the night awake in order to prevent the destruction of a house," said another inhabitant from the Vila Autódromo community.[11]

The study results show a situation of total absence of transparency, mostly caused by the Municipal Administration of Rio de Janeiro, as one of the largest legacies of the 2016 Olympics for the city (Article 19, 2015, p. 33). They also show the difference between the idea of unlimited access to information, promoted by the Brazilian law, and the reality found in Rio de Janeiro. Nevertheless, this is not an exception. A number of researchers have been questioning the neoliberal promise of unprecedented access to information that would lead to greater economic equity (Borgman, 2003). After all, this promise depends on institutions that are part of social, economic and political dynamics, which determine access to information for different social groups. The Law of Access to Information also brings up the question of the concentration of information by the State. Some of the work around Bourdieu's notion of field understands the State as an entity that plays the role of monopoly, through the use of violence by force or by symbolic matters. In this sense, we could talk of different kinds of capital, like economic capital, cultural capital and information capital, among others, as part of state appropriations in the context of access to information.

The sustainability discourse about Rio 2016 Olympic Games and media power

Since the moment in which the choice of Rio de Janeiro as the 2016 Olympics host was announced, the mainstream media, politicians and several analysts have been emphasising the opportunities from investment growth in the city,

> highlighting the possibilities of solving large problems such as those of urban mobility and the recovery of degraded spaces for housing, commerce and tourism, as in the case of the harbour area. The population of the city, however, has already realized that the project Rio Olympic City, which comprises the developments for the 2014 World Cup, and the 2016 Olympic and Paralympic Games, as well as large projects such as Porto Maravilha, will not generate the promised benefits.
>
> (Dossier Mega-Events and Human Rights Violations in Rio de Janeiro, 2015, p.8)

While we observed a lack of access to information and participation, the official discourse was built around the promotion of the economy and growth in the city, their sustainable legacy and shared benefits. This has similarities with other discourses around mega-events in different parts of the world (Gaffney, 2013, Boykoff 2016). The Western Zone of Rio de Janeiro, where BRT Transolímpica is located, was presented by the Municipal and Federal Administration as the "heart of the Rio 2016 Games" in the Sustainability Plan of the mega-event.[12] According to the Federal Government, a total area of 40,000 m² was built for sport activities in the region, mostly concentrated in only one neighbourhood: Barra da Tijuca.[11] Since the election of Rio de Janeiro was announced, the local government, with the support of the Federal Government, started a big propaganda programme that emphasized the opportunities for investment and economic growth in the city, presenting the Western Zone as an area of expansion. Mainstream media played a key role in spreading this view, highlighting the potential of the Olympics to resolve important problems, such as urban mobility (De Almeida, Marchi Junior and Pike 2014). Besides the propaganda about the benefits of the Olympics for the city inhabitants, the sustainability of the mega-event has been also emphasized. The Brazilian candidacy to the 2014 World Cup and to the 2016 Olympics were based on a series of "sustainability" commitments (see Plano de Gestão da Sustentabilidade dos Jogos Rio, 2016), including various conservation projects, minimization of the impacts of the Olympics, innovations, sustainable materials for construction and the promise of reducing impacts in ecosystems.

However, according to our analysis, there was no discussion or participation of the population in the decision-making process about access to natural resources or discussions on collective management of the territories. Instead of that, in the process of construction planning, environmental aspects were usually approached as isolated issues or combined with environmental law to legitimize the relocation of communities and their resettlement in distant areas, ignoring their relations with the territory and the city. This has been happening in Rio's Western Zone, causing social-spatial exclusion and segregation (Santos Junior and Montandon, 2011, p. 41). These impacts have been previously seen also in other cities that hosted mega-events. Usually, mega-events promote capital expansion to areas not yet explored (Malfas et al., 2004), for example, through the process of land speculation. It is important to understand these processes through the concept of accumulation by dispossession (Harvey, 2003). In this chapter, the most important dimension is the symbolic part of dispossession, namely the marginalization of certain discourses and the construction of mainstream social-environmental discourses as part of the reproduction of power asymmetries and the preparation for capital accumulation.

The concept of territory and territorialities (Enne and Gomes, 2013), if expanded to the meanings and symbolic construction of spaces by people, is also important to understand the wider context. The Western Zone of the city has an agrarian history made of migrants from many Brazilian rural areas that have been established there and started to grow food for the rising city. This history is also a history of struggles for the rights on land and political organization associated with other peasant movements in the country, and workers' movements in the city (Santos and Ribeiro, 2007). Most people living in communities in the Western Zone nowadays, in the past known as Sertão Carioca, inherited not only the territory but also the cultural costumes and collective practices on land and natural resources, such as the cultivation of food gardens. These are now disappearing, as people are evicted from these territories.

In reaction to official discourses celebrating the legacy of large-scale infrastructural improvements and economic benefits, alternative media have reported a series of negative outcomes of such mega-events. They have pointed out rising land values and rent increases fuelling the displacement of residents; slum clearances that imply violent evictions and forced relocation; the militarization of public spaces, bypassing of laws and planning measures; temporary suspension of assembly and association rights; enormous public expenditures in structures of arguable utility; and public indebtedness to cover inflated expenses (Cohre, 2007; Rolnik, 2009). However, the influence of these reports is limited because Brazil has one of the most concentrated mass media outlets in the world. The role of media in public discourses regarding the links between the Olympics and urban change has been frequently overlooked, and emphasis has been largely paid to Olympic city-making and neoliberal entrepreneurialism (Vainer, 2011), gentrification through large-scale redevelopment projects (for example, Coaffee, 2011), reproduction of growth machine politics (for example, Castro, 2011) and acquisition of symbolic capital through city branding politics (for example, Broudehoux, 2007).

To sum up, although the sustainability discourse was a constant part of public discourse, key social and environmental issues were absent from the debates in the case of the Olympic Games in Rio de Janeiro. This is what most of the data analysed show in the case of the BRT Transolímpica. Looking at the results of the study on access to information mentioned above and taking into account all the references that point at human rights violations and huge impacts in the environment caused by the BRT Transolímpica works, there is enough evidence to denounce the marginalization of some alternative perspectives and discourses, including those of the inhabitants directly affected by the project and their counter-narratives. Drawing on the idea of symbolic power (Bourdieu, 1989), it is important to highlight the role of media (as a form of power) in accumulation by dispossession (Harvey, 2003). Furthermore, there is a dimension of this process that deserves our attention:

accumulation by *symbolic* dispossession. This idea can help explain the absence of discourses, the criminalization of social movements and the invisibilization of narratives that result on symbolic violence in the media context. Overall, conflicts in the communities mentioned here are reported in the media in such a way so that power asymmetries are ignored and the reasons of conflicts are concealed.

Conclusion

This chapter shows that the lack of information leads to lack of participation and to the restriction of other important human and social rights. If there is no information, public participation in public debates is compromised as well as any real possibility for the population to influence the decision-making process. This is made worse by the combination of lack of information with lack of communication in the context of mass media concentration, where there is almost no space for alternative narratives.

Looking into the social and environmental dimensions of the case of BRT Transolímpica, it seems clear to me that this is more than just an urban conflict; it is rather a social-environmental conflict. According to Scotto (1997), social-environmental conflicts are disputes that involve, in implicit or explicit ways, the access to environmental resources and social tensions between collective and private interests. These conflicts would emerge from the appropriation of spaces and lands, or of collective resources by specific social actors, attending to individual – or collective – interests. In many situations, conflicts arise when the meaning and the use of a certain territory by a specific group occurs to the detriment of the meanings and uses that other social groups may employ for assuring their social and environmental reproduction and their lives (Zhouri, 2014, p. 7). By understanding the absence of access to information as a key aspect of the severe impacts of the Olympics in the communities in the Western Zone of Rio de Janeiro, this chapter invites us to pay more attention to social-environmental conflicts that result from the violation of rights that affect people's possibilities of influencing decisions.

Notes

1 The first version of this paper was presented at the ECPR Graduate Student Conference – University of Tartu, 2016. In that moment, the author was a Guest Researcher at the Environmental Policy Research Centre, at the Free University of Berlin, as part of the German Chancellor Fellowship Program, supported by the Alexander von Humboldt foundation.

2 Article on TV Brasil, a Public Broadcast: http://tvbrasil.ebc.com.br/reporterbrasil/bloco/olimpiada-custarar-391-bilhoes.

3 Data obtained from the Municipal Secretary of Construction Work (SMO – in portuguese Secretaria Municipal de Obras), through a direct Request of Information made by the author in March 2015. Nevertheless, news reports show an increase in the costs of the BRT, in relation to the initial forecasts, in total of at least 2.2 billion. See https://extra.globo.com/noticias/rio/corredor-brt-transolimpico-funciona-meia-bomba-21304722.html.

4 For a detailed history of the mega-events in Brazil, see Gaffney (2015).

5 Direct data, obtained from the Municipal Administration, through the Access to Information Law, part of the study "Rio 2016: Violations to Access to Information in the case of BRT Transolímpica", Article 19, launched in July 2015. The author of this article was the researcher responsible for the study. The coordination of the research was from Mariana Tamari, from NGO Article 19. Larissa Lacerda, researcher at Ippur-UFRJ, was an assistant researcher.

6 Link to the study (available in Portuguese): http://artigo19.org/wp-content/uploads/2015/07/Relat%C3%B3rio-BRT-Transol%C3%ADmpica.pdf

7 Article 19 is an NGO focused on Human Rights, Freedom of Expression and public transparency.

8 After two decades of mobilization from the civil society, in 2011, the Law of Access to Information (in Portuguese – Lei de Acesso à Informação – LAI), Law number 12.525, was approved. In May 2012 it was implemented, after established a regulation. More information on the implementation of the Law is available in the article "Law of Access to Public Information – Political and Informational Dimensions". Available at: http://reposito rios.questoesemrede.uff.br/repositorios/bitstream/handle/123456789/1736/A%20 LEI%20DE%20ACESSO.pdf?sequence=1. Last view on 20.4.2017

9 Links: http://prefeitura.rio/web/transparenciacarioca; http://riotransparente.rio.rj.gov.br; http://www.rio.rj.gov.br/web/transparenciadamobilidade/. The website Olympic Transparency was out of service during the entire period of the study. It is important to mention that the analysis refers to the period from March to June 2015.

10 Link: acessoainformacao.gov.br

11 Some international newspapers also covered the eviction stories. More information on this article from *The Guardian* newspaper: www.theguardian.com/ world/2015/jun/03/forced-evictions-vilaautodromo-rio-olympics-protests#

12 The definition of the group in the document is: stakeholders directly involved in the achievements of the Olympics. According to the municipal administration, they are ranked as here: 1) Athletes, 2) National Olympic and Paraolympic Committee, 3) Olympic and Paraolympic Families, 4) Media, 5) Broadcasters, 6) Public, 7) Commercial Partners, 8) Work Force, 9) International Sport Federations.

References

Borgman, C. (2003) *From Gutenberg to the Global Inormation Infrastructure: Access to Information in the Networked World*. Los Angeles: University of California.

Bourdieu, P. (1989) *O Poder Simbólico*. Rio de Janeiro: Bertrand Brasil.

Boykoff, J. (2016) *Power Games: A Political History of the Olympics*. London: Verso.

Broudehoux, A. (2007) Spectacular Beijing: The Conspicuous Construction of a Olympic Metropolis. *Journal of Urban Affairs* 29 (4), 383–399.

Centre on Housing Rights and Eviction) (2007) *Fair Play for Housing Rights: Mega-Events, Olympic Games and Housing Rights*. Available at: www.cohre.org/mega-events. [Accessed January 2013.]

Coaffee J. (2011) Urban Regeneration and Renewal. In J. Gold and M. Gold (eds), *Olympic Cities*. New York: Routledge. Pp. 180–193.

Comitê Popular da Copa e Olimpíadas no Rio (CPCOR) (2013) *Dossiê Megaeventos e Violações de Direitos Humanos no Rio de Janeiro*. Available at: http://bit.ly/DossieRio2013

Comitê Popular da Copa e Olimpíadas no Rio (CPCOR) (2014) *Dossiê Megaeventos e Violações de Direitos Humanos no Rio de Janeiro*. Available at: http://bit.ly/DossieRio2014

Enne, A. and Gomes, M. (2013) É tudo nosso: disputas culturais em torno da construção da legitimidade discursiva como capital social e espacial das periferias do Rio de Janeiro. In P. Passos, Aline Dantas and M. Mello (orgs), *Política cultural com as periferias: práticas e indagações de uma problemática contemporânea*. Rio de Janeiro: IFRJ.

Fundação Oswaldo Cruz and Federação de Órgãos para Assistência Social e Educacional (2014) *Mapa de Conflitos Envolvendo Injustiças Ambientais e Saúde no Brasil*. Available at: www.conflitoambiental.icict. fiocruz.br. [Accessed 15 July 2014.]

Gaffney, C. (2013) Between Discourse and Reality: The Un-sustainability of Megaevent Planning. *Sustainability* 5 (9). Available at: https://doi.org/10.3390/ su5093926

Gaffney, C. (2015) *The Mega-event City as Neo-liberal laboratory: The Case of Rio de Janeiro*. Available at http://periodicos.pucminas.br/index.php/percursoacademico/article/view/ 8074/8680.

Harvey, D. (2003) *The New Imperialism*. Oxford: Oxford University Press.

Malfas, M., Theodoraki, E. and Houlihan, B. (2004) Impacts of the Olympic Games as Mega-Events. *Municipal Engineer. Journal of the Institution of Civil Engineers*, 209–220.

Rolnik, R. (2009) *Report of the Special Rapporteur on Adequate Housing as a Component of the Right to an Adequate Standard of Living, and on the Right to Non-discrimination in this Context*. Geneva: United Nations General Assembly.Santos, L and Ribeiro, J. (2007) O que querer vender quer dizer: urbanização e conflitos de terra através dos classificados imobiliários do Sertão Carioca (1927−1964). *Revista IDeAS Interfaces em Desenvolvimento, Agricultura e Sociedade* 1 (1), 78–84.

Scotto, G. (1997) (eds) *Conflitos ambientais no Brasil: natureza para todos ou somente para alguns?* Rio de Janeiro: IBASE/Fundação Heinrich Böll.

Vainer C. (2011) Cidade de exceção: reflexões a partir do Rio de Janeiro. *Anais do XIV Encontro da Associação Brasileira de Planejamento Urbano e Regional*, 14.

Zhouri, A. (2014) *Mapping Environmental Inequalities in Brazil: Mining, Environmental Conflicts and Impasses of Mediation*. desiguALdades.net Working Paper Series 75, Berlin: desiguALdades.net International Research Network on Interdependent Inequalities in Latin America.

10

THE POLITICAL ECOLOGY OF URBAN SPACE IN TRANSITION

Sam Beck

Introduction

Political ecology addresses the political economic relationships of people with the natural environment under capitalism, mostly how humans are positioned to play a role in natural environmental calamities to generate profit margins for those who control the means of production. It is not very common to address the political ecology of a human-made calamity in an urban social and built environment (see Heynen, 2013). My focus on this chapter is on the people who occupy an urban space defined by three different populations, all of them in-migrants to Williamsburg, Brooklyn, during the dramatic changes brought about by gentrification and displacement that materialized from 1990s to 2017. Each social group was involved in an effort to locate, reproduce and sustain itself within Williamsburg usually in competition with the others. Each sought to control a geographic domain of its own and justified their legitimacy in this space as historically determined (Latinos), based on the idea of social cohesion (Hasidic Jews) or the power of the real estate market (gentrifiers).

Hispanics have been settling in Brooklyn even before World War Two, but they made their demographic presence felt in the great migration of Puerto Ricans from the island home to Williamsburg as United States citizens in the late 1950s and 1960s. Dominicans arrived as immigrants from the mid-1960s. The Jewish Hasidim arrived as Holocaust survivors at about the same time as Puerto Ricans, initially joining a Jewish population mixed with Irish, Germans and Italians, who already had a presence in Williamsburg before World War Two and then displaced them. A population I can only identify as predominantly "gentrifiers" or "newcomers" drifted into Williamsburg starting in the late 1980s, increasingly in the 1990s and powerfully as "hipsters" and the more affluent "yuppies" and luxury condo investors after 2005.

Both Latinos and Hasidim occupied housing and commercial space left behind by white ethnics. The hipsters' – mostly artists – initial impact was not particularly great. They squatted in abandoned factories and warehouses or rented apartments without escalating real estate prices as they did later on. As one long-time Latino told me, "They fit into the neighbourhood." Their early presence, much like ethnic working-class communities, caused chain migrations. They attracted others, notably non-artists who followed them and caused a flood of people moving into Williamsburg looking for affordable housing. This caused real estate pressures felt by everyone who had settled there before them. Latinos embraced the early newcomers. The Hasidim ignored them. The rezoning of the waterfront in 2005 brought on a luxury housing boom that attracted more affluent and international investors.

The neoliberal city and its impact on different populations: the case of Williamsburg

The confluence of events that some would say started in the 1930s and into the 1970s served as the preconditions to the demise of social liberalism and the rise of the period of neoliberalism and austerity. New York City experienced spatial, physical and human socioe-conomic devastations over the course of the last 70 years everywhere except in Manhattan's economic centre. In the 1970s the withdrawal of private and public capital caused the discontinuation of vital urban infrastructure in New York City's periphery settled by low-income people of colour. The policies of "benign neglect", "greening" and "planned shrinkage" were implemented in those parts of New York City that were not seen as "vital" to the emerging urban regime. Large tracts of land were laid to waste. The media uniformly characterized the people as criminals and a drain on the economy. It was in those areas of the City where people of colour found housing they could afford, where over decades and generations they built the social fabric of community and their respective cultural commons that held in place relationships of family, kinship and neighbourliness. It was here that the spatial and physical reconfiguration of "inner city" neighbourhoods[1] took place.

In Williamsburg, it was the Latinos living in high density who suffered most severely. First it was the 1970s abandonment and then the drug economy in the 1980s. In the millennium, they continued to suffer the consequences of economic and social dislocation policies that drove development and favoured the affluent and the politically connected. The semi-isolation of Williamsburg in the 1950s to 1980s created the context for landlords to despoil and abandon housing in which Latinos could afford to live. These conditions generated revitalization. According to David Harvey:

> Surplus absorption through urban transformation has . . . a darker aspect. It has entailed repeated bouts of urban restructuring through "creative destruction." This nearly always has a class dimension, since it is usually the poor, the underprivileged, and those marginalized from political power that suffer

FIGURE 10.1   Luxury housing construction is taking place along the East River with extraordinary views of the East River, the Williamsburg Bridge and Manhattan's skyline. This project is one piece of a multi-building and public access park being built by Two Trees in the former Domino Sugar Factory site. Community negotiation produced an agreement to include 30% "affordable" units

Author: Sam Beck

first and foremost from this process. Violence is required to achieve the new urban world on the wreckage of the old.

(Harvey, 2013, p. 16)

Williamsburg had a unique physical connection to Manhattan and was well positioned as a beachhead for capital investment after successes in Park Slope and

DUMBO. The Williamsburg Bridge and multiple subway lines made the East River obstacle irrelevant. Williamsburg's demographic and physical configuration fused social groups (Latinos, Hasidic Jews and Hipsters) into competing socio-cultural and economic entities focused on housing availability. It became fiercer with the 2005 waterfront re-zoning. As the more affluent moved into the area, the working poor scrambled to locate affordable housing elsewhere. Religious and socio-cultural unity protected the streets on which the Hasidim lived. They took advantage of their ability to raise capital and the real estate market conditions that New York City policies created and that the newcomers brought with them.

The "creative class" (Florida, 2014) was the initial driving force for gentrification, as artists located adequate space and conditions for their particular creative endeavours and as hangers and students followed to seek low-cost housing and participate in the "hip" lifestyle. Easy public transportation access to Manhattan and a modernized landscape of luxury housing and retail amenities of restaurants, bars and cafes attracted the more affluent and more hipsters. As real estate prices increased, everyone except the most affluent was impacted. By 2005, those most affected were Hispanics who lived in areas of decline and where competition for real estate was most intense. Artists who found affordable living and studio space early on felt the impact as well. Public artists who used local wall space to paint murals were increasingly being pushed out of the neighbourhood as their walls were torn down, replaced with housing for newcomers.

The Hasidim much like the Latinos felt the pressures of a housing shortage due to their high poverty rates. However, the Hasidic community, unlike the Hispanic community, took care of its own through a structured communal system of redistribution. In the 2010s the cost of housing in Williamsburg was so high that the Hasidim started to move in larger numbers into satellite communities in upstate New York and New Jersey. Members of the Latino community moved to areas of affordability in New York City, and migrated to Pennsylvania, Florida and other parts of the country.

Paradoxically, the foundation for capital reinvestment of the millennium was laid down by working poor Latinos who took advantage of funding made available to them through a myriad of federal programmes associated with the War on Poverty.[2] It is this funding that gave rise to the important Latino-oriented community-based organizations (CBOs) of Williamsburg in the 1970s. The Hasidim also took advantage of the resources offered by the government through the efforts of the United Jewish Organization (UJO) of Williamsburg established in 1966 (Marwell, 2007).

By the time I arrived in Williamsburg in the late 1990s distinct neighbourhoods with socio-culturally defined boundaries were in place. The waterfront had the first luxury apartment towers in which the affluent lived. The Northside with old and new construction housed apartment-sharing hipsters. The Southside (*Los Sures*) was solidly Latino. South Williamsburg still held century-old two-, three- and four-storey row houses (brownstones) and multistory apartment buildings that the Hasidim called their own. Some of the most prominent commercial streets catered to the specific populations who lived nearby. While Northside shopping attracted anyone who had the means, Spanish stores were located in *Los Sures*. Hasidic stores were located in South Williamsburg on Lee Avenue. North (N) designated streets separated hipsters and yuppies from *Los Sures* with more streets increasingly encroached upon by the affluent. With some exceptions Broadway separated the Hispanic neighbourhood from the Hasidim with the Hasidim crossing over encroaching on *Los Sures. Los Sures* was emptying of Latinos by the encroachments of non-Latinos from the North and South.

Latinos

The absence of employment and the disappearance of union jobs with deindustrialization impoverished Latinos who migrated to Brooklyn for work and improved lives along the industrial waterfront. A minority of youths and young men were involved in the underground but highly visible drug culture created by street organizations (gangs) who brought about turf wars and death. People did the best they could in a neighbourhood left to its own devices (see Echeverria 1984 film). The Catholic churches responded with alternative activities for the youth. Those Hispanics who were better off left *Los Sures* for better housing and safer neighbourhoods.

FIGURE 10.2   Ubiquitous bodegas remain part of the Latino Southside (Los Sures)

Author: Sam Beck

Bryan Karvelis, the charismatic priest of the Transfiguration Church, organized the youth into alternative gangs. They learned to repair houses that landlords allowed to fall into disrepair. He inspired his parishioners to take control over their own community and take responsibility for the community's well-being. He spearheaded a number of Latino service institutions that by the time I came to the neighbourhood had saved the neighbourhood from further decay and formed the spiritual and organizational bulwark of resistance to gentrification.

Hasidim

The Williamsburg Hasidim created a densely packed exclusionary socio-economic and religious enclave. By the late 1990s South Williamsburg was Hasidic. The Hasidim followed pro-natal customs and the leadership encouraged the replacement of the population lost during the Holocaust. This resulted in nuclear families with, on average, eight children and as many as seventeen. A community leader told me, "The population doubles every ten years." Exponential population growth pushed their demand for housing in areas adjacent to where the Hasidim already lived.

The demand for housing in their community was so great that Hasidic leaders used their political clout of accessing their community's block votes to access politicians. They gained land use variances and acquired ownership over publicly owned properties on which they built large apartment buildings and schools. The religious leadership collaborated with Hasidic community housing developers to access the capital to build housing for the community at a price that made subsidy to the poor possible. Hasidic housing developers built market rate housing for affluent gentrifying newcomers, dedicating some of their profits to support charities and affordable housing for their community's growing population. Hasidic real estate investors are considered as "some of the industry's most active and powerful players" (DeLaRosa and Samtani, 2016).

FIGURE 10.3 Hasidic children feel safe on sidewalks in their community where they may play without adult supervision

Author: Sam Beck

The immense cultural divide has not stopped them from transforming key neighbourhoods into yuppie central where rents and sales prices have skyrocketed. From the second quarter of 2008 to the second quarter of 2016, the average apartment sales price in Williamsburg doubled – from $668,956 to $1.3 million (ibid.). Even in 2008 when the real estate market turned downward, both development and lending slowed down. Confidence in the area decreased, and capital was withdrawn from real estate. Many projects stopped even when foundations were dug

FIGURE 10.4 Lee Avenue is the central commercial street for the South Williamsburg Hasidic community

Author: Sam Beck

out and exposed outlining that indicated the start of a luxury building. Luxury condominiums could not be sold and were turned into rental units instead. A few Hasidic real estate investors "doubled down" and bought undervalued properties cheap. In 2010, when properties returned to the prices before 2008, they made huge profits (ibid.).

Williamsburg Hasidim's social organization is a cultural assemblage formed by the largest and most influential group, the Satmar. This community is strikingly different from other ethnic or religious, even other Orthodox Jewish, communities. They organized themselves as a cultural, religious, political and economic entity with state-like features, everything from loan associations, to law enforcement, to a Hasidic-only bus service and an organizational structure that determines how everyday life is lived. Charitable giving, *tzedakah*, is part of their moral code and is a way of subsidizing low-income families who also take advantage of the state-operated welfare system. The United Jewish Organization (UJO) of Williamsburg and North Brooklyn was established in 1966 and came to serve the Hasidic community, coordinating charitable giving and distribution among other activities.

Hipsters and Yuppies

Historically, artists were seen in the academic literature as the advancing tide of gentrification, and gentrification has become a field day for real estate speculators and developers. Artists may signal the encroachment of gentrification by identifying attractive places that inspire others to move there. However, it is government policies that provide incentives to developers to build housing, whether market rate or affordable. This was the case along the waterfront, but also further inland. Under a special programme, developers receive tax credits when their developments are built with 80% market rate units and 20% affordable units. The movement of the more affluent into a low-income neighbourhood was an important economic development strategy for the City. While the Latino community was glad for the 20% affordability, they pushed for 30%. In either case, the disaggregation of Latino families represents a loss of political power.

Waterfront luxury housing created a need for transportation between Brooklyn and Manhattan. Privately operated water taxis with NYC subsidies helped make this possible. A few blocks from the water on North 7th Street and Bedford Avenue is the first Brooklyn L train stop out of Manhattan. In the mornings and at the end of the workday, a flood of "hipsters" used this train stop. In 2013 it was here that Dunkin' Donuts opened its first shop. The opening of a Whole Foods supermarket was completed in 2016 at the same time that the Apple store celebrated its opening across the street. The L train, travelling west, follows 14th Street across Manhattan with a major transportation hub stop at Union Square near the campuses of NYU, the New School, and Cardozo School of Law with thousands of students.

The areas around the L train stops in Brooklyn became centres of housing modernization and the growth of boutiques selling everything from specialty cheese to vintage clothing, tony restaurants (for example, Aska or Renard), bars and pricey

FIGURE 10.5   In the hipster-dominated parts of Williamsburg appear the signs of a Latino community that asserts its presence and persistence

Author: Sam Beck

coffee shops. New construction of multi-storey rental apartments and condominiums popped up like mushrooms after a rain. The Great Recession of 2008 only briefly interrupted a building boom; by 2012, the boom had continued.

By 2014, the impact of gentrification pushed artists out of Williamsburg where the cost of studios and rentals reached the prices of Manhattan. By this time, they had L and G subway stop communities in Bushwick and Bedford-Stuyvesant. The affluent purchased condominiums overlooking the East River. Young women pushing baby carriages and window-shopping on Bedford Avenue joined hipsters who locked their bicycles at the Bedford L train entrance. Gentrification on Williamsburg's Northside is complete.

Gentrification in the neoliberal city: ethnic neighborhoods in transition

Latino resistance to gentrification and their effort to stop or slow down displacement has not arrested gentrification in *Los Sures*. The Latinos who remained in Williamsburg were those who owned their own houses or apartments, secured housing for themselves in market rate buildings or lived in subsidized housing of one sort or another. Yet the struggle continued. Latinos were fighting landlords who sought to illegally expel tenants from rent-stabilized buildings. They advocated for the inclusion of affordable units in any new construction in the neighbourhood. And Latinos organized politically to compete with the Hasidim for properties to build affordable housing.

Local Latino community-based organizations formed Mobilization Against Displacement (MAD) as waterfront re-zoning was being discussed. This was a response to the waterfront rezoning process (Depaolo and Morse, 2016). Churches United emerged at about this time, created as the only Williamsburg non-profit organization dedicated to advocate for affordable housing. This important organization was initially founded as a grassroots coalition of Catholic churches when the waterfront was being re-zoned in 2005 to empower people who were facing displacement futures to gain self-confidence and to see themselves with the power to bring about change. Church leadership was an important part of the executive board as Churches United became an effective organization.

Father Jim O'Shea, a Roman Catholic priest, led Churches United. He used the pulpits of North Brooklyn churches to mobilize their parishioners into an effective voting block much like the one formed by the UJO. Father O'Shea, much like Father Bryan Karvelis, was quite intentional in also developing an organic lay leadership to create community empowerment from the bottom up. Latino immigrants were mobilized to become activists in their own lives and to believe they have the dignity of anyone else and could be change agents by involving them in large-scale demonstrations, spectacles that successfully sought to influence politicians and housing developers.

Speaking for all Hispanic neighbourhood CBOs, Churches United insisted in gaining access to a seat at the table as a decision-maker of *Los Sures* development. This was not an act of resistance, but an act of inclusion. This involved access to affordable housing for Latinos, a long-standing issue because the Hasidim acquired access at a much higher rate. Even when this matter was litigated as a case to prevent further racial segregation and despite court decisions favouring Latinos, the Hasidim continued to benefit. Racially based housing discrimination favouring whites, gentrifiers and the Hasidim was widespread in Williamsburg in the past and it remained so.

When Churches United leadership changed to Churches United for Fair Housing (CUFFH) Father O'Shea was forced to resign. A lay leadership replaced that of the clergy to escape the will of the Bishop of Queens and Brooklyn. This transition was caused by the conflict between the Latino community, led by Churches United, and the Hasidim's UJO over a large property that was to be redeveloped and that was to include affordable housing units (see Beck, 2016, pp. 26–27).

The relationship between the Hasidim and the *Los Sures* Latinos was similar to the relationship that Latinos had with the hipsters and yuppies. Both are the cause of Latino displacement. However, while class identified the "newcomers" (the affluent), ethno-religious identity identified the Hasidim (ultra-Orthodox Jews). Latinos were perceived as an ethnicity and a class (Spanish and working poor). The dynamic between them was most often understood as very different. The Hasidim

FIGURE 10.6 Brooklyn Legal Services A located at crossroads where the Hasidim, Latinos and Hipsters intersect

Author: Sam Beck

were never characterized as gentrifiers. Their engagement with Latinos was identified as a fight for a limited resource between two ethnic groups. As such, the Hasidim used "anti-Semitism" as a tool to silence and attempt to immobilize Hispanics. Hispanics used "Hasidic racism" as the source of displacing Latinos.

The "Broadway Triangle" became the latest cause of dispute between Latinos and the Hasidim. Churches United played a principle role in fighting for a place

FIGURE 10.7   The Southside Puerto Rican owners of this residence kept the fortifica-
tion fence, a reminder of a dangerous past

Author: Sam Beck

in the decision-making process related to the disposition of the largest tract of land
in Brooklyn available for housing that included private and City properties. The
politics of the times were such that the Broadway Triangle housing project was to
be handed over to UJO. This would have been a windfall financially and would
mean the expansion of Hasidic territory by creating housing exclusively for the
Hasidim. Even with legal action that should have prevented any construction on
this wedge of real estate that could have provided hundreds of affordable units of
housing for both Latino and Hasidic families, the matter has not been resolved over
the course of ten years. The Hasidim-owned private properties in the Triangle and
those acquired after litigation became exclusionary Hasidic housing and a Hasidic
school for girls.

   With the leadership of Churches United, the Broadway Triangle Community
Coalition (BTCC) was established in 2008 headed by Juan Ramos, one of CUFFH's
founders. It was a multi-racial group of forty churches, civic groups and not-for-
profit organizations. This group represented the three neighbourhoods on all sides
of the Broadway Triangle, Williamsburg, Bushwick, and Bedford Stuyveant. The
fight was with the City who awarded the Broadway Triangle to the UJO, directly
or indirectly violating the Fair Housing Act by enabling the Hasidim to continue
residential segregation through their form of exclusionary housing.

FIGURE 10.8   Spray can graffiti art is lost as the walls on which they are created are turned into rubble

Author: Sam Beck

This was the result of several actions: first, the city consulted with a single Hasidic organization (UJO), representing only a segment of the community, to design the re-zoning. Then, in a no-bid process, it chose that organization to co-develop and market the affordable housing on city property. That housing was to be low-rise buildings with many large apartments, primarily addressing the needs of Hasidic families at the expense of families of colour (Ramos et al., 2015). This form of favouritism, where the UJO allied Hasidim benefit from being able to deliver a block of votes to the politicians willing to provide what the Hasidic leadership wants is playing itself out again, even as the Broadway Triangle issue remains unresolved. The very large Pfizer Pharmaceutical Company building, across the street from the Broadway Triangle, that was purchased by a UJO associated housing development company is to be converted into housing for the Hasidim. Here again, the Latino-led Broadway Triangle Community Coalition is seeking to stop the expansion of Hasidic exclusionary housing and the expansion of the Hasidic neighbourhood.

Latinos continue to occupy housing in Williamsburg, much of it owned and managed by Southside United, HDFC and remains affordable as a result of the community's efforts to stabilize *Los* Sures housing in the 1970s and 1980s. Latino CBOs strive to retain and create affordable housing for its constituents. Hasidic families in *Los Sures* moved into relatively new government-subsidized owner-occupied row housing interspersed with Latino families. Newly built and gutted rehabed buildings in *Los Sures* are occupied by newcomers who afford market rate rents where two-bedroom apartments are priced as high as $4,000 a month or more.

Modern styled housing is a sign of a changing neighbourhood reflecting a changing aesthetic. This holds true in each of the three neighbourhoods, hipster, Latino or Hasidic. Another changing aesthetic also is apparent when traversing these neighbourhoods. Only a few years ago, spray can art was painted on exterior walls by young Latino artists, usually without permission from owners. At present, exterior walls are being covered with murals painted by Hipster artists commissioned by a café, bodega or market. Of the commemorative spray can murals chronicling the death of young men killed during the conflicts during turf wars of the 1980s and 1990s only a few remain on the Southside. Graffiti, spray-painted by young men leaving their black marks in the neighbourhood to advance their reputation among peers, continue to appear, but less so in the gentrified Northside or the Hasidic neighbourhood (see Beck, 2015).

The Latinos are being squeezed out of their community where they saved the buildings in the era of planned shrinkage and when they created their cultural commons. According to Elizalde, "census data show the rapid displacement of Latinos from Williamsburg. In 2000, Latinos made up 36 percent of the neighborhood's population. That dropped to 27 percent in 2010" (2013). The media portrayed Williamsburg as a new frontier ripe for economic development, paying little heed to the pre-existing population. Williamsburg is discussed as if artists from Manhattan brought art to a place that did not have any. Of course, this is far from the truth. Latino artists flourished in Williamsburg and still do. The El Puente High School for Peace and Justice employs artists who work with students on community projects.

For Latinos living in Williamsburg, only some resent the intrusion of newcomers. When hipsters were flooding into the community, they were perceived as intrusions into their neighbourhood because the threat of rent increases was all too real. At present, Latinos are less concerned about their presence, although people get visibly upset when it comes to the absence of affordable housing in an environment where rent prices continue to escalate because newcomers are willing to pay prices that Latino families cannot afford. A more affluent population brought upscale commerce that includes a higher quality of fruit and vegetables being sold. Ubiquitous bodegas are now called "delis", forced to modernize to stay competitive. While all appreciate better quality food, Latinos complained about the increasing costs of shopping. They are pleased with the cultural diversity present in the neighbourhood, increased safety and higher quality shops.

Policy makers and developers are reshaping the Latino cultural commons to suit gentrifiers. The Hasidim create their own cultural commons and a built environment that suit their needs and aesthetics. In the mid-2010s, Latinos who remained in the community did not see gentrifiers necessarily as a bad thing because they saw them as increasing their quality of life and that of their children, "exposed to diversity" as some say. However, displacement caused by gentrifying processes is unappreciated because it is destructive of their way of life and the social and cultural interdependence that Latino communities created over the course of multiple generations. According to Waitzkin, "when working class people lose their homes . . . [they] often suffer a deep and lasting grief that derives as much from the loss of their social networks as from their destruction of their homes" (2000, p. 101; Fullilove, 2016).

The Hasidim experience was quite the opposite of the Hispanics. Their natural population increases made the need for affordable housing as important a policy matter as it was for Latinos and hipster artists and their followers. Their community and religious insularity generated some notable events as they made contact with people outside of their community. The Hasidim prohibit men from looking at women perceived as improperly dressed and have at times posted fliers in their store windows that told women who are dressed with arms, legs, midriffs and chests uncovered not to enter their shops. Bike lanes that the city painted through their community in order to make Brooklyn more biking friendly upset the Hasidim because the men would be exposed to "underdressed" hipster (*Artisten*) women (Idov, 2010).

Tension between Latinos and the Hasidim were particularly great around housing. When talking to Latinos who remember successes in accessing public-funded housing, they always talk about Robert Clemente Housing. When urban renewal in the 1960s and 1970s razed scores of old buildings in favour of high-rise housing projects, Latino residents grew rightfully suspicious that most of the new apartments were going to the Hasidim. One night in 1974, just before the federally subsidized Roberto Clemente Houses were to open, 500 Latinos occupied the buildings. It took a 1977 consent decree to stipulate that 51% of the project's apartments would go to Latino families (Hevesi, 1994).

Public housing disputes in Williamsburg have festered since the 1970s where the ethnic imbalance favoured the Hasidic community through what Marty Needelman of Brooklyn Legal Services A identified as a "system of 'money and favors'", a comment disputed by the Hasidic Rabbi David Niederman, UJO'S executive director. Not under dispute is that 68% of Williamsburg housing project residents have been Hasidic Jews for decades, when most of the 200,000 or so people on the waiting list for such housing are either black or Latino (Leagle, 1978; Hays, 1991). What could not be disputed is that the neighbourhood is home to one of the highest concentrations of Section 8 housing vouchers in the city, according to federal data analyzed by WNYC – a US radio station – and the *Daily News*. Section 8 housing is a voucher system that allows private landlords to rent apartments at fair market rates to low-income tenants issued by the US Department of Housing and Urban Development. In several of Williamsburg's Hasidic census tracts, Section 8 tenants compose more than 30% of residents, a level reached only in scattered pockets of the Bronx (Seville, 2016).

Artists are also fighting gentrification. A well-known artist in Bushwick, Jules de Balincourt, failed to form an organization of artists in 2013, who would buy buildings and form cooperatives to secure living and studio space for themselves. In 2016, the Brooklyn Museum hosted the "Brooklyn Community Forum on Anti-Gentrification and Displacement". Artists are as vulnerable as the Latinos because they too are dependent on affordable rents to remain in the neighbourhood and continue to live and work in the community of artists they created.

Conclusion

The commons had its origins before capitalism, when agriculturalists and pastoralists shared use rights of commonly held properties like pastures and forests, which they regulated cooperatively. In an urban built environment, the commons take on public domains with symbolic significance in which social groups create their identities and their cultures and where they locate their physical boundaries (Nonini, 2007). It is the social group that not only defines space, but the physical space that defines the social group.

I previously worked in Providence, Rhode Island where the Fox Point neighbourhood was settled for more than 100 years by Cape Verdean-Americans. Unfortunately, they lived in housing next to Brown University. Much of it is housing to which the historic preservation movement gave great value. Moreover, Urban Renewal and "slum removal" policies destined Cape Verdean displacement as low-income people of African descent. In the 1980s, as they were being replaced by affluent whites in the 1980s, Cape Verdeans understood what was happening as "Nigger Removal". They understood this as an act of racism and classism (Beck, 1992). Resistance took on the form of community mobilizing events and demonstrations. Yet, by the early 1990s gentrification was complete. What was happening in Williamsburg was different. Here it is a matter of Latino removal with a set of different dynamics.

In any case, gentrification redefines space to fit the aesthetic values of the affluent. It is a matter of class. Latino resistance to gentrification in Williamsburg manifested itself with street festivals that displayed Puerto Rican, Dominican and Mexican identities. Latino-dominated Roman Catholic processions also took place.

El Museo de Los Sures was created as a public space for Latinos to use as an art gallery and a reminder that Hispanics were in Williamsburg before the gentrifiers came and that they remain. In the face of capitalism's essential element, private ownership of property, the symbolic, cultural, space must be considered a viable arena of resistance to counter the hegemonic power of neoliberalism manifested by the economy of gentrification and displacement that produces ethno-racial cleansing. It is also a way of creating history, leaving recorded tracks in time.

In reviewing and delineating some of the features that defined the three social groups and their interactions, I provided a description of a cultural landscape in which the built environment gives expression to the three group's aesthetic and economic values. Most importantly, their respective ecological adaptations within their particular part of Williamsburg and, even more important, their relationship to one another were conditioned by political and economic forces not of their own making, but to which they responded. They were positioned by city government policies and relationships with politicians to compete for scarce resources, housing and real estate that defined each social group's boundaries.

In the urban context that I described, ethno-racial conflicts are not naturally occurring; neoliberal market conditions and political dynamics produced them. Government policies bring about corporate investments and real estate speculation in attractive working-class areas of urban decline where land values are underpriced. It is for this reason that activists fighting gentrification must identify and alter government policies to reduce or deflect the conflicts they produce by stabilizing and expanding the availability of affordable housing and creating unity that cuts across ethno-racial, religious, and class lines.

The particular New York City political ecology being played out in Williamsburg advantaged the affluent and the Hasidic cultural commons and the people who created them to the detriment of the Latinos and their landscape, increasingly defined by gentrification and displacement. The more inroads made into the Southside by the affluent Northsiders and the Hasidic enclave dwellers from the South, the more Latinos were displaced. What not so long ago that Williamsburg was identified as a Latino neighbourhood. The density of the Hasidic community, its exclusionary housing and its exclusive socio-cultural nature inhibited anyone else from living in their neighbourhood and prohibited gentrification within the confines of the "Hasidic neighbourhood". The typical gentrifier would not consider living in a Hasidic neighbourhood. The Hasidim have created an ecological niche that excluded everyone else and appeared to be as successful as the gentrifiers in expanding into the Latino-built environment without being called out as gentrifiers.

Gentrification that causes displacement is based on market principles that move capital from one investment area into another seeking profits. The long-term result is the replacement of one population by another. In the short term such areas become the most diverse in urban environments, often seen by locals and hipsters as an attractive aspect of their neighbourhood. Gentrification is not a "natural" occurrence because it is policy makers who make decisions about government investments and it is politicians who make laws that regulate housing. The result is the creation of segregated neighbourhoods because those with limited income are able to live only in places they can afford.

The Hasidim developed the most successful strategy against gentrification by consolidating housing in a neighbourhood in which their co-religionists live and expanding into neighbouring areas. Hasidic developers are also joining in the gentrification process by building market rate luxury housing for the affluent. Co-religionist housing developers collaborate with their community's leadership to gain access to real estate by applying pressure on politicians who need the Hasidic vote. Latino-led CBOs that represent Latino interests enter into disputes with Hasidic developers, leaders and the UJO for properties that become available for affordable housing development. Although Latino organizations have been successful in litigating Hasidic-led segregation, housing discrimination and abusive landlord strategies to illegally evict tenants to bring about gentrification, enforcement is ignored, or it takes so long that even successful litigation is ineffective. As Marty Needleman says, "the law is what you can get away with".

I started bringing my students to Williamsburg in the 1990s to carry out community service among the Hispanic CBOs, particularly Churches United for Fair Housing, and remained in the community ever since. In the process of launching itself as a new organization with the legacy of Father Jim O'Shea's Churches United, the young executive director, Rob Solano, operated the organization with volunteers, my students, an executive board and no budget. I became a member of the CUFFH board. Over a ten-year period, with the support of the most influential Latino organizations, Latino politicians and foundation funds, he built up the CUFFH staff with 15 paid staff members who participate in the struggle for affordable housing in every form possible and more recently against illegal displacement with a budget of almost $1 million.

Juan Ramos, the chairman of the Broadway Triangle Community Coalition and the recently appointed executive director of Southside United, HDFC (*Los Sures*), Marty Needleman, the decades long Chief Counsel of Brooklyn Legal Service Corporation A, and many other community leaders and grassroots people continued to come together to participate in what may look like a fight *against* gentrification. Those who do so may even use the language of *fighting against gentrification*, but they are doing something quite different. They are looking to reproduce the cohesion of a Latino community and their cultural commons. They are fighting *for* community, a way of life and their cultural commons, a sense of identity with the space they occupy, where they live and engage others, their family members, fictive kin and neighbours who share their way of life and where strangers are welcomed and embraced.

In an economy in which the profit-motive drives ambition and conflicts with the desire to sustain and reproduce community, the struggle for community among Latinos can only survive in a place like Williamsburg when people are able to secure housing and live in concentration as a population in significant enough numbers to sustain their sense of identity as a community with a common neighbourhood.

This may be achieved only through relatively large-scale community managed housing to provide the critical mass in which social cohesion may occur. Placing individuals and households in affordable units provided by luxury housing developers may relieve the pressures of displacement among a few individuals and families, but it does not solve the efforts to stabilize community. Resistance to gentrification is resistance to displacement. The struggle for cultural continuity must continue![3]

Notes

1 This is a term used to identify low-income urban neighbourhoods of colour.
2 The War on Poverty was President Lyndon B. Johnson's legislation in response to the high national poverty rate to bring about poverty reduction.
3 I want to thank my friend and colleague Carl Maida for supporting my work. I am grateful to my life partner, Marianne A. Cocchini, who pushed me into considering how my anthropology can serve the people who I engage in research. My Romanian experience, funded by IREX and the University of Massachusetts Department of Anthropology, brought me into contact with Roma scholar/activist/politician Nicolae Gheorghe who showed me a model for academic public engagement. I also want to recognize the many people in North Brooklyn who have embraced me, taught me about their community and made me a member, especially Father Jim O'Shea, Rob Solano, Marty Needleman, Juan Ramos, Diana Reyna, Ron Schiffman, Gary Schlesinger and Sara Stern.

References

Beck, Sam (1992) *Manny Almeida's Ringside Lounge: The Cape Verdean Struggle for Their Neighborhood.* Providence, RI: GAVEA-Brown Publications.

Beck, Sam (2015) Urban Transitions: Graffiti Transformations. In Sam Beck and Carl Maida (eds), *Public Anthropology in a Borderless World.* New York: Berghahn. Pp. 314–350.

Beck, Sam (2016) Knowledge Production and Emancipatory Social Movements from the Heart of Global Hipsterdom. Special Issue, Toward Communities of Practice in Global Sustainability. *Anthropology in Action* 23 (1): 22–30.

Brooklyn, NY – Amid Ringing Church Bells and Muslim Calls to Prayer, Bed-Stuy Synagogue Ticketed for Shabbos Siren (2016) Brooklyn New York.com. http://www. voisizneias.com/252430/2016/10/26/brooklyn-ny-amid-ringing-church-bells-and-muslim-calls-tp-prayer-bed-stuy-synagogue-ticketed-for-shabbos-siren. [Accessed 9 August 2018.]

DeLaRosa, Yoryi and Hiten Samtani (2016) *Learning and Earning: Hasidic Brooklyn's Real Estate Machers. The Real Deal.* [Accessed 9 August 2018.]

Depaolo, Philip and Sylvia Morse (2016) Williamsburg: Zoning Out Latinos. In Tom Agnoti and Sylvia Morse (eds), *Zoned Out! Race, Displacement, and City Planning in New York City.* New York: terreform. Pp. 72–94.

Echeverria, Diego (1984) *Los Sures.* [Film shot and produced by Echeverria.]

El Puente (n.d.) El Puente Arts Overview. http://elpuente.us/content/el-puente-arts-overview. [Accessed 17 May 2017.]

Elizalde, Elizabeth (2013) In Williamsburg, Efforts to Preserve Latino Culture. Brooklyn News Service. http://journalism.blog.brooklyn.edu/in-williamsburg-efforts-to-preserve-latino-culture/. [Accessed 17 May 2017.]

Florida, Richard (2014) *The Rise of the Creative Class* (Revised and expanded). New York: Basic Books.

Fullilove, Mindy (2016) *Root Shock: How Tearing Up City Neighborhoods Hurts America, And What We Can Do About It.* New York: New Village Press.

Harvey, David (2013) *Rebel Cities: From the Right to the City to the Urban Revolution.* London: Verso.

Hays, Constance, L. (1991) Housing Fight in Brooklyn is Settled. *The New York Times.* www.nytimes.com/1991/06/06/nyregion/housing-fight-in-brooklyn-is-settled.html. [Accessed 19 May 2017.]

Hevesi, Dennis (1994) Hasidic and Hispanic Residents in Williamsburg Try to Forge a New Unity. *The New York Times.* www.nytimes.com/1994/09/18/nyregion/hasidic-and-hispanic-residents-in-williamsburg-try-to-forge-a-new-unity.html. [Accessed 18 May 2017.]

Heynen, Nik (2013) Urban Political Ecology 1: The Urban Century. Progress in Human Geography. http://phg.sagepub.com/content/early/2013/08/28/0309132513500443. [Accessed 18 May 2017.]

Idov, Michael (2010) Clash of the Bearded Ones: Hipsters, Hasids, and the Williamsburg Street. *New York Magazine.* http://nymag.com/realestate/neighborhoods/2010/65356/. [Accessed 18 May 2017.]

Iversen, Kristin (2014) The Poorest Parts of Brooklyn Are . . . In Williamsburg? Brooklyn. http://www.bkmag.com/2014/01/09/the-poorest-parts-of-brooklyn-are-in-williamsburg/. [Accessed 18 September 2018.]

Leagle (1978) Williamsburg Fair Housing v. New York City Housing. Leagle. No. 76 Civ. 2125 (CHT; 450 F. Supp. 602 (1978)). www.leagle.com/decision/19781052450F Supp602_1954.xml/WILLIAMSBURG%20FAIR%20HOUSING%20v.%20NEW%20 YORK%20CITY%20HOUSING. [Accessed 18 May 2017.]

Marwell, Nicolle P. (2007) *Bargaining for Brooklyn: Community Organizations in the Entrepreneurial City.* Chicago: University of Chicago Press.

Murphy, Doyle (2013) "Dunkin Donuts Comes to Bedford Ave. Is this the Official End of Williamsburg? www.nydailynews.com/new-york/brooklyn/williamsburg-runs-dunkin-article-1.1525155. [Accessed 16 May 2017.]

Nonini, Donald M. (2007) *The Global Idea of "The Commons."* New York: Berghahn.

Ramos, Juan, Needelman, Martin S. and Krishnan, Shekar (2015) Black, White and Wrong all Over: De Blasio Sides with Segregation in Brooklyn's Broadway Triangle. *Daily News.* 22 July. www.nydailynews.com/opinion/ramos-needelman-krishnan-black-white-wrong-article-1.2299581. [Accessed 7 August 2017.]

Seville, Lisa Riordan (2016) Hasidic Neighborhood in South Williamsburg is a Top Beneficiary of Section 8, but Some Question Whether Law is Strictly Followed. *Daily News.* 17 May. www.nydailynews.com/new-york/hasidic-neighborhood-b-klyn-top-benefi ciary-section-8-article-1.2639120. [Accessed 20 May 2017.]

Waitzkin, Howard (2000) *The Second Sickness: Contradictions of Capitalist Health Care.* Maryland: Rowman & Littlefield Publishers.

11

ENVIRONMENTAL JUSTICE CLAIMS AND DIMENSIONS IN ANTI-MEGAPROJECT CAMPAIGNS IN EUROPE

The case of the Forum Against Unnecessary and Imposed Megaprojects

Alfred Burballa-Noria

Introduction

The term "megaproject" became popular in academic literature from the early 2000s onwards after the publication of two key works: one by Altshuler and Luberoff (2003) and another by Flyvbjerg et al. (2003). A commonly accepted definition is the one given by Gellert and Lynch (2003, pp. 15–16): "projects which transform landscapes rapidly, intentionally, and profoundly in very visible ways, and require coordinated applications of capital and state power". These works pointed out several elements constituting the problematic and complex nature of megaprojects, such as rent-seeking intentions by its proponents, under-estimation of costs, over-estimation of demand, exclusive decision-making processes and insufficiently acknowledged social and environmental impacts. Further research has confirmed that those negative components are indeed associated with the process of megaproject development and implementation (Flyvbjerg, 2005, 2014; Fainstein, 2008). As the global context is defined by increasing investment in new physical infrastructure (Beckman and Gil, 2009), megaproject development, even in the global north, is re-emerging as a contentious issue (Temper, 2014) around which antagonistic parties confront one another, producing a dichotomy of winners and losers (Macharis and Nijkamp, 2013).

One of the categories of megaprojects defined by Gellert and Lynch (2003) are infrastructure megaprojects. Examples of contested megaprojects of this type in Europe include a new airport development in Nantes (Pieper, 2013), a new train station in Stuttgart (Novy and Peters, 2012) and several high-speed railway (HSR) developments, such as HS2 in England. The opposition campaigns that accompany the implementation of these megaprojects have been explored from different, although not necessarily contradictory, perspectives within the existing literature, for example, as struggles of resistance to neoliberal processes (Robert, 2014) and particularly accumulation by dispossession (Harvey, 2003) or as part of the global environmental justice agenda (Martínez-Alier et al., 2014) pushed by an emerging international/global Environmental Justice Movement (Martínez-Alier et al., 2014; Greyl et al., 2013).

In response to this wave of contention resulting from megaproject development, a cross-country alliance has been forged: a European network of campaigning groups opposing megaprojects known as the "Forum Against Unnecessary and Imposed Mega Projects" ("the UIMP network" or "the network" henceforth) (Ariemma and Burnside-Lawry, 2014; Presidio Europa No TAV, 2014). How has the concept of environmental justice been linked to these particular conflicts in academia to date? Martínez-Alier et al. (2014) classify the network into the category of urban and transport environmental justice ("EJ" henceforth) with the groups involved pursuing a multi-faceted agenda. Equally, the denomination of megaprojects as unnecessary/useless and imposed can be categorized as a component of a new EJ vocabulary set that emerged as a result of the praxis of a number of EJ organizations across the globe (Martínez-Alier, 2015). In parallel, when analysing two examples of megaproject-related conflicts, della Porta and Piazza (2008, p. 5) identify "the conceptualisation of a new model of development defined in terms of 'environmental justice'..., ungrowth and sustainable development".

Despite such observations connecting anti-megaproject campaigns and the EJ framework, a deeper examination of the claims and arguments put forward by the groups opposing megaprojects should be conducted in order to suggest further linkages between them – in particular at a time when the EJ conceptualization has been expanded beyond distributional demands. Moreover, assessing how EJ claims are shaped over time constitutes a further element of interest when applying an EJ framework (Urkidi and Walter, 2011) in the sense that they can capture some of the dynamics unfolding and account for a more robust understanding of the analysed disputes. Towards this end, this chapter will analyse how EJ claims and dimensions are framed and articulated in anti-megaproject campaigns, and so test whether the EJ conceptualization advanced by Schlosberg (2007) – explained in section 2 – matches with the discursive practice of the European groups that comprise the UIMP forum – analytical focus of the present research. The relevance of such an exercise lies as well in the fact that these opposing platforms do not explicitly identify with the concept of EJ.

The EJ analytical framework and the European context

The term "environmental justice" first emerged out of the anti-toxic campaigns and civil rights activism in the USA during the 1980s (Walker, 2012) that denounced the higher rates of environmental or health risks and burdens suffered by certain communities, for instance, marginalized communities, relative to other segments of society (Greyl et al., 2013). In this case, the claims made referred to the distributional dimension of justice, which is essentially the allocation of benefits and harms. Subsequently, the term broadened considerably, first to incorporate a component of social justice encompassing elements of class, race and gender (Taylor, 2000), and, second, to integrate the struggles of the global south in opposition to environmental destruction also defined as the "environmentalism of the poor" (Anguelovski, 2015, p. 169).

Today, the term has been adapted variously by academics, activists and institutions and applied to a wide range of environments (Walker, 2012). As Walker observes, EJ "is situated and contextual, grounded in the circumstances of time and place hence defying universal definition" (p. 11). With the emergence of grassroots resistances and movements for the protection of the environment throughout the world, some authors have added other elements to the concept to broaden its accessibility so that it now reflects the full spectrum of claims raised by these groups. This has been accomplished by adopting a particular definition of justice that "encompasses the expressed concerns of EJ groups, the conception of justice to the nonhuman world, and the recent contributions of justice theory" (Schlosberg, 2007, p. 8).

The incorporation of two further dimensions – participation and recognition – has ultimately helped to bolster this broad conceptualization of the term. Schlosberg (ibid.), for example, argues that insufficient recognition and constraints to participation constitute a source of injustice. Indeed, the literature emphasizes the need to recognize collective identities and cultural practices (Schlosberg, 2004), noting the particular relevance of recognition for indigenous communities (Urkidi and Walter, 2011). Indeed, recognition is directly linked with participation; as Schlosberg (2004, p. 19) puts it, "If you are not recognised, you do not participate." In this vein, the participation or procedural dimension of EJ alludes to the institutional processes that facilitate the inclusion of individuals or collectives in the decision-making processes that, to a greater or lesser degree, affect their lives. In sum, the three identified dimensions of EJ that will be utilized in the analytical process are: distribution, participation and recognition.

Such an evolved conceptualization of EJ enables the utilization of the term as a lens through which to analyse a diverse range of socio-environmental conflicts that chime with the plethora of issues being addressed by a multi-faceted EJ agenda (Martínez-Alier et al., 2014), urban and transportation questions among them. When considering conflicts over infrastructure development in Europe, one may think that the participation of different stakeholders in infrastructure planning and access to information should have been normalized as a result of the implementation of the EU legislation and the Aarhus Convention[1] (McCracken and Jones, 2003, cited in Walker, 2012). However, as the aforementioned examples of conflicts over megaproject development indicate, flaws and limitations persist within this decision-making framework. The following section will present the UIMP network as the object of study along with the analytical methodology utilized.

The UIMP network and the analytical method

The analytical process employed in this chapter will focus on categorizing the claims and arguments subscribed to by the UIMP network according to the above-mentioned three dimensions: distribution, recognition and participation. The

UIMP network has its origin in the convergence of several groups from across Western Europe opposing high-speed railway (HSR) developments. Its foundational document is the Charter of Hendaye (2010). Subsequently, other groups opposing other types of infrastructures and megaprojects joined the network. As a consequence, some of the assertions contained in the documents must be considered in relation to opposition against HSR. Martinez-Alier et al. (2014, p. 40) describe the coalition as follows:

> There is now a growing "European Forum against Imposed and Useless Projects" (Grands Projets Inutiles et Imposés). In 2012 it held its 2nd meeting with 8,000 participants against the planned airport of Notre Dame-des-Landes. This took place over five days in Brittany near Nantes from 7 to 11 July. The 3rd Forum was held in summer 2013 in Stuttgart, the site of a resistance movement against a grand, new, superfluous train station.[2]

This network has been chosen on the assumption that, by connecting and sharing the experiences of various groups opposing megaprojects, its work has generated a synthesis of meanings and experiences. To carry out the examination, the documents produced by the network (see Table 11.1) will be examined qualitatively through a thematic analysis process employing the computer software package NVivo. As part of the analytical process the claims stated by the network will be employed to generate themes that ultimately will be linked to the three EJ dimensions underpinned by the previously described theoretical framework. The chapter will also draw on observations carried out by the author during the last four forums organized (2013–2016).

Claims and dimensions of Environmental Justice in the UIMP network discourse

The following analysis of the EJ dimensions identified in the arguments expressed by the UIMP network is divided into two subsections. The first brings together

TABLE 11.1 Documents produced by the UIMP network considered in the analysis (source: author)[3]

Document	Acronym
Charter of Hendaye (2010)	CH
Final Declaration 2012	FD2
Charter of Tunis (2013)	CT
Final Declaration 2013	FD3
Final Declaration 2014	FD4
Final Declaration 2015	FD5
Final Declaration 2016	FD6

Author: Alfred Burballa-Noria

recognition and participation. The second deals with equity and the distribution of the impacts generated by megaproject development. The explanatory model presented in Figure 11.1 enables the visualization of the generated themes and its relation among them and with the three EJ dimension analytical framework.

a) Participatory and recognition claims

This section will explore those claims that relate to participation and recognition.

In the discourse advanced by the UIMP network, references to the lack of transparency as well as the diffusion of biased and untruthful information abound:

> We denounce the opacity with which the governments and the administrations act (CH).
>
> [We] confirm that . . . governments and administrations operate in obscurity (CT).
>
> [T]he official justification for the construction of these new lines is constructed systematically resorting to false hypotheses about the traffic and the socioeconomic yield, as well as to an underestimation of the costs of accomplishment in order to [better 'sell'] a project whose real utility has not been demonstrated; on the contrary, numerous studies have proven the non[-]relevance of these projects in economic and social terms (CT).
>
> [O]ne of the features that unites large works and their promotion consists [of] false data and unrealized and unrealizable economic projections (FD5).

The network's discourse also suggests that a binding and inclusive debate has been omitted by those public institutions that must promote it. Their stance is therefore to appeal to the states not only to address this defect but also to do so in such a way that the discussion is not about one particular project but about the model that underpins the planning and projection of infrastructures:

> During the discussions they [participants] identified at international level . . . the same prevention of democratic debate (FD3).
>
> We demand that the Governments of France, Italy and Spain . . . undertake a real[. . . public debate on a European scale on the model of transport, territorial planning and organisation of our society that underlie[s] this unrestrained development of HSR lines (CH).

Two essential points emerge from these observations in relation to participation and decision-making processes: on the one hand, the very nature of these megaprojects makes participation problematic, given that relevant frameworks such as the Aarhus Convention are ignored; on the other, specific actors can exercise their capacity for leverage and influence the decision-making process of governments. These two points express the basis on which the term "imposed" was grounded:

> These projects are unable to lead to the participation[4] of the population in decision processes (CH).

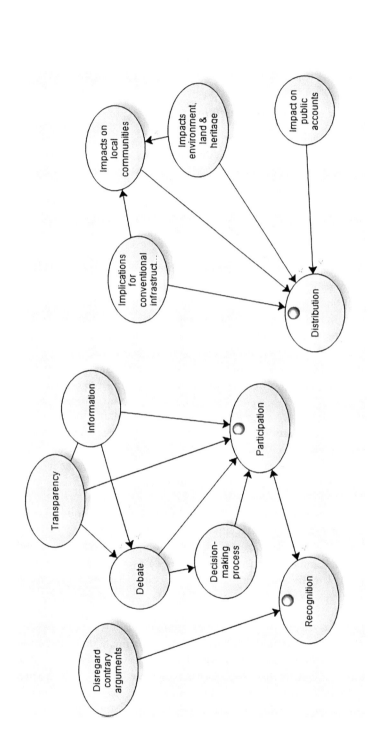

FIGURE 11.1 Explanatory model of the qualitative analysis generated with NVivo

Author: Alfred Burballa-Noria

> [T]hese projects exclude the effective participation of the population in the decision-making process (CT).
>
> [These projects are] imposed because they are implemented through the systematic denial of citizen participation accounted for in the Aarhus Convention which is part of the legislation of all European countries and of the EU itself (FD5).
>
> [These are] companies that, through lobbying, influence political decision-making to obtain exceptional measures to get around all legal obstacles (CT).
>
> [D]uring the Forum, special emphasis was put on the role of the industrial and financial lobbies that influence the European Commission in a decisive and uncontrolled way (DF5).

Furthermore, the network states that instead of spaces for participation and the confrontation of ideas, the response from governments is to repress and criminalize those who express them:

> [The groups gathered to] [d]enounce the repression inflicted on the inhabitants and activists (FD2).
>
> We recognise[d] that we are all facing state repression and we reject the criminalisation of activists (FD4).
>
> [The issues discussed included the] exacerbation of repression and the denial of democracy disguised as legality (FD6).

In response to these observations, possible strategies for addressing the lack of consideration towards megaproject dissenters and local communities are proposed:

> [S]olutions are possible by attributing the final part of the decision-making process to the populace directly affected, a fundamental factor for real democracy and local autonomy (CT).

The last component to be outlined in this subsection refers to the perception of the groups within the network of the recognition they receive when addressing the competent institutions. According to the documents analysed, in addition to the deliberate failure to establish participatory mechanisms in relation to decision-making as discussed above, these institutions have treated activists and local communities with disregard and marginalized from public opinion. They express "scorn [for] the arguments and proposals of the citizens" (CH), "deny them access to the means of communication" (CT) and "treat proposals by citizens with contempt" (CT).

b) Distributional claims

Under the heading of the distributional dimension fall a series of claims which can be clustered into four generic categories amongst which there is some degree of overlap. The first of these relates to impacts on the environment, the land and the local heritage:

> [The opposed projects involve] destruction of natural spaces and agricultural lands, a new barrier of harmful effects and degradation of the environment (CH).
>
> [T]he destruction of wildlife areas [. . .] and of cultural and artistic heritage: they do harm and cause degradation, environmental pollution generating irreversible damage to the environment (CT).
>
> During the discussions they [participants] identified at [the] international level [. . .] the same environmental devastation (FD3).
>
> [M]egaprojects are the instrument of neoliberal policies for the predation of the planet's resources (FD5).

The second category corresponds to claims about the impacts on local communities, particularly that those individuals who live close to where a megaproject is constructed must put up with certain negative impacts that such projects generate. Although these are not specified, it can be assumed that they refer to impacts such as an increase in noise, dust and pollution and also loss of aesthetic value. When local communities are expropriated from lands, a link with the previous category can be established.

> These projects constitute an ecological, socioeconomic and human disaster for the territories they cross: . . . with important negative impacts for the residents (CH).
>
> [Megaprojects] have serious negative consequences for inhabitants (CT).

Rather than persist with this model, the potentialities of a different paradigm of development should be explored:

> Solutions are possible . . . by giving preference to the proximity and re-localization of the economy, protection of agricultural land, energy-use moderation and the transition toward de-centralized, renewable energy sources (CT).

Referring specifically to HSR developments, the third category of claim are those that describe the negative implications that the new developments will have on the conventional transport network:

> [T]he priority granted to the HSR is done . . . to the detriment of the traffic of proximity and of the priority in the maintenance and development of the existing railway networks, which are neither maintained nor optimized so as to develop a transport of freight that would irrigate the territories and a public service of transport accessible to all (CH).

This claim reverberates as well with the second category of claims regarding the negative impact of megaprojects on local communities in the sense that a progressive abandonment and deterioration of the local/regional network would also involve a negative impact for those communities that benefit from the conventional network. The final category concerns one of the characteristics that according to the network define the megaprojects they oppose: the claim that they are unnecessary (or, alternatively, useless). Unnecessary for communities they may be, but, according to the network, there are various benefits to be accrued from such projects: for example, the concession of loans to fund the cost associated with their implementation and construction, and through different mechanisms of corruption. These in turn lead to the loss of public funds that could be allocated to social spending; what's more, such spending generates public debt, which further reduces public spending as funds are redirected to pay off debt.

> [T]he realization of these useless projects is increasingly at the expense of public coffers: they produce enormous debts and don't generate economic benefits, concentrating wealth and impoverishing society (CH).
>
> During the discussions they [participants] identified at [the] international level . . . the same waste of public money in the interest of the few, the same future public debts (FD3).
>
> Megaprojects . . . increase the debt of every nation (FD5).
>
> It was pointed out that megaprojects generate corruption which is theft of public resources (FD5).

Discussion and conclusions

In Section 3, the connections between anti-megaproject campaigns in Europe and the EJ framework derived from the identification of its three dimensions (distribution, participation and recognition) were outlined. A thematic analysis was then conducted, utilizing the charters and declarations issued by the UIMP network, a transnational resistance network established "to counterbalance transnational mega projects" (Ariemma and Burnside-Lawry, 2014, p. 3). Through the identification of key themes, the interweaving of the discourse emerging from the UIMP network documents has been pointed out.

In relation to the distributional dimension, four themes were identified. Although no specific reference is made, the theme of territorial and environmental impacts appears obvious, given the use of unequivocal language, such as "degradation", "devastation", "destruction", "irreversible damage" and "predation of the natural resources". Importantly, there is no mention in these documents of instruments such as the EIA studies.

The second theme to emerge concerns the effects of megaprojects on local communities. By employing terms such as "negative impacts" and "negative consequences", such claims convey that the livelihoods of the local communities will be seriously affected by the programmed infrastructure development, suggesting a potential link with the "environmentalism of the poor" referenced in Section 2. At the same time, this theme overlaps with claims that denounce the deterioration of conventional transportation networks providing a local and regional service to these communities.

The last claim in this category regards the perceived excessive public spending that creates a burden for public finance in two respects. First, such projects are seen to be of limited usefulness; that is, the service provided by the new infrastructure is already covered by an older network and therefore is considered unnecessary, despite the new one being more modern and faster. Such a stance conveys an endorsement of the degrowth perspective that rejects ecological modernization and green growth projects as outlined by Kallis et al. (2015). Second, the negative implications in terms of cost of opportunity are denounced, particularly given the general context of the austerity policies being implemented across Europe. Also, in one of the most recent declarations, corruption is identified as another element that is associated with megaproject development and that further contributes to the fundamental injustice of the model.

The participatory dimension, as represented in the network's discourse, has three prominent, interrelated elements: information and transparency, organization of proper and accessible debates and the consideration of inclusive decision-making processes, which includes the demand for self-determination by the affected communities. The situation can be summarized as follows. The initial phases of the project are characterized by opaque procedures that are denounced by opponents. Subsequently, when the project is presented to the public, the exercise is seen as propaganda, supported by biased evidence; moreover, the public is given no opportunity to address or debate the issues publicly as the institutions provide no space for a confrontation between opposing arguments. On the contrary, these decision-making processes are permeable to the influence of certain powerful lobbies or elite groups. Likewise, the network also contends that in conducting these processes, the relevant institutions appear to ignore internationally recognized legal instruments such as the Aarhus Convention. To make matters worse in terms of participation, it is not uncommon to identify a response from the public institutions geared towards criminalization and repression of opposing groups.

The corollary to this examination is the identification of the recognition dimension. In this vein, the UIMP network states that their demands and arguments are despised by institutions and megaproject promoters and that mainstream media ignore their position. This lack of recognition leaves opposing groups in a difficult position if they are ever to be perceived as legitimate actors by the larger citizenry, a situation that is challenged by paradigms such as post-normal science (Kallis et al., 2015; D'Alisa and Kallis, 2015).

In terms of the lessons to be learned from the present analysis, from a scholar perspective, it emerges that the overall critique towards megaproject development processes, although with different terminology, matches with critical accounts advanced by scholars (for example, Flyvbjerg et al., 2003). Second, the EJ framework based on the three basic aforementioned principles identified by Schlosberg (2007, 2004) is confirmed as a valid analytical tool for comprehending not only global south mobilization processes (for example, Urkidi and Walter, 2011) and conflicts over resource extraction and waste disposal (Martínez-Alier et al., 2014) but also more concealed global north grass-roots initiatives articulated through multidimensional frames (although with clear links to ecologist movements, the environmental dimension is transcended by a more complex range of issues being at stake, such as democratic and transport rights) that also have implications in the growth of the social metabolism.

Nonetheless, as noted in Velicu and Kaika (2015), this perspective is limited in itself to the extent that portrays justice as a static element usually to be demanded or allocated. Hence, in the view of the authors this perspective has to be challenged if communities attempt to develop new imaginaries and associated practices of political equality. In that sense, as the present examination focused on a case-study of a transnational network whose partners belong to different geographical areas (unlike the case-study chosen by the mentioned authors), it did not aim at theorizing on the politics of the movements but in locating their discourses and narratives into the EJ framework as the UIMP network had been identified as a component of the global EJ movement. In order to theorize on the politics of these movements it seems more appropriate to analyse each single platform or movement in their place of origin as the authors did for Rosia Montana or other authors did for the No TAV movement (Leonardi, 2013) in the understanding that the political praxis of these movements will be better understood in their main context of action.

Furthermore, the analysis conducted facilitates devising the evolution of environmental networks such as UIMP. Departing from the focus on one single issue, opposition against HSR developments, the network was capable to grow, transcending the initial issue as frames of reference shared with other partners were identified jumping to the transport theme − as other projects appeared, for example, station, airport − but also other types of megaprojects identified in the literature − mines, dams, casinos (see other megaproject categories in Gellert and Lynch, 2003). In that sense, the EJ framework emerges as a consistent tool to provide further cohesion to the constellation of platforms and movements mobilizing against harmful projects across the planet; through a narrative based on the EJ principles activists can identify common grounds for the construction of common agendas and shared identities. The platforms forming the UIMP network could then consider the suitability of incorporating into their narratives or frames of reference mentions to EJ or more specifically to "transport justice" drawing on some of the theoretical elaborations on the subject.

As one of the focuses for practitioners is to build alliances among the wide array of social movements (Martínez-Alier et al., 2014) an example to take into consideration is the evolution of the anti-HST campaign in the Basque Country. As the single-issue campaign declined, through the last events organized, activists tried to establish bonds with other collectives involved in social and environmental issues (as observed by the author in the 2016 campaign event named "Txirrinka"[5]). In such a process of alliance-building the EJ framework could be drawn on to strengthen the underlying discourse and shared narrative of the process.

To conclude, as the critiques towards the EJ approach suggest, it should not be taken as a definitive framework and instead should be further problematized, in particular considering rationalities that clash with the traditional ones of the market, of development and of growth. This should enable to transcend pre-given frameworks and consensus-oriented politics that prevent transformative change from happening. Notwithstanding its limitations, it is believed that providing an account based on the EJ framework of anti-megaproject campaigns is a first step in this direction.

Notes

1 *Aarhus Convention on Access to Information, Public Participation and Access to Justice in Environmental Matters* done at Aarhus (Denmark) on 25 June 1998. It was signed by the European Commission the same year and its requirements "translated into EU law in Directive 2003/35/EC" (Hartley and Wood, 2005, p. 321).
2 Three further editions of the Forum have been celebrated: Rosia Montana (Romania) at a proposed site for a gold mine in 2014; Bagnaria Arsa (Italy) hosted by an anti-HSR committee in 2015; and Bayonne (France) in 2016, also hosted by a platform opposing a HSR project.
3 FD2 (French), FD5 (Italian) and FD6 (Italian) are not available in English. Fragments utilized in this analytical exercise are translated by the author.
4 Better expressed in English as: . . . *unable to provide opportunities for the participation of* . . .
5 http://ahttxirrinka2016.blogspot.co.uk/

References

Altshuler, A. and Luberoff, D. (2003) *Mega-Projects. The Changing Politics of Urban Public Investment*. Washington, D.C.: Brookings.

Anguelovski, I. (2015) Environmental Justice. In G. D'Alisa, F. Demaria and G. Kallis (eds), *Degrowth: Vocabulary for a New Era*. Oxon: Routledge. Pp. 60–63.

Ariemma, L. and Burnside-Lawry, J. (2014) Transnational Mega Projects and Transnational Resistance Networks: Democratic Participation and Communicative Action – the No TAV Movement and the Lyon–Turin High-speed Rail Project. In *23rd World Congress of Political Science, "Challenges of Contemporary Governance" 19–24 July*, Montreal.

Beckman, S. and Gil, N. (2009) Infrastructure Meets Business: Building New Bridges, Mending Old Ones. An Introduction to the Special Issue. *California Management Review* 51 (2), 6–29.

D'Alisa, G. and Kallis, G. (2015) Post-Normal Science. In G. D'Alisa, F. Demaria and G. Kallis (eds), *Degrowth: Vocabulary for a New Era*. New York and London: Routledge. Pp. 217–220.

della Porta, D. and Piazza, G. (2008) *Voices of the Valley, Voices of the Straits: How Protest Creates Communities*. Oxford and New York: Berghahn Books.

Fainstein, S.S. (2008) Mega-projects in New York, London and Amsterdam. *International Journal of Urban and Regional Research* 32 (4), 768–785.

Flyvbjerg, B. (2005) Machiavellian Megaprojects. *Antipode* 37 (1), 18–22.

Flyvbjerg, B. (2014) What You Should Know About Megaprojects and Why: An Overview. *Project Management Journal* 45 (2), 6–19.

Flyvbjerg, B., Bruzelius, N. and Rothengatter, W. (2003). *Megaprojects and Risk: An Anatomy of Ambition*. Cambridge: Cambridge University Press.

Gellert, P.K. and Lynch, B.D. (2003) Mega-projects as Displacements. *International Social Science Journal* 55 (175), 15–25.

Greyl, L., Vegni, S., Natalicchio, M., Cure, S. and Ferretti, J. (2013) The Waste Crisis in Campania, Italy. In H. Healy, J. Martínez-Alier, L. Temper, M. Walter and J.-F. Gerber (eds), *Ecological Economics from the Ground Up*. London: Routledge. Pp. 273–308.

Hartley, N. and Wood, C. (2005) Public Participation in Environmental Impact Assessment – Implementing the Aarhus Convention. *Environmental Impact Assessment Review* 25 (4), 319–340.

Harvey, D. (2003) *The New Imperialism*. New York: Oxford University Press.

Kallis, G., Demaria, F. and D'Alisa, G. (2015) Introduction. Degrowth. In G. Kallis, F. Demaria and G. D'Alisa (eds), *Degrowth: Vocabulary for a New Era*. Oxon: Routledge. Pp. 28–45.

Leonardi, E. (2013) Foucault in the Susa Valley: The No TAV Movement and Struggles for Subjectification. *Capitalism Nature Socialism* 24 (2), 27–40.

Macharis, C. and Nijkamp, P. (2013) Multi-criteria Multi-actor Analysis in Evaluating Mega-projects. In H. Priemus and B. van Wee (eds), *International Handbook on Megaprojects*. Cheltenham, UK and Northampton, USA: Edward Elgar. Pp. 242–267

Martínez-Alier, J. (2015) La ecología política y el movimiento de justicía ambiental. *Ecología Política. Cuadernos de Debate Internacional* 50: 55–61.

Martínez-Alier, J., Anguelovski, I., Bond, P., Del Bene, D., Demaria, F., Gerber, J. F. and Yánez, I. (2014) Between Activism and Science: Grassroots Concepts for Sustainability Coined by Environmental Justice Organizations. *Journal of Political Ecology* 21, 19–60.

Novy, J. and Peters, D. (2012) Railway Station Mega-Projects as Public Controversies: The Case of Stuttgart 21. *Built Environment* 38 (3), 128–145.

Pieper, A. (2013) Land Grabbing in France: The Case of the Notre-Dame-des-Landes Airport. In *Land Concentration, Land Grabbing and People's Struggles in Europe*. Amsterdam: Transnational Institute. Pp. 78–81.

Presidio Europa No TAV (2014) *About the No TAV Movement and Beyond . . . A Comprehensive Essay*. Available at: www.presidioeuropa.net/blog/tav-movement/

Robert, D. (2014) *Social Movements Opposing Megaprojects. A Rhizome of Resistance to the Neoliberal Hydra?* Degree Project in Urban and Regional Planning, Royal Institute of Technology Stockholm.

Schlosberg, D. (2004) Reconceiving Environmental Justice: Global Movements and Political Theories. *Environmental Politics* 13 (3), 517–540.

Schlosberg, D. (2007) *Defining Environmental Justice: Theories, Movements, and Nature*. New York: Oxford University Press.

Taylor, D.E. (2000) The Rise of the Environmental Justice Paradigm. *American Behavioral Scientist* 43 (4), 508–580.

Temper, L. (2014) *Environmentalism of the Dispossessed: Mapping Ecologies of Resistance*. PhD thesis, Universitat Autonoma de Barcelona.

Urkidi, L. and Walter, M. (2011) Dimensions of Environmental Justice in Anti-gold Mining Movements in Latin America. *Geoforum* 42 (6), 683–695.

Velicu, I. and Kaika, M. (2015) Undoing Environmental Justice: Re-imagining Equality in the Rosia Montana Anti-mining Movement. *Geoforum* 84, 305–315.

Walker, G. (2012) *Environmental Justice: Concepts, Evidence and Politics*. London and New York: Routledge.

PART III

The economic valuation of nature

From academic debates to activist action

12

ISOLATION AND ABSTRACTION TO TACKLE DEFORESTATION

The problem of theory as a practical problem in environmental issues

Mario Hernandez-Trejo

Introduction

In this chapter, I argue for the critical engagement of scholars and activists in environmental policy design and implementation. I depict some of the different applications of a model of efficient land use coined in the 19th century: von Thünen's model. This theory has been widely accepted among economists, set the basis for key concepts in economics, such as marginal utility, provided a basis for forestry techniques and informed the designing of policy tools for forests conservation. Given its influence, I trace the application of von Thünen's model among economists, and how it evolved in spatial targeting models to improve the effectiveness of payments for ecosystem services (PES) schemes.

The main aim of this analysis is not reviewing the academic literature based in von Thünen's concepts, but showing how these theoretical principles promote an ideal way of organizing the territory based on assumptions of economic rationality and the isolation of land use from its context. My interest in illustrating the relatively successful transfer of these ideals over generations of economists and policy makers helps us to consider environmental policy-making and academic practice as political arenas. Thus, I follow the approach of political ecology in examining how scientific knowledge and policy making merges into a hybrid political project, namely *market environmentalism*: a set of ideas, policies, techniques and actors that share the assumption that markets are cost-effective tools to regulate the interaction between people and the environment.

Political ecologists that have been immersed in environmental policy making have shown that the advance of market environmentalism is not a coherent and homogeneous project. As Dempsey and Robertson (2012, p. 759) put it for the case of environmental policy based on the ecosystem services framework: despite its expansion and predominance, there are "frictions and discontinuities" in market environmentalism that open spaces of engagement for alternative political positions. The national-scale PES programme in Mexico provides a good example of this: its origins are closely related to the development of neoliberal conservation in Mexico; ideally, the advocates of PES in Mexico see the problem of deforestation and water provision as a matter of implementing a compensation scheme for ecosystem services (for example, watershed protection) between individual buyers (for example, downstream inhabitants in a watershed) and sellers (for example, upstream owners of forests).

Yet, far from meeting the above ideal criteria, the PES programme in Mexico is actually rooted in a government-led mechanism, that is, the taxing system, thus the government is the actor who not only sets the price of the ecosystem services but also pays a monetary incentive funded through taxes to the owners of forest to preserve the ecosystem services that benefit water users. Despite the original definition of PES by environmental economists as a transaction of well-defined ecosystem services between individuals, the actual functioning of these increasingly important environmental policies relies on the relationship between government institutions, political organizations and international agencies, among others.

As research based in political ecology has shown, the fact that the Mexican PES programme is embedded in the conflictive functioning of the state, opened spaces for political organizations to intervene and promote alternative visions on the relationship between people and the environment (McAfee and Shapiro, 2010). In other words, the frictions and discontinuities in the advance of market environmentalism should be seen as a platform to do politics. In this chapter, I try to contribute to such interventions by analysing the mechanisms through which the promoters of market-based conservation use particular instruments of policy making to depoliticize environmental issues such as deforestation. In this sense, I consider political ecology as a lens to highlight the power relationships underlying environmental change, as a useful critical tool for environmental politics.

But political ecologists are also immersed in the neoliberal conundrums they aim to disentangle. This is why, before looking at Von Thünen, in the following section I will posit my position with regards to the relationship between environmental policy, academic research and activism. Section three provides a brief account of the assumptions of von Thünen's model and identifies some hints to understand the political position of its author. Section four depicts how these assumptions and political positions were reproduced by environmental economists and policy makers based at the World Bank. Section five looks at how a specific instrument in market-based environmental policy, namely the spatial targeting of PES in Mexico, relies on von Thünen's assumptions and fails to achieve its goal, that is, to increase the efficiency of the payments by avoiding the enrolment of forested areas that would be preserved in the absence of payments. Finally, the last section takes the critique to environmental economics as a practical problem and suggests some fields of action for political ecologists.

The problem of theory as a practical problem in political ecology

It is my sense that the debates that stem from a strict division between scholars and activists obscure the fact that all environmental research is developed in a political context. As this chapter suggests, even the most technical and abstract academic works on the environment, such as theories and models based on environmental economics, are immersed in a political dynamic. Correspondingly, the assertion that critical scholarship is frequently detached from political participation should not lead to indifference on the role of university-based researchers. On the contrary, we should demand politics-relevant analysis in political ecology. As social scientists, political ecologists have endeavoured to make generalizations from a variety of empirical cases related to environmental issues; these theorizations allow to grasp broader processes in which the particular cases are immersed. Nonetheless, recent debates in this field have warned against the risk of posing theoretical categories that are not contributing to an accurate understanding of environmental issues, such as the financialization of ecosystems conservation.

A recent paper compares the stance of the "critics" and the "promoters" of neo-liberal conservation. The former claim that conservation schemes such as ecosystem services markets can be categorized as forms of commodification of nature and capital accumulation, whereas the latter endorse the investment of private capital in conservation to develop green economies (Dempsey and Suarez, 2016). The authors analyse the scale and scope of conservation finance and contrast their findings with the discourse of both groups. Firstly, they conclude that flows of conservation investment remain marginal and "largely unprofitable" (Dempsey and Suarez, 2016, p. 667); second, they argue that both the critics and the promoters have developed a rhetoric that overestimates and idealizes the scale of conservation finance. In other words, conservation may not be a big business, and the theoretical framing of conservation as a means to capital accumulation remains "more fiction than fact" (ibid.), but, still, critics and promoters develop a narrative and conceptualization of neoliberal conservation as a generalized strategy to make a profit.

This paradox raises concerns on the risk for critical scholarship to remain marginal in the process of shaping environmental agendas by privileging the construction of concepts at the expense of concretized theoretical explanation. It also seems to suggest that, on the one hand, the promoters of mainstream conservation are endorsing the dominant paradigm in environmental governance, that is, market environmentalism, and, on the other, the critics may miss points of entry for a substantial debate on environmental issues and action research by developing innocuous arguments. However, it is important not to dismiss academic research *a priori* when it has mainly a theoretical character; on the contrary, whether critical or not, we should aim to analyse it from a sociological perspective: Where does it come from? What are the context and the social relationships that provide a basis for it? I would argue that these questions help to overcome the idea that theory occurs in an institutional vacuum and to assess its socio-political relevance. But, most importantly, they help us to identify fields of action to intervene and debate to contest neoliberal conservation. Following N. Bukharin, I would say that we should address "the problem of theory as a practical problem" (Bukharin, 2002 [1931]).

There is a significant body of literature in political ecology that depicts how policy makers, scientists, governments and agencies promote market environmentalism. In other words, the theories that justify market-based conservation have been studied sociologically to a large extent. Yet, to engage in environmental policy making and action research, we also need to understand its logic. As Bukharin puts it, it is not enough to explain the class character of a certain theory; we also need "to proceed to an exhaustive criticism on the *internal* phases of the [theoretical] system" (Bukharin, 1927, p. 8; emphasis in the original). Following this method, in my research, I trace in neoclassical economics the roots of models for efficient land use in which policies such as PES are based. I highlight the idealist character of these theories, its inability to explain environmental change and human behaviour and how they often inform ineffective environmental policies.

This chapter explains how these flaws are reproduced in environmental policy making and environmental economics. Given the increasing importance of environmental economics in shaping environmental agendas, and the parallel failure of market environmentalism in tackling degradation and environmental conflicts, it is pertinent to posit the question of whether or not it is time for political ecologists to participate in political arenas, such as education, to promote different methods and approaches to understand the links between the environment and economic systems. Therefore, the last section of this chapter considers the syllabus of economics programmes and the politics within universities as relevant practical problems for political ecologists.

Von Thünen, the "isolated" economist

In the mid-18th century, J.H. von Thünen, an economist from Pomerania, in Northern Germany, was systemically keeping records of costs and returns on his own Junker estate. Von Thünen was concerned with finding the most efficient system of land management to conduct his enterprise. Among other enquiries, he studied two practical aspects of forestry: calculating the optimal period from planting to cutting down stands of forests for timber production, and the optimal location for forestry. He concluded that a period of 42 years allows the forester to maximize profits, and suggested that forestry should be developed from 4 to 7.3 miles from the consumption market due to the high yields per unit of land and low production costs (von Thünen, 2009 [1863]). Von Thünen arrived at the first conclusion by analysing the effects on profit of the recurrent selective removal of trees to improve the growth rate of the remaining crop trees, and to the second conclusion through the comparison of the transport costs of different land uses. He drew in at least two assumptions: first, that "the diameter of the tree is the standard for the normal interval and the need for space" (von Thünen, 2009 [1863], p. 73); this surmise allowed him to calculate the age of timber stocks for the successive removal of trees. And, second, that there is a single consuming centre; based on this idea he compared the costs and returns from different land uses to suggest a spatial organization for them. He focused mainly on transport costs to indicate that returns are higher in areas closest to markets because transport costs are lower. A concentric number or rings were used by von Thünen to illustrate a prototype of an efficient use of land, organizing competing land uses according to their transport costs. Each ring represents a type of land use in a distance-based gradient, in which the city is located in the centre. The costs increase as economics activities are realized farther from the city.

Stemming from these assumptions, von Thünen isolated certain factors of reality to transform them into mathematical expressions. For instance, the different elements that influence the location of timber production: ecosystemic diversity, transport networks and so forth are abstracted and the only factor taken into account are transport costs expressed in figures of prices and distance. As von Thünen (1966 [1876], p. 3) puts it, his "imaginary assumptions"isolate a variable as if other co-determining factors are uniform. Subsequently, he incorporates empirical data from the records of his enterprise to operate what present-day economists consider "the world's first economic model" (Hall, 1966, p. xxi).

But von Thünen was not researching in isolation. Given the importance of forestry in 18th-century Pomerania for fuel and building, and the imports of timber from Scandinavia, his concerns on the management of woodlands were shared by foresters and economists. He reproduced the inquisitions of his critics in a kind of monologue worth reading because it shows not only von Thünen's method, but also his stance towards the critique of his imaginary assumptions, and towards the qualms on the applicability of his ideal model of land management:

> [T]he mere practitioner will say:

> > What use to me is the knowledge of a law that depends
> > entirely upon a series of assumptions that can never be
> > found in reality? Here trees of equal diameter and
> > equal growth are assumed, all of which are perfectly
> > and equally distributed through a wood, without the
> > slightest clearing; constant and steady thinning is also
> > assumed, whereas in practice thinning can be done
> > only after periods of several years. What use can I make
> > of studies which, like these, are based upon entirely
> > ideal circumstances?

> To which I reply:

> > These investigations directed to the natural laws governing
> > forestry relate to practical silviculture as pure
> > geometry relates to applied.
> > Pure geometry is based upon entire fictions: points without
> > extension, lines of no width − none of these can be

> found in reality. Nonetheless, pure geometry is the irrefutable
> foundation of practical geometry, and without the
> former the latter would be nothing but trial and error.'
>
> *(von Thünen, 2009 [1863], p. 73)*

This monologue shows at least two aspects of von Thünen's method and political position. The first one refers to the distance that the author is putting between the economist and the practitioner; the former provides "the foundations" for practice through ideas, whereas the latter passively "makes use of studies" for concrete modes of action. This perspective presents a picture where the economist appears to be outside the processes he is analysing. His role is that of the expert who provides a prescription of how an economic agent should think, how to value and make decisions. The economist appropriates for himself the role of the expert who instructs economic agents on how they should make sense of values and the environment. The second aspect concerns the use of abstractions, which von Thünen' represents with the metaphor of geometry, as the starting point for determining agricultural location+n. Rather than a tool for understanding a process or social fact, von Thünen's model is a mathematical expression of an ideal form of land use in which empirical data may fit, or not, and this will determine the efficiency of a particular system. The conception of the real begins and ends in the imaginary.

It seems to be contradictory that von Thünen presents an optimal model of land use management knowing beforehand that the assumptions in which it is built cannot be found in reality. What is the point of proposing a location for forestry assuming that there is one consumption market, and at the same time knowing that there are many other? Despite von Thünen's acknowledgment that his land use model is imaginary, the influence of his work spans from fundamental theoretical perspectives, such as neoclassical economics, to technical aspects of forestry practice and environmental policy-making, also including trends in economic geography and environmental history. Why a perspective that detaches facts from their context and expresses processes, such as the trade of agricultural products, in terms of geometry has so much impact? Why a perspective that expresses socio-environmental change in terms of geometry is influential?

I would argue that divorced from reality, von Thünen's method entails a normative model, that is, an idea of how a rational actor ought to behave economically. In the subsequent sections, I will analyse how the mobilization and adaptation of von Thünen's model by experts in land use management and environmental policy making seek to legitimize a normative model that promotes determined patterns of territorial organization. I will focus on the variations of von Thünen's model as applied by environmental economists to improve the effectiveness of payments for ecosystem services (PES) schemes. I will highlight how the abstractions and assumptions in which these models rely inform land use management programmes that play a role in socio-ecological processes by diffusing lessons on how institutions and land owners should behave. The actors, models and techniques (for example, policy instruments like mapping) that advocate for conservation schemes such as PES render forest owners as profit maximizers who, in order to optimize the outputs of this type land use, should respond to economic incentives and make decision-making based on calculations of costs and benefits. As claimed by von Thünen, space is represented in these models, and thus in the policies they inform, as homogeneous and divisible by points and lines, which provide the basis for the optimal decision-making that would lead to the implementations of techniques to achieve an efficient allocation of resources.

Von Thünen's brain children at the World Bank

"I love von Thünen above all my masters" wrote A. Marshall (cited in Hall, 1966, p. xi) in about 1900. The legacy of Marshall has had a significant impact: the concept of marginal utility, among other insights, were diffused in Marshall's textbooks that were dominant for years. He drew in von Thünen's idea of the margin to explain the behaviour of consumers about prices. According to Marshall, the benefit that a consumer obtains from a product decreases as consumption increases. Thus, there is a point where one unit of a product does not generate any benefit, in other words, a margin that functions to determine the value of a good. As mentioned in the previous section, von Thünen was interested in determining the optimal location for competing forms of land use and, using transportation costs, he calculated the points where the production of a good or service would not be profitable. The same idea of a margin was applied to forestry, namely to the determination of the period for cutting down of stands of trees for the maximization of profits from timber production.

In the mid-1970s, another influential economist, Nobel Prize laureate and textbooks author P. Samuelson, took von Thünen's concern on forestry to continue the debate with foresters on the best time to harvest a stand of trees. He incorporated to the calculation of rotation periods the value of land. In his discussion with foresters, Samuelson (1976, p. 467) argues that "managerial economics" (Samuelson, 1976, p. 467) on forestry omits the value of land and opportunity costs by focusing only on the maximization of rents from the stands of trees. For him, the optimal maximization of rents also depends on the price of land, not only of forests. The conclusions by Samuelson with regards to the rotation period in forestry differ from von Thünen's, but, overall, they share the idea of short rotation periods as inefficient regarding optimal land management. Samuelson praises von Thünen as "a prophet way ahead of his own times" (2009, p. xiii), and with the confidence of the textbook writer he asserts: "Yes. Science does advance funeral by funeral. And science does advance also birth by birth. Von Thünen's brain children live and proliferate" (p. xiv). His statement was to be confirmed.

In the preamble of the Rio Conference in 1992, Southern countries were debating with the position of Northern countries on a global agreement on forest conservation. The former, headed by Malaysia and India, argue that it was unfair to carry the costs of conservation when the latter cleared their forests during their industrialization (Adams, 2008). The *Forests Principles* defined during the Conference lack clear commitments in terms of forests conservation, but there was a call "for scientific assessment and management of environmental impacts of forestry" (Adams, 2008, p. 96). These agreements, along with concerns about the effects of land use change raised in the Convention on Climate change, were endorsed by institutions such as the World Bank, an institution that channelled economic resources for conservation through mechanisms like the Global Environment Facility. Along with the financing of conservation, research grounded in environmental economics was bolstered by the World Bank. In the 1990s amidst the wave of the neoliberalization of economies in Latin America, economists based in the Environment Department and the Policy Research Department of the World Bank were focused in finding sustainable and efficient models for land use.

Von Amsberg (1994) looked at the relationship between the variations of the price of timber and land use patterns to forecast the effects of policy interventions such as log export bans. The author applies von Thünen's approach on valuing competing land uses (managed and unmanaged forests), and follows his assumption that "a given piece of land is put to the use in which it will yield the highest returns" (von Amsberg, 1994, p. 3). Similarly, Schneider (1995, p. vi) uses von Thünen's model of efficient land use to propose "policies to rationalize the settlement and development" in areas such as the Amazon, where large tracts of uninhabited land "act as a magnet for both squatters and entrepreneurs in search of new economic opportunity", posing threats to the environment. One of the most influential studies in this trend of von Thünian studies on land use and environmental issues is the one by Chomitz and Gray (1996). The authors assess the effects of road building on deforestation in Belize. Their aim is to develop a spatial model to "locate roads so as to spur development while minimising induced deforestation" (p. 488). They use mainly the variables of soil quality and transport costs. With regards to the latter, they follow von Thünen in assuming that spatial differences in agricultural prices are linked to variations in transport costs to the market. Thus, depending on the distance from the market and the type of soil, "roads will favor forest clearing for commercial crops, while others will stimulate the spread of shifting cultivation" (p. 507). To different degrees, all of these authors applied von Thünen's insights to predict the behaviour of landowners in relation to land use. Eventually, this approach would unfold into environmental policy.

Von Thünen at the margins. Fixing PES programmes in developing countries

Two of the most representative schemes of payments for ecosystem services (PES) were shaped by von Thünen's understanding of land use. Designed from the late 1990s to the early 2000s, the PES programmes of Costa Rica and Mexico are government-led, national-scale environmental projects focused on halting deforestation. The environmental rationale to preserve forest is the provision of ecosystem services, such as carbon sequestration or watershed protection. Both are based on the payment of economic incentives as a means to induce landowners to preserve forested land. In this section, I will focus on a specific mechanism included in the PES schemes of both countries, although I will refer only to the Mexican case: spatial targeting. This is one of the outcomes of the concern of policy makers to make an effective PES programme through directing the payments to specific forested areas. The environmental economists involved in the designing and assessment of the programme, some of them based in the World Bank, applied the assumptions of von Thünen's model of efficient land use to spatial targeting, and that is why I will provide more details on the logic of this model.

During the initial implementation period of the Mexican PES programme, the policy makers redesigned specific mechanisms of the programme due to the need to avoid the wastage of funds and improve the capacity of the monetary transactions to change the behaviour of forest owners with regards to land use (Alix-Garcia et al., 2008; Muñoz-Piña et al., 2011). As mentioned previously, spatial targeting aims to increase the efficiency of payments on the environment and the wealth of landowners by mapping the spatial distribution of ecosystem services and socio-economic conditions to focus economic incentives on specific locations. One of the tools for spatial targeting in the Mexican PES programme is the deforestation risk index whereby the priority forested areas for enrolment are identified as the ones located closer to the market, which is assumed to be a city. This index is based on a model of efficient land use rooted in von Thünen's notion of land rent. Just as World Bank economists have applied von Thünen's model to assess PES programmes following the example of Chomitz and Gray (see Pagiola, 2011), the Mexican policy makers designed the deforestation risk index drawing in the same assumptions (Muñoz-Piña et al., 2004, 2008).

Von Thünen developed a model of efficient land use drawing on the Ricardian notion of differential rent, that is,

> the difference in the price at which the produce of the poorest land must be sold in order to cover costs (the tenant-farmer's profit and interest being always included in the costs), and that at which the produce of the best land can be sold.
>
> *(Marx, 1982 [1851], p. 258)*

In other words, the marginal lands function as a parameter because any fertility above represents more productivity. Von Thünen (1966 [1876]) elaborated on this notion to stress that the price of an agricultural product depends on transports costs and thus on distance from the market. This fact, von Thünen argues, will influence the intensity of production. According to this author, the optimal character of an intensive system in one place, or an extensive system in another place, depends on the distance from the consuming market. Despite the differences between Ricardo and von Thünen, both highlight the role of the relative advantage of a place compared to the most marginal in terms of the variations of price, and the effects of this fact in the productivity of land (Ricardo) or land use (von Thünen). They argue that the productivity (Ricardo) and an optimal allocation of land (von Thünen), and the land price, can be increased if the costs of higher productivity, or transportation, are lower than the potential increase in the rent.

Von Thünen's model of optimal allocation of land uses, based on the notion of land rent described above, was applied by environmental economists to design a set of criteria for defining the areas where payments for conservation should be allocated. The spatial targeting model of land use by Pagiola (2011) and Muñoz et al. (2004) is based in von Thünen's idealization of the spatial organization of economic activities, mainly because the authors take into account transportation costs, as an element that must be considered in economic decisions related to land use, and because it reproduces the abstraction process of depicting economic activities in terms of points and lines with a monetary value. To paraphrase von Thünen: pure geometry set the foundation for practical geometry to tackle deforestation in a PES scheme.

The model for the PES programme compares the returns from three forms of land use: forestry (on-site benefits as logging and harvesting of non-timber products), agriculture, and conservation depicted as "off-site benefits [like] carbon sequestration [and] water protection" (Pagiola, 2011, p. 7). It assumes that returns are higher in areas closest to markets because transport costs are lower. It concludes that forestry is the most inefficient land use because, compared to the other two land uses, the returns for forestry are lower than a) agriculture in areas close to the market, and b) the conservation of ecosystem services (for example, watershed protection), if the value of the positive externalities of preserved forest is taken into account. This means that a profit seeker prefers to engage in agriculture instead of forestry as he gets closer to the market. Thus, deforestation is supposed to decrease in areas far from the market, but returns from off-site benefits, that is, ecosystem services, if higher than agriculture returns, will make deforestation fall even with urban proximity.

The model for the spatial targeting of PES evolved into a deforestation risk index presented in the form of maps that are used to assess the applications for PES by forests owners. The plots proposed for enrolment in the programme are rated according to criteria expressed graphically in a map, such as their location in relation to areas considered as poor in socio-economic terms, their proximity to a natural protected area, or the market. The effectiveness of these methods has been low; the assessments of the Mexican PES programme show that it is still reaching areas that would be preserved even in the absence of payments (Alix-Garcia et al., 2014). A recent policy-relevant study concluded "that the average risk of deforestation among enrolled properties remains somewhat below the national average across of forested lands" (p. 7).

At this point it is worth recalling the monologue in which von Thünen vindicates the status of "pure geometry" over "practical geometry". He wonders in a pedagogical tone: "What use can I make of studies which, like these, are based upon entirely ideal circumstances?" (von Thünen, 2009 [1863], p. 73). From the above account of the reproductions and applications of von Thünen's insights by orthodox economists, we can answer that the use of these models has influenced the way in which socio-environmental issues, such as deforestation, has been framed, that is, addressing environmental issues through techniques based on imaginary assumptions. This approach also reinforces the position that the environmental economist is the expert who is outside the processes he is looking at. Just like von Thünen in his monologue prescribes "pure geometry" to "the mere practitioner", and places himself out of politics, the policy makers of the Mexico PES scheme blame the organizations that promoted alternative criteria to allocate PES, and the "lack of understanding of the economics of deforestation among technical foresters" (Muñoz-Piña et al., 2011, p. 109) as the main obstacles to improve the efficiency of the programme. Environmental economists place themselves out of environmental politics.

Finally, I would argue that the "trial-and-error" approach to environmental policy ("practical geometry" to use von Thünen's metaphor) has underpinned the development of "pure geometry". In other words, without the failure of spatial targeting for fostering conservation in areas close to the city, which is caused by a territorial organization that reproduces an uneven development (that has not been analysed here), von Thünen's model would not be re-created and diffused through generations of economists who will learn and internalize the same idealist theoretical assumptions. This confirms Bukharin's statement: "Historically: the sciences 'grow' out of practice, the 'production of ideas' differentiates out of the 'production of things'" (Bukharin, 2002 [1931]).

Concluding remarks (and poliTICS-relevant recommendations)

The problem of mainstream environmental policy and the theories that endorse it is not abstraction itself. To a varying degree, all fields of knowledge rely on abstractions; this methodological process allows the separation of processes and facts from their contexts to understand the features that they share and make generalizations. This chapter is aimed at critically illustrating how the theorizations of neoclassical economics frame socio-environmental issues in terms of pure technical operations. For instance, regarding the conservation of forests in the context of competing land uses, the environmental economists stem from imaginary assumptions to define the criteria for the allocation of economic incentives that offsets opportunity costs. The apparently neutral technical advice by economists assumes that the behaviour of forests' owners relies on the calculation of opportunity costs and that all goods are private goods in a homogeneous space. This chapter shows that the level of abstraction in von Thünen's model leads to a "geometrical" understanding of environmental issues, where the deforestation risk in a plot is inferred from a set of points and lines associated with monetary values.

The chapter also depicts how this way of addressing land use change proliferated among economists in different contexts, and constituted a common tool in environmental economics applied to mainstream environmentalism. The relatively successful transfer of this product of science into mainstream environmental policy was exemplified with the Mexican PES programme. I use the word "relatively" because the development of market environmentalism is not a consistent political project by neoliberal governments, economists and other actors. It has been contended and it is failing to a large extent in halting environmental degradation. Nonetheless, as the case shows, the neoclassical paradigm among economists, who hold key positions to shape the environmental agenda, prevails.

How can we contribute to overcome this paradox? I consider that trying to encompass both the methodological and the sociological critique on market environmentalism is only one part of the problem. Political ecologists need to engage in politics to socialize the insights that may help to subvert the market-based perspectives that, despite its unprofitability, prevail in contemporary environmental governance. For political ecologists based in academia, one of the first steps to bridge the gap between theoretical cognition and practice is to act on the politics and economy of their universities. Even though the critique on mainstream environmentalism and its idealism is helpful: "The dispute over the reality or non-reality of thinking that is isolated from practice is a purely scholastic question" (Marx, 1992 [1845], p. 422).

One example, related to the topic of this chapter, of a field of action where academic political ecologists can contribute is the syllabus of economics programmes. Criticizing the academic indifference on the global financial crash of 2008, a group of economics students based in Manchester, UK, pointed out:

> The economics we were learning seemed separate from the economic reality that the world was facing … We examined how its mainstream had begun to be dominated by a certain kind of economics, often referred to as neoclassical, at the expense of other approaches.
>
> *(PCES, 2017)*

In 2011–2012, this group of students organized the Post-Crash Economics Society and demanded a reform in the curriculum of the University of Manchester to open a space for alternative approaches to economic thinking. Their claims were echoed in other universities and similar students societies were created by independent students. To varying degrees, these organizations intervene in the politics of the universities, making the students societies real platforms for participation in relevant education problems. Concerning political ecologists, the teaching of economics is important to environmental politics to the extent most of the environmental policy interventions are based on environmental economics, which incorporates the environment in a neoclassical economic analysis. In other words, to a large degree, environmental economics is market environmentalism's lab.

The Post-Crash Economics Society criticize the role of economists in political problems as follows: "the technical language and tools of economists obscure political judgements and subtly redefine the goals of political problems, in turn excluding the public and other important stakeholders from the policy process" (Earle et al., 2017, p. 9). Based on the above account of the relationship between environmental economics and deforestation, I consider that critical scholarship should aim not only to expose the contradictions that entail stemming from geometry to address global issues such as deforestation or climate change. It should also seek to explain why the experts that provide geometric advice are influential to the degree that their insights play a role in legitimizing market environmentalism. If political ecologists want to be consistent with the foundations of their field, that is to challenge apolitical ecologies, the first step is not to remain at the margins.

References

Adams, W.M. (2008) *Green Development Environment and Sustainability in a Developing World.* New York: Taylor & Francis.

Alix-Garcia, J., Aronson, G., Radeloff, V., Ramirez, C., Shapiro, E., Sims, K. and Yañez, P. (2014) *Environmental and Socioeconomic Impacts of Mexico's Payments for Ecosystem Services Program.* Environmental and Socioeconomic Impacts of Mexico's Payments for Ecosystem Services Program. 3ie Final Report, International Initiative for Impact Evaluation-CONAFOR, New Dehli.

Alix-Garcia, J., de Janvry, A., Sadoulet, E. and Torres, J.M. (2008) Lessons Learned from Mexico's Payment for Environmental Services Program. In Lipper, L., Sakuyama, T., Stringer, R. and Zilberman, D. (eds), *Payment for Environmental Services in Agricultural Landscapes.* Rome: FAO-Springer. Pp. 163–188.

Bukharin, N. (1927) *The Economic Theory of the Leisure Class.* New York: International Publishers.

Bukharin, N. (2002 [1931]) *Theory and Practice from the Standpoint of Dialectical Materialism,* Marxists.org. Available at: www.marxists.org/archive/bukharin/works/1931/diamat/ [Accessed 10 December 2016.]

Chomitz, K.M. and Gray, D.A. (1996) Roads, Land Use, and Deforestation: A Spatial Model Applied to Belize. *World Bank Economic Review* 10 (3), 487–512.

Dempsey, J. and Robertson, M.M. (2012) Ecosystem Services: Tensions, Impurities, and Points of Engagement with Neoliberalism. *Progress in Human Geography* 36(6), 758–779.

Dempsey, J. and Suarez, D.C. (2016) Arrested Development? The Promises and Paradoxes of "Selling Nature to Save It". *Annals of the American Association of Geographers* 106 (3), 653–671.

Earle, J., Moran, C. and Ward-Perkins, Z. (2017) *The Econocracy. The Perils of Leaving Economics to the Experts.* Manchester: Manchester University Press.

Hall, P. (1966) Introduction. In Hall, P. (ed.), *Von Thünen's Isolated State: An English Edition of Der istolierte Staat.* Oxford: Pergamon Press. Pp. xi–xliv.

Marx, K. (1982 [1851]) A Letter to Frederick Engels, London, 7 January 1851. *Marx and Engels Collected Works.* Lawrence & Wishart.

Marx, K. (1992 [1845]) Theses on Feuerbach. *Early Writings.* London: Penguin Books.

McAfee, K. and Shapiro, E.N. (2010) Payments for Ecosystem Services in Mexico: Nature, Neoliberalism, Social Movements, and the State. *Annals of the Association of American Geographers* 100 (3), 579–599.

Muñoz-Piña, C., Fernández, J.C., Jaramillo, L. and Esteva, G. (2004) Pixel Patterns of Deforestation in Mexico: 1993–2000. INE Working Paper Series, vol. 0401. Instituto Nacional de Ecología, Mexico.

Muñoz-Piña, C., Guevara, A., Torres, J.M. and Braña, J. (2008) Paying for the Hydrological Services of Mexico's Forests: Analysis, Negotiations and Results. *Ecological Economics* 65 (4), 725–736.

Muñoz-Piña, C., Rivera, M., Cisneros, A. and García, H. (2011) Challenges of the Targeting of the Payments for Environmental Services Programme in Mexico [Retos de la focalización del Programa de Pago por los Servicios Ambientales en México]. *Revista Española de Estudios Agrosociales y Pesqueros* (228), 87–113.

Pagiola, S. (2011) Using PES to Implement REDD. PES-Learning paper 2011–1, World Bank, Washington, D.C.

Post-Crash Economics Society (PCES) (2017) *The University of Manchester Post-Crash Economics Society* [Online]. Available at: www.post-crasheconomics.com/ [Accessed 29 May 2017.]

Samuelson, P.A. (1976) Economics of Forestry in an Evolving Society. *Economic Inquiry* 14, 466–492.

Samuelson, P.A. (2009) Thünen: An Economist ahead of His Times. In U. van Suntum (ed.), *The Isolated State in Relation to Agriculture and Political Economy. Part III: Principles for the Determination of Rent, the Most Advantageous Rotation Period and the Value of Stands of Varying Age in Pinewoods.* Hampshire: Palgrave. Pp. xii–xiv.

Schneider, R.R. (1995) *Government and the Economy on the Amazon Frontier.* Washington, D.C.: World Bank.

von Amsberg, J. (1994) *Economic Parameters of Deforestation.* Washington, D.C.: World Bank.

von Thünen, J.H. (1966 [1876]) The Isolated State. In P. Hall (ed.), *Von Thünen's Isolated State: An English edition of Der istolierte Staat.* Oxford: Pergamon Press.

von Thünen, J.H. (2009 [1863]) *The Isolated State in Relation to Agriculture and Political Economy. Part III: Principles for the Determination of Rent, the Most Advantageous Rotation Period and the Value of Stands of Varying Age Pinewoods.* New York: Palgrave Macmillan. Pp. 1–298.

13

NATURAL CAPITAL ACCOUNTING (NCA)

Roles in corporate environmental stewardship

Les Levidow

Introduction: valuing "natural capital" for what?

For several centuries nature has featured economic metaphors from anthropomorphic projections. In late 1700s Germany, "rational forestry" simplified the complex biological dynamics of forest stands as a scientific-managerial basis to maximize wood production for economic return (Scott, 1998, pp. 11–22). Market competition has been naturalized: "all organic beings are striving to seize on each place in the economy of nature" (Darwin, 1859, p. 90). This capitalist metaphor informed the new science of ecology: "the body of knowledge concerning the economy of nature . . . the study of all those complex interrelationships referred to by Darwin as the condition of the struggle for existence" (Haeckel, 1866, p. 9). Since the 18th century, claims on nature have cited shifting personifications, for example, as an organism, mechanism, market, constitutional lawyer, selective breeder and so forth (Williams, 1980). Such metaphors perform contending claims and so readily become disputed.

Likewise, financial metaphors have become prevalent in regulating natural resources since the 1990s. UN institutions have promoted tradeable instruments, such as carbon credits, biodiversity offsets and payments for ecosystem services. As a financial metaphor, "natural capital asset" highlights the source of ecosystem services on which economic activities depend (TEEB, 2008; UNEP, 2011, p. 16). Together they face threats of resource degradation, resulting from the economic "invisibility of nature". Natural capital stocks, for example, are "invisible engines of sustainability" (UNEP, 2011, p. ii). To render these assets more visible and thus protect them, natural capital accounting (NCA) has been elaborated in various ways.

The global justice movement has denounced such financial concepts as weapons of neoliberal globalization, arguing that the natural capital concept "serves to permit the commodification of nature" (BankTrack, 2012; People's Summit, 2012;

No to Biodiversity Offsetting, 2013; WDM, 2013). As a form of "nature pricing", natural capital accounting (NCA) ignores the communities who help to maintain ecosystem services; indeed, such concepts "obscure the social context" of resource flows and usage (Unmüßig et al., 2012, p. 28).

According to such critics, moreover, "natural capital" depoliticizes the issues: "This economization of nature changes how it is viewed and ultimately undermines political action, which really ought to be committed to public welfare and all nature's functions" (Unmüßig, 2014, p. 12). NCA avoids or displaces state responsibility for resource protection: good intentions around natural capital are entirely understandable, but reinforcing the idea that everything has a price will not engender the ability to treat the natural world differently . . . Overcoming the invisibility of nature would be better rectified through taxation, regulation and government intervention (Director of WDM, now Global Justice, NCI, 2015, p. 27).

As many critics note, resource degradation has worsened because extractive industrial development models have benefited some interests at the expense of others, meanwhile weakening regulatory controls (Apostolopoulou and Adams, 2015; Büscher et al., 2014; Heynen et al., 2007; Bresnihan, 2017). Market-type schemes purport to avoid or compensate for environmental harm, yet they help to weaken state regulation and enforcement. Put ominously, "the goal is to transform environmental legislation into tradable instruments", argues a Brazilian NGO, the BVRio Environmental Exchange (cited in Heinrich Böll Foundation, 2016). With such perspectives, critics have questioned the corporate interest in nature accounting, linked with tradeable permits.

By contrast to those schemes, natural capital accounting (NCA) has remained somewhat marginal to the wider controversy. NCA has been proposed for three different contexts: national policy frameworks for nature conservation, tradeable permits, and business strategies around resource dependencies (NCC, 2016). The latter is the focus of this article, which asks: amidst local conflicts over industrial activity, how does corporate NCA matter for the use and degradation of natural resources?

As a summary answer, this article argues that NCA informs corporate strategies for "green supply chains" and environmental stewardship. By identifying multistakeholder dependence on natural resources, corporate NCA casts local communities as fellow dependants on "shared assets". This multi-stakeholder process potentially marginalizes critics and depoliticizes resource conflicts. Thus, NCA warrants scrutiny from the environmental justice movement. This analysis draws on critical perspectives about neoliberal conservation agendas, as outlined next.

Neoliberal conservation agendas: critical perspectives

Financial instruments for natural-resource management have been theorized within broader concepts such as "free market environmentalism", "neoliberal conservation" or "neoliberalising nature". The latter involves the privatization and marketization of biophysical reality, with the state and civil society groups either facilitating this or regulating only the worst consequences. Ecological fixes are devised in the name of remaking, conserving or expanding nature (Castree, 2008, pp. 142–143, 150). Internal state contradictions are addressed "by off-loading responsibilities to the private sector and/or civil society groups", as if the latter provided environmental protection in lieu of interventionist states (pp. 146, 149).

As an early global scheme of nature accounting, the Kyoto Protocol created tradeable carbon credits, entitling permit-holders to pollute the atmosphere. When it became controversial, this scheme was denounced as commoditizing nature. Yet such schemes do not create novel surplus value: "emissions rights do have an exchange value and a use value, but they do not represent value" (Felli, 2014, p. 268). Tradeable credits, therefore, redistribute value. Hence, "the distribution and circulation of these entitlements through market-based mechanisms should not lead us to treat them as 'commodities', but rather as a form of rent" (p. 254). This relates to Marx's concept, "the price paid to the owner of natural forces or mere products of nature" for the right to use them, as necessary conditions of production – likewise, by analogy, a company's entitlement to pollute. The carbon-trading system arose from an inherent tension: governments across the world have faced the contradiction between the need to ensure the reproduction of the conditions of production (and of social reproduction), which would mandate drastic reductions in greenhouse gas (GHG) emissions, and the need to ensure that they retain capital within their boundaries, which generally requires as few regulations as possible (p. 258).

A cap on GHG emissions would restrict a key condition of production, so they were a focus of rival capitalist claims and thus rent-seeking. Although the Protocol set a political limit on global emissions, the distribution among producers "is regulated by the law of value", that is, by financial power, thus depoliticizing the global use of space and resources. This role complements the wider neoliberal project of "non-decision making in economic processes" by allocating resources according to investors' ability to pay rather than regulatory criteria (Felli, 2015, p. 655). Thus, the scheme sustains or even intensifies unequal power relations.

Tradeable permits exemplify a broader process that could be called "depoliticization by economization", whereby multiple environment values are reduced to a single unit of valuation (Adaman and Madra, 2014). As well documented, REDD+ forest credits have often intensified conflicts over natural resources and land use. Nevertheless, these schemes expand because they offer Corporate Social Responsibility (CSR) and marketing benefits to companies buying the carbon credits, such as Kering and Coca-Cola. Although the scheme brings extra reputational risks, companies seek carbon credits to support environmental claims for corporate supply chains or to offset risk from investments in potentially stranded carbon-intensive assets (Laing et al., 2015, pp. 3–4). Indeed, "green supply chain" is the new buzzword replacing "sustainable consumption", as firms recognize the need to protect their brands and sales through environmental claims such as "carbon neutrality" and "deforestation-free" (Kill, 2016, p. 114).

Analogous instruments have been devised for nature conservation. The 1992 Convention on Biological Diversity (CBD) was seen as potentially constraining business' access to natural resources, especially through regulatory limits and benefit-sharing arrangements. To avoid such constraints, business cooperated with non-governmental conservation organizations (NGCOs) to develop entrepreneurial strategies around "market mechanisms" for allocating access to sites of "nature as capital", for example, schemes paying for ecosystem services. Funds from US AID and the UN's Global Environmental Facility helped expand these roles of NGCOs, especially the International Union for Conservation of Nature (IUCN), World Wildlife Fund (WWF) and Conservation International (MacDonald, 2010).

Through joint biodiversity initiatives, NGCO-business partnerships have helped to give companies the imprimatur of environmental stewards. Meanwhile, NGCOs themselves have become corporate-like entities (Corson, 2010). Their contribution is recognized by companies, which seek such collaborations "as necessary risk management to protect their reputations and markets and as a way to open up new markets" (Robinson, 2012, p. 969).

Through the asset metaphor, nature is equated with financial investment and its returns and becomes a billable service provider (Sullivan, 2013). Valuing natural capital "makes nature legible by abstracting it from social and ecological contexts and making it subject, and productive of, new market contexts" (MacDonald and Corson, 2012, p. 159). Financial metaphors imply that "the environment can be considered, valued, and managed as an asset like any other" (Coffey, 2016, p. 215).

By highlighting and naturalizing a market return on investment, the asset-metaphor helps to promote specific types of economic activity and stakeholder participation. A survey of neoliberal conservation practices found a chameleon-like flexibility in creating "both environmentally and market-friendly subjects". Local people "are increasingly now being incorporated into conservation every time they conduct their new conservation-friendly livelihood activities". Many initiatives have been "working within the lives of rural people, changing their behaviour", especially by appealing to economic rationales (Holmes and Cavanagh, 2016, pp. 204, 206). Thus, market logics, linking economic and environmental benefits, play many potential roles in legitimizing resource access. Let us examine what this means for NCA.

Promoting the asset metaphor for nature

As a flexible metaphor, natural capital has been given diverse meanings and roles over several decades (for example, Pearce et al., 1989; MEA, 2005; Porritt, 2006). It was originally promoted as an extra persuasive tool for environmental protection. According to the UK environmentalist Jonathan Porritt, for example, "if there is any genuinely sustainable variant of capitalism, then it will need to work within the conceptual and linguistics conventions that people are now so familiar with", for example, natural capital (Porritt, 2006, p. 113).

For development theorists "natural capital" has meant a resource empowering community development for better livelihoods through sustainable development. Conversely, "human capital" enhances "natural capital" within a wider framework for analysing the institutional design and societal governance of natural resources.

A multi-faceted capital became a "ready metaphor" to capture the range of "enabling conditions" that development-conservation advocates may promote in order to achieve desired aims (Wilshusen, 2014, p. 129). Such metaphors highlighted various forms of labour and power relations, but these became obscured by later versions of natural capital.

Set up by the G7, The Economics of Ecosystems and Biodiversity (TEEB) studies have promoted natural capital evaluation, understanding natural resources as assets-stocks delivering flows of ecosystem services, analogous to financial capital yielding dividends. According to TEEB's problem-diagnosis, nature is the "GDP of the poor"; poverty is worsened by ecosystem loss. So this must be alleviated in order to ensure "the right of the world's poor to livelihood flows from nature which comprise half of their welfare or more" (TEEB, 2008, pp. 4–5, 31). As a plea for fairness, "social justice will be threatened if the world continues to deepen the gulf between those who have the use of ecological goods and services and those who do not" (p. 25).

In this perspective, ecosystem services flow from natural capital, seen as stocks or assets – separate from human activities, except for "maintenance and restoration costs" (TEEB, 2008, p. 32, diagram). Given that "you cannot manage what you do not measure", governments must promote "ecosystem-biodiversity accounting in physical and monetary terms" (pp. 6, 54). The TEEB initiative had been sponsored by the Convention on Biodiversity, whose 2010 Conference of Parties (COP) promoted several TEEB reports on a metaphorically resonant website, the Bank of Natural Capital. At the 2010 COP in Nagoya, natural-capital valuation was portrayed as a "win–win solution" for the environment, the economy and the poor.

In the TEEB and UNEP perspectives, natural capital acquires human-like powers to deliver services, thus anthropomorphically projecting financial assets on to nature: "In more economic terms, it can be said that ecosystem services flow from 'natural capital stocks' (also sometimes termed 'natural assets'), like interest or dividends from the financial stocks" (ten Brink et al., 2012, p. 5). Social relations in maintaining nature are reified as relations between things, by analogy with labour being reified by financial capital assets. This double-metaphor has been promoted for global development agendas: "The development path should maintain, enhance and, where necessary, rebuild natural capital as a critical economic asset and as a source of public benefits" (UNEP, 2011, p. 16). The "natural capital" metaphor has been taken up by some national policy frameworks and by the private sector.

Natural capital accounting (NCA) has been promoted for and by many business organizations, including the World Business Council for Sustainable Development (WBCSD). The strategic rationale links natural, financial and reputational assets of business. According to a UNEP report, "environmental stress tests" can inform company decisions on investment and supply chains. Such tests would help to avoid "disorderly market responses" to both financial and reputational threats, for example, from "the rise of the civil society divestment movement". It advised business that "environmental regeneration will need to be placed within the price system of the real economy" (UNEP, 2015, pp. 15, 4), implying little scope or need for improvement outside nature-pricing. Next let us examine business contexts for NCA.

Strategizing green supply chains versus business threats

Drawing on the "natural capital" metaphor, the new TEEB for Business Coalition sought a shift in corporate behaviour towards preserving natural and social capital. It formalized earlier collaborations of non-governmental conservation organisations (NGCOs) with business, now linking the WBCSD, the IUCN, the WWF and others. As a potential incentive for companies, it highlighted that environmental externalities must be further internalized to protect competitiveness (see Maxwell, 2013). On this rationale, NCA can anticipate future changes in a business's dependence on ESS and adjust its strategy accordingly.

TEEB for Business Coalition was expanded and rebranded as the National Capital Coalition (NCC). Again, the prevalent problem-diagnosis, "economic invisibility has been a major reason for the neglect of natural capital" (NCC, 2014, p. ii). The Coalition soon decided to draft a Natural Capital Protocol, "a comprehensive guide to measuring and valuing natural capital in business decision-making" (see NCC, 2015a). The Protocol would start by understanding the business case, impacts and dependencies, risks and opportunities. Such aims set the priorities for identifying relevant activities that would benefit from "ecosystem services".

What have been the drivers and benefits of such a standard Protocol? According to the NCC's first director, business wants to make "smarter" decisions. Ecosystem services are the Achilles' heel of the economy, so they must get their "ankles covered". By identifying potential impacts on natural capital, the Protocol will help management to make the right decisions (van der Gaag, 2014). Greater competition for resources "endangers corporation reputations and marketability of products" (CISL, 2015: 17). Some companies seek a first-mover advantage in securing their supply chains (NCC Director, interview, 1 May 2015).

The Protocol distinguishes between its putatively neutral methods and their specific application by each company. Such assumptions are shared by conservation experts jointly drafting the Protocol: The method must look with both lenses (society and business) at the same resources, without any moral judgement on choices. The valuation method aims to be neutral regarding any interpretation or application, even though neutrality may be difficult to achieve (interviews, Conservation Intl members of NCP's Technical Group, 23 June 2015). Likewise, the accounting methods are separable from ethical judgements (interview, WWF, 23 June 2015). Indeed, NGCOs see their role as ensuring value-neutral methods.

Despite the putative neutrality of NCA, some insiders emphasize its special relevance to market instruments. According to a business liaison staff member:

> . . . natural capital valuation could help with the tradable credits already in place. It could help current ones by carrying out a valuation exercise, e.g. of

restored wetlands to feed into a wetlands bank, or create potential for a new market.

(interview, NCC-WBCSD, 29 June 2015)

Likewise, "NCA can potentially play an important role in developing and implementing market-based instruments, such as payment for ecosystem services and biodiversity offset markets", according to a business consultancy (Spurgeon, 2014, p. 6).

Regardless of any such scheme, NCC member companies seek methods relevant to supply-chain and marketing strategies. The Protocol warns companies that their agro-food assets "could become stranded by threats to critical ecosystems" (NCC, 2016, p. 9, citing Oxford University, 2013). As a strategic response,

> businesses in the food and beverage sector can use natural capital assessments to inform decisions such as where to grow and invest capital, or withdraw and divest assets, or how to weigh environmental constraints for new or different business models.

(NCC, 2016, p. 56)

Competitive advantage includes "intangible benefits", for example, "reputational benefits from own-brand differentiation" (ibid.). According to the NCC, the Natural Capital Protocol (NCP) has been elaborated through exemplary practices and pilot studies by several companies (especially Olam, Kering, and Coca-Cola). Let us examine each company's reputational risks which generated interest in the NCP, complementing its CSR strategy.

The agro-food conglomerate Olam International advertises its environmental policy as "Growing Responsibly". Yet its plantations were being criticised for deforestation and land rights abuses (Oxfam Australia, 2014, p. 40; FERN, 2016, p. 11). In response to such criticism, it became the first company globally to complete a High Conservation Value (HCV) assessment according to the HCV Resource Network System. Olam aimed for 100% compliance with the Roundtable on Sustainable Palm Oil certification by 2020. The company's technical partners include the WWF (Olam, 2016, p. 6). As one of the NCC's business engagement partners, in 2015 Olam helped to develop and test the NCP's Food and Beverage Sector Guide led by the IUCN (ibid: NCC, 2016). After Olam's discussion with its NGO critics, especially the World Resources Institute and Mighty Earth, their protest campaign was suspended, and likewise any further land clearing of Gabon's forests for palm and rubber plantations. Meanwhile they would jointly find 'common ground . . . on a sustainable and prosperous path forward' (Mighty Earth, 2017).

Kering, a large group encompassing textiles and luxury goods, underwent reputational problems in the early 2000s. Its subsidiary Puma faced NGO protest for causing environmental degradation and labour exploitation. Puma soon took remedial measures on both issues; these became precedents for the entire Kering Group of companies (Baumann-Pauly et al., 2016). For its public relations strategy, one subsidiary funded a film warning against ecological damage, released on World Environment Day, while also cross-promoting environmentally sustainable products (La Redoute, 2009; Tarpley, 2016, pp. 107–108). In parallel, Kering's Gucci Group decided to eliminate all paper made from Indonesian rainforests and plantations, in partnership with the Rainforest Action Network (Kering Group, 2009).

In 2012, Kering set ambitious environmental targets for 2016, for example, as regards leather traceability, gold sourcing, water pollution, chemical use and carbon emissions. To guide its efforts, the company developed "economic profit and loss" (EP&L) methods. A specific focus was the company's Puma brand of denim products; its Re-Cut Project redesigns the process "to waste less, recycle more and steer our materials through a more efficient chain". This brand piloted NCA methods, which were later incorporated into the NCC's framework: "We have now fully integrated this pioneering natural capital accounting tool into our business . . . as we explore different options to improve the sustainability of our supply chain." Using such methods, the Group achieved a 10% reduction in impact intensity from 2012 to 2015 (Kering Group, 2015, pp. 3, 7). Here the reputational stakes remain implicit.

Coca-Cola has faced even greater reputational damage from complicity with death squads (Killer Coke, 2004) as well as for "drinking" the world dry through large-scale water extraction (War on Want, 2007). From the latter wake-up call, the company announced an aim to replenish all of its products water use by 2020. In 2015, the company announced that it had nearly achieved this goal, thus making its production "water neutral" (Kent, 2016). The calculations integrate the methods of Natural Capital and ESS to evaluate water replenishment projects: "Our projects provide benefits" for enhancing the company's role in water stewardship (Denkstatt and Coca-Cola Company, 2016, p. 8).

To avoid water stress, Coca-Cola devises a Source Water Protection Plan (SWPP), for which "we engage the community, local government, civil society and other businesses to look for ways to collaborate" (Coca-Cola, 2016). This programme is carried out "with local communities and governments and other respected third-party partners" (Coca-Cola, 2015), for example, WWF and Nature Conservancy. Thus, again NGCOs play a crucial role in legitimizing the expert methods for identifying multi-stakeholder dependence on natural resources, as a basis for a company to claim environmental stewardship. Despite these efforts, in 2015 several Indian village councils demanded that the company stop using groundwater, and then India's National Green Tribunal ordered the company to close plants that were violating environmental laws (India Resource, 2016). Coca-Cola continues to undergo financial and reputational damage, despite its CSR efforts.

Depoliticizing resource conflicts?

As shown in the examples above, global business has sought NGCOs as partners for many environmental initiatives, especially those related to NCA. In this process, the International Union for Conservation of Nature (IUCN) has played a key role. As advertised at IUCN's World Conservation Congress: "business is increasingly recognized as part of the solution, and NGOs are more than ever willing to discuss and collaborate with business" (see WBCSD, 2012). The IUCN not only expects that the Natural Capital Protocol will "help businesses understand the risks and opportunities that arise from accounting for natural capital in their decision-making processes" but also projects its social and environmental aims on to business: "we will ensure that the Protocol becomes a valuable and critical tool for the business community to contribute to IUCN's mission of a just world that values and conserves nature" (IUCN, 2014).

The IUCN also played a central role in the Natural Capital Protocol, which elaborates a method for its Business Engagement Partners (BEPs) to identify "natural capital impacts and dependencies across a supply chain". It emphasizes prospects "to unlock hidden value in the supply chain", especially by reframing resource issues around "commercial opportunity" and creating "shared value with stakeholders" (NCC, 2015a). Such an approach is expected to enhance the reputation of BEPs and thus their social "licence to operate" (NCC, 2015b).

Indeed, the financial stakes are reputational, given that companies remain vulnerable to public protest. Relative to other environmental approaches,

> natural capital gets more traction with finance departments. At one time, 80% of companies' value was tangible, i.e. on the books. But now it's only 20%; the rest depends on its reputation. Through natural capital accounting, we become aware of negative impacts and how to fix any problems. Otherwise outsiders will push us to do so.
>
> *(NCC Director, interview, 1 May 2015)*

This warning is reinforced by nature conservation groups: "A company may face blockages from consumer or community action", among other reasons for its decision-making to consider natural capital implications (interview, WWF, 23 June 2015).

Threats and opportunities for business have been elaborated by several expert reports. When companies seek to grow, they encounter several limits, including natural capital costs imposed through regulation, social campaigns and shortages. A company can turn risks into business opportunities by reconsidering supply-chain strategies, towards a "resilient sourcing strategy" and "stewardship" interventions (Trucost, 2016, p. 2). By positioning "their business for a low carbon, resource efficient future", they can "demonstrate the shared value they are creating for stakeholders and customers" (p. 12).

According to the report's lead author, business interest in natural capital has several motives and aims:

> NCA brings all natural resources within a common framework . . . The accounting methods focus on tangible but non-proprietary assets; these are more at risk and less under a company's control than proprietary ones. NCA helps a company's Sustainability Unit to obtain engagement from its Finance Unit, e.g. by monetising resource dependencies, or by signalling potential

jeopardy of its social licence to operate. Such methods have gained much interest from companies in resource "hot spots", especially societal conflicts around water, such as Coca Cola in India or the Columbian coffee industry after a long civil war.

(interview, Trucost, 26 August 2016)

Thus, NCA can inform company strategies to gain a stewardship reputation by engaging community representatives and restructuring supply chains.

It is important to point out here that accounting methods describe natural resources through a universal "equivalency". In essence, environmental effects become "'profit and loss"; biodiversity becomes a "portfolio" conferring resilience on ecosystems, almost as if these were proprietary assets. In the name of contextual-izing environmental issues, other stakeholders are relegated to impacts of potential damage or scarcity (CISL-Kering-NCP, 2016). In the Coca-Cola example above, nature-accounting likewise turns water into homogeneous quantities that can be substituted and replenished, separately from community maintenance, thus render-ing the latter invisible; water becomes a natural capital "asset".

By contrast, one TEEB report highlighted ontological tensions inherent in NCA. "If valuing biological resources is a tool to improve *in situ* conservation, it assumes that local stakeholders have sufficient incentives to maintain a given ecosystem against other competing uses", so contradictory drivers warrant atten-tion. Yet nature accounting readily separates people from nature by "simplifying its meaning and value to human societies" (Brondízio and Gatzweiler, 2010). This caveat has been echoed by some NGCO experts who, for example, argued that "the valuation methods should make visible the labour [of natural capital mainte-nance], especially in a local context, though the relations can get buried in multiple metrics" (interviews, Conservation Intl members of NCP's Technical Group, 23 June 2015). Indeed, ecosystem services are generally attributed to natural "assets", while communities protecting common readily become invisible.

Likewise, as recognized by some participants, economic language has political limitations for fairness issues: "the capital metaphor has the disadvantage that it cannot encompass shared resources, and sometimes capital is destroyed. . . . There is a justice challenge if multinational companies value natural capital only for its dividends, at the expense of indigenous people and small businesses" (interview, NCC ex-Director, 10 March 2015). Indeed, tensions arise around "shared assets", given that many uses are conflictual. Yet the NCC's documents emphasize win–win scenarios, as if corporate investment in natural capital will necessarily protect ecosystem services and their multiple uses.

Conclusion: natural capital accounting for greening supply chains

Giving a price to nature has become a contentious means of supposedly protecting natural resources. Controversy has focused mainly on tradeable credits, which offer proprietary rights to pollute or to access resources. These instruments facilitate business strategies for rent-seeking, that is, privileged access to natural resources, while depoliticizing environmental conflicts. Such schemes complement efforts at weakening environmental regulation and/or reducing it to tradeable permits.

By contrast, natural capital accounting (NCA) confers no proprietary rights and shows little sign of being applied for such a purpose. Advocated for protecting the natural resource base, NCA has been criticized for commoditizing nature. Yet the latter role has remained elusive and seems a remote prospect. So what role may NCA play?

Some of the same companies have taken up tradeable credits and NCA and may have different but complementary roles within CSR strategies. NCA informs corporate decisions about greening supply chains, in turn supporting claims for environmental stewardship (for example, Denkstatt and Coca-Cola Company, 2016; Trucost, 2016; as theorized by Corson, 2010). As a key incentive, business access to natural resources faces several threats (for example, over-exploitation, rival stakeholder claims, climate change, more stringent regulation and reputational damage). These may jeopardize basic conditions of its production process, analogous with restrictions on GHG emissions (Felli, 2014). NCA frameworks help to anticipate a company's future resource dependencies, conflicts, vulnerabilities and reputational damage. NCA identifies the "ecosystem services" and thus "shared assets" on which companies and local communities alike depend, thus making some aspects of nature more visible. Given communities' roles in maintaining the natural resource base as a commons their roles are readily fetishized as inherent properties or "services" of "'natural capital assets". A local community thereby becomes (at most) a fellow beneficiary and dependant of ecosystem services.

Through that process, a company may better legitimize its efforts to manage "shared assets", for example, to appropriate resources *as if* they were proprietary. It may reconsider its strategies for supply chains and multi-stakeholder relationships. It may relocate, limit or remediate resource degradation, in strategic ways enhancing their competitive advantage and claim for environmental stewardship. An NGCO-business partnership may help incorporate community representatives into a company's economic logic, thus marginalizing critics of company agendas. Such potential roles exemplify forms of neoliberalzing nature, that is, "off-loading responsibilities to the private sector and/or civil society groups" (Castree, 2008). In such ways, the "natural capital" metaphor can serve to depoliticize societal conflicts around natural resources (cf. Holmes and Cavanagh, 2016). Each outcome remains contingent on specific actors, potentially intensifying resource conflicts (e.g. Cola Cola) or else softening them (Kering and Olam).

What are the practical implications for environmental justice groups? NCA methods have been informing corporate strategies for "green supply-chains" within broader strategies to strengthen and stabilize access to natural resources. Such strategies have endemic tensions, for example, around community roles in maintaining natural resources and thus proprietary claims for "shared assets". Although NCA may help companies to depoliticize societal conflicts, the overall process may inadvertently politicize them. Such tensions offer opportunities for interventions that would highlight community-dependent commons, as a basis for alliances promoting different economic metaphors and development pathways.

Acknowledgements

Helpful editorial comments were received from Romain Felli, Jutta Kill, Larry Lohmann and the two editors of this volume.

References

Adaman, F. and Madra, Y. (2014) Understanding Neoliberalism as Economization: The Case of the Environment. In Y. Atasoy (ed.), *Global Economic Crisis and the Politics of Diversity*. London: Palgrave Macmillan. Pp. 29–51.

Apostolopoulou, E. and Adams, W.M. (2015) Neoliberal Capitalism and Conservation in the Post-crisis Era: The Dialectics of "'Green'" and "'Un-green'" Grabbing in Greece and the UK. *Antipode* 47, 15–35.

BankTrack (2012) Position on the Natural Capital Declaration. www.banktrack.org/show/news/banktrack_position_on_the_natural_capital_declaration

Baumann-Pauly, D., Scherer, A.G. and Palazzo, G. (2016) Managing Institutional Complexity: A Longitudinal Study of Legitimacy Strategies at a Sportswear Brand Company. Journal of Business Ethics 137, 31–51.

Bresnihan, P. (2017) *Valuing Nature – Perspectives and Issues*, Research Series Paper No. 11: Dublin: National Economic and Social Council.

Brondízio, E.S. and Gatzweiler, F.W. (2010) Socio-cultural Context of Ecosystem and Biodiversity Valuation. In P. Kumar (ed.), *The Economics of Ecosystems and Biodiversity Ecological and Economic Foundations*. London and Washington, D.C. Pp. 150–181: Earthscan, www.teebweb.org/our-publications/teeb-study-reports/ecological-and-economic-foundations

Büscher, B., Dressler, W. and Fletcher, R. (2014) *Nature™ Inc. Environmental Conservation in the Neoliberal Age.* Tuscon: University of Arizona.

Castree, N. (2008) Neoliberalising Nature: The Logics of Deregulation and Reregulation. *Environment and Planning A* 40, 131–152.

CISL (Cambridge Institute for Sustainability Leadership) (2015) *Doing Business with Nature: Opportunities from natural capital.* Cambridge Institute for Sustainability Leadership, Report by the Natural Capital Leaders Platform, Available at: https://www.cisl.cam.ac.uk/resources/publication-pdfs/doing-business-with-nature.pdf

CISL-Kering-NCP (2016) *Biodiversity and Ecosystem Services in Corporate Natural Capital Accounting: Synthesis Report.* Cambridge: Cambridge Institute for Sustainability Leadership.

Coca-Cola (2015) Collaborating to Replenish the Water We Use. Available at: www.coca-colacompany.com/stories/collaborating-to-replenish-the-water-we-use

Coca-Cola (2016) Mitigating Water Risk for Communities and for Our System. Available at: www.coca-colacompany.com/stories/mitigating-water-risk-for-communities-and-for-our-system

Coffey, B. (2016) Unpacking the politics of natural capital and economic metaphors in environmental policy discourse, *Environmental Politics* 25:2, 203–222.

Corson, C. (2010) Shifting environmental governance in a neoliberal world: US AID for conservation. *Antipode* 42 (3), 576–602.

Darwin, C. (1859) *On the Origin of Species by Means of Natural Selection.* London: J. Murray.

Denkstatt and Coca-Cola Company (2016) Natural Capital Accounting: The Coca Cola Water Replenishment Program. Available at: http://naturalcapitalcoalition.org/wp-con tent/uploads/2016/07/Denkstatt_Natural_Capital_Accounting.pdf

Felli, R. (2014) Climate Rent. *Historical Materialism* 22, 251–280.

Felli, R. (2015) Environment, Not Planning: The Neoliberal Depoliticisation of *Environmental* Policy by Means of Emissions Trading. Environmental Politics 24 (5), 641–660.

FERN (2016) *Financing Land Grabs and Deforestation: the role of EU banks and investors.* Brussels: FERN.

Haeckel, E. (1866) *Generelle morphologie der organismen.* Berlin: G. Reimer.

Heinrich Böll Foundation (2016) *A New Nature in the Wake of the Green Economy,* New Economy of Nature Programme. Available at: www.boell.de/en/2016/10/10/new-nature-wake-green-economy?dimension1=ds_oekonomie_natur_en

Heynen, N., McCarthy, J., Prudham, S. and Robbins, P. *(2007) Neoliberal Environments. False Promises and Unnatural Consequences.* London: Routledge.

Holmes, G. and Cavanagh, C.J. (2016) A review of the social impacts of neoliberal conservation: Formations, inequalities, contestations, *Geoforum* 75, 199–209.

India Resource (2016) Campaign to Hold Coca-Cola Accountable. Available at: www. indiaresource.org/campaigns/coke/index.html

International Union for Conservation of Nature (IUCN) (2014) IUCN Leads the Way towards Valuing Nature in Business. Available at: www.iucn.org/?uNewsID=17183

Kent, M. (2016) Our Water Wake-up Call; What Will be Yours? 9 September. [CEO, Coca-Cola]. Available at: http://naturalcapitalcoalition.org/our-water-wake-up-call-what-will-be-yours/

Kering Group (2009) Gucci Group Commits to Protecting Indonesia's Rainforests. Available at: www.kering.com/en/press-releases/gucci_group_commits_to_protecting_indo nesias_rainforests

Kering Group (2015) *Environmental Profit & Loss (E&PL): 2015 Group Results.* Available at: www.kering.com/en/sustainability/news/natural_capital_protocol_launch

Kill, J. (2016) *The Kasigau Corridor REDD+ Project in Kenya: A Crash Dive for Althelia Climate Fund.* Re:Common. Available at: www.recommon.org and Counter Balance, www. counter-balance.org

Killer Coke (2004) http://killercoke.org

La Redoute (2009) La Redoute soutient le film «Home». Available at: www.kering.com/ sites/default/files/sites/default/files/press-release/CP_LaRedoute_HOME.pdf

Laing, T., Taschini, L. and Palmer, C. (2015) *Understanding the Demand for REDD+ Credits.* Centre for Climate Change Economics and Policy Working Paper No. 218. Grantham Research Institute on Climate Change and the Environment Working Paper No. 193. www.lse.ac.uk/GranthamInstitute/publication/understanding-the-demand-for-redd-credits/

MacDonald, K.I. (2010) The Devil is in the (Bio)diversity: Private Sector "E'ngagement"' and the Restructuring of Biodiversity Conservation. *Antipode* 42 (3), 513–550.

MacDonald, K.I. and Corson, E. (2012) '"TEEB Begins Now"': A Virtual Moment in the Production of Natural Capital. *Development and Change* 43 (1), 159–184.

Maxwell, D. (2013) Q & A with Dr Dorothy Maxwell, Director of TEEB for Business Coalition. Available at: www.accountingforsustainability.org/community/dialogues/q-a-with-dr-dorothy-maxwell-director-of-the-teeb-for-business-coalition/

MEA (2005) Millennium Ecosystem Assessment, *Ecosystems and Human Well-being: Synthesis.* Island Press, Washington, DC.

Mighty Earth (2017) Olam and Mighty Earth agree to collaborate on Forest Conservation and Sustainable Agriculture in Highly Forested Countries, 21 February. Washington, D.C.: Mighty Earth, http://www.mightyearth.org/olam-and-mighty-earth-agree-to-collaborate/

Natural Capital Coalition (NCC) (2014) *Valuing Natural Capital in Business. Taking Stock: Existing Initiatives and Applications.* Available at: https://naturalcapitalcoalition.org/wp-content/uploads/2016/07/Valuing_Nature_in_Business_Part_2_Taking_Stock_WEB.pdf.

Natural Capital Coalition (NCC) (2015a) *Developing the Natural Capital Protocol and Sector Guides for Business.* Available at: https://naturalcapitalcoalition.org/protocol/sector-guides/

Natural Capital Coalition (NCC) (2015b) *The Natural Capital Protocol: Feedback Report from Business Engagement Partner Interviews.* Available at: https://naturalcapitalcoalition.org/wp-content/uploads/2015/06/Natural-Capital-Coalition-Business-Engagement-Partner-Interview-Report.pdf

Natural Capital Coalition (NCC) (2016) *Natural Capital Protocol: Food and Beverage Sector Guide.* Available at: http://naturalcapitalcoalition.org/wp-content/uploads/2016/07/NCC_FoodAndBeverage_WEB_2016-07-12.pdf

Natural Capital Initiative (NCI) (2015) *Natural Capital Initiative 2015: Valuing our Life Support Systems 2014. Summit Summary Report.* Available at: www.naturalcapitalinitiative.org.uk/wp-content/uploads/2015/06/Valuing-our-Life-Support-Systems-summit-report.pdf

No to Biodiversity Offsetting! (2013) http://no-biodiversity-offsets.makenoise.org/

Olam (2016) *Corporate Responsibility and Sustainability Report 2015.* Singapore: Olam International, http://olamgroup.com/wp-content/uploads/2014/02/16395-Sustainability-Report-2016-Exec-summary_V17_20p_lowres.pdf

Oxfam Australia (2014) *Banking on Shaky Ground: Australia's Big Four Banks and Land Grabs.* Carlton, Victoria, Australia: Oxfam Australia.

Oxford University (2013) *Stranded Assets in Agriculture: Protecting Value from Environment-Related Risks.* Stranded Assets Programme, Smith School of Enterprise and the Environment. Available at: www.smithschool.ox.ac.uk/research-programmes/stranded-assets/Stranded%20Assets%20Agriculture%20Report%20Final.pdf

Pearce, D., Markandya, A., Barbier, E. (1989) *Blueprint for a Green Economy.* London: Earthscan.

People's Summit (2012) Final Declaration, People's Summit at Rio+20 for Social and Environmental Justice in defence of the commons, against the commodification of life, https://globalforestcoalition.org/wp-content/uploads/2012/07/PeoplesSummit-Final Declaration-ENG.pdf

Porritt, J. (2006) *Capitalism as if the World Matters.* London: Earthscan.

Robinson, J.G. (2012) Common and Conflicting Interests in the Engagements between Conservation Organizations and Corporations. *Conservation Biology* 26 (6), 967–977.

Scott, J.C. (1998) Seeing Like a State: How Certain Schemes to Improve the Human Condition Have Failed. New Haven: Yale University.

Spurgeon, J.P.G. (2014) *Comparing Natural Capital Accounting Approaches, Data Availability and Data Requirements for Businesses, Governments and Financial Institutions: A Preliminary Overview.* Final report to the EU Business and Biodiversity Platform, performed under the ICF contract.

Sullivan, S. (2013) Banking Nature? The Spectacular Financialisation of Environmental Conservation. *Antipode* 45 (1), 198–217.

Tarpley, D.B. 2016. *The Compendium Veribellum: Ruminations on the Written Word from the Realm of the Cabbage King.* Fattafinga Productions.

The Economics of Ecosystems and Biodiversity (TEEB) (2008) *The Economics of Ecosystems and Biodiversity: An Interim Report*, edited by Pavan Sukhdev, Study Leader, Brussels:

European Commission. Available at: http://ec.europa.eu/environment/nature/biodi versity/economics/pdf/teeb_report.pdf

ten Brink, P., Mazza L., Badura T., Kettunen M. and Withana S. (2012) *Nature and its Role in the Transition to a Green Economy*. TEEB. Available at: www.teebweb.org/wp-content/ uploads/2013/04/Nature-Green-Economy-Full-Report.pdf

Trucost (2016) *Growing Business Value in an Environmentally Challenged Economy*.

United Nations Environment Programme (UNEP) (2011) *Towards a Green Economy: Pathways to Sustainable Development and Poverty Eradication*. Available at: www.unep.org/ greeneconomy/Portals/88/documents/ger/ger_final_dec_2011/Green%20Econo myReport_Final_Dec2011.pdf#

United Nations Environment Programme (UNEP) (2015) *Pathways to Scale: Aligning the Financial System with Sustainable Development*. Available at: http://unepinquiry.org/wp-content/uploads/2015/04/Aligning_the_Financial_System_with_Sustainable_Develop ment_3_Pathways_to_Scale.pdf

Unmüßig, B. (2014) *On the Value of Nature: The Merits and Perils of a New Economy of Nature*. Berlin: Heinrich Böll Foundation.

Unmüßig, B., Sachs, W. and Fatheuer, T. (2012) *Critique of the Green Economy*. Brussels: Heinrich Böll Foundation. Available at: www.boell.eu/downloads/Critique_of_the_ Green_Economy.pdf

Van der Gaag, P. (2014) Protecting the Achilles Heel of our Economy, speech at Natural Capital Initiative (NCI) conference, November. Available at: www.youtube.com/ watch?v=U4W0w31r_cw

War on Want (2007) Coca-Cola: Drinking the World Dry. Available at: www.waronwant. org/media/coca-cola-drinking-world-dry

WDM (2013) World Forum on Natural Capital: The Great Nature Sale. [Global Justice Now] Available at: www.globaljustice.org.uk/sites/default/files/files/resources/nature_ sale_briefing.pdf

Williams, R. (1980) Ideas of Nature. In R. Williams, *Problems in Materialism and Culture*. London: Verso. Pp. 67–85.

Wilshusen, P.R. (2014) Capitalising Conservation/Development: Dissimulation, Misrecognition and the Erasure of Power. In B. Büscher, W. Dressler and R. Fletcher (eds), *Environmental Conservation in the Neoliberal Age*. Tucson, AZ: University of Arizona. Pp. 127–157.

World Business Council for Sustainable Development (WBCSD) (2012) *Key Highlights: WBCSD at IUCN's World Conservation Congress*, World Business Council for Sustainable Development, Jeju, South Korea, 6–15 September 2012.

14

OFFSETTING FOR WHOM?

Re:Common

Introduction

Corporations involved in extractive industries, industrial agriculture and construction of large-scale infrastructure, International Financial Institutions, such as the World Bank and the European Bank for Reconstruction and Development, international conservation NGOs and a growing number of governments are increasingly employing a strategy known as "biodiversity offsetting". They claim that this will help protect biological diversity because for every hectare of land that is destroyed through their operations, the biodiversity related to another hectare of land will be protected or restored elsewhere (World Rainforest Movement & Re:Common, 2016). Thus, by using offset metrics losses of biodiversity at one place would be compensated by protecting or restoring an "equivalent" amount of biodiversity somewhere else.

Most offset projects have, as direct consequence, the restriction of local access and use of the land, with the underlying reason that projects' developers have to demonstrate that there is an improvement in the way that land is being used solely due to the offset project. In most cases, the implementation of biodiversity offsetting schemes is fiercely advocated by projects' developers and sponsors, as an antidote to the "'irrational'", "'undiscriminate'" and "'inefficient'" traditional use of land by communities, whom there is a structural incentive to blame for the biodiversity degradation that the offsets are supposed to counter. In the same cases, income-generating alternatives to alleviate the loss of access to the land used for offset projects are promised but do not materialize, while restrictions are put in place that limit communities' ability to self-sustain.

Examples from the ground demonstrate that biodiversity offsets eventually result in a double land grab, because land is taken away by corporations from communities not only for the mine or the plantation or infrastructure development, but also for the area they plan to use for the biodiversity offset project, and the damaging effects are directly experienced by communities living on both sites.

This article looks into the case study of a biodiversity offsetting project implemented by the mining company Rio Tinto: the QMM in Madagascar. A reference is also made to another case study of a biodiversity offsetting project by Rio Tinto, the Oyu Tolgoy in Mongolia. The article explores the construction of the Rio Tinto '"Net Positive Impact"' narrative and then continues with some questions about the purpose of measuring in offsetting. It eventually calls for a re-thinking of the role that NGOs, activists and engaged academia could play in relation to a complex situation framed to allow "turbo-capitalist" extraction from communities and nature.

The conclusion addresses a fundamental question of justice. It highlights the need to understand that corporations are using market-based instruments, like biodiversity offsetting, to find a new social licence to destroy the common wealth while leveraging the role of the State to ensure that public opposition will not stop the destruction. We furthermore argue that the creation of new laws allows environmental destruction to proceed through the use of compensation mechanisms, like biodiversity offsetting, obscuring the existence of unfair power relations and the violation of basic rights of the poorest. The inevitably partisan question for activists and engaged academics that this chapter raises is: which side are they on?

The case of QMM in Madagascar: one telling example for all

The Rio Tinto QMM biodiversity offset project in the Anosy region of southeastern Madagascar, one of the most biologically and culturally diverse islands in the world, is probably the most widely advertised offset project in the mining sector. It is intended to compensate for biodiversity loss resulting from the destruction of a unique and rare coastal forest at Rio Tinto QMM's ilmenite mining site at Fort Dauphin, also in the Anosy region, by introducing restrictions to local forest use in Bemangidy-Ivohibe, some 50 kilometres to the north of the mining site.

A joint Re:Common and World Rainforest Movement (WRM) field investigation in September 2015 aimed to collect the views of villagers living in the vicinity of one of the three sites of the QMM project. In particular, we visited communities living near one of the three sites that make up the Rio Tinto QMM biodiversity offset plan for the company's ilmenite mine in Fort Dauphin.

Re:Common is a collective engaged in investigation and public campaigning against corruption and destruction of territories in Italy, Europe and the rest of the world. We denounce and oppose the consolidation of the extractivist society, rooted in the systemic extraction of wealth from the territories, in the dispossession of communities and the impoverishment of billions of people globally.[1]

The World Rainforest Movement (WRM) is an initiative set up in 1986 by a group of activists from different countries to facilitate, support and reinforce the struggle against deforestation and land grabbing in countries with forests and forest-dependent communities.[2]

We together are among the civil society organizations that in 2013 promoted and signed a declaration to "Stop Biodiversity Offsetting" signed by hundreds of grassroots and civil society groups globally. We felt the urgency to meet the communities on the frontline of new biodiversity offsetting projects, and understand with them the real implications of this false solution to biodiversity loss caused by the expansion of extractivism.

Our field investigation found that the reality around the offset site we visited is very different from the picture presented in the glossy brochures that have been distributed internationally. In particular, subsistence livelihoods of villagers are made even more precarious by the creation of the biodiversity offset. Interviews with villagers confirmed that restrictions on the forest use had been imposed without negotiation and with little regard for the fact that until then the forest had been almost the unique source of survival for the people of the area. Income-generating alternatives to alleviate the loss of access to the forest had been promised but have yet to materialize, while severe restrictions on community forest use are already in place. A meeting with conservation NGOs in charge of implementation revealed also that ethically deplorable methods have been used to ensure compliance with these restrictions (more in World Rainforest Movement & Re:Common, 2016).

Residents of the village of Antsotso in particular are left in a dire situation as a result of the Rio Tinto QMM biodiversity offset. They lost the land used to grow their staple food, manioc, at the edge of the forest. The only place left for them to grow manioc now are nearby sand dunes. Manioc production in the sand dunes is not going well, and new fields had to be established that require two hours' walking from the village along a narrow strip of sandy soil along the beach to reach them. Yields are poor due to the sandy soils, which are not suitable for the basic food production that the community needs. Access to the staple source of protein, fish caught in the lagoons and ocean along the coast, is also jeopardized because restrictions on forest use mean that villagers have no access to trees needed to carve canoes to replace worn ones no longer suitable to take out on the water. As a result of the Rio Tinto biodiversity offset project at Bemangidy-Ivohibe, families with no cash income to buy food are left without sufficient food to feed their families.

The biodiversity offset linked to the Rio Tinto QMM ilmenite mine in Madagascar has been widely advertised as a biodiversity offset model, but what we found at the site was anything but exemplary. The claim by Rio Tinto and its partners that this biodiversity offset initiative could contribute to a "Net Positive Impact" on biodiversity in the region affected by the QMM ilmenite mine is misleading, to say the least, and the forest restrictions imposed on local communities are raising serious human rights, health and food insecurity issues at the biodiversity offset site. A further field investigation carried out one year later by Re:Common in the same area, in September 2016, demonstrated that the situation is far from improving. Daily survival for the villagers is becoming increasingly challenging, and this is starting to create a serious climate of social unrest in the area.

Rio Tinto and the construction of its Net Positive Impact narrative

Rio Tinto is a British–Australian mining corporation with headquarters in London, UK. It is involved in the mining of iron ore, copper, bauxite, uranium, coal and diamonds on six continents, and conflicts associated with Rio Tinto mining operations are many. Rio Tinto's corporate sales in 2015 (approximately $34.8 billion) were more than three times bigger than the gross domestic product (GDP) of Madagascar in the same year.

It was back in 2004 at the Third IUCN[3] World Conservation Congress in Bangkok that the Rio Tinto Group went far beyond a show of a great interest in biodiversity offsets, and launched its biodiversity strategy (Rio Tinto 2004), committing to achieve a Net Positive Impact (NPI) on biodiversity through its operations worldwide. In this framework, QMM's ilmenite extraction project in Fort Dauphin in the South of Madagascar, was chosen as a pilot site for testing tools to achieve and quantify NPI on biodiversity because of Madagascar's highly endemic and threatened biodiversity, and the risks and opportunities on the site (BirdLife International 2011). Thus, the choice for the implementation of the project fell on such a unique and complex ecosystem, where the supposedly ecologically destructive "environmental Other" (World Rainforest Movement and Re:Common, 2016), represented once again by local communities who have been relying on the forest for decades, is seen as the real problem:

> Madagascar is among the richest countries in the world in terms of biodiversity, where poverty, however, leaves no alternative for communities than turning to natural resources to survive. This high pressure causes massive destruction of natural habitats and includes Madagascar in the red zone (hotspot) for risk on biodiversity.
>
> *(Rio Tinto, 2014)*

It is exactly its alliances with credible conservation groups and academia that allows Rio Tinto to gain international respect and recognition as a champion of biodiversity protection, and to paradoxically claim, in a 2009 company press kit about the operations in Madagascar, that its ilmenite mine "has come to rescue the unique biodiversity of the littoral zone of Fort Dauphin" (QIT Madagascar Minerals SA Press Kit, 2009)[4]

To rescue biodiversity in Madagascar, Rio Tinto involved the International Union for the Conservation of Nature (IUCN), Kew and Missouri Botanical Gardens, international and Malagasy conservation NGOs (including the national partner of BirdLife International), and a Biodiversity Advisory Committee with members from academia and conservation NGOs. These groups, as service providers, contributed to grant enormous credibility to the biodiversity offset project internationally and to take on offset implementation at the local level.

This story began in 2001, when the partnership between the multinational and BirdLife International was established, in order for BirdLife to assist RioTinto in the development and implementation of its biodiversity strategy and its goal of Net Positive Impact on biodiversity at its mining operations (BirdLife International 2011). But the elaboration of a convincing biodiversity offsetting strategy is not an easy task. Accounting for biodiversity gains and losses in a credible manner, combining scientific and conservation values with economic and cultural principles, requires the involvement of very diverse stakeholders at multiple levels, and needs to be grounded in both scientific and culturally sensitive information. In this framework, the designing of the NPI strategy for the Rio Tinto QMM ilmenite project required in-depth research to obtain crucial biological and socio-economic information from potential offset sites within the Anosy region of Madagascar, and in this quest for the perfect spot Tsitongambarika did match all the requirements: high biodiversity value, thus an important conservation area, the principal watershed for the region, and a strong ecosystem goods and services provider to ensure the economic and cultural well-being of the surrounding population. Plus, it was already in the plans of the State to turn it into a protected area.

A well-equipped army of Malagasy and international scientists from Missouri Botanical Garden, Rio Tinto QMM (QIT Madagascar Minerals, QMM) and the Malagasy NGOs Asity Madagascar and Madagasikara Voakajy during 2005 and 2006 started visiting extensively the Tsitongambarika forest to conduct a series of biodiversity surveys, coordinated by BirdLife International, and funded through BirdLife's partnership with Rio Tinto. Moreover, botanical inventory activities were carried out in technical collaboration with the Missouri Botanical Garden (MBG), Rio Tinto QMM and BirdLife International. An inventory of all plant species encountered was conducted using the standard protocol for botanical sampling developed and adopted by MBG, together with biodiversity metrics that help quantifying the scale of biodiversity loss at the mining site. The metrics also help defining the size and characteristics of the biodiversity offset that was required for the mining company in order to prove that it provided the necessary compensation. Overall, all these granted scientific legitimacy and accuracy to the whole process. Other examples, like the one in Box 14.1, show this is quite a common issue nowadays.

BOX 14.1 ANOTHER EXAMPLE . . . AND MORE TO COME: *MONGOLIA, THE CASE OF OYU TOLGOI*

The Oyu Tolgoi open pit and underground copper mining project, the largest mining investment ever licensed in Mongolia, has been the first project to highlight a biodiversity offset action in its Environmental Impact Assessment and related biodiversity management plan, under the guidance of The Biodiversity Consultancy of Cambridge. Oyu Tolgoi is 66% controlled by Rio Tinto and project costs are about $10 billion and the mine will account for about 30% of Mongolia GDP. The project EIA was published in 2013 by the Mongolian environmental ministry, after the government modified the environmental law of the country on the advice of the World Bank by introducing the option of biodiversity offsetting. A specific biodiversity offset plan has been agreed by the project sponsor, including specific measures, such as: a monitoring plan for some endangered species in the project area – namely Khulan, black tail gazelle and some birds – and an anti-poaching plan involving different authorities. An international civil society fact-finding mission in April 2015 detected that the actual offsetting project is still under preparation and faces many uncertainties – including how to implement the new environmental law and its financing. Project production for export to nearby Northern China is ongoing with severe environmental impacts since January 2013 without any offsetting taking place yet.

Measuring nature: why, and for whom?

In light of what was described above and in facing this increasingly worrying tendency, several researchers, activists and practitioners have started to consider the question of whether or not assigning economic values to social and environmental phenomena may be a "good thing". This often implies the unrolling of very elaborated research projects focused on the measurement and quantification of biodiversity losses, questioning how to put them to a use that will lead to outcomes that serve the public and conservation interest.

A number of critical analyses are being developed on how values are made and how valuation systems work in several areas of social and environmental policy, and increasingly detailed accounting systems and biodiversity metrics are being developed.

We do not simply evade this discussion by leveraging the ethical rejection of the principle according to which "the only means of protecting nature is by exposing its economic value". By starting from a more political economy perspective, we could argue that more basic and fundamental questions on the actual creation and extraction of value through these new proposed mechanisms, based on including natural capital into the accumulation equation, have not been thoroughly addressed yet. Thus, we could respond to those engaging in this exercise by questioning the very efficiency of the proposed mechanisms in the long run.

In particular, using analogies with the experience of the carbon markets, we could wonder how, even in the perspective of capitalist accumulation, a broad demand could be created for biodiversity offsets that would be able to produce the consolidated revenue stream necessary to make the "offset or biodiversity credits" both financially appealing in the long run and efficient as a market-based mechanism for biodiversity conservation. From a more comprehensive capital accumulation perspective, we would argue that it is not clear how "biodiversity markets" would help to reorganize production and society at large in order to generate more surplus value and profits to boost accumulation. Moreover, beyond the technical dimension of measurement, from a global market perspective we would question whether nature measurement is part of a large scheme to build the "capital enterprise" of a new cycle able to create value, or whether it is just functional to the financialized turbo-capitalism in search of new quick and dirty extra profits (at a time of crisis of accumulation) while moving from one bubble to another as long as possible, or whether direct profits are the point at all, or just cheap "regulation"? In short, such a mechanism may contribute to create new forms of financial rents that are completely delinked from the generation of any new economic value, despite being related to extractive projects and operations, such as in the case of carbon trading and related markets (Felli, 2014).

We thus would conclude that we doubt that financialization of nature, and its deploying mechanisms such as biodiversity offsetting, can effectively create some value beyond the short-term simple extraction/predatory attitude/upward redistribution. However, it is not in the merit of the efficiency and effectiveness of these mechanisms that we would like to build our argument in this case, but rather on questioning the very purpose of measuring, thus re-thinking the role that NGOs, activists and engaged academia could play in relation to this complex situation.

We would like to propose the perspective that focusing on measuring and cost/benefit analyses carries with it the implicit risk of evading, or getting distracted from what we consider more fundamental questions. We question the ways in which academia and conservation NGOs are tied to an operational matrix that is defined by business and remain indifferent to the consequences on the lives of humans and nature. Areas that indeed are precious thanks to the dynamic interdependent relationship to nature that communities were able to define and maintain for thousands of years. Biodiversity offsetting is a concept developed to appropriate such areas and extract the maximum out of it, within the theoretical boundaries of a legal system appropriately changed to make it possible.

Questioning the political economy of biodiversity offsetting and the economic valuation of nature

Beyond the critique of biodiversity offsetting as a concept and the absurdities that are inevitable in the process of abstracting complex and dynamic natural habitats into equivalences based on questionable metrics and units, insights and knowledge gained through direct exposure to the reality of biodiversity offset implementation confirm that the real objective behind these schemes is not protecting nature but rather allowing further destruction to be carried on undisturbed through some new legitimization or even legalization of potential environmental crimes.

The questionable – and still unproven – exercise of giving an economic value to nature may be regarded as a smokescreen to hide the actual motivation for certain business to engage in its development – including through funding research programmes and nice "protection" grants or collaboration for conservation groups. The Rio Tinto case could suggest that the economic benefit of offsetting programmes does not lie in the potential offsetting market to be developed, but rather on the continuation of the destructive core business of the mining company, which intrinsically has to devastate nature to extract minerals in any part of the world, without any actual rehabilitation or mitigation possible, in particular in the case of mining in or close to unique biodiversity hotspots. Such devastation is de facto green-washed thanks to biodiversity programmes.

More than that, it is an impossible, unequal equation, where local communities are taking on the burden of a double land grab with the paradox of regenerating the often-damaged image of the involved companies. In contrast, these companies not only are presented as champions in nature conservation, but they even get internationally acclaimed for improving biodiversity conditions in their operations' sites, with the support of well-accredited researching centres, conservation NGOs and academia. To the point that more mining is publicly framed as a way to better protect endangered biodiversity! (See also Apostolopoulou and Adams, 2017.)

And the real motivation for governments to support this – including by actively engaging in modifications of the legal framework or whatever else is needed to facilitate breaches of the boundaries of otherwise protected areas – may be the increased income from licensing and compensation, as well as a more stringent control over communities and territories where otherwise the state was not physically present. Now environmental NGOs and private security of the company – or the militaries working for them – do supply to this vacuum by closing up spaces where more communal ways of organizing life in interdependency with nature have been experienced for thousands of years. Their conservation activity expands into the policing of territories and communities who are becoming new targets of more or less explicit repression and violence by the state.

In the case of Madagascar and the communities in Antsotso, areas of forest around which communities were organizing their life are now forbidden territories for them. And this is being imposed on them "for the protection of the forest" through conservation NGOs. Such restriction, which as we have seen before has a devastating impact on their lives, appeared in a way that they could not connect neither to the activities of Rio Tinto, nor to the State. However, it is deeply connected to both. The ultimate result is that their lives are now under a type of control that they have not experienced before, and that without access to the forest, the people of this community will be slowly forced to move away.

This convergence of interests between corporations and governments poses us a more simple but crucial question about who really benefits from the implementation of these mechanisms. This question, more than those around measuring nature and its economic value, cannot be evaded anymore and should be brought back at the centre of any discussion on these matters.

Beyond the predatory role of financialization applied to nature for further and quicker extraction of wealth from territories – as mentioned above – it is getting more evident that more physical extraction from territories is requested by new mining projects or large dams in biodiversity-rich areas (more often in the global South) as well as infrastructure projects – such as motorways or housing developments – in more anthropized areas (more often in the global North) where protected areas represent the few remained hotspots of biodiversity. In both cases increased physical extraction and transformation of territories requires sacrificing and destroying already-protected areas or untouched ones. At the same time there is the urgency to overcome growing opposition by local communities on the ground, whether in more urbanized areas in the global North or remote areas in the global South. Hence the need for corporations to find a new social licence to destroy the common wealth, leveraging the role of the State in ensuring that popular opposition will not stop the new destruction.

But the State is required for something more structural for making this new destruction possible. That is in making it legally possible as well as justified in the name of a "public interest" reframed to accord with the imperative to privatize. In short, biodiversity offsetting is an example of privatization of the law by the law, in the sense that those allowed to pay (through implementing an offset project) for destroying nature in violation of environmental law in force, that is, a protected natural reserve or a park, can legally commit what would be treated as an environmental crime if it were committed by anyone who cannot afford to pay for an offset. It is not by chance, in fact, that most governments in different parts of the world are rushing, sometimes under the lobbying of the World Bank or major investors, to change their environmental law to include biodiversity offsetting.

A final "partisan" question

Beyond the legalization of biodiversity and nature destruction in favour of corporate interests and the repressive attitude of governments bent on controlling territories and local communities, evidence gathered on the ground also raises a basic and fundamental question of justice.

We simply consider unacceptable that peasant families lose their livelihoods so that the world's largest corporations can increase their profits, at a time when profitable investments are fewer and fewer, and that neither the companies nor the conservation partner organizations consider it necessary to inform villagers of the real reasons behind the restrictions imposed on the use of their territories. Knowledge of existing unfair power relations and violations of basic rights of the poorest raises an inevitably partisan question for activists and engaged academics: Which side are they on, and on what basis do they identify their allies?

We believe that offsetting functions effectively as a ploy to avoid discussing in a transparent and democratic way authentic alternatives to a development model that works only for the few at the expense of the many.

With this in mind, we believe it is crucial for activists, as much as engaged academics, not to waste precious time searching for creative and elaborate ways to modify the functioning of a mechanism that should be rejected instead, be it for the development of a new mine, of a highway, a dam or any further innovative step to grant turbo-capitalist accumulation based upon the extraction of wealth (and sovereignty) from territories and communities.

Notes

1 http://www.recommon.org
2 http://www.wrm.org.uy
3 The International Union for Conservation of Nature is the world's oldest and largest global environmental organisation, with almost 1,300 government and non-governmental organisations as members.
4 Suivi environnemental – Un bilan positif des cinq premières années, N. 002 Magazine semestriel QMM, Octobre 2014 http://www.riotintomadagascar.com/pdf/fasimainty oct14.pdf

References

Apostolopoulou, E. and W. Adams (2017) Biodiversity Offsetting and Conservation: Reframing Nature to Save It. *Oryx* 51, 23–31.

BirdLife International (2011*) Tsitongambarika Forest, Madagascar. Biological and Socio-economic Surveys, with Conservation Recommendations*. Cambridge: BirdLife International. Available at: www.birdlife.ch/sites/default/files/documents/BirdLife-2011-Tsitongambarika-book-En.pdf

Felli, R. (2014) On Climate Rent. *Historical Materialism* 22 (3–4), 251–280

Fennell, D. (2003) *Ecotourism: An Introduction*. London and New York: Routledge.

Hodge, I.D. and W.M. Adams (2014) Property Institutions for Rural Land Conservation: Towards a Post-Neoliberal Agenda. *Journal of Rural Studies* 36, 453–462.

QIT Madagascar Minerals SA Press Kit (2009) A Mine at the Rescue of the Unique Biodiversity of the Littoral Zone of Fort Dauphin.

Rio Tinto (2004) Rio Tinto Biodiversity Strategy – Sustaining a Natural Balance. Available at: www.riotinto.com/SustainableReview/Landaccess/programmes/Biodiversity/pdf/BiodiversityStrategy.pdf

Suivi environnemental – Un bilan positif des cinq premières années, N. 002 Magazine semestriel QMM, Octobre 2014, www.riotintomadagascar.com/pdf/fasimaintyoct14.pd

World Rainforest Movement, Re:Common (2016) Rio Tinto's Biodiversity Offset in Madagascar. Double Landgrab in the Name of Biodiversity? Available at: www.recommon.org/eng/new-report-rio-tintos-biodiversity-offset-madagascar/

World Rainforest Movement, Re:Common (2016) Rio Tinto in Madagascar: A mine Destroying the Unique Biodiversity of the Littoral Zone of Fort Dauphin. Available at: http://wrm.org.uy/wp-content/uploads/2016/06/Article_Rio_Tinto_in_Madag ascar.pdf

World Rainforest Movement and Re:Common (2016) Rio Tinto's Biodiversity Offset in Madagascar. Double Landgrab in the Name of Biodiversity? Available at: www.recom mon.org/eng/new-report-rio-tintos-biodiversity-offset-madagascar/

15

NATURE IS OUR RIGHT

Framing a new nature protection debate in Europe

Sandra Bell and Friedrich Wulf

Introduction: why a new approach to conserving nature?

For a long time as NGOs we have tried to save nature, by setting aside and managing protected areas as well as appealing to politicians. Many of the 30 national Friends of the Earth organizations across Europe are working to protect specific nature sites, and getting involved with practical action while at the same time leading political campaigns to halt destruction or address the drivers of biodiversity loss. We have won a network of protected areas, and better protection for some species, and recently we've successfully defended important laws that protect nature. But still biodiversity continues to decline at an alarming rate. We are facing increasing challenges to convince politicians at all levels to make the right decisions for nature. Our analysis is that we not only need to step up this action – we need to change our approach, too. And at a time that governments are beginning to wake up to the economic value of nature, we need to reclaim the true value of nature to all of us.

How economists value nature

The economists who are now taking an interest in nature say that we've failed to reverse biodiversity decline because we have failed to recognize the economic value of nature. "The crisis of biodiversity loss can only begin to be addressed in earnest if the values of biodiversity and ecosystem services are fully recognised and represented in decision making," says environmental economist Pavan Sukhdev, lead author of the well-known TEEB study. To some extent Friends of the Earth agrees with this analysis – nature underpins our economy yet gets scant recognition for all the services it provides us with for free. But we have serious concerns about how this has been taken on board. For example, in the UK, the Natural Capital Committee (2015, p. 1) talks about fully integrating the environment into the economy and, alarmingly, suggests the prioritization of protection of nature by "focusing on those areas with the highest economic benefits". And now plans are being made that draw on this new way of valuing nature and making decisions about its protection.

There are many reasons for not using the "value of nature" only in economic terms, not least that as humans we have a connection with nature that cannot be described in a spreadsheet. And we cannot value nature for its intrinsic value if we have to always put a price on it. Even from a selfish perspective there is a high risk in using the short-term approach of economics and applying it to nature and natural systems. It shows, for example, that we have the ability to identify a handful of bee species that currently contribute the highest economic returns in terms of providing pollination services to crops. But in a changing climate we may need completely different bee species to pollinate our crops in the future. So, a decision to prioritize conservation of the most useful species and ignore the rest would be disastrous for our future food security, as well as morally wrong.

Friends of the Earth does not reject every connection of nature to the economy – it can be useful to demonstrate that nature can provide cost-effective flood protection, for example. But we do reject the notion that decisions about protecting nature are made on the basis of its contribution to economic growth alone. Friends of the Earth is also concerned that assigning price tags or metrics to nature allow it to be traded – in schemes such as biodiversity offsetting that put forward a flawed notion that nature, in all its complexity, is something that can be measured, exchanged and replaced in another location.

How people value nature

We are therefore promoting a different way to talk about the value of nature to people, and another way to connect biodiversity to society, not as a tradeable and exchangeable commodity we must pay for, but as a fundamental right for everyone, rooted in what people tell us about what they value about nature. When we ask people why they care about nature they have an emotional response – they never mention monetary value. This is just a small selection of comments from Friends of the Earth supporters: "Saw puffins for the first time by the score, also fulmars, kittiwakes, razorbills, greater black backed gulls. The place is magic. I wish I could live there"; "Being in nature restores my sanity half the time! Even if it's just in the back garden. The smells, sights sounds and feelings of the nature just to be found there is wonderful"; "Standing knee deep in the fast flowing streams in the black of a warm July night, as the sea trout run the river – it's a great experience"; "Ta' Kantra is magical. As kids, we'd sleep under the stars close to the cliff's edge, wake up at day break and dive into the sea".

A new debate needed – Nature is Our Right

We need a new public debate to frame public understanding of the importance and relevance of nature. That is why Friends of the Earth Europe (FoE Europe) is launching a new framing for its campaigns centred on the key message that having nature in our lives is a right and a necessity for everyone – *Nature is Our Right*. The aims of FoE Europe's "Nature is our Right" approach are: to frame a new nature protection debate across Europe – based on citizens' rights to benefit from and experience nature and the social value of nature, to give voice to people's growing desire, and demand for, more and better nature in their lives, not less, and to increase public and political support to protect nature.

In framing a new debate, we want to steer discussion away from having to justify nature protection as making good business sense, or being "good for the economy". Nature should be protected for its intrinsic value – and also for the wider immeasurable benefits it brings to people – our sense of wonder, and our health and well-being in being connected to nature. We also want to demonstrate that nature is irreplaceable. So, the idea that habitats and species are tradable and that damage in one place can simply be replaced in another place, as in biodiversity offsetting proposals, is a breach of people's and communities' right to local nature in their lives and on their doorsteps.

Why do we need a new framing for nature now?

More and more assessments show that nature is in fast decline and most of the natural life support eco-systems we rely on for our health, well-being and society are in a poor and degraded condition, from our declining bees to the degraded health of our soils and seas. The latest "state of nature" reports show that more than 60% of the EU's protected species and 77% of the EU's habitat types are in bad shape, and that, since 2010, irreversible biodiversity loss has continued largely unabated (European Environment Agency, 2015). A large proportion of species are at risk of extinction.

Nature is a resource and a social justice issue

This is an issue that affects us all. Protection or destruction of nature has deep effects on people and communities, and people's rights. Nature is the basis of our lives, from cleaning our water and air, to protecting us from flooding, to providing us with fertile soils to produce food and bees to pollinate our plants. A healthy and sustainable society relies on our looking after it. The complacent status quo is not an option. We have a vision that we can only realize if many more people become engaged – that nature is thriving, not just surviving, across Europe, with benefits for us all. This will need the leadership, policy and practical actions of all governments – prompted by public demand for our right to nature – so that nature flourishes, threats to nature are reversed and everyone can access, enjoy and gain from thriving nature. To realize our vision we need to mobilize new sectors of civil society across Europe, beyond the traditional conservationist constituency – and to do that we need to talk about nature in a way that people can relate to.

Nature is absolutely essential for everybody's mental and physical health and well-being and children's development (see Figure 15.1; see, for example, Brink et al., 2016). Access to nature has multiple benefits for mental health, as well as indicators of physical health, such as blood pressure, obesity levels and even life expectancy. When it comes to child development, access to nature and green space

FIGURE 15.1   Connecting to nature: children exploring the forest near Darmstadt, Germany

Author: Luka Tomac, Friends of the Earth Europe, www.natures-keepers.org

provides children with cognitive, emotional and physical benefits, such as increased ability to concentrate, improved academic performance, reduced stress and aggression levels and reduced risk of obesity (see Box 15.1). Inequalities in health are linked to access to nature, in all stages of life: pre-birth, childhood, adult life and old age.

But too often it is marginalized, poor and/or ethnic minority communities with the least power and money who are denied the ability to enjoy and experience nature, and the proven benefits that nature brings us. People living in areas with high deprivation are more likely to have less access to green spaces and fewer opportunities for healthy activities (Marmot, 2013 and Box 15.2). Everyone should have access to high-quality, thriving nature.

BOX 15.1 BENEFITS OF ACCESS TO NATURE

"But if outdoor play itself is so good for children, why do they need to leave the playground and explore beyond its boundaries? Because unlike playgrounds created by a human designer, natural environments allow children to play in far more varied and imaginative ways. Compared with man-made playgrounds, the natural world is highly complex, with lots of places to hide

> and explore; it is untidy, which may be off-putting for adults, but adds to its attraction for children; and above all it is dynamic, varying from day to day, season to season and year to year."
>
> Natural Childhood report, Stephen Moss,
> National Trust, 2012, p. 8

Being close to nature and activities in nature improve self-reported well-being of disadvantaged groups. More and more initiatives are using nature and green spaces for green exercise and for health therapies. Inequality in mental well-being is 40% narrower among people who report good access to green areas, compared with those with poorer access (Mitchell et al., 2015).

Existing inequalities in access to nature would be made worse by policies like biodiversity offsetting that have no mechanism for taking into account the impact on local communities as nature is treated as something that can be shifted around from one location to another to suit developers, irrespective of its value to local people.

BOX 15.2   POWER, MONEY AND ACCESS TO NATURE

"[I]n areas where more than 40 per cent of residents are black or minority ethnic there is 11 times less green space than in areas where residents are largely white."

CABE, Community Green, 2010, p. 4

What do we want to change as a result of re-framing our campaigns?

By engaging more people in practical and political action we want to achieve some specific outcomes:

- *More people will be empowered and inspired to act for themselves to stand up for nature.*

Many people across the globe are already standing up for our right to nature, and for vital laws to protect nature – for all of us and for future generations. They may be standing up for a local nature site, or they may be local practical actions like planting wildflowers – crucially such local actions can involve people who do not regard themselves as conservationists but as people who care about their locale and the health of their children. If people get interested in practical environmental action, they may well go on to engage in more political actions later. We have collected some great examples of people acting in their communities in our Nature's KEEPERS project. From a high-profile campaign, with Europe-wide support, to stop toxic dumping in the Førde fjord in Norway to a group of committed local people planting wildflowers on a scale that transformed their town in England ordinary people are standing up for nature (see Figures 15.2 and 15.3).

All these actions big or small, practical or political are valuable actions for nature. We hope to see many more "nature's keepers or champions" come forward across Europe.

- *More people from diverse sectors of society will act.*

To fully protect Europe's nature, we need to convince politicians to back a right to nature for all citizens, and fundamental reform of our industrial food and farming system. We will not achieve change on the scale required without mobilizing more people than are currently involved in nature campaigns. By reframing the debate we have the opportunity to reach out and involve new groups of people – doctors, nurses, health professionals, teachers motivated by public health and education – and their representative organizations – and parents concerned about their children's health and (lack of) contact with nature.

- *Strong and ambitious nature policies are needed to secure people's rights to nature.*

FIGURE 15.2   Standing up for nature: Anne-Line Thingnes Førsund, Norway

Author: Luka Tomac, Friends of the Earth Europe, www.natures-keepers.org/

FIGURE 15.3   Standing up for nature: Victoria Harvey, UK

Author: Luka Tomac, Friends of the Earth Europe, www.natures-keepers.org

Friends of the Earth Europe has identified several priority policy demands that are set out briefly below. We have a better chance of achieving these if people engage with nature campaigns and if politicians and decision makers understand the true value of nature to our well-being. Vice versa, having good legal frameworks in place and working provides people with the necessary instruments to claim their right to nature, and makes it easier for them to engage for nature. According to FoE Europe, these are the main steps that must be taken to achieve this:

- *The laws that protect nature must be better enforced across Europe.*

In December 2016 the European Commission concluded that the EU nature directives are effective when they are properly implemented – that they are "fit for purpose". This welcome statement followed a public campaign backed by more than 520,000 people across Europe. It will now be essential to improve implementation and enforcement of the laws, including designating protected nature sites, better management of nature sites (management plans and funding) and clamping down on illegal activity and threats to protected nature. This is necessary because there still are too many special places being damaged or threatened by inappropriate development. As well as having an unacceptable impact on species that are meant to be protected in law, these schemes also threaten local communities' natural heritage, their connection to their local landscape or their access to a natural environment that we now know is crucial to our well-being. Two case studies from different

FIGURE 15.4   Standing up for nature: Dermot Hickson, Northern Ireland, UK

Author: Declan Allison, Friends of the Earth England, Wales and Northern Ireland

ends of the EU show examples of such important places that are threatened by development but protected by EU legislation and where its strong implementation could make all the difference: the case of the motorway construction in Kresna Gorge in Bulgaria and the case of the highway construction in Heaney Landscape, in rural Northern Ireland.

Governments must do much more to tackle the drivers of biodiversity loss

Governments need to step up action to address inconsistent policies that undermine nature and the internationally agreed goal to halt biodiversity loss. In particular, industrial farming, and energy production are having devastating impacts on nature. In Europe it will be essential to change policies such as the next Common Agricultural Policy. Nature underpins farming, so it is counter-productive for farming to be destroying the very systems that it relies upon, such as healthy soil and natural pest control. The EU must use the opportunity of the next revision of its Common Agricultural Policy (CAP) to move away from incentivizing industrialized and intensive farming practices, towards one that supports sustainable farming and food production with nature restored, not destroyed.

Rural as well as urban communities have a right to experience thriving nature in the countryside. Yet intensively farmed land, although green in appearance, can be largely devoid of biodiversity. For example, several recent studies have shown that bee diversity in towns and cities can be as high as, or even greater than, nearby rural areas (see, for example, Urban Pollinators Project, 2015). Bees are a good example of how nature provides us with specific services but also contributes to the sense of well-being we experience in contact with nature, for example, by pollinating wild and garden flowers. But bees are in trouble. Europe needs a pollinator strategy to protect European bees and pollinators that are especially affected by industrial farming practices and by the growing effects of climate change.

Governments need to ensure proper, sufficient and independent funding

. . . for nature, nature conservation and restoration. Given that a healthy and sustainable society and economy is dependent on our looking after nature, such funding should be regarded as an investment in a sustainable economy and our future well-being.

Governments must not put a price on nature

Turning nature into a product or a service that can be sold off, privatized or traded will just make the problem worse. Biodiversity offsetting offers an indicative example of the consequences of policies that attempt to put a price to nature and its destruction. Such schemes aim to make up for biodiversity loss in one area by financing restoration or protections in another. By promising to restore or even increase biodiversity elsewhere to compensate for its destruction, such mechanisms risk facilitating nature destruction in the first place, delivering a "licence to trash" while tranforming biodiversity into a tradeable commodity.

Reduce overconsumption and stop infinite growth

Last but certainly not least, it will be essential to address overall consumption and growth. The mantra of never-ending economic growth on a finite planet increases pressure on land and nature. Governments need to change their way of measuring progress, abolish gross domestic product (GDP) and reduce ecological footprints by pushing for a circular economy, sharing and leasing, encouraging recycling by pay-as-you-throw and by reducing taxes on labour while increasing those on materials. The policy and lifestyle changes required to protect and restore nature are profound, but they are achievable if enough people are convinced that nature is not a luxury but something that is essential to us all – that nature is a right for absolutely everyone.

Conclusion

Nature must be better valued – in social, cultural and economic terms – and given more and proper weight in political decisions. Nature underpins the economy and our well-being, and needs much better protection to avoid continued decline and ultimately ecosystem collapse. However, Friends of the Earth Europe opposes any proposal that integrates nature into the markets.

Nature is important and valuable in its own right, but there seems to be no place for this thinking in the current proposals of governments. Our vision is about people accessing and enjoying nature and living in harmony with nature. The ultimate way to protect nature is to address the core issues and drivers that destroy it; much better implementation of existing international obligations, EU and national laws; and good governance at the local level. But all these will require a profound political shift. To achieve this, we need to reframe the debate about the value of nature, and reclaim what nature means to us. And we need to mobilize many more people and wider sectors of society. We believe we can do this by connecting to people's wider concerns, showing how valuable nature is for everybody's health and well-being and presenting nature not as a privilege: Nature is Our Right.

References

Brink P., Mutafoglu K., Schweitzer J-P., Kettunen M., Twigger-Ross C., Baker J., Kuipers Y., Emonts M., Tyrväinen L., Hujala T. and Ojala A. (2016) *The Health and Social Benefits of Nature and Biodiversity Protection*. A report for the European Commission (ENV.B.3/ETU/2014/0039), Institute for European Environmental Policy, London/Brussels.

CABE - Commission for Architecture and the Built Environment (2010) *Community Green, Using Local Aces to Tackle Inequality and Improve Health*. Available online: https://www.designcouncil.org.uk/resources/report/community-green

European Environment Agency (2015) State of Nature in the EU. Results from reporting under the nature directives 2007–2012. Technical report No 2/2015., 173 pp.

IMA-Europe (2015) *Response to Evidence Gathering Questionnaire for the Fitness Check of the Nature Directives*. Online document, available at: http://ec.europa.eu/environment/nature/legislation/fitness_check/index_en.htm

Marmot M., (2013). *Review of Social Determinants and the Health Divide in the WHO European Region: Final Report*. World Health Organization.

Milieu IEEP and ICF, (2016) Evaluation Study to support the Fitness Check of the Birds and Habitats Directives, 668 pp.

Mitchell, R.J., Richardson, E.A. and Pearce, J.R. (2015) Neighborhood Environments and Socioeconomic Inequalities in Mental Well-Being. *American Journal of Preventive Medicine* 49 (1), 80–84. doi: 10.1016/j.amepre.2015.01.017.

Moss, S. (2012) *Natural Childhood*, National Trust report.

Natural Capital Committee (2015) *The State of Natural Capital*, Third report to the Economic Affairs Committee.

Sukhdev, P. (2010) Putting a Value on Nature Could Set Scene for True Green Economy. *The Guardian*. Available at: www.theguardian.com/commentisfree/cif-green/2010/feb/10/pavan-sukhdev-natures-economic-model

The Economics of Ecosystems and Biodiversity (TEEB) (2010) *The Economics of Ecosystems and Biodiversity: Mainstreaming the Economics of Nature: A Synthesis of the Approach, Conclusions and Recommendations of TEEB.* Available at: www.theguardian.com/commentisfree/cif-green/2010/feb/10/pavan-sukhdev-natures-economic-model

Urban Pollinators Project (2015) *Urban Pollinators Research.* Published in Proceedings of the Royal Society B, University of Bristol.

16

NATURE'S RIGHTS AND EARTH JURISPRUDENCE – A NEW ECOLOGICALLY BASED PARADIGM FOR ENVIRONMENTAL LAW

Mumta Ito and Massimiliano Montini

Introduction

The experience gained over the last 50 years in the evolution of environmental law has shown that its current structure is inadequate to face the challenges of our time. At best it can slow the rate of destruction, but it cannot prevent or reverse it. This is why a new ecologically based approach to law is needed, grounded on the protection of the integral functioning of ecosystems as a whole as its main objective, protecting all human and non-human beings, on the same legal (and practical) footing. This proposed approach, based on the principles of Earth Jurisprudence, aims at recognizing the intrinsic legal value of nature per se, independently from its "utility" to human beings. Some examples of this new approach in action can be seen in recent national legislation in Ecuador, Bolivia, New Zealand and the USA as well as the Draft EU Directive produced by the charity Nature's Rights as the subject of a European Citizens Initiative that we will touch on further below.

The failure of environmental law

Why environmental law has failed to protect nature

In the last 40 years alone – the time from which the first major environmental laws were enacted – we have extinguished 52% of the global populations of all species (according to WWF's Living Planet Index), climate change is upon us and the world's ecosystems are collapsing. The evolution of environmental law, despite producing a huge quantity of legislation has not been able to reverse the destructive transgression of planetary boundaries. The main reasons for the substantive failure of the current regulatory regime for environmental protection, which may be observed at international, at regional (for example, European Union) as well as at national level in most domestic jurisdictions, is due to the fact that environmental law has been so far largely designed to fit in with the dominant economic model. Such a model places economic growth (at all costs) at the top of the political agenda, despite its possible negative consequences in social and environmental terms. More specifically, environmental regulation has been shaped on the basis of the assumption that it should work as a tool to address and manage the most relevant negative "externalities" caused by patterns of economic development based on the dominant economic model, without any critical form of assessment of the economic model itself. This has led to the current situation, which is characterized by an ample and widespread corpus of legislation for environmental protection that, despite addressing in great detail the most important environmental issues, is often not concretely contributing to reverse the negative trends that characterize the global and the local environmental situation.

What is therefore absolutely necessary is to understand the real and profound reasons that are causing such a "crisis of effectiveness" of environmental law or, in other terms, to understand why environmental law, despite its high level of sophistication and its broad coverage, and despite being generally complied with at international as well as at regional and domestic levels, is not delivering the hoped and expected positive results in terms of effective environmental protection.

Outdated paradigms

Our modern legal system, within which the current environmental law regulatory system has been developed and is implemented, operates within the following outdated paradigms:

- Mechanistic (that is, viewing the world as made up of separate unconnected objects – like items in a shopping cart – rather than a complex interconnected whole – like a human body – that gives rise to a siloed approach).
- Anthropocentric (that is, viewing the world as existing solely for the use of human beings – this is where ideas about "natural resources" and "natural capital" derive, basing nature's value on its utility to humanity rather than on its intrinsic value).
- Adversarial (competitive/retributive model where one party wins at the expense of another).

None of these paradigms reflect the full scientific reality of how natural systems operate. This gives rise to the illusion of a "power-over" relationship with Nature that has led to our current predicament.

The main cause of the failure of environmental law is deeply rooted in the Western legal tradition and its Cartesian mechanistic and reductionist approach, which has provided the foundations for the development of environmental law since its very beginning. The said approach is also characterized by a marked anthropocentrism, which tends to promote or, at least, not to question the tendency of humans to dominate and exploit Nature as if we were separated from it, rather than trying to respect and live in harmony with all other species present on Earth as an integral part of Nature (the Earth community). In other words, it may be said that environmental law had developed through the years within a cultural attitude of dominance and separation of human beings over nature, which is in profound conflict with the reality of the situation. We are Nature and we depend on Nature for our very existence.

The most notable example of such a culture of dominance is represented by the widespread use of the property paradigm also in relationship with Nature, which reduces it to a mere object of property. This is then built on in the Green Economy, which promotes its further commodification through the introduction of tradable market-based instruments establishing transferable property rights over different aspects and functions of Nature that we look at further below.

Law facilitates economics

In ancient times, law facilitated human values – today law facilitates economics. Perhaps it may be said that law in our society is shaped by and is dependent on economic choices and priorities. The main problem today is that law is facilitating the application of an economic paradigm of unlimited growth that is coupled with the destruction of Nature. In this way, law contributes to undermining the source of life.

Our economic paradigm is based on one key concept, namely valuing Nature as a resource for human consumption, and this is where ideas like "natural resources" and "natural capital" come from. However, Nature is infinitely valuable – because it is the source of life. Our health and well-being are integral to the health and wellbeing of Earth. We cannot have a viable human economy that destroys Earth because one derives from the other. The logical conclusion is societal collapse.

The European Union has committed to strive towards an absolute decoupling of economic growth from environmental destruction. To achieve this, we need innovative laws that recognize the intrinsic value of nature and the way to do that is through legal personality and enforceable legal rights. In order to change the game, we also need to change the rules that govern the game – and that means the structure of law.

The problem with our current structure of law

Nature is treated as an "object" under the law – either property or fair game unless special rules apply. However, this approach – which in the past has been applied to slaves, indigenous people, women and children who were also deemed by law to be "objects" – has several practical drawbacks that make it almost impossible for people and governments to protect Nature using the law.

The law does not recognize a relationship between us and the rest of Nature. Law governs relationships but only between "subjects" of the law and the prima facie position is one of no obligations or legal duty of care towards Nature. As a result, anybody has the right to destroy Nature that does not belong to anyone, and property owners have the right to destroy ecosystems on their property – unless the law specifically says otherwise. This leaves Nature "outside" the system and fundamentally unprotected. So, we are left with the impossible task of reactively legislating to carve out protections, rather than proactively creating the legal frameworks needed to create true sustainability.

The end result is piecemeal protection and a reductionist approach. This ignores the uncertainty and unpredictability involved in dealing with interconnected living systems. A good example of this is our endangered species protection system that relies on listing which species are under threat, a process that takes years of scientific research. However, according to UNEP (the United Nations Environment Programme), we are losing 150 to 200 species each day – in the time it takes to update the lists it is already too late. Also, in a radically interconnected world who is to say which species is a "VIP" and what the loss of a seemingly insignificant species would have on the ecosystem as a whole?

Another consequence is that environmental issues are dealt with almost exclusively by the planning and administrative courts. This means that only technical arguments about decision-making processes can be put forward rather than an examination of all of the wide-ranging issues involved with dealing with interconnected living systems. In the case of local development, the only conversation that can happen in court is whether the correct planning procedure was followed, and the outcome is simply a referral back to the planners. There is an implicit assumption in our system that development is beneficial, but environmental impact has to be quantified and proven, even though scientists agree that it is impossible to do so because of the complexity and unpredictability of interconnected living systems, favouring a precautionary approach.

The only avenue left in law is if a disaster happens and people litigate – the courts will compensate people for proven monetary loss. However, under the current environmental legal regime, it is very difficult to restore the damage caused to Nature because there is no clear relationship in law between humans and the rest of Nature.

There are also problems with enforcement, piercing the corporate veil, the lack of flexibility in sanctions and the fact that a model of law that is adversarial and retributive does little to uncover the root cause of the problem and co-create solutions. Finally, it leads to a cultural attitude of separation from Nature that is at the root of our environmental crisis.

Our current system of law is missing an overarching framework that puts our existence on this planet into its proper context. This means that there is no legal requirement for governments to formulate policies that prioritize the health and integrity of ecosystems and integrate this requirement across all levels and sectors of society. Accordingly, environmental decisions are made exclusively at the micro-level under individual planning cases with no regard to the cumulative effect of such decisions in eroding ecosystems and Earth system resilience as a whole.

In Figure 16.1 the diagram on the left is the usual model for sustainability. The problem with this model is that it assumes that each circle can exist independently of the others. In reality the only one that can exist without the others – is Nature.

The diagram on the right is therefore more accurate. It shows a natural hierarchy of systems because without Nature there is no people and without people there is no economy.

This then leads to a natural hierarchy of rights with Nature's rights as our most fundamental rights because Nature forms the underlying basis of all life on Earth, then human rights as a subsystem of Nature's rights – and then property or corporate rights as a subsystem of human rights.

In the model on the right, the rights are in service of one another rather than in conflict – working synergistically to protect the integrity of the whole. In this model human activities have to be beneficial for humans as well as Nature – or it's not viable in the long run.

Nature's rights and its underlying philosophy of Earth Jurisprudence are creating the fundamental legal framework for this to happen.

Counter-balancing corporate power

The above diagram is in stark contrast to what we are seeing in the world today with corporate and human rights in conflict and Nature's rights left out of the picture completely. Rights are a tool for addressing power imbalances. At present there is an imbalance between the large corporations and everybody else. The current trend for corporations to sue governments for trying to protect people or Nature – such as the Bayer Syngenta case against the European Union's ban on

CURRENT SUSTAINABILITY MODEL

RIGHTS OF NATURE MODEL

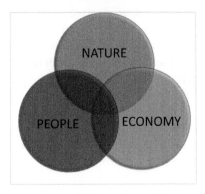
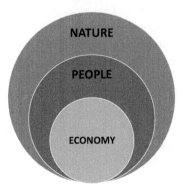

FIGURE 16.1   Towards a hierarchy of rights

Authors: Mumta Ito and Massimiliano Montini

three neonicotinoid pesticides linked to the deaths of millions of bees – is only likely to continue.

Furthermore, while big multilateral trade agreements like Transatlantic Trade and Investment Partnership (TTIP) and Trans-Pacific Partnership (TPP) have been set back by the election of President Trump, others like the Comprehensive Economc and Trade Agreement (CETA) are going ahead and additional bilateral trade agreements are under constant negotiation.

Also, we are seeing the financialization of nature – monetizing ecosystems by creating property titles out of the various functions of nature to form the basis of cash flows that can be traded on the capital markets. This is coupled with flawed methodologies – like biodiversity offsetting that assumes that interconnected living ecosystems are interchangeable like banknotes – which could have dangerous consequences, as is examined in the section below.

These trends have the potential to greatly accelerate the destruction. Bringing Nature in as a stakeholder in its own right is a powerful counter-balance to corporate dictatorship. It empowers people and governments to stand for Nature – the underlying basis of our economy and our lives – and to protect future generations using a different structure of law.

The current crisis and the way forward: commodification and financialization of Nature or Rights of Nature?

Option 1: The commodification and financialization of nature

It is evident in the growing trend towards the commodification and financialization of Nature that our governments and financial institutions recognize that regulation has failed to halt environmental destruction. However, their "solution" is to leave the future of our ecosystems – and therefore the lives of our future generations – in the hands of market forces.

Realizing that the value of Nature has been left out of economic equations, the components and functions of Nature, including biodiversity, are now being priced and assigned an economic value that forms the basis for the creation of financial instruments that can be traded on capital markets. These instruments are often acquired by corporations to offset their overuse, degradation or pollution of the environment, or even to further profit from trading them. Pollution permits, natural capital bonds, biodiversity banks and offsetting mechanisms already exist. Essential prerequisites for the commodification and financialization are pricing Nature, characterizing Nature's functions as "ecosystem services" and redefining Nature as "natural capital". This approach has several drawbacks that could seriously accelerate the rate of destruction:

- Ecosystems are living systems – each one is unique and interconnected. It is not possible to destroy one and mitigate by restoring another somewhere else without destabilizing the whole.

- Offsetting speeds up the planning process – it is based on the assumption that the damage to biodiversity can be reduced or even eliminated, and that it does not matter where damage occurs. This is a reductionist approach that is out of alignment with the radically interconnected and unique Nature of ecosystems.
- Segregation and pricing of the interconnected components of an ecosystem is an artificial construct. It does not reflect the reality of how ecosystems operate, their cumulative function or their true value in the web of life.
- The system favours the status quo by legitimizing environmental destruction. Instead of encouraging corporations to change their ways, it allows the same actors to make additional profits through financial speculation.
- Decision rights over how to live in a territory and manage the ecology are increasingly transferred from the local sphere to multi-nationals and financial institutions. This could lead to profit-driven speculation. If a company stands to profit from the price of clean air going up, then it will invest in activities that ensure that clean air is scarcer and in high demand in the future. In the case of biodiversity, investors can profit from speculation on the extinction of species, as if it were a game.
- All markets are susceptible to crashes – in the case of Nature-based financial products, crashes could have disastrous consequences for the underlying "conservation" project when the land is repossessed.
- Conservation policy is decided by what is more profitable rather than what is best for the ecology as a whole.
- Carbon credits and reduced emissions from deforestation and forest degradation (REDD) (similar mechanisms) have been ineffective in halting climate change or deforestation.

There have been different forms of the commodification and privatization of Nature over history, such as the policies that privatize biodiversity itself and other tools like intellectual property mechanisms that lay claims to genetic or biochemical elements. Today we are witnessing a new wave of privatization through the invention of natural capital. In this context, large corporations are pushing for reforms in international and national policies to enable their control of biodiversity. This new wave of privatization of Nature cannot be controlled under the existing structure of law. We need the fundamental and systemic transformation that rights of Nature offer as a powerful counter-balance to corporate excess.

Option 2: Nature's Rights

Nature's Rights shifts the paradigm by reversing the structure of law that treats Nature as an object separate to us – which is the root of the problem – by recognizing Nature as a rights-bearing subject of the law equal to humans and corporations. This is the game-changing step that brings Nature into our governance system as a stakeholder in its own right and transitions us into a whole-systems framework of law. Instead of reactively legislating to carve out protections, we start with the premise that all of life is protected and we carve out the level of human activity that is acceptable to maintain the dynamic balance, thereby moving towards a natural contract between Earth and humanity. On a practical level, rights of Nature would bring the following changes to our legal system:

- It provides an overarching context for our existence as part of Earth as a whole, enshrining interdependence in law and a legal requirement for this context to be embedded in all levels of society. It recognizes that the economy is a subsystem of human society, which is a subsystem of Earth.
- It empowers people to pro-actively reject governmental actions that permit unwanted and damaging development to occur by enabling us to assert the rights of those ecosystems that would otherwise be destroyed.
- It goes to the heart of our economic system by valuing Nature intrinsically. Property rights are no longer absolute; they are qualified by the rights of the ecosystems and species living there.
- It creates a relationship in law with the rest of Nature, a legal prerequisite for a duty of care. This enables obligations towards Nature, including the obligation to restore the damage.
- Rights are a legal tool for addressing power imbalances (for example, slaves, indigenous people, women and children). Currently, the imbalance is between the corporations, financial institutions and everyone else. It is the only effective counter-balance in the face of policies that concentrate corporate power, such as CETA, TPP, TTIP, and financializing Nature.
- It creates a fundamental basis for the human right to life because without Nature humans cannot exist and develop.

Promoting an ecologically based approach to law

Paving the way to a different approach to law

Nature's Rights is a holistic and ecologically based approach to law that is underpinned by the principles of Earth Jurisprudence. Its purpose is to establish a mutually enhancing presence on Earth through embedding these principles in all aspects of our lives and society. The Earth Jurisprudence, which inspires the different approach to law suggested by the Nature's Rights proposal within an ecological law perspective, can be distilled into the following key principles:

- Wholeness – the Earth is a living being – a single Earth Community webbed together through interdependent relationships. All life has inherent value and Earth has thresholds and limits.
- Lawfulness – Earth is part of the universe, which is ordered and operates according to its own laws that govern all life, including human beings.
- Duty of Care – Earth Jurisprudence is a living law – a way of life, guided by moral responsibilities. We have a duty of care to all present and future members of the Earth Community to contribute to its integrity and well-being.

- Nature's Rights – Earth and all of the Earth Community have three inherent rights: the right to exist, the right to habitat, and the right to fulfil their role in the ever-renewing processes of life.
- Mutual Enhancement – relationships within the Earth Community are reciprocal, a cycle of giving and receiving.
- Resilience – all healthy living systems have the ability to grow, evolve and adapt to change and disturbance, without losing inner coherence. To learn from Nature and understand natural laws, we must become eco-literate and engage other ways of knowing – feeling, sensing and intuition.

Practicing this approach to law requires that we make decisions that prioritize the long-term ecological interests of the whole and of future generations, over short-term financial gains.

Seeds of the new emerging paradigm

Given that our current legal and economic models have been ineffective in halting the widespread destruction of the biosphere, more and more countries are looking at rights for Nature as a way forward. A new emerging paradigm of an ecologically based approach that enshrines Nature's rights in law may be observed. For a comprehensive list of these laws and policies and links to the relevant official documents see www.harmonywithnatureun.org/rightsOfNature/. Here are some of the most relevant examples at the time of writing:

- **UN level:** The UN has a Harmony with Nature Department to promote rights of Nature. In 2010, Bolivia presented a Universal Declaration for the Rights of Mother Earth. Since then there have been various UN resolutions moving in this direction, such as the General Assembly Resolution 70/208 of 22 December 2015, which formally recognizes the principles of Earth Jurisprudence.
- **Supranational level:** The Earth Charter, adopted in 2000 under the global initiative of several civil society groups, advocates the respect for "Earth and life in all its diversity".
- **National level:** Ecuador (Constitutional recognition of the rights of Nature and holistic concept of "well-being"); Bolivia (Law recognising the Rights of Mother Earth, an alternative economic framework and an Ombudsman for Mother Earth);
- **National court decisions:** New Zealand, Ecuador, India, Argentina. These decisions expand our jurisprudence by recognizing the concept that an organism or a manifestation of Nature such as a river has inherent rights that can be recogniszd in law. In Ecuador in 2011 the first rights of Nature court victory won a successful injunction against the government to stop polluting a river through defending the river's rights in court. In India, the case of *T.N Godavarman Thirumulpad Vs. Union of India & Others* (2012) is known for the opinions of Judges K.S. Radhakrishnan and Chandramauli Kr. Prasad who asserted that

environmental justice could be achieved only if we drift away from anthropo-centric principles. In 2017, the Uttarakhand High Court granted the Ganga and Yamuna rivers legal personality and rights along with the Gangotri (largest glacier in Asia) and Yamunotri glacier. Colombia's Constitutional Court has recognized the Atrato River basin as having rights to "protection, conserva-tion, maintenance and restoration". In 2018, the Supreme Court of Justice of Colombia also issued a historic ruling by granting rights to the Colombian Amazon Region along the same lines as those given to the Rio Atrato.

- **Local/Municipal/Regional level:** More than 36 USA municipalities, including Santa Monica in their Sustainability Rights Ordinance, Pittsburgh, New Mexico State. In the USA, these laws recognize the rights of commu-nities and the rights of ecosystems side by side, and they subordinate corpo-rate interests. Such laws in the USA have successfully banned fracking locally. Moreover, cities such as São Paolo, Brazil and Mexico City have also adopted laws that recognize Nature's Rights, and national laws with regional applica-tion have been passed in New Zealand, Australia, Belize and the list is growing.
- **National parks:** Te Urewera National Park in New Zealand is a subject of the law with legal personality as well as Mount Taranaki.
- **Customary law:** Legal recognition of indigenous governance and sacred sites – mainly in Africa (for example, Benin Sacred Forest Law 2012 – protects the living law and promotes community ecological governance).
- **Policy:** IUCN has adopted resolutions on the rights of Nature and included rights of Nature in their 2017–2020 work programme.

How can we make this happen?

Historically, legal rights have never been granted easily from those in power. They have to be claimed by the people. In Europe we now have the beginnings of a form of participatory democracy – thanks to Regulation 211/2011 (the "European Citi-zens Initiative"), which is the first instrument in the world that allows citizens to pro-pose laws at a trans-national level. One million statements of support across at least seven Member States enables citizens to propose items for the EU legislative agenda.

To this effect, Mumta Ito and colleagues have produced a Draft EU Directive to show how a framework for rights of Nature and ecological governance could work at the EU level and they are organizing a European Citizens Initiative to pro-pose it for inclusion in the EU legislative agenda. In March 2017 her organization Nature's Rights held a conference in the European Parlimanent that was co-hosted by MEPs from three different political parties to introduce the initiative. The rights are collective – applying to the ecosystems or species as a whole. The main points covered are as follows:

- The right to life and to exist.
- The right to maintain the integrity of its natural cycles, vital processes and capacity for regeneration.

- The right to habitat.
- The right to naturally evolve and to preserve the diversity of life.
- The right to preservation of the functionality of the water cycle.
- The right to timely and effective restoration.

Additionally, the proposal provides for:

- A legal duty of care.
- Legal personality.
- Procedural rights around standing, representation and enforcement.
- A human right to a healthy environment in a rights of Nature context.
- Stripping of rights or privileges of corporations that subordinate the rights of physical people and Nature.
- Ombudsman, amicus curiae, training of all judiciary in environmental matters, special courts and tribunals, problem-solving approach, restorative justice and a wide range of enforcement powers, like piercing the corporate veil, joint director and shareholder liability, restoration.
- Reviewing national laws to integrate across all policy areas.
- Ecological governance, including ecological impact tracing and landscape classification with restoration obligations.
- Phasing out subsidies to industries that infringe the rights of Nature and diversion of those subsidies towards industries that align with the rights of Nature.
- A ban on trade agreements that infringe the rights of Nature.

Although society has talked about sustainability for decades, there is no current legal framework that has achieved this. The NGO Nature's Rights is building international support to proactively promote the paradigm shift in law needed to meet the challenges of our time and to develop alternative frameworks based on an ecological approach to law, which promotes legal recognition of Nature's rights as the first step.

Conclusion

To counteract the excessive use of the property paradigm with respect to Nature, we believe that environmental law needs to be profoundly revised from its very foundations, in order to shift towards an ecological approach. This should be based on Earth Jurisprudence, which considers the health and integrity of ecosystems as a prerequisite for healthy and sustainable patterns of human development. The new emerging paradigm is to be grounded in experiential understanding of human beings as an integral part of the Earth community – our flourishing and survival interdependent with the flourishing and survival of the ecosystems that provide and maintain the basic conditions for life (a principle that also underpins the widely embraced Earth Charter Initiative). It would place ecosystems and other species on the same legal (and practical) footing as corporations and human beings. A practical tool that provides a bold first step towards achieving this is the legal recognition of other species and ecosystems as subjects of the law with enforceable rights. This would act as a counter-balance to corporate rights and as a strong support to our most fundamental human right – the right to life. How can we have a right to life if that which gives us life doesn't have a corresponding right to life?

Only if such a shift occurs, will environmental law be able to make an effective contribution to the protection of the health and integrity of the ecosystems that support and maintain the conditions for life on Earth. There are natural laws that govern life. When laws take these into account, we can create peace, prosperity and harmony for all. When laws are not aligned with these, we almost inevitably create a spiral of destruction, as we are seeing in the world today. All societies that have ignored this truth have perished. We have a choice to reverse this fatal end. Let's grasp it.

Notes

About Nature's Rights: Nature's Rights (previously Rights of Nature Europe) is a young international non-profit organization committed to establishing rights of nature in law and policy in Europe and around the world. Among its innovations is a Draft EU Directive to codify nature's rights into European law.

About ELGA: The Ecological Law & Governance Association (ELGA) was recently established as a network of academics, professionals and organizations committed to tackling the causes, and not just the symptoms, of global environmental degradation. It aims to support the creation and implementation of ecological law and governance from a wide ecological perspective, rather than from a narrow economic, utilitarian and anthropocentric perspective.

Bibliography

Barlow, M. (2013) *Blue Future: Protecting Water for People and the Planet Forever.* New York: The New Press.

Berry, T. (1999) *The Great Work: Our Way into the Future.* New York: Bell Tower.

Berry, T. (2002) Rights of the Earth: Recognising the Rights of All Living Things. *Resurgence* 214. www.resurgence.org/magazine/issue214-challenge-at-johannesburg.html

Bosselmann, K. (2016a) *The Principle of Sustainability. Transforming Law and Governance* (2nd edn). London and New York: Routledge.

Bosselmann, K. (2016b) *Earth Governance. Trusteeship of the Global Commons.* Cheltenham and Northampton: Edward Elgar.

Burdon, P. (2011) *Exploring Wild Law. The Philosophy of Earth Jurisprudence.* Kent Town: Wakefield Press.

Capra, F. and Luisi, P.L. (2014) *The Systems View of Life. A Unifying Vision.* Cambridge and New York: Cambridge University Press.

Capra, F. and Mattei, U. (2015) *The Ecology of Law. Toward a Legal System in Tune with Nature and Community.* Oakland: Berrett-Koehler.

Cullinan, C. (2002) Human Governance Must Be Consistent with Universal Laws. *Resurgence* 214. www.resurgence.org/magazine/issue214-challenge-at-johannesburg.html

Cullinan, C. (2003) *Wild Law: A Manifesto for Earth Justice.* Totnes: Green Books.

Diamond, J. (2005) *Collapse: How Societies Choose to Fail or Succeed*. New York and London: Penguin.

Ito, M. (2014) Being Nature – Extending Civil Rights to the Natural World. *Ecologist*.

Ito, M (2015) The Legality of Extinction – How Far Can the Law Protect Endangered Species? Lexis Nexis, Lexis PSL.

Ito, M. (2016) Rights of Nature. Why Do We Need It? *Permaculture Design Issue 99 Ecological Restoration*, 48–51.

Ito, M. (2017) Breakthrough Legal Framework Can Save the Biosphere Before it's Too Late. *Ecohustler*. www.ecohustler.co.uk/2017/04/19/breakthrough-legal-framework-can-save-biosphere-late/

Ito, M. (2017) Nature's Rights: A New Paradigm for Environmental Protection. *Ecologist*. https://theecologist.org/2017/may/09/natures-rights-new-paradigm-environmental-protection

Jackson, T. (2009) *Prosperity without Growth. Economics for a Finite Planet*. London and New York, NY: Earthscan (Routledge).

Jørgensen, S.E., Fath, B.D., Nielsen, S.N., Pulselli, F.M. and Bastianoni, S. (2016) *Flourishing within Limits to Growth. Following Nature's Way*. London and New York: Earthscan (Routledge).

Linzey, T. with Campbell, A. (2009) *Be the Change. How to Get What you Want in Your Community*. Layton: Gibbs-Smith.

Montini, M. (2014) Revising International Environmental Law through the Paradigm of Ecological Sustainability. In F. Lenzerini and A. Vrdoljak (eds), *International Law for Common Goods: Normative Perspectives in Human Rights, Culture and Nature*. Oxford: Hart Publishing. P. 271.

Montini, M. (2016) The Double Failure of Environmental Regulation and Deregulation and the Need for Ecological Law. *Italian Yearbook of International Law XXV*, 265.

Montini, M. and Volpe, F. (2016) Sustainable Development at a Turning Point. *Federalismi* 21, 1.

Montini, M. and Volpe, F. (2017) Regulation for Sustainability: Promoting an Ecology-based Approach. *Federalismi* 3, 1.

Rühs, N. and Jones, A. (2016) The Implementation of Earth Jurisprudence through Substantive Constitutional Rights of Nature. *Sustainability* 8, 174.

Stone, C.D. (2010) *Should Trees Have Standing? Law Morality and the Environment* (3rd edn). New York: Oxford University Press.

Stutzin, G. (2002) Nature's Rights: Justice Requires that Nature Be Recognised as a Legal Entity. *Resurgence* 210.

The Council of Canadians, Fundación Pachamama and Global Exchange (2011) *The Rights of Nature: The Case for a Universal Declaration of the Rights of Mother Earth*.

Tucker, E. and Grim, J. (2014) *Thomas Berry: Selected Writings on the Earth Community*. New York: Orbis Books.

Various Authors (2012) *Rights of Nature: Planting Seeds of Real Change*. Global Exchange.

17

NATURES, RIGHTS AND POLITICAL MOVEMENTS

Larry Lohmann

Natures fit for capital

The word *nature* has a lot of meanings, and they are always changing. For Raymond Williams (1983, p. 219), it was "perhaps the most complex word in the [English] language". Distinguishing nature from what is not nature is an unending struggle. When we grow crops, are we dealing with nature or something that is not nature? Maize, rice and potatoes have been with us for millennia, we influencing (creating) them and they influencing (creating) us. When we look at a forest, we are almost always looking at something that has been shaped by millennia of human burning, planting, sharing, cultivating and gathering. Are we looking at nature or at something that is not nature? Or at both? In what circumstances do we even want to ask such questions?

I think about what it is for me to remember my way home. My eyes fall on that familiar rock, I lift my head and there is that old tree in the distance, and after that there will be two more streets, the bend in the road and then the building with the butcher shop. Is my memory something that I have inside me that is separate from nature, or is my memory also in nature – in the pathway, the rock, the tree and the streets? No need to travel to Melanesia (Strathern, 1980) or the Amazon (Viveiros de Castro, 1998) to find places or circumstances in which nature/culture bifurcations to which we may have grown accustomed suddenly look odd.

Nevertheless, our schoolteachers told us that behind all the different things human beings do there is an unchanging background consisting of things like atoms and energy. Human societies are like characters in a cartoon. Captain America walks around in the foreground, but the background often stays pretty much the same from frame to frame. This background, our schoolteachers said, is called "nature". So, we're surprised when we learn that for many Amazonian societies, it is, roughly speaking, the background that is culture, and what move around in the foreground are natures (Viveiros de Castro, 1998; Kohn, 2013).

Which raises the question: what are the reasons for dividing nature from society in the peculiar way that our schoolteachers advocated, and to say that this is the most important distinction there is? In societies dominated by capital there are in fact many such reasons, probably more than there ever were before. These reasons tend to be "free-floating" in the sense spelled out by Daniel Dennett (2018). They don't presuppose intelligent, intentional prior design, comprehension or even consciousness. They are unlikely to be reasons that individual capitalists, for example, can be said to "have". They don't necessarily need a Descartes to articulate them. But they're adaptive for the accumulative environments that have proliferated especially since the 16th century, which they continually modify in turn. They are there in the way people and things act (Zizek, 1991; Marx, 1976 [1867]) even if not in what they believe. For example, human beings are divided from land so that they can be put to work and produce surplus that becomes profit. Various processes result in the half-successful creation and re-creation of supposedly non-natural humans who can make commodities out of supposedly non-human natures, which are created and re-created through similarly half-successful procedures. The bifurcation is then sharpened and generalized globally through fossil-fuelled mechanization (Huber, 2008) and thermodynamics (Lohmann and Hildyard, 2014; Caffentzis, 2013). Relationships are reconfigured in millions of ways that result in the emergence, by the 19th century, of relata (Barad, 2007, pp. 136ff.), consisting of real abstractions (Moore, 2015, pp. 30, 55–56, 197) known as "resources" (potential or actual) and "labour" (potential or actual), that is, of new forms of non-human and human. For example, when people move into centres of mechanization, the land they leave behind changes as well as the people themselves. Farmland changes into large-scale plantations, mineheads or reservoirs. Fertility of the agricultural fields that remain changes from being a matter of manuring, firing and rotation with local cultivars towards being more a matter of importing guano from Peruvian islands, saltpeter from the Atacama, or Haber-Bosch nitrates from gas extracted from new fracking sites in the US. Each import entails certain kinds of treatment of human beings and land far from the fields where the new fertilizer itself changes the soil structure. Animals change over time, too. The 19th century saw a difference in the treatment of horses when they became part of the steam economy (Forrest, 2017), and the 20th century in the treatment of cattle and chickens when they were isolated and amassed on feedlots and factories, their recourse to commons cut off and their rates of growth reorganized according to the free-floating rationales of capital. The domestic beast-that-can-be-tortured was part of a nature that was as artifactual as the mythical, purely wild deer and buffalo of the "primordial" Americas (Hribal, 2012; Mann, 2006; see also Berger, 2009).

Almost by definition, resources are passive and under threat from society. To survive the threat, they have to be "managed sustainably" by experts who inhabit an ancestral line that stretches back at least to the 18th-century European foresters working to keep insular colonial plantations productive (Grove, 1997). To put it another way, sooner or later many resources have to become as "renewable" as possible. Alternatively, the "populations" to which resources are counterposed have to be surveyed, reorganized, "digitized" and trimmed (or expanded). Or certain resources have to be cut off from contact both with ordinary people, and, to some extent, with individual capitals, and placed under legislation establishing protected areas or other special reserves. Such actions – usually undertaken by states – embellish, embroider, elaborate and strengthen existing Cartesian bifurcations still further, adding their bits to help produce the "nature" and "society" of educated people, which seem always to have been there and to be "separate from the practices in which they are brought into being and reproduced" (Mitchell, 2002, p. 296).

These capitalist environmentalisms – together with regulation more generally – tend to generate their own imaginary featuring powerful managerial agents situated above both nature and society that can step in to govern their mutual relations. In one limiting case, this even includes fantastical agents charged with "ending capitalism" while keeping capitalist nature more or less as it is. (For a contrast between such "global" imaginaries and alternative "spherical" imaginaries, see Ingold, (2000).) Law, mapping, school curricula, statistics, economics, climatology and other disciplines and institutions help to stage, produce, format and secure a bifurcation of the world into implementation and plans, material and discursive, real and abstract, material and technological, violence and law, "exchange and rules for exchange", "objects and ideas, nature and culture, reality and its representation, the nonhuman and the human" (Mitchell, 2002, pp. 10, 82–83). "Biopower" (Foucault, 2003), in tandem with its more recent complement "geopower" (Yanez, 2018; Bonneiul and Fressoz, 2016; see also Moore, 2015; Robertson, 2004), add immense detail and density to these reifications. Maintaining these bifurcations – which are manifested in innovations such as "the economy" (an object datable very roughly from the 1930s) and "the climate" (a similar object emerging over a longer period) – is itself, as Timothy Mitchell (2002) argues, key to maintaining elite power in contemporary capitalist societies. But the reasons for their entrenchment remain free-floating and generally evolutionary and need not invoke either "agency" or "structure".

A new stage: ecosystem services

A further stage in this history – one of special contemporary interest – is ecosystem services. This particular new nature, and the "free-floating" reasons for its emergence, have evolved in a context of crisis afflicting earlier capitalist environmentalisms. Later 20th-century overaccumulation saw increasing reliance on the production of waste-based consumption as a means of absorbing surplus (Pineault, 2016; Foster, 2011) at the same time that post-1970 environmental legislation was promulgated in what amounted to both a symptom and a cause of the "maxing out" (Moore, 2015, pp. 119–120, 226) of free waste sinks that industrial capital had long relied on. Exchange of ecosystem services was expressly designed as a way of cheapening that regulation (Lohmann, 2006) – which from its earliest days had been questioned as a dangerous check on economic growth (Lane, 2015, p. 28) – or making it more flexible, "reasonable" and streamlined from the point of view of commercial developers (Robertson, 2004). Instead of reducing their environmental impact at home, businesses could now comply with environmental norms and laws by buying low-cost units of environmental compensation (CO_2 emissions reduction equivalents, units of bat conservation, units of watershed quality, internationally transferred mitigation outcomes and so on) from the other side of the country or the other side of the globe. That helped align regulation more closely with neoliberal business models in which profit rates had to depend more heavily on crude dispossession, neo-extractivism, wage reductions, financial engineering and speculation and plunder of the public sector.

To make this possible, however, non-human nature needed once again to be reconfigured and reimagined. In addition to the cheap labour and cheap resources that capital had always created and depended on, nature/society dichotomies were now modified and re-enlisted to accommodate mass production of tokens whose use-value was to provide cheap, flexible regulatory relief. The extractive and pollution pipelines that conventional environmental regulation had threatened to pinch off were repaired by novel, standardized products derived from further, second-order appropriations of nature. For example, power plants in Europe could "offset" their greenhouse gas emissions by quantifying and colonizing the photosynthetic capacity of tracts of land in Latin America, Africa or Asia. Corporations could also mine the future for such units by claiming – via arcane numerologies paralleling those deployed by the "quants" of the new finance (Lohmann, 2010, pp. 233–237, 242–246) – that their investments in ecosystem services were preventing a measurably greater increment of environmental degradation from occurring elsewhere, and that their purchase of these digitized increments of "avoided degradation" would cancel out the destructiveness of their own activities. The relative cheapness of such units was not – or not entirely – a given, legislated fact, but emerged largely out of a predictable dynamic of rent-seeking lobbying and regulatory capture; informal, improvisatory negotiation (Robertson, 2007); and entrepreneurial competition to find the most efficient means of mass-producing destruction-compensation tokens, often involving ingenious manipulation of numbers. Prices in carbon markets, for example, generally start out very low and then decline spectacularly: pollution allowance prices under the European Union Emissions Trading Scheme have declined by a factor of at least six over its lifetime, hitting significantly negative figures for many large industries (Pearson, 2010), while prices of the United Nations carbon offsets used in the scheme have dropped by a factor of more than 100. Few basic commodities – even those most associated with plummeting prices, such as coffee – can match this triumph of cost reduction.

The new nature consisting of ecosystem services thus emerged in a context that joined burgeoning neoliberal responses to profit crisis traceable to stunted growth in labour productivity (Moore, 2015; Caffentzis, 2013) with a "great acceleration" in environmental destruction (Steffen et al., 2015; Angus, 2016; Melathopoulos and Stoner, 2015). But its appearance also owed a great deal to – and is contributing to the further development of – a third factor: the "geopower" mentioned above. Geopower manifested itself in, for example, post-war ecosystem science and the supercomputer-driven global circulation models (GCMs) that enable and constrain the work of the Intergovernmental Panel on Climate Change (IPCC). While the groundwork for both developments had been laid long before in European colonial science (Anker, 2001) and what James Beniger (1986, p. vi) calls the 19th-century "control revolution" tied to the emergence of thermodynamic energy, significant recent factors were post-Second World War systems and cybernetic thinking influenced by military and nuclear-state preoccupations with command, control, communication, feedback and means for wholesale mechanization of interpretative labour (Elichirigoity, 1999, pp. 33–36; Edwards, 2013; Haraway, 1991, pp. 62–68; Gane, 2006; Nelson, 2015). GCMs helped paint an ever more indelible picture of a coherent global climate system "locked into an endless dance of adaptation" with an external, equally blocklike global social system (Taylor, 2015, p. 39; see also Carey, 2014 and Fogel, 2004, p. 109), which both responded to and was supposed to control and manage it (Elichigoity, 1999, p. 37). Ecosystem studies, for their part, came under growing pressure to develop into an "econoscience" in which "conventional market accounting units and ecosystem accounting units" would be merged in a way that could make national and international trading in ecosystem services credible in environmental terms (Boyd and Banzhof, 2007, p. 626). Thus, the new "nature" defined as ecosystem services included not just species, but also digitized units of "species-equivalents" that could be exchanged one for another to provide the same services to society that less information-intensive conventional regulation would have provided, but more cheaply. It included not just molecules, but also "molecule-equivalents" certified by the IPCC to be "equally" destabilizing to the climate and thus tradeable for one another according to their "global warming potentials" (GWPs). For example, it no longer exhausted the definition of a nitrous oxide molecule to say that it consisted of one nitrogen atom and two oxygen atoms; had certain distinctive, complex effects on global climate; and so forth. Today, a nitrous oxide molecule is also, climatologically speaking, 0.003 carbon dioxide molecules, 0.114 methane molecules and 17.953 CFC-11 molecules (IPCC, 2015, pp. 87–88). The subject matters of natural sciences shifted, in other words, when different species and greenhouse gases began to have to confront each other as service commodities in the way that linen, in becoming a commodity, had to confront coats, corn and iron in certain new ways (Marx, 1976 [1867], pp. 132ff.). To become an acceptable candidate for salvation, capital's nature itself had to become – in parallel with the human subjects of Foucault's biopower – something that geopower was capable of "making live or letting die" as well as something sovereign corporations or states could "let live or make die" (Foucault, 2003, p. 241; Ojalammi and Blomley, 2015, p. 53).

The partial reinvention of "nature" in terms of ecosystem services was simultaneously, of course, a partial reinvention of the "society" counterposed to it under the rule of capital. In the course of helping capital overcome regulatory blocks to investment, the averaged, "liquid" nature (Buscher, 2014) defined by an expanded set of market-friendly environmental equivalences finds a counterpart in the averaged, "statistical" person (Heinzerling, 2000) whose fears (Sunstein, 2009) and suffering can be fluently costed out even while specific individuals or communities succumb to uncertainty or disease. Under a geopowered regime of environmental services, the neoliberal state can convert polluting factories, airports or extraction sites into statutorily "non-polluting" installations that local residents have fewer legal rights to challenge, without having to stem a single effluent stream. At the same time, new styles of "social" discipline come into play (Osborne, 2015; Pena-Valderrama, 2016; West, 2006) in the distant locations that produce the offsets that "neutralize" effluents or extinctions. Each "double grab" performed by an offset (see Re:Common, this volume) is also double in the sense of amounting to a grab of both "nature" and "society".

Rights to nature

One element missing from the short history of natures sketched above is rights. Natures are partly composed of rights and rights are partly composed of natures. Every history of natures is a history of rights, and vice versa.

For example, the rights of access that form part of the set of relations in which the ecologies of various common irrigation systems in Asia are suspended are tied to obligations not only to common welfare but also to spirits of water, rice, and other aspects of the landscape (Chatchawan and Lohmann, 1991, pp. 102–105). The "bundles of rights" that are commonly held to constitute private property, by the same token, cannot become a reality without the various "bundles of powers" that constitute access (Ribot and Peluso, 2003, p. 153). Those powers in turn rely on technologies that have specific ecological effects. In the modern era, strong private rights over extensive stretches of land have depended, among other things, on the availability of hedges, fences and other labour-saving technologies of exclusion and border-construction that have a marked impact on the face of the landscape and its inhabitants' relationships (Blomley, 2007). State or public rights over protected areas also go hand in hand with selectively exclusionary techniques and the construction of distinctive "wildernesses" (Neumann, 1998; Lohmann, 1999). The mapping of territories to facilitate the exercise of rights of conquest, ownership or appropriation helps create putatively null spaces made distinct from the material relationships that formerly constituted them (Sack, 1986). Rights over the electromagnetic spectrum, too, depend on possession by the state of technologies to control and generate the relevant aspects of nature. Even the alienable rights to use your own person that characterize labour power, together with the rest of capital's social relations, become generalized globally only through conflict-ridden fossil-fuelled technologies that reshape non-human as well as human nature (Huber, 2008). The technology-assisted violence associated with creating and enforcing differential private property rights that thinkers as varied as Norbert Elias and David Graeber (2015) see as largely "stored behind the scenes of everyday life" (Elias 2000 [1939]: 238–239) is a violence that makes not only human but also non-human beings what they are.

As one may expect from the history of natures sketched earlier in this chapter, novel elaborations of capitalist nature tend to go hand in hand with the emergence of novel varieties of rights. In the 1940s, for example, it would have seemed outlandish to presume that there could exist rights to global carbon-cycling capacity that could be parcelled out among nation-states. Yet by the year 2000, when ecosystem services had become an aspect of nature, such rights were legally entrenched in global environmental policy (Lohmann, 2006), carrying with them all sorts of financial and environmental consequences. No amount of fences, hedges and cadastral surveys would have been sufficient to make these rights a reality. They become possible only with, for example, continuous emissions monitoring systems (Cole, 2002), satellite imaging, new enforcement systems (Rose, 2003) and a supercomputer-powered conception of Earth as a "vast machine" (Edwards, 2013) endlessly cycling carbon under the controlling eye of nation-states. Just as tradeable wetland-destruction rights ownable by corporations require the production of mounds of "scientifically incoherent" data and propositions that can "circulate in the networks of law and economics" (Robertson, 2006, pp. 375, 377), so, too, ownable rights to use the atmosphere to dump carbon dioxide in (as well as, perhaps at some point in the future, recognized political rights to geoengineer) presuppose a nature that processes of highly mechanized interpretation carried out in part by "intelligent infrastructure" (Jordan, 2018) can "see", even if others cannot.

The *rights to nature* referred to in the title of this volume could not have emerged, and could not continue to emerge today, except through such concrete, science-laden histories. As a rule, *rights to nature* as a concept becomes possible only where it becomes possible to recast a wide range of practices and phenomena as if they were relationships between humans and things – between, roughly speaking, Cartesian subjects and Cartesian objects, *persona* and *res* (Tigar and Levy, 1977, pp. 268–269) – whether those humans are peasants or corporate heads and whether those things are rice fields or Ferrel cells pictured in GCMs. Rights to nature, that is, tend to be part of integrated packages that also include fetishized relata bearing labels such as "resources", "hectares", "nature reserves", "units of functional lift" or "the global climate".

The extent to which *human* rights come out of this same troubled history, while under-explored, should not be under-estimated. To oversimplify drastically, human rights and the relata that are their subjects tend to precipitate out of the conflicts and compromises that accompany the emergence of packages that include natures of a roughly Cartesian, anti-commons type. Just as London's public parks are no more (if no less) than a residue of embattled commons (Thompson, 1990, pp. 63, 96–184) governance of which passed, over decades and centuries, to middle-class and then municipal organizations (Lefevre, 1910), so, too, a good many of the human rights associated with efforts to limit sovereign power, institute welfare states, combat racism and so forth contain substantial residues (if only residues) of commons-based efforts at self-defence following partial dispossession that have then been reconstituted under other authorities (Linebaugh, 2009; McDermott, 2007). By the same token, some of the first self-identified environmental justice movements tended to present themselves by default as advocating equal human rights to nature (unpolluted air, for example), for the time being leaving latent or inexplicit any underlying opposition to rights to nature (or human rights) themselves. Many mainstream climate justice intellectuals – including delegates to international climate change negotiations as well as academics – have followed suit, basing their work on notions of equal (human) rights to fetishized objects, such as carbon dioxide molecules, development, climate finance, climate risk or economic growth (for example, Baer et al., 2009; Roberts, 2001).

Rights of nature on the "middle ground"

More thoroughgoing resistance to the rights-to-nature framework, of course, does exist in many forms. One form that has become particularly prominent recently are movements for the rights *of* nature, more or less explicitly conceived as opposed to capitalistic rights *to* nature (Ito and Montini, this volume; see also Republic of Ecuador, 2008, Pecharroman, 2018, Arsel, 2012; cf. Stone, 1974). What lessons does the story of rights to nature hold for these movements?

One lesson is that whatever rights of nature may be, conflicts will arise when they are interpreted as rights of any of the abstract natures that have developed under the rule of capital. For example, do natural resources have rights? That amounts to a strange way of talking insofar as natural resources are as a rule constituted in a way that serves commodity production and industrial development, and any rights granted to them would have to be strictly and quantitatively conditioned in order not to hobble capital accumulation.

Similarly, do ecosystem services have rights? That sounds even stranger. Wage workers have rights, but what would it mean for capitalist work itself to have rights? And yet that is what ecosystem services are (Robertson, forthcoming) – the capital-ized work of non-humans, organized in part around the goal of helping to immu-nize private or public industries against environmental laws that governments have passed since the later 20th century. If, on the other hand, it is ecosystem service *providers* that are held to be the holders of rights of nature, other problems arise. For example, how will rights *of* nature be able to challenge capitalistic rights *to* nature if they are modelled on the rights wage labourers have had to fight for? Are there to be non-human labour movements and non-human labour relations boards? If so, what form would these take?

Perhaps, then, the nature that has rights is commons (see Partridge, this volume). But this is not really coherent either. If commons are reinterpreted as a species of natural resource management, as Elinor Ostrom (1990) controversially does, then the difficulties mentioned above with the notion of "rights of resources" re-emerge. If, by contrast, commons are seen as "those parts of the environment for which customary law exact[s] specific forms of community respect", which lie "beyond [people's] own thresholds and outside of their own possessions", which are "not perceived as scarce", and to which people "ha[ve] recognized claims of usage, not to produce commodities but to provide for the subsistence of their households" (Illich, 1983), then the notion of "the rights of commons" seems peculiar in other ways. One difficulty is that such a notion awkwardly assimilates "forms of community respect" to a model of negotiation between relata (Barad, 2007, pp. 136ff.) that emerge from specifically capitalist relationships. This difficulty arises perhaps in its sharpest form where, as is often the case, commons practices are inextricable from a sense of the sacred, whether human or non-human. As one indigenous lawyer puts it, because the cosmos is sacred, to say that it has rights is insulting, like saying that God has rights (Saldamando, 2015). Thus while "common rights" is a comprehensible, fairly unproblematic term insofar as it encompasses diverse notions of mutuality, deference and customary respect, "rights *of* commons" is less so. Language attributing rights to *territorios* (in the sense used in indigenous Latin America) runs into similar contradictions.

Attributing rights to various elements or aspects of nature rather than nature in the round tends only to complicate the issue. Very roughly, most specific elements or aspects of capital's natures can be subsumed under the same categories that apply to the whole: "resource", "protected object", "ecosystem service". That makes it problematic to propose rights that can be possessed by specific parcels of land or specific animals, geological formations, deoxyribonucleic acid (DNA) sequences, rivers or plants, or their various activities, with some humans sometimes a partial exception. Under some commons regimes, meanwhile, many aspects of nature also remain more or less in the same framework of the sacred that covers the whole. Yet under other commons or liminal regimes, rights can be attributed to elements or aspects of nature even if not to the whole. For example, although animals may in some circumstances be sacred and removed from the realm of rights altogether, they are also often beings over which humans have rights but that also have their own rights. On the cusp of the early modern era, animals were not only not yet resources in the contemporary sense; famously, they were also often even put on trial for various misdeeds and could be defended in court (St. Clair, 2011). Contemporary animal rights movements are in part a conscious retort – but one that tends not to invoke the sacred – to the increased industrial resourcification of animals particularly following the Second World War. Recent defences of the rights of rivers also belong to this odd, evolving "middle ground" (White, 2011 [1991]) where capitalistic, commons, religious and rights traditions are all uncertainly in play and subject to ad hoc transformations.

Accordingly, the political difficulties of finding or creating a nature that could be an unequivocal subject of rights are not likely to be relieved simply by restricting the focus to elements or aspects of various natures. Should we then just give up this line of enquiry? If "recognizing rights of nature" is no substitute for – and may even undermine – efforts to support and build on existing tangles of commons relationships in their millions, and if the real issue is how to stimulate discussions and other actions directed at more mutually respectful ways of living and being *tout court*, perhaps nature talk should simply be dispensed with. Perhaps the concepts both of rights and of nature are burdened with just too much historical baggage to be usefully retooled as instruments in struggles opposing rights-to-nature frameworks.

But this is probably too hasty a conclusion. The political reality is that many who participate in movements that criticize natural resources and ecosystem services continue to feel a need, in current contexts of public debate, to develop general "oppositional" concepts (Haraway, 1991, pp. 155–156) of nature that are as abstract, general and simplified as those represented by phrases such as "natural resources" and "ecosystem services". Of course, "commons" itself is one such term (Lohmann and Hildyard, 2014, p. 66), adapting for general use a tradition specific to historical struggles in Europe and Asia and seldom even called by that name there. However, in addition to being equally highly contested, "commons" may still be too obscure in the minds of many middle-class activists and academics to be used as an effective lever in official and international debates, especially since capital has its own free-floating reasons for defending various versions of "commons" (Caffentzis, 2004, 2013; Federici, 2004). At the same time, the active "middle ground" (White, 2011 [1991]; see also Liu, 2006, 2000, 1996) where structures of nature as resources or ecosystem services cannot quite be entrenched by force is currently a lively and fertile site where new and invented congruences – however ludicrous or equivocal (Viveiros de Castro, 2004) – are positing different and provisional "natures" that may at least be stepping-off points for future cooperation and struggle, or moments in a longer process of what Boaventura de Sousa Santos (2005, p. 20) calls the "dialogical and political work" of translation among social movements. As a gesture of kindness offered by commoners and indigenous peoples to potential allies who have grown up under the sign of "rights to nature", advocacy of "rights of nature" may still turn out to be capable of preparing the ground for more radical practices of interpretation and re-interpretation.

References

Angus, I. (2016) *Facing the Anthropocene: Fossil Capitalism and the Crisis of the Earth System.* New York: Monthly Review Press.

Anker, Peder (2001) *Imperial Ecology: Environmental Order in the British Empire, 1895–1945.* Cambridge, MA: Harvard University Press.

Arsel, M. (2012) Between 'Marx and Markets'? The State, the 'Left Turn' and Nature in Ecuador. *Tijdschrift Voor Economische En Sociale Geografie* 103 (2), 150–163.

Baer, P., Athanasiou, T., Kartha, S. and Kemp-Benedict, E. (2009) Greenhouse Development Rights: A Proposal for a Fair Global Climate Treaty. *Ethics, Place & Environment* 12 (3), 267–281.

Barad, K. (2007) *Meeting the Universe Halfway: Quantum Physics and the Entanglement of Matter and Meaning.* Durham, NC: Duke University Press.

Beniger, J. (1986) *The Control Revolution.* Cambridge, MA: Harvard University Press.

Berger, J. (2009) *Why Look at Animals?* London: Penguin.

Blomley, N. (2007) Making Private Property: Enclosure, Common Right and the Work of Hedges. *Rural History* 18 (1), 1–21.

Bonneiul, C. and Fressoz, J.-B. (2016) *The Shock of the Anthropocene: The Earth, History and US*, trans. D. Fernbach. London: Verso.

Boyd, J. and Banzhaf, S. (2007) What are Ecosystem Services? The Need for Standardized Environmental Accounting Units. *Ecological Economics* 63, 616–626.

Buscher, B. (2014) Nature on the Move I: The Value and Circulation of Liquid Nature and the Emergence of Fictitious Conservation. In B. Buscher, W. Dressler and R. Fletcher (eds), *NatureTM Inc.: Environmental Conservation in the Neoliberal Age.* Tucson: University of Arizona Press. Pp. 183–204.

Caffentzis, G. (2004) *A Tale of Two Conferences: Globalization, the Crisis of Neoliberalism and Question of the Commons.* Presentation at the Alter-Globalization Conference, San Miguel de Allende, Mexico, 9 August.

Caffentzis, G. (2013) *In Letters of Blood and Fire.* Oakland: PM Press.

Carey, M. (2014) Science, Models, and Historians: Toward a Critical Climate History. *Environmental History* 19, 354–364.

Chatchawan T. and Lohmann, L. (1991) The *mueang faai* Irrigation System of Northern Thailand. *The Ecologist* 21 (1), 101–106.

Cole, D.H. (2002) *Pollution and Property: Comparing Ownership Institutions for Environmental Protection.* Cambridge: Cambridge University Press.

Dennett, D.C. (2018) *From Bacteria to Bach and Back: The Evolution of Minds.* London: Penguin.

de Sousa Santos, B. (2005) The Future of the World Social Forum: The Work of Translation. *Development* 48 (2), 15–22.

Edwards, P. (2013) *A Vast Machine: Computer Models, Climate Data, and the Politics of Global Warming.* Cambridge, MA: MIT Press.

Elias, N. (2000 [1939]). *The Civilizing Process: Sociogenetic and Psychogenetic Investigations.* Trans. Jephcott, E. Oxford: Blackwell.

Elichirigoity, F. (1999). *Planet Management: Limits to Growth, Computer Simulation, and the Emergence of Global Spaces.* Evanston: Northwestern University Press.

Federici, S. (2004) *Caliban and the Witch: Women, the Body and Primitive Accumulation.* Oakland: Autonomedia.

Fogel, C. (2004) The Local, the Global, and the Kyoto Protocol. In S. Jasanoff and M.L. Martello (eds), *Earthly Politics: Local and Global in Environmental Governance.* Cambridge: MIT Press. Pp. 103–126.

Forrest, S. (2017) *The Age of the Horse: An Equine Journey through Human History.* New York: Atlantic.

Foster, J.B. (2011) The Ecology of Marxian Political Economy. *Monthly Review* 63 (4), 1–16.

Foucault, M. (2003) *Society Must be Defended: Lectures at the College de France, 1975–76,* trans. D. Macey. New York: Picador.

Gane, Nicholas (2006) When We Have Never Been Human, What is to be Done?: Interview with Donna Haraway. *Theory, Culture and Society* 23 (7–8), 135–158.

Graeber, D. (2015) *The Utopia of Rules: On Technology, Stupidity and the Secret Joys of Bureaucracy.* London: Melville House.

Grove, R.H. (1997) *Ecology, Climate and Empire: Colonialism and Global Environmental History, 1400–1940.* Cambridge: White Horse Press.

Haraway, D. (1991) *Simians, Cyborgs and Women: The Reinvention of Nature.* London: Free Association Books.

Heinzerling, L. (2000) The Rights of Statistical People. *Harvard Environmental Law Review* 24, 189–207.

Hribal, J. (2012) Animals are Part of the Working Class Reviewed. *Borderlands* 11 (2), 1–37.

Huber, M. (2008) Energizing Historical Materialism: Fossil Fuels, Space and the Capitalist Mode of Production. *Geoforum* 40, 105–115.

Illich, I. (1983) Silence is a Commons. *Co-Evolution Quarterly,* Winter.

Ingold, T. (2000) Globes and Spheres: The Topology of Environmentalism. In *The Perception of the Environment.* New York and London: Routledge. Pp. 209–218.

Intergovernmental Panel on Climate Change (IPCC) (2015) *Climate Change 2014: Synthesis Report. Contribution of Working Groups I, II and III to the Fifth Assessment Report of the Intergovernmental Panel on Climate Change.* Geneva: IPCC.

Ito, M. and Montini, M. (2018) Nature's Rights and Earth Jurisprudence – A New Ecologically-based Paradigm for Environmental Law. This volume.

Jordan, M.I. (2018) Artificial Intelligence – The Revolution Hasn't Happened Yet. *Medium.* Available at: https://medium.com/@mijordan3/artificial-intelligence-the-revolution-hasnt-happened-yet-5e1d5812e1e7.

Kohn, E. (2013) *How Forests Think: Toward an Anthropology beyond the Human.* Berkeley: University of California Press.

Lane, R. (2015) Resources for the Future, Resources for Growth: The Making of the 1975 Growth Ban. In B. Stephen and R. Lane (eds), *The Politics of Carbon Markets.* New York: Routledge. Pp. 27–50.

Lefevre, G. (as Lord Eversley) (1910) *Commons, Forests and Footpaths.* London: Cassell.

Linebaugh, P. (2009) *The Magna Carta Manifesto: Liberties and Commons for All.* Berkeley: University of California Press.

Liu, L.H. (1996) *Translingual Practice: Literature, National Culture, and Translated Modernity – China, 1900–1937.* Stanford: Stanford University Press.

Liu, L.H. (ed.) (2000) *Tokens of Exchange: The Problem of Translation in Global Circulations.* Durham, NC: Duke University Press.

Liu, L.H. (2006) *The Clash of Empires: The Invention of China in Modern World Making.* Cambridge, MA: Harvard University Press.

Lohmann, L. (1999) *Forest Cleansing: Racial Oppression in Scientific Nature Conservation.* Sturminster Newton: The Corner House.

Lohmann, L. (2006) *Carbon Trading: A Critical Conversation on Climate Change, Privatisation and Power.* Uppsala: Dag Hammarskjold Foundation.

Lohmann, L. (2010) Uncertainty Markets and Carbon Markets: Variations on Polanyian Themes. *New Political Economy* 15 (2), 225–254.

Lohmann, L. and Hildyard, N. (2014) *Energy, Work and Finance.* Sturminster Newton: The Corner House.

McDermott, J.F.M. (2007) Producing Labor-power. *Science and Society* 71 (3), 299–321.

Mann, C.C. (2006) *1491: New Revelations of the Americas before Columbus.* New York: Vintage.

Marx, K. (1976 [1867]) *Capital,* vol. 1. London: Penguin.

Melathopoulos, A.P. and Stoner, A.M. (2015) Critique and Transformation: On the Hypothetical Nature of Ecosystem Service Value and its Neo-Marxist, Liberal and Pragmatist Criticisms. *Ecological Economics* 117, 173–181.

Mitchell, T. (2002) *Rule of Experts: Egypt, Technopolitics, Modernity.* Berkeley: University of California Press.

Moore, J. (2015) *Capitalism in the Web of Life: Ecology and the Accumulation of Capital.* London: Verso.

Nelson, S.H. (2015) Beyond *The Limits to Growth*: Ecology and the Neoliberal Counterrevolution. *Antipode* 47 (2), 461–480.

Neumann, R.P. (1998) *Imposing Wilderness: Struggles over Livelihood and Nature Preservation in Africa.* Berkeley: University of California Press.

Ojalammi, S. and Blomley, N. (2015) Dancing with Wolves: Making Legal Territory in a More-than-human World. *Geoforum* 62, 51–60.

Osborne, T. (2015) Tradeoffs in Carbon Commodification: A Political Ecology of Common Property Forest Governance. *Geoforum* 67, 64–77.

Ostrom, E. (1990) *Governing the Commons: The Evolution of Institutions for Collective Action.* Cambridge: Cambridge University Press.

Partridge, T. (2018) The Commons as Organizing Infrastructure: Indigenous Collaborations and Post-neoliberal Visions in Ecuador. This volume.

Pearson, A. (2010) *The Carbon Rich List: The Companies Profiting from the EU Emissions Trading Scheme*. London: Sandbag.

Pecharroman, L.C. (2018) Rights of Nature: Rivers that Can Stand in Court. *Resources* 7 (1), 13–27.

Pena-Valderrama, S. (2016) *Entangling Molecules: An Ethnography of a Carbon Offset Project in Madagascar's Eastern Rainforest*. PhD thesis, Durham University, Available at: http://etheses.dur.ac.uk/11475/.

Pineault, E. (2016) *Growth and Over-accumulation in Advanced Capitalism: Some Critical Reflections on the Political Economy and Ecological Economics of Degrowth*, paper presented at the 5th Degrowth conference, Budapest, 31 August.

Re:Common (2018) Offsetting for Whom? This volume.

Republic of Ecuador (2008) *Constitution of 2008*. Georgetown University Political Database of the Americas. Available at: http://pdba.georgetown.edu/Constitutions/Ecuador/english08.html.

Ribot, J. and Peluso, N. (2003) A theory of Access. *Rural Sociology 68 (2),* 153–181.

Roberts, J.T. (2001) Global Inequality and Climate Change. *Society & Natural Resources* 14 (6), 501–509.

Robertson, M.M. (2004) The Neoliberalization of Ecosystem Services: Wetland Mitigation Banking and Problems in Environmental Governance. *Geoforum* 35, 361–373.

Robertson, M.M. (2006) The Nature that Capital Can See: Science, State, and Market in the Commodification of Ecosystem Services. *Environment and Planning D* 24, 367–387.

Robertson, M.M. (2007) Discovering Price in All the Wrong Places: The Work of Commodity Definition and Price under Neoliberal Environmental Policy. *Antipode* 39 (3), 500–526.

Robertson, M.M. (forthcoming) Ecosystem Services as Nature's Workfare. *Annals of the Association of American Geographers*.

Rose, C. (2003) Romans, Roads and Romantic Creators: Traditions of Public Property in the Information Age. *Law and Contemporary Problems* 66, 89–110.

Sack, R.D. (1986) *Human Territoriality: Its Theory and History*. Cambridge: Cambridge University Press.

St Clair, J. (2011) Let us Now Praise Infamous Animals. In J. Hribal, *Fear of the Animal Planet: The Hidden History of Animal Resistance*. Oakland: AK Press. Pp. 1–20.

Saldamando, A. (2015) Personal communication.

Steffen, W., Broadgate, W., Deutsch, L., Gaffney, O. and Ludwig, C. (2015) The Trajectory of the Anthropocene: The Great Acceleration. *The Anthropocene Review* 2 (1), 81–98.

Stone, C.D. (1974) *Should Trees Have Standing? Toward Legal Rights for Natural Objects*. Los Altos: William Kaufman, Inc.

Strathern, M. (1980) No Culture, No Nature: The Hagen Case. In C. MacCormack and M. Strathern (eds), *Nature, Culture and Gender*. Cambridge: Cambridge University Press. Pp. 174–222.

Sunstein, C.R. (2009) *Laws of Fear: Beyond the Precautionary Principle*. Cambridge: Cambridge University Press.

Taylor, M. (2015) *The Political Ecology of Climate Change Adaptation: Livelihoods, Agrarian Change and the Conflicts of Development*. New York: Routledge.

Thompson, E.P. (1990) *Customs in Common: Studies in Traditional Popular Culture*. New York: The Free Press.

Tigar, M. and Levy, M.R. (1977) *Law and the Rise of Capitalism*. New York: Monthly Review Press.

Viveiros de Castro, E. (1998) Cosmological Deixis and Amerindian Perspectivism. *Journal of the Royal Anthropological Institute* 4 (3) 469–488.

Viveiros de Castro, E. (2004) Perspectival Anthropology and the Method of Controlled Equivocation. *Tipití* 2 (1), 3–22.

West, P. (2006) *Conservation Is Our Government Now: The Politics of Ecology in Papua New Guinea.* Durham: Duke University Press.

White, R. (2011 [1991]) *The Middle Ground: Indians, Empires, and Republics in the Great Lakes Region, 1650–1815.* Cambridge: Cambridge University Press.

Williams, R. (1983) *Keywords.* London: Penguin.

Yanez, I. (2018) Personal communication.

Zizek, S. (1991) *For They Know Not What They Do: Enjoyment as a Political Factor.* London: Verso.

PART IV

Tracking alternatives to the neoliberal agenda

Radical environmentalism
and community action

18

THE COMMONS AS ORGANIZING INFRASTRUCTURE

Indigenous collaborations and post-neoliberal visions in Ecuador

Tristan Partridge

Introduction

Countless community initiatives around the world have been based on shared access to communally held land and water and the cooperative management of these productive resources. Such "commons regimes" – particular ways of managing socio-environmental relations (Kenrick, 2009) – have been embodied and developed across diverse socio-cultural contexts and historical moments. Here, I focus on experiences in the indigenous community of San Isidro in Ecuador's Cotopaxi province. Seizing opportunities at a time of national political change, community-members in San Isidro revived forms of cooperative action to further the construction of an irrigation water pipeline, completed in 2009. This community infrastructure project had its source in collectively owned land and served to distribute water for use in agriculture among participating households. In addition to these physical resources, the project also depended on (and generated) certain social resources and collaborative relations. Elsewhere, similar social systems that support cooperation have been called "social infrastructures" (Berlant, 2016, p. 402). I use the term "organizing infrastructure" because, in San Isidro, these particular strategies and forms of organizing have been central to the successful management of the pipeline project and have been put to use in further community collaborations. In this chapter, I highlight how the community management of commons resources in San Isidro strengthened this organizing infrastructure and I relate these community-level dynamics to national political changes since 2006, an era characterized by post-neoliberal visions and rhetoric.

In highland Ecuador, collective actions led by indigenous groups have both precipitated and responded to moments of political change. This has been particularly visible when legal institutional change sought to formalize or redefine the potential for political cooperation and the governance of historically shared resources – both in terms of social organizing (for example, the 1937 Law of the Communes) and in relation to natural resources (during land reform processes in the 1960s and 1970s) (Becker, 1999; Lucero, 2003). More recently, following the presidential election of left-leaning economist Rafael Correa in late 2006, the country's political climate shifted again – also influenced by indigenous political actions (Becker, 2011a) – with the result that visions for fashioning a post-neoliberal era became central to how social, environmental and economic policies were designed. As this chapter argues, the successful implementation of these revalorized political visions at the national level depends significantly on the labour, cooperation and social resources of indigenous and rural communities.

The commons as emergent collaborative space

Analyzing the commons and studying lived examples of how common-pool resources are governed, shared and appropriated – particularly those structured through voluntary and collaborative forms of organizing – have been vital tools for better understanding how cooperation is negotiated and how collective initiatives emerge and sustain themselves (Ostrom, 1990). The commons has also gained traction as a concept to re-orientate political action. In some analyses, the commons operates as an unspecified, utopian concept applied in relation to the institutions and infrastructures that distribute or deliver mass resources (Berlant, 2016). Other analyses have explored and critiqued the relevance of the commons concept as a domain of political thinking-and-action that aims at radical redistribution and liberation from capital (Hardt and Negri, 2009) and/or pursues decolonization and deprivatization (Virno, 2004; Harney and Moten, 2013; Berlant, 2016). As a result, "the commons" often refer to an emergent political space or project that fosters creativity and cooperation (Alessandrini, 2012). As we shall see in the Ecuadorian case discussed below, where communities made use of political and constitutional changes at the national level, there are parallels between the idea of emergent political spaces and the systems of cooperation applied in San Isidro in order to sustain the community's pipeline project.

However, in studying any of these broad parallels between commons regimes elsewhere in the world and the particular context of highland Ecuador in the 21st century, we must acknowledge the long regional history of indigenous struggle and community organizing that has at different times fought to defend, reinstate and sustain shared resources and particular means for their management. Such organizational and self-management work undertaken by indigenous communities has supported collaborative action despite differences within and between groups – and although such work is typically geared towards distinct objectives with unpredictable or uneven consequences for those involved, it has also frequently been central to supporting a broader political goal of collaborative self-determination (Colloredo-Mansfeld, 2009, p. 213).

Collective control over shared resources has also supported communities in achieving and maintaining territorial autonomy and legal recognition – using both together as a basis for pursuing collective interests through interactions with the state and, critically, with other communities and organizations (Lyons, 2006, p. 13). As noted below, the terrain for negotiations between the state and indigenous, marginalized and environmental groups has shifted in the last decade as governmental politics began to engage with long fought-for issues and ideas, for example, through nominal support for the Kichwa indigenous concept of Sumak Kawsay (Buen Vivir in Spanish), which proposes relationships of respect and care among humans, communities and Nature (Zimmerer, 2012). Reflecting concerns about how the concept of "the commons" is being picked up and used, the risk of cooption is ever-present: "As with the real commons . . . the concept itself has been the object of many manipulations and appropriations mostly by the institutions that have made the abolition of communal property their mission" (Federici, 2011, p. 42). In this chapter, I focus not on rhetorical appropriations of the commons but specifically on praxis in a particular context, placing these practices in the broader political context of Ecuador.

The "post-neoliberal" political context and constitutional change

After periods of intense political instability, Ecuador ratified a new national constitution in 2008. Its contents were marked by the ambitions of a political movement and administration that explicitly sought to contest neoliberalism through the construction of "socialism for the twenty-first century", an undertaking that then-president Rafael Correa not only endorsed but for which he also evangelized on the international stage and that, crucially, he declared to be necessary in order to end neoliberalism as the "perverse system that has destroyed our democracy, our economy and our society" (Burbach, 2007). Neoliberal economic policies in the 1990s, together with the move to abandon the national currency and adopt the US dollar in 2000, were among the events that led to both increased political volatility and the resurgence of social movement mobilizations – actions that removed a succession of neoliberal presidents from power, particularly from 1997 to 2007 (Becker, 2011b, p. 26).

Post-2008, the Correa administration pursued a political project – promoted under the name of the *revolucion ciudadana* or "Citizens' Revolution" – which sought to systematize what many activists and analysts referred to as "post-neoliberalism" via increased social spending and renewed claims for national sovereignty (Clark, 2015). This marked a sea change in Ecuadorian politics. Food sovereignty was to guide national agricultural policy – rejecting large-scale intensive agribusiness in favour of small-scale production for the domestic market – and the constitutional process that incorporated such progressive ideas was itself deliberately decentralized, participatory, and responsive to the demands of social movement organizations (Peña, 2015). While still focused on growth, constitutional economics addressed issues of economic plurality and redistribution (Radcliffe, 2012). Other markers of the "post-neoliberal" era also extended beyond economic policies: there was a re-valorization of expertise and academic knowledge (Nelms, 2015), and constitutional change in 2008 provided a "critical juncture" for indigenous movements to "decolonize the country's political structures" (Becker, 2011a, p. 48). That Buen Vivir (Sumak Kawsay) was to guide national development policy (as detailed below) also marked a "radical break" since development plans would no longer depend primarily on their "potential profitability" (Gudynas, 2013, p. 181).

Critiques abound questioning what the "post-" in "post-neoliberalism" signifies in the case of Ecuador. Analysts note, for example, that under Correa the country has seen private sector-led extractivist economic activities continue, albeit with more explicitly pro-poor policy and rhetoric (Walsh, 2010; Kennemore and Weeks, 2011; Goodale and Postero, 2013). Here, however, my focus is not on the delimiting question of whether "the post-neoliberal is, in fact, neoliberalism reinvented" (Nelms, 2015, p. 111). Instead, what is of interest is how specific communities have negotiated and responded to these shifts, and have carved out new political spaces within a changing political arena and in relation to the 2008 Constitution.

Indigenous peoples' social movement organizations have been key civil society actors in moments of political upheaval and constitutional reform across the Andean region (Van Cott, 2003). In Ecuador, an indigenous uprising in 1990 firmly placed indigenous concerns within the national political arena and was followed by repeated calls for the country's constitution to undo the monopolistic powers of a small governing elite, to create a more participatory and inclusionary political system and to declare Ecuador a plurinational state – a multi-cultural society that formally recognizes diverse indigenous territories, cultures, organizations and systems of justice (CONAIE, 1991; Becker, 2011a, pp. 47–53, 2011b, p. 14f.). While tensions persisted between the visions of a post-neoliberal Citizens' Revolution and the pluri-national political priorities put forward by indigenous organizations and activists (Becker, 2011a), the influence of indigenous groups on the 2008 Constitution can be traced in further ways, particularly with reference to collective rights and ideas about development.

For example, Article #57 of the constitution (under *Heading II, Chapter 4:* "Rights of Communities, Peoples and Nationalities") specifies 21 collective rights for indigenous communities, organizations, registered *comunas* and nationalities – including protected rights to occupy inherited lands and territories and to maintain collective control over the use, administration and conservation of land resources held in common (AC, 2008; Partridge, 2016a). The constitution also introduced a chapter on the "Rights of Nature" (*Heading II, Chapter 7:* "Derechos de la naturaleza") with reference to the indigenous Kichwa concept of "Pacha Mama" (or Mother Nature/*Pachamama*) "of which we are a part and which is vital to our existence" (AC, 2008, p. 15). Officials involved in the writing of the constitution have noted that putting forward Nature's Rights involves not a retreat from transforming Nature in order to improve living conditions (particularly of marginalized and exploited groups) but instead

> to investigate and talk with Nature, always appreciating that we are immersed
> in it . . . [consolidating] a new form of interrelation of human beings with

Nature . . . an attitude of identification with Nature, far from ownership and dominance, and very close to curiosity and love.

(Acosta, 2010, p. 2)

Although the relationship between collective control over land and the protection of Nature's rights varies considerably across different contexts, Article #57 also contains provisions for state support of localized practices of biodiversity conservation.

Another indigenous Kichwa concept that featured heavily in the 2008 Constitution was that of *Sumak Kawsay* (or *Buen Vivir* in Spanish) – a multiple concept that translates roughly into English as *harmonious living* or *living well together* (Acosta, 2016). The country's *Development Plan* was to be structured around guaranteeing the "realization" of Buen Vivir or Sumak Kawsay (as in Article #275 and following sections of the Constitution that outline elements of a "harmonious co-existence" with Nature). This clearly marked a radical break from prior development objectives and their political emphasis on neoliberalism, deregulation and extractivism (Aguinaga et al., 2013). Instead, Buen Vivir came to stand for particular values and, in translation from Sumak Kawsay, acquired constitutional meanings that variously brought together notions of "social justice, inclusion and equality" (Zimmerer, 2012, p. 602). Specific articles in the constitution mirrored these broad objectives, for example, to promote a politics of redistribution to provide all farmers with access to land and water (#218); to apply systems of science, technology, innovation and ancestral knowledge to improving quality of life for all beings (#385); to prioritize intergenerational responsibility (#400); and to protect fundamental rights to water (#413) and to a healthy, ecologically balanced environment (#14) (AC, 2008; Partridge, 2016a, 2017).

Such significant constitutional aspirations, however, have not only tested notions of political possibility at the national level. They have also created new political spaces and challenges for communities such as San Isidro. In addition to protections for indigenous groups against discrimination and racism – not all of which have been consistently applied or sustained in the ensuing years – Article #57 of the 2008 Constitution included legal protection for indigenous lands used in common. It was following the introduction of these constitutional measures that the community of San Isidro opted to register legally with the state as a *comunidad* in 2009 and thus to benefit from, for example, legal support in counteracting the misappropriation of communal land or water resources (Partridge, 2016a, 2016b). Managing these "commons", however, requires specific forms of social organizing and collaborative labour – as described in the following section.

San Isidro: action and shared infrastructures

San Isidro, at an average altitude of 2950 metres above sea level, is located in the foothills of the western range of mountains that run north–south along the length of Ecuador. The Andean climate is dry with rainfall concentrated around the months of October and March. Although the climate is usually relatively stable year-round, rainfall patterns have become more erratic and less reliable in recent years – something that many residents put down to global climate change. At the time of fieldwork (2010–11), the population of San Isidro was 492 people living in 92 registered households. On average, 85 of those households participated in a community project that brought many benefits: a collectively managed irrigation system that has transformed agricultural production in this semi-arid Andean climate. Even though maintaining this irrigation system involves more hard work for San Isidro residents than those living in six neighbouring communities who also share the water, this increased labour requirement has been key to its success – boosting community co-ownership and demanding effective, cooperative organizing.

Describing this system as commons-based infrastructure emphasizes the coincidence of social and physical relations that it both generates and requires. Here, I highlight how collective resource management of shared water and land has strengthened San Isidro's "organizing infrastructure". In particular, there are four factors of managing these common resources that have supported the success of the pipeline project and have strengthened a shared basis of cooperative relations and techniques: (i) *skills* and the ability to draw on and share in-house expertise; (ii) the *scale* of the project: enabled by cross-community cooperation it has accessed greater government funding; (iii) *regularity* of related work requiring greater investments of time and money both personally and communally; and (iv) *inclusivity*, which has increased community buy-in within San Isidro. The history of acquiring and controlling shared natural resources (land and water) also influences how this commons-based project has emerged and has been sustained – particularly with regard to water and the *páramo* uplands. The *páramo* in Ecuador refers to high-altitude, wetland moors that play a vital role in hydrological cycles by absorbing and releasing rainfall. San Isidro battled for many years to secure its own irrigation water supply from an area of *páramo* just over 1000 hectares in size that the community now owns collectively, known by its Kichwa name, Chaupi Urku.

There were two main efforts to launch a community irrigation project in San Isidro before the successful bid in 2009. The first came after the Ecuadorian Government had nationalized all water resources in 1972 creating INERHI (Ecuadorian Institute of Water Resources) and had introduced subsequent measures to, at least nominally, support localized irrigation water projects. In the early 1990s, San Isidro applied to INERHI for support in locating and delivering water from the *páramo*. However, a rival bid from La Playa (a neighbouring community) was successful, at the cost of San Isidro's chances. It is important to note that almost 20 years later the La Playa project was no longer fully functioning since it highlights some of the skills that San Isidro had access to and could cultivate that supported the eventual success of their later project. The original construction in La Playa had been rushed without conducting necessary engineering surveys. A lack of technical experience among those responsible had meant professional engineers had to be hired in as consultants on any repair work, which was prohibitively expensive. By contrast, in San Isidro, a former community president (Don Jorge Llumiquinga) was a trained technician for the regional water infrastructure agency. He could be hired at a more affordable daily rate (to work on identifying and expediting any necessary repairs) and, critically, could train others in the community – input and skills that have been used increasingly throughout San Isidro's efforts to secure community access to irrigation water.

In the late 1990s, a second venture negotiated a deal whereby San Isidro would protect *páramo* sources (through grazing management and native tree-planting to maintain groundwater levels) used by a number of plantations downstream, in exchange for water concessions (OPIJJ, 2009, pp. 130–131). Unfortunately, government authorization was refused (from CNRH, the National Council of Water Resources, that replaced INERHI in 1994).

The third, and successful, venture came following the creation of INAR (National Institute for Irrigation) in 2007 by the recently elected Correa government, an institute created to focus on small-scale agricultural production. Further protections for small farmers and indigenous groups were written into the 2008 constitution, as detailed above. In January 2009, San Isidro was part of a successful joint application to INAR, different to previous bids due to its scale: rather than addressing the water needs of only one community, the application was made through the local representative political body OPIJJ (Organization of Indigenous Communities in Jatun Juigua) proposing a system that would benefit seven different communities. Consequently, it was significantly larger than most of the projects in the local area, at just over $1.5 million (other regional projects usually amounted to *c*.$200,000). The new pipeline would provide 50 litres per second (lps), and this would be split evenly between (i) Yacubamba (the largest community in the area) along with five satellite communities, and (ii) San Isidro, which would receive 25 lps (compared to 4 lps previously).

This was a good deal for San Isidro, but one that was hard won. In order for this inter-community agreement to be settled, water for the project would be sourced only from San Isidro land – higher up in the *páramo* hills and more difficult to access. This would require more maintenance work and performing that work would be more demanding and time-consuming, given the distances involved. Part of the deal was also that San Isidro would take on primary responsibility for this maintenance work. All of which placed great demands on San Isidro residents, both in terms of collective labour involved in maintaining the 20 kilometres pipeline, and the managerial work required to coordinate those efforts.

Project participation was governed and administered by members of the San Isidro community council, in discussion with regular "assembly" meetings for all participating households. Meetings took place at least once a month, but given the overlap in community membership and pipeline membership (the vast majority of households fitted both categories), even meetings called for other purposes may find a pipeline-related item on their agenda. At least one member or representative of each of the 85 households participating in the pipeline project was expected to attend each meeting. One issue that came up repeatedly during the course of my fieldwork was whether the community should pay a full-time water-system manager. This would require more financial contributions from all members each month, but would reduce the number of weeks/days each household would have to spend in the *páramo* engaged in maintenance work. Ultimately, however, the community-assembly decision was made to save money on a manager's salary and to maintain current levels of labour contributions from all project members.

Decisions were made by majority vote – one vote per household – and were based on extensive deliberations. Assembly meetings typically lasted for at least two or three hours, sometimes running to eight hours and into the night. Everyone who wanted to speak was invited to do so, although this relied on the facilitation skills of a community council member (often the secretary), usually seated at the head table in the community meeting house. A series of lists and accounts kept track of who had worked when, and who had paid (and how promptly) their monthly contributions to the ongoing costs of the pipeline. These costs, after any available government funding for maintenance, were divided evenly between all participating households. Carrying out such managerial tasks on a day-to-day basis fell first to the community council (whose members are elected by community vote every two years). However, ultimate responsibility for decisions and decision-making processes fell to the community as a whole – negotiated through the assembly meetings.

Labour and pipeline maintenance primarily feel into two categories: (i) as part of occasional collective work-parties (*mingas*), a form of cooperative labour that has been practiced in the region for centuries, or (ii) in smaller groups during regular, week-long shifts. *Mingas* had been crucial to the pipeline's construction, and had since taken place in the *páramo* when large-scale maintenance work was required – a handful of times per year up to 100 people would spend a weekend there. The isolation of the huts in the *páramo* meant that all essential elements of everyday life had to be planned for and provided during these *mingas*. In such a remote spot, everyone's most immediate needs and interests were brought together, and everyone relied on the same means for meeting them. Food – cooked and shared communally – was limited to what was made available to everyone, and to what could be carried up from the village. These became important, shared experiences. The remoteness of the *páramo* also typified the week-long shifts of work, which were taken in turn according to a rota. More regular than the *mingas*, these shifts involved three people from three different member-families living and working together from Sunday to Sunday in an isolated hut built specifically for this project. When three people were there each week, this worked out at roughly two shifts of one week per household, per year.

While these demands were significant, they had actually contributed to the success – thus far – of the project. Maintenance and project management responsibilities required member-households of the pipeline to devote more of their time, money and effort to its operation than any other collective undertaking on an ongoing basis had demanded in the past. People's engagement with the project was thus more regular than in past scenarios. It was also the case that a greater number of households participated than in previous projects, and this *inclusivity* had combined with the abovementioned *skills* and elements of *scale* resulting in revived forms of cooperation – both within and between communities. Whether the pipeline will continue to function successfully in the longer term remains to be seen but, now eight years in, this project has already outlasted a number of other community endeavours and illustrates the potential endurance of co-ownership and commons-based initiatives.

The commons as organizing infrastructure

This chapter has highlighted how different resources held in common became the basis of both physical and social forms of infrastructure vital to the realization of a range of social and political goals. The commons in the experiences described here refer both to the natural resources at the heart of San Isidro's pipeline project and the social resources that are required to maintain and sustain it – including voluntary labour schedules, cooperative decision-making processes, regular participation in assembly meetings and collective work-parties. Together, these contribute to the "organizing infrastructure" in San Isidro – a set of practices, skills, techniques and forms of organizing that can be (and have been) put to use in other actions and collaborations. As we have seen, this community-operated irrigation system sources water from communally held land and requires regular cooperative labour from participating households. As a result, the project has both tested and strengthened collective organizing within the indigenous community concerned. The commons is both a material basis (land and water) and a mode-of-interacting underpinning San Isidro's organizing infrastructure.

This chapter has also outlined some of the factors that distinguish the current project from previous attempts at securing a supply of irrigation water for the community – related to skills, scale, regularity and inclusivity – and the role these factors have played in the success-so-far of this collaborative project. Evidence for how this organizing infrastructure has been put to use in further ways is found in more recent mobilizations for water justice and against land misappropriation. For example, San Isidro residents collaborated with neighbouring communities to organize protest marches and to launch a successful legal campaign that stopped an export-oriented broccoli plantation diverting local water resources away from local communities (Partridge, 2017). Within San Isidro itself, the community has repeatedly used assembly meetings and deliberations to address long-running conflict with a neighbouring landowner regarding land boundaries and ownership – also using *mingas* to construct fences, repave roads or redirect irrigation channels when required due to the nature of the dispute (Partridge, 2016a). Having social systems and forms of organizing infrastructure in place has helped make these actions and others like them successful in their aims.

The timing of these recent developments in community praxis and collective action in San Isidro is linked to political shifts at the national-level. Through their collaborative work on the pipeline project, San Isidro residents have realized a number of objectives that the 2008 Constitution aimed to achieve: applying ancestral practices, prioritizing intergenerational responsibility, protecting fundamental rights to water, sustaining an ecologically balanced environment (through grazing management in the *páramo*, and increasing family-scale agriculture at home) and, ultimately, improving quality of life not only for those participating in the project but also for those plants and animals that also benefit from more sustainable farming and irrigation practices.

This historical context highlights both the diverse forms of ongoing indigenous struggle against systematic marginalization in Ecuador as well as constitutional changes that, at least nominally, offered increased forms of legal and institutional support for indigenous communities (including increased availability of funding for irrigation projects). In this sense, San Isidro's community-operated irrigation system is both an expression of collaborative potential and an illustration of how a network of communities seized these emergent political opportunities – where different elements of "the commons" were indeed the basis for an emergent political space that fosters collaboration (Alessandrini, 2012). Such fraught and shifting political dynamics also reflect how post-neoliberal ideas – including some of the far-reaching concepts contained in the 2008 Constitution regarding "harmonious living" – continue to rely for their actualization on the commitment, cooperation and labour of diverse communities such as San Isidro.

Acknowledgement

I am grateful to people in San Isidro, OPIJJ and MICC, without whom this ongoing research would not be possible. I also acknowledge financial support during the writing of this chapter from the Spanish Ministry of Economy and Competitiveness, through the "María de Maeztu" programme for Units of Excellence (MDM-2015–0552).

References

AC (2008) *Constitución Del Ecuador*. Quito, Ecuador: Asamblea Constituyente.

Acosta, A. (2010) Hacia la Declaración Universal de los Derechos de la Naturaleza: Reflexiones para la acción. *Revista AFESE* 54, 11–32.

Acosta, A. (2016) Repensar el mundo desde el Buen Vivir. In *Degrowth in Bewegung(en)*, Chapter 04, 1–11.

Aguinaga, M., Lang, M., Mokrani, D. and Santillana, A. (2013) Debates on Development and its Alternatives in Latin America: A Brief Heterodox Guide. In M. Lang and D. Mokrani (eds), *Beyond Development: Alternative Visions from Latin America*. Quito, Ecuador: Fundación Rosa Luxemburg and Transnational Institute. Pp. 41–59.

Alessandrini, D. (2012) Immaterial Labour and Alternative Valorisation Processes in Italian Feminist Debates: (Re) Exploring the "Commons" of Re-production. feminists@ law 1 (2).

Becker, M. (1999) Comunas and Indigenous Protest in Cayambe, Ecuador. *The Americas* 55 (4), 531–559.

Becker, M. (2011a) Correa, Indigenous Movements, and the Writing of a New Constitution in Ecuador. *Latin American Perspectives* 38 (1), 47–62.

Becker, M. (2011b) *Pachakutik: Indigenous Movements and Electoral Politics in Ecuador*. Lanham: Rowman & Littlefield Publishers.

Berlant, L. (2016) The Commons: Infrastructures for Troubling Times. *Environment and Planning D: Society and Space* 34 (3), 393–419.

Burbach, R. (2007) *Ecuador: The Popular Rebellion Against the "Partidocracia" and the Neo-Liberal State*. Quito, Ecuador: CENSA.

Clark, P. (2015) Can the State Foster Food Sovereignty? Insights from the Case of Ecuador: Can the State Foster Food Sovereignty? Insights from Ecuador. *Journal of Agrarian Change* 16 (2), 183–205.

Colloredo-Mansfeld, R. (2009) *Fighting Like a Community: Andean Civil Society in an Era of Indian Uprisings*. Chicago: University of Chicago Press.

CONAIE (1991) Anteproyecto de ley de nacionalidades indígenas del Ecuador, 1988 (Confederación de Nacionalidades Indígenas del Ecuador: CONAIE). In J. Juncosa (ed.), *Documentos Indios: Declaraciones y pronunciamientos*. Quito, Ecuador: Abya Yala, Pp. 202–212.

Federici, S. (2011) Women, Land Struggles, and the Reconstruction of the Commons. *WorkingUSA* 14 (1), 41–56.

Goodale, M. and Postero, N. (2013) *Neoliberalism, Interrupted: Social Change and Contested Governance in Contemporary Latin America*. Stanford: Stanford University Press.

Gudynas, E. (2013) Transitions to Post-extractivism: Directions, Options, Areas of Action. In M. Lang and D. Mokrani (eds), *Beyond Development: Alternative Visions from Latin America*. Quito, Ecuador: Fundación Rosa Luxemburg; Transnational Institute. Pp. 165–188.

Hardt, M. and Negri, A. (2009) *Commonwealth*. Cambridge, MA: Harvard University Press.

Harney, S. and Moten, F. (2013) *The Undercommons: Fugitive Planning & Black Study*. London: Minor Compositions.

Kennemore, A. and Weeks, G. (2011) Twenty-First Century Socialism? The Elusive Search for a Post-Neoliberal Development Model in Bolivia and Ecuador. *Bulletin of Latin American Research* 30 (3), 267–281.

Kenrick, J. (2009) Commons Thinking. In A. Stibbe (ed.), *The Handbook of Sustainable Literacy: Skills for a Changing World*. Dartington: Green Books. Pp. 33–38.

Lucero, J.A. (2003) Locating the "Indian Problem" Community, Nationality, and Contradiction in Ecuadorian Indigenous Politics. *Latin American Perspectives* 30 (1), 23–48.

Lyons, B.J. (2006) *Remembering the Hacienda: Religion, Authority, and Social Change in Highland Ecuador*. Austin: University of Texas Press.

Nelms, T.C. (2015) "The Problem of Delimitation": Parataxis, Bureaucracy, and Ecuador's Popular and Solidarity Economy. *Journal of the Royal Anthropological Institute* 21 (1), 106–126.

Organization of Indigenous Communities in Jatun Juigua (OPIJJ) (2009) *Recorriendo el Camino de Nuestros Abuelos*. Cotopaxi: Ecuador: Organización del Pueblo Indígena de Jatun Juigua con la cooperación de Visión Mundial Ecuador.

Ostrom, E. (1990) *Governing the Commons: The Evolution of Institutions for Collective Action*. Cambridge and New York: Cambridge University Press.

Partridge, T. (2016a) Rural Intersections: Resource Marginalisation and the "Non-Indian Problem" in Highland Ecuador. *Journal of Rural Studies* 47, 337–349.

Partridge, T. (2016b) Water Justice and Food Sovereignty in Cotopaxi, Ecuador. *Environmental Justice* 9 (2), 49–52.

Partridge, T. (2017) Resisting Ruination: Resource Sovereignties and Socioecological Struggles in Cotopaxi, Ecuador. *Journal of Political Ecology* 24, 763–776.

Peña, K. (2015) Social Movements, the State, and the Making of Food Sovereignty in Ecuador. *Latin American Perspectives*, 0094582X15571278.

Radcliffe, S.A. (2012) Development for a Postneoliberal Era? Sumak Kawsay, Living Well and the Limits to Decolonisation in Ecuador. *Geoforum* 43 (2), 240–249.

Van Cott, D.L. (2003) Andean Indigenous Movements and Constitutional Transformation: Venezuela in Comparative Perspective. *Latin American Perspectives* 30 (1), 49–69.

Virno, P. (2004) *A Grammar of the Multitude: For an Analysis of Contemporary Forms of Life.* Cambridge, MA and London: Semiotext.

Walsh, C. (2010) Development as Buen Vivir: Institutional Arrangements and (De)colonial Entanglements. *Development* 53 (1), 15–21.

Zimmerer, K.S. (2012) The Indigenous Andean Concept of Kawsay, the Politics of Knowledge and Development, and the Borderlands of Environmental Sustainability in Latin America. *PMLA* 127 (3), 600–606.

19

ILLEGAL CAMPING ON "STOLEN NATIVE LAND"

Amanda K. Winter

Introduction

This chapter presents and analyzes two cases of what was deemed "illegal" camping (in tents) on public land, on what is sometimes referred to as "stolen native land" in Vancouver, unceded Coast Salish Territories. The first case is a socio-economic response to the housing crisis by locals camping in tents (commonly referred to as a tent city/tent city squat) in Oppenheimer Park, located in Vancouver's Downtown Eastside. In the second case, environmental activists camped in tents to resist an oil pipeline in the Burnaby Conservation Mountain in Greater Vancouver. By examining these events, which took place about the same time and less than 15 kilometres apart, I shed light on the lessons learned from resisting the neoliberal environmental agenda through the various subjectivities at play.

The irregular use of "stolen native land" is telling of the disconnect between social and environmental resistance, at least in Vancouver, but more generally across North America and beyond. I make this more general claim because I imagine that part of the disjuncture between social and environmental resistance is the dominant idea that humans are separate from nature, and this is perhaps more pronounced in a traditional "urban" setting (see Lefebvre, 2003). This conventional idea is not bound to Vancouver but is a prominent fixture in current Western thought. As Harvey (1996, p. 427) writes,

> it is almost as if a fetishistic conception of "nature" as something to be valued and worshipped separate from human action blinds a whole political movement to the qualities of the actual living environments in which the majority of humanity will soon live.

It is then important to contest neoliberalism and approach these justice concerns in a way that does not reinforce dichotomies such as indigenous/non-indigenous and "pristine nature"/urban. This approach is important given the current dissonance in certain movements that conceptualize the environment as an entity without humans, and prioritize its protection over social concerns.

This chapter will demonstrate how each term in the title is then a piece of the puzzle of this disconnect. Illegality corresponds to power through the way in which the tents are deemed illegal and why. Camping in tents on public land are acts of resistance against the neoliberal privatization of land, the related housing crisis and the regulation of public space. Camping is seen as an abnormal activity involving community living, semi-permanence and the portrayal of an uncleansed image according to the state (see Kennelly, 2015 on the poverty cleansing tactics used in Vancouver). Stolen native land gives attention to Vancouver's colonial past and present, raising questions of urban indigeneity, and maintains the viewpoint of land as a property that can be stolen and commodified.

Considering Canada's colonial history and resource extraction based economy, the resistance examples in this chapter are situated within Canada's "quest for 'energy superpower' status" (Veltmeyer and Bowles, 2014, p. 59). Natural resource extraction motivated genocidal practices, as Canada's economy has depended on forests and mining – and with it the settler removal, displacement and dispossession of Indigenous peoples. Barker (2009, p. 336) describes the current context of Canada's "hybrid" colonialism as "a cross between old imperial conquest of land and resources and new imperial conquest of social reality". The government's current position to rectify the effects of such a conquest is now through "recognition and reconciliation". Writing against such policies, Indigenous scholar Coulthard (2007, p. 439) claims that this approach "promises to reproduce the very configurations of colonial power that Indigenous peoples' demands for recognition have historically sought to transcend". Ongoing debates and struggles over natural resource development have and still are occurring across multiple levels of government.

A major city of Canada's British Columbia (BC) province, and close to the United States' northwest border, Vancouver has a population of about 600,000 with approximately 2.4 million in the greater region (Statistics Canada, 2011). As a relatively "young" city, Vancouver was, in settler terms, founded as a mining village in 1886, where xʷməθkwəy̓əm (Musqueam), Sḵwx̱wú7mesh (Squamish) and Səl̓ílwətaʔ/Selilwitulh (Tsleil-Waututh) Indigenous peoples lived for thousands of years. Many activists today, through a gesture of symbolic solidarity, will provide their address not as BC, but as CST: Coast Salish Territories.

While Canada is not typically viewed as environmentally friendly, Vancouver is famed as a sustainable and green city. Further relevant for the resistance examples in this chapter is the City of Vancouver's quest for the title of the "Greenest City in the World". This involves a municipal action plan with environmental, energy, transport, food and waste goals. The environmental movement in Vancouver is explained by Choudry (2010, p. 100) as dominated by white liberal NGOs that ignore colonialism, while they strive for their privileged version of a "just society". In fact, most Canadian environmental groups "make only passing mention of its effects on Indigenous communities" (Preston, 2013, p. 44). This disconnect, along with the municipality's focus on green city goals, and Canada's colonial history that is largely predicated on displacement through natural resource extraction, all form the important context for the examples discussed in this chapter.

I collected data as a non-Indigenous activist-researcher (outsider-participant) through autoethnographic participation in Vancouver in the fall of 2014. The overall purpose of my field research was to examine the construction and contestations around Vancouver as a "green" city. I transcribed and open coded field notes, media, emails, news articles and Facebook posts where I realized the striking similarities yet juxtaposition of these two camping events. I visited Oppenheimer Park before, during and after the tent city, including the day of its forced injunction and removal. I was also an active participant in the Burnaby Mountain protests. After briefly describing both examples I explore their differences, and then discuss the imagined borders and subjectivities between the two camps. The goal here is to push scholars and activists to be aware of and reflect on how groups of people are represented in their justice demands, and, further, how the environment is framed as connected (or not) to such groups.

Case 1: Tent city and the actually existing Indigenous

Today the Downtown Eastside (DTES) "is often used metonymically for urban poverty, positioned as a dead zone within the city", although the area was key to the region's early imperial growth, where workers flocked to the sawmill and railroad yards (Burnett, 2014, pp. 157–158). In general, contentions seem to amass in the DTES, or as a *Vancouver Observer* journalist describes it: "welcome to the Downtown Eastside, the locus of arguments over gentrification, aboriginal rights, addiction, poverty, and who really runs City Hall" (Yerman, 2014). With a high percentage of homeless persons, acquired immune deficiency syndrome (AIDS) and drug use, this former "skid row" area is characterized as one of North America's worst slums. The Oppenheimer area in the DTES has a 13% Indigenous population (compared to 2% overall in Vancouver) and 70% low-income residents (City of Vancouver, 2013). With low-income residents still unable to afford SROs (Single Resident Occupancy units), 5% of dwellings are owned in Oppenheimer (compared to 48% in Vancouver), with 32% of the DTES homeless population identified as Indigenous. As such, tent cities, anti-gentrification and anti-poverty activism are typical fixtures in this part of Vancouver (see Blomley, 2003).

The Oppenheimer Park tent city (this case of camping herein referred to as Oppenheimer) in the Downtown Eastside began with about 10 tents in July 2014. Instead of obeying orders from the Vancouver Police Department to vacate the public park, more campers joined. The tent city lasted about four months with conservative estimates reaching 100 tents (150 people). The campers – (mostly DTES locals) saw living in tents as a dignified and self-sufficient alternative to SROs – the typical assistance offered by local government to address the housing affordability crisis that has rocked Vancouver since 2007. During a meeting with Vancouver City Councillors, representatives from the tent city demanded immediate action to deal with homelessness in the city, with measures such as improving the conditions of the SROs and providing permanent, rather than temporary, subsidized housing.

This particular tent city (see Figure 19.1) was deemed illegal and forcibly removed in October 2014. As I idly watched the City tear down the tent city (see Figure 19.2), I asked another bystander what they will do with all of the belongings,

FIGURE 19.1 Oppenheimer Park Tent City Squat (August 2014)

Author: Amanda K. Winter

FIGURE 19.2 Oppenheimer Park Tent City (October 2014 – 'Eviction Day')

Author: Amanda K. Winter

and he pointed to the row of garbage trucks – "they will throw it away, it's all trash anyway". Those living on the streets, for whom "sustainable" simply means surviving day to day, have their life in public spaces increasingly regulated so that the city may maintain its attractive appearance, as demonstrated in the tent city evictions (see Kennelly, 2015).

Case 2: No more pipelines on stolen native land

In 2011, Kinder Morgan, the energy company who manages the existing Trans Mountain pipeline that runs from Edmonton to Vancouver, put forth a proposal to twin/expand this particular pipeline. This would triple the capacity (from approximately 300,000 to 890,000 barrels of oil daily) and require a physical enlargement of the Burrard Inlet to accommodate for the increase of tankers needed to transport this corrosive oil from the Alberta tar sands (see Figure 19.3). The expansion project required initial survey work in the Burnaby Mountain Conservation Area (less than 15 kilometres east of the DTES). When this survey work began in 2014, as true to the liberal environmentalist movement of the region, Kinder Morgan was met with resistance by a host of locals, municipal government, Indigenous and non-Indigenous folks.

Burnaby Residents Opposed to Kinder Morgan Expansion (BROKE) was formed in response to the pipeline proposal. They used traditional methods of educational outreach, canvassing and rallies and were involved in municipal politics. They were joined by the Vancouver Eco-socialists Group (VESG) (a long-standing, small group dedicated to various "system change" efforts), and by Rising Tide Vancouver Coast Salish Territories (a direct action, justice-oriented group), all of whom met under the newly established (in fall 2014) umbrella group called Climate Convergence. These groups consisted mainly of white, middle-aged residents and retirees, joined by a few students and Indigenous people. From a younger demographic, an anarchist group dubbed The Caretakers built a resistance encampment directly on top of one of the sites that Kinder Morgan was set to bore, which physically prevented Kinder Morgan from conducting their survey work. This included a main camp site (see Figure 19.4) with others bringing private smaller tents, for 24/7 watch over the mountain, to "defend the land" (this case of camping herein referred to as Burnaby).

Kinder Morgan replied with an over $5 million dollar SLAPP suit (Strategic Lawsuits against Public Participation), naming five defendants as well as BROKE and associated "John and Jane Does". The company also sought an enforcement order, the typical method used to deter the public from engaging in public affairs. BROKE responded:

> [O]nce again we see that Kinder Morgan is attempting to block OUR access to OUR land against Burnaby by-laws. We need to rise up and stop this travesty and protect our rights to freedom of assembly. How can a federally appointed tribunal rule to ignore municipal by-laws, give a corporation

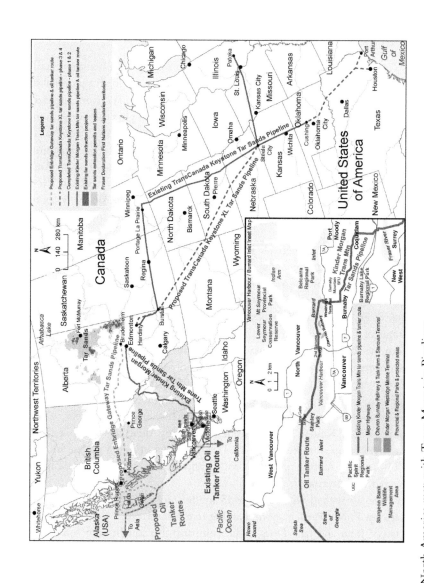

FIGURE 19.3 North America map with Trans Mountain Pipelines

Author: Wilderness Committee, 2014

FIGURE 19.4   Protest signs in front of the Burnaby Camp

Author: Amanda K. Winter

the right to clear cut, survey and block access to residents? It's an archaic interpretation of federalism when local people have no say in protecting the environment.

(October 2014, email; capitalization in the original)

In a *Vancouver Observer* interview, Lynne Quarmby (one of the defendants, a professor at the nearby Simon Fraser University) was asked about the lawsuit and if she was worried that Kinder Morgan would seize her house:

[W]hat is the value of owning my home and having retirement savings, if our world is spiraling into this negative space? If there's no freedom of speech in Canada, and we continue accelerating climate change. If there's no intergenerational justice. If there's no global justice – then what's the value of my *home*?

(Prystupa, 2014; emphasis added)

The activists' demands in this case, with slogans like "No More Pipelines on Stolen Native Land", were not only against oil and environmental degradation, but also strategically in support of Indigenous rights. The immediate demand was to stop the construction of the Trans Mountain Expansion Project pipeline. The resistance events escalated from rallies, to direct action, a lawsuit and a Supreme Court trial. Some meetings had as few as five to ten people, growing to an estimated 800 that attended the rally against the initial injunction in November 2014. The injunction was enforced, the camp was forcibly removed and Kinder Morgan was allowed to conduct survey work on Burnaby Mountain.

The nature of camping in neoliberal resistance

From what I have briefly outlined above, the Oppenheimer camp can be seen as a socio-economic resistance, in particular to housing – where Burnaby land defenders were protecting natural resources in line with environmental justice. The following three further differences demonstrate the various subjectivities at play.

The first difference concerns the role of the local government in determining the legality of the camping. In Oppenheimer, the City of Vancouver was against the camp and ordered the injunction; indeed, the local government was the target of the resistance. In Burnaby, the City of Vancouver was in support of the camp and against the pipeline, opposing the energy corporation and federal and provincial governments – and the City of Burnaby declared the energy company's activities illegal. Here, the local government became an ally of the resistance.

The second difference concerns the socio-materiality of the tents and their camp sites, especially their removal. Oppenheimer was lined with garbage trucks, city workers in high-vis vests and shopping carts with the locals' belongings. In Burnaby, Federal riot police in full weaponized uniform protected Kinder Morgan, made more than 100 arrests and erected a fence around the work site. There were more rallies, chants and even the building of a totem pole. After the removal, the donated camp materials collected from Burnaby were placed into a van and later used for other environmental resistance activities across British Columbia. Further to this, the Oppenheimer tents symbolized a home, whereas in Burnaby the tents symbolized obstruction, not personal homes, which connects to the final difference.

The third difference concerns the actors involved, which tell us a lot about the time and space differences between survival and sustainability. Those involved with Oppenheimer were local residents doing it for themselves, as a survival tactic – with a micro-local time–space continuum – it was a daily resistance regarding the politics of that city block. Those involved with Burnaby ranged: many were local, some students and professors, some travelled across Canada and the US, my housemates, grandmothers, eco-socialists, some who told me their haunting first-hand stories of the tar sands. As many discussions were based on establishing a long-term, worldwide fight against oil pipelines, it was clear that those involved felt the weight of global climate change, that they felt a part of a global environmental effort within a specific local context. Burnaby was long term in every direction, as the discourse of "no more pipelines on stolen native land" suggests time immemorial with the Indigenous support and future generations with their concern for climate change.

The above differences, along with the concern that only in Burnaby was the notion of "stolen native land'" evoked, show two sets of seemingly dichotomous subjectivities that emerge through these examples: Indigenous–non-Indigenous and urban–nature. The imagined borders between Burnaby and Oppenheimer play a role in constructing the subjectivities, which attach to material geographies (Harvey, 1996). Located in Vancouver's slum, the city-ness becomes the dominating factor for the Oppenheimer subjectivity. Urban subjectivities are often countered to the rural, agrarian and "nature". The urban is often portrayed as unnatural, where humans are not a part of nature, and thus cities as our habitats are, by extension, unnatural.

The typical Indigenous subjectivity has been dominated by an "eco-noble savage" idea that the Indigenous peoples are close to and harmonious with "nature": "if located anywhere, native people are frequently imagined in the past or in nature. In either case, they are placed outside the city" (Blomley, 2003, p. 114). In Oppenheimer, camping obstructed the image of a clean public park in the city, where the homeless are rendered ambiguous, vulnerable and unwelcome in such a place (see Dooling, 2009). Oppenheimer may be an extreme case of an "unnatural" setting, as Masuda and Crabtree (2010, p. 656) describe the perception of the DTES as "an appalling social and aesthetic blight on an otherwise much-envied global metropolis". Not only is the area considered "unnatural", but a blight on the city itself. Camping at the Burnaby Mountain is socially and spatially different, as the act fits with the "nature" subjectivity, thus there was little concern for upholding an image of cleanliness, rather of corporate access to natural resources. Since cities are then seen as "unnatural", and Indigenous people are associated with "nature", this leaves little political space for the justice concerns of the actually existing urban Indigenous population.

These subjectivities and the juxtaposition of the cases illustrate what can be deemed as a weakness in such resistances. Dooling (2009, p. 632) asks an important question: "how might integrating social and environmental justice agendas inform a concept of justice that recognizes the complexity of the city's spatial dialectics?" One response to this, in the context of the above cases that demonstrate a disconnect between social and environmental agendas, is to consider these resistances as responses to neoliberal environmentalism and its increasing connection to urbanization. Taking down the borders between the cases, and between the city and nature, may allow us to view Greater Vancouver as stolen native land, pushing scholars and activists to consider these connections. This is important as the involved subjectivities play a role in framing justice demands in such resistances.

Discussion

The city's spatial dialectics relate to Canada's economy, colonialism and urbanization. The above examples come at a crucial time as Brenner (2014) claims that while the Alberta tar sands are not often associated with urbanization, they do indeed represent (planetary) urbanization – challenging conventional conflations of the urban and the city. Brenner (2014, p. 27) writes that the aerial image of the tar sands

> takes us far away from the large, dense, vertical landscapes of cityness, into a zone in which the earth's surface has been layered with a viscous sludge,

traversed by muddy roads twisting around ponds filled with huge accumulations of toxic waste.

(Brenner, 2014, p. 27)

The recent transformation and commodification of the tar sands support capitalist expansion and the accumulation of capital in cities.

Arboleda (2015) stresses that the social and physical change that comes with such extraction makes the "urban" an important identifying characteristic. Re-examining the map in Figure 19.3, the subjectivities may be traced along the pipelines: as capital circulates via oil through the pipelines, those directly affected are displaced. Preston (2013, p. 43) writes that the idea that the tar sands are beneficial for the economy works to "obscure and normalise ongoing processes of environmental racism, Indigenous oppression and violence. And Alberta's tar sands, notably the Athabasca deposits, provide a particularly demonstrative site where these politics play out with every barrel of bitumen extracted from Indigenous territories".

Vancouver in this light is not a bounded city, but an exchange point, which re-conceptualizes borders where oil goes from pipeline to tanker, where Indigenous peoples go from reservation to the DTES. In their *Mainlander* article, Wallstam and Crompton (2014) explore the sustainability dissonance and deem Vancouver as the "city of perpetual displacement". They claim the same party (Vision Vancouver) responsible for overseeing their green city plans has also been complacent:

> Ignore the fact that tanker traffic has doubled in the Burrard Inlet under Vision's watch, up by over 100%. Set aside the fact that Vancouver has among the lowest business property taxes in the world, making it a haven for the majority of the world's mining corporations. Overlook the fact that Vision Vancouver's big answer to the global climate crisis is green business and tax breaks for venture capitalists. Focus instead on the fact that Vision Vancouver has created the "greenest city in the world." Vancouverites are now living under a progressive, green government – or at least you would think if you followed the recent rhetoric of leaders in Vancouver's liberal NGO environmentalist movement.

The authors continue by questioning the consistency of environmental resistance:

> [I]f the struggle to defend the land is defeated, and if Indigenous people are displaced into the cities, the solidarity comes to an abrupt end . . . The choice to dismiss or champion different types of dispossession is only possible from a position of privilege.

Thus, the trend of mainstream, liberal NGO environmentalism in Vancouver invis-ibilizes the ongoing settler colonialism and is a challenge for achieving justice (see also Choudry, 2010). Burnaby Mountain may represent a "pristine, bourgeois wil-derness" that often takes the centre of mainstream debates. This level of protest and activism is missing in the Downtown Eastside, which in this light seems too urbanized to represent such pristine nature, although this is where Indigenous peoples have been displaced to.

As indicated by these authors, this is not the first example of such dissonance. During my involvement in the Burnaby resistance I noticed several comparisons and discussions about the Clayoquot Sound protest, deemed one of Canada's most successful and large civil disobedience acts. During "Clayoquot Summer" in 1993, approximately 10,000 protesters including non-Indigenous and Indigenous peoples protested the government-approved clear-cutting of 70% of the Sound's forests. During that time, environmental activists sided with Indigenous peoples against corporations, yet when the Indigenous peoples wanted to harvest the forests, the environmentalists were against this (Barker, 2009), again illuminating the dissonance that Wallstam and Cromptom discuss above.

This is where concepts of solidarity can be explored to harness the power of resistance through camping, as a method to claim a right to space. Solidarity across the subjectivities and social-environmental divides could be a way for these efforts to become a radical alternative to neoliberal environmentalism. The non-Indigenous activist groups made it clear that the issue was not reconciliation or giving Indigenous peoples their cut of the profit. By concentrating on the "stolen" and "'unceded" nature of Burnaby Mountain, activists directed attention to who benefits from the exploitation of the land and how. However, navigating the non-Indigenous subjectivity remains difficult (see, for example, Memmi's (1974) portrayal of how the social context of colonization places barriers on those who call for a systemic change). Refusing colonialism as a non-Indigenous person could conceivably include a range of activities from signing petitions to more radical actions. However, radical choices may have significant consequences for indigenous activists. This is useful to understand the tensions between non-Indigenous and Indigenous peoples, as many non-Indigenous activists recognized their position of privilege and grapple with how to proceed. Using Memmi's theory, Gale (2014) examines efforts among Israeli and Palestinian peace activist groups, tracing their movement from acts of co-existence to *co-resistance*, wherein the goal was no longer to simply live together, but to politically oppose the occupation. However, she describes a "paradoxical reality" where the leftist colonizer is "politically ineffective", especially in galvanizing large resistance groups, resulting in a choice between "evil and uneasiness" (Memmi, 1974, pp. 85–87).

Conclusion

The examples discussed above involve camping in tents on public land as acts of resistance to state-corporate power. This juxtaposition of two examples from Vancouver, a Canadian settler city on unceded Coast Salish Territory, makes a profound statement about the detachment of social from environmental justice concerns in the current colonial flavour of Vancouver's "liberal environmentalist movement". The first example was a tent city in a public park in Vancouver's slum, an area with a disproportionately high number of Indigenous peoples. Those involved saw living in tents as a dignified way to bring attention to the housing crisis. The second example was of environmental activists camping directly on the site where an energy company planned to conduct survey work for their tar sands oil pipeline on a conservation mountain in Greater Vancouver. In the first example, in what is often understood as a typical urban environment, there was little attention to the survival concerns of actually existing Indigenous and marginalized people. In the second example, in the "pristine natural" environment of Burnaby Mountain, Indigenous and non-Indigenous activists came together to demand "no more pipelines on stolen native land" – garnering international attention and transnational solidarity.

This chapter raised questions, such as: why is Burnaby Mountain considered "stolen native land", but the Downtown Eastside not? What kinds of imaginings and subjectivities are employed in the construction of borders between Burnaby and Oppenheimer? What would *co-resistance* (Gale, 2014) against neoliberalism look like if both Oppenheimer and Burnaby were considered stolen native land? Tent city squats and environmental activism, especially against fossil fuel infrastructure, and in particular against the tar sands, are not unique to Vancouver, and thus the answers to these questions are important for many other places across the globe.

Although as mentioned these cases were quite different in their trajectories, involved communities and tactics, there is a common underlying thread to what they are resisting: the neoliberal commodification and privatization of land. Both groups resorted to camping as resistance, as it symbolizes a stake and a relationship with the land. Both camps resisted neoliberalism and there was space for solidarity and new ideas of a just urbanization. The camps on their own demanded space and made declarations of their positions against current injustices. The Burnaby camp has been described as a "new activist community operating generally outside the disciplining of commodified and colonial space" (Hornick, 2015, p. 7). Choudry (2010, p. 101) claims that while non-Indigenous Canadians are relatively privileged, "the sense of betrayal, loss of sovereignty and despair felt among many non-Indigenous people affected by free market capitalism" can provide "a window of opportunity to build solidarity with Indigenous peoples".

To move away from problematic dichotomies, such as Indigenous/non-Indigenous and "pristine nature"/urban, we need to pay attention to our justice demands, the way we frame the environment and the underlying connections that exist when we rethink conventional borders. Moreover, scholars and activists need to be aware of the consequences of framing the environment as an entity without humans sidelining social concerns. These findings ultimately offer insights regarding the delicate nature of solidarity in the climate justice movement, the expectations of particular social groups, and the importance of Indigenous rights as part of calls for systemic change and climate justice.

Acknowledgements

I would like to thank the Central European University (CEU) Budapest Foundation for their financial support. I also deeply appreciate the discussions and suggestions from Tamara Steger and CEU's ACT Just Research Group.

References

Arboleda, M. (2015) Spaces of Extraction, Metropolitan Explosions: Planetary Urbanization and the Commodity Boom in Latin America. *International Journal of Urban and Regional Research* 40 (1), 96–112.

Barker, A. (2009) The Contemporary Reality of Canadian Imperialism: Settler Colonialism and the Hybrid Colonial State. *The American Indian Quarterly* 33 (3) (summer), 325–351.

Blomley, N. (2003) *Unsettling the City: Urban Land and the Politics of Property*. New York: Routledge.

Brenner, N. (2014) *Implosions/Explosions: Towards a Study of Planetary Urbanization*. Berlin: JOVIS.

Burnett, K. (2014) Commodifying Poverty: Gentrification and Consumption in Vancouver's Downtown Eastside. *Urban Geography* 35 (2), 157–176.

Choudry, A. (2010) What's Left? Canada's "Global Justice" Movement and Colonial Amnesia. *Race & Class* 52 (1), 97–102.

City of Vancouver (2013) Downtown Eastside Local Area Profile. Available at: http://vancouver.ca/files/cov/profile-dtes-local-area-2013.pdf

Coulthard, G. S. (2007) Subjects of Empire: Indigenous Peoples and the 'Politics of Recognition' in Canada. Contemporary Political Theory 6 (4), 437–460.

Dooling, S. (2009) Ecological Gentrification: A Research Agenda Exploring Justice in the City. *International Journal of Urban and Regional Research* 33(3), 621–639.

Gale, L. (2014) "The Coloniser Who Refuses": Co-resistance and the Paradoxical Reality of Israeli Solidarity Activists. *Journal of Peacebuilding and Development* 9 (2), 49–54.

Harvey, D. (1996) *Justice, Nature and the Geography of Difference*. Malden: Blackwell.

Hornick, B. (2015) A View from Burnaby Mountain: Naomi Klein's This Changes Everything. *Countours Journal*. Simon Fraser University Institute of the Humanities, Spring. Available at: http://blogs.sfu.ca/departments/humanities-institute/wp-content/uploads/2015/04/ContoursSpring2015.6-19.pdf

Kennelly, J. (2015) "You're Making our City Look Bad": Olympic Security, Neoliberal Urbanization, and Homeless Youth. *Ethnography* 16 (1), 3–24.

Lefebvre, H. (2003) *The Urban Revolution*. Minneapolis: University of Minnesota Press.

Masuda, J. and Crabtree, A. (2010) Environmental Justice in the Therapeutic Inner City. *Health & Place* 16, 656–665.

Memmi, A. (1974) *The Colonizer and the Colonized*. London: Earthscan Publications.

Preston, J. (2013) Neoliberal Settler Colonialism, Canada and the Tar Sands. *Race & Class* 55 (2), 42–59.

Prystupa, M. (2014) Vancouver Observer. SFU Scientist Worries She'll Lose Home, over Kinder Morgan Lawsuit. Available at: www.vancouverobserver.com/news/sfu-scientist-worries-shell-lose-home-over-kinder-morgan-lawsuit-video

Statistics Canada (2011) Census Metropolitan Area of Vancouver, British Columbia. Available At: www12.statcan.gc.ca/census-recensement/2011/as-sa/fogs-spg/Facts-cma-eng.cfm?LANG=Eng&GK=CMA&GC=933

Veltmeyer, H. and Bowles, P. (2014) Extractivist Resistance: The Case of the Enbridge Oil Pipeline Project in Northern British Columbia. *The Extractive Industries and Society* 1 (1), 59–68.

Wallstam, M. and Crompton, N. (2014) The Mainlander. Pipelines and Elites: The Politics of Greenwashing in Vancouver. Available at: http://themainlander.com/2014/11/11/pipelines-and-elites-the-politics-of greenwashing-in-vancouver/

Wilderness Committee. (2014) Kinder Morgan Pipeline Route Maps. Available At: www.wildernesscommittee.org/kinder_morgan_pipeline_route_maps

Yerman, J. (2014) Developer Dollars, Community Policing, and Cruddy "Little SROs": The Talk at Carnegie Centre. *Vancouver Observer*, 24 October. Available at: www.vancouverobserver.com/news/developer-dollars-community-policing-and-cruddy-little-sros-real-talk-carnegie-centre

20

GERONTOCRACIES OF AFFECT

How the "politics of austerity" have reshaped elder environmental radicalism

Mary Gearey

Introduction

Think for a moment of your own inherent perspective on ageing. Are elders, in your eyes, from your experience, venerable, wise, connected and connecting? Or are they insular, out of touch, myopic in vision – both physically and metaphorically? Are the elderly the ones who got us into our current global environmental mess? Were they too concerned with jobs, property and prestige to intercede when environmental degradation became apparent – are the younger generations reaping what they have sown? Or have these elders too been enmeshed within processes that have restricted their ability to self-determine – to choose a different way to form communities, to utilize resources or to develop economies? We need to pause for a moment to question why age in these neoliberalized times increasingly bears a stigma throughout the global North.

Our ability to imagine environmental radicals is connected intimately with age – the presumption being that the radical young are doers – and that the radical old are thinkers. Within this chapter I ask you to consider why our older community members are often excluded from scholarship concerning environmental activism. Moving from a reflection on our responses to the possibility of elder environmental activism to focusing on empirical research undertaken within the River Adur valley in West Sussex in the UK, this chapter invites, or even incites, you to revisit dominant presumptions and to appreciate the radical interventions, actions and performances of our community elders. These unsung heroes and heroines exist and perform across different temporalities and spatialities. It is suggested in this chapter that it is central government funding cuts to local authority spending that has prompted a resurgence in radical elder activism. Kitson et al. (2011, p. 292) have described this widespread public spending contraction in many developed economies as exhibiting "geographies of austerity" as the pattern is currently replicated across many countries. The impact is that there is less public money for road maintenance, education, social housing, waterways management and environmental stewardship. As explored below, the fieldwork reveals the different inventive, collaborative and unexpected ways that community elders have worked together to champion the needs of the environment. What they have created can be described as "gerontocracies of affect" – freeform of elder lead consortia based around an ethics of care, in which custodianship for the environment is the central axiom.

Deep ecology, eco-socialism, eco-feminism and the rise of the elder environmentalists

The adverse position of elders within societies heavily influenced by neoliberal regimes is explored within a range of literatures (Heller, 2003; Goerres, 2009; EC, 2007; Segal, 2013; Whelehan and Gwynne, 2014). To age is to decline, to become unproductive, to lessen valuable contributions to societies that are increasingly pivoted on speed and adaptability. Zygmunt Bauman's work captures this dexterity by describing it as "liquid modernity" (2000); everything is in flux, moving, changing – our economies, our environment, our connections with others, our embodied selves. As a result, the tropes of the young – flexibility, responsiveness, vigour – are elevated, whereas the connotations of ageing are negative. Age classifies, and as it does so it limits and proscribes who can and who should not or cannot participate in modern society and in what ways.

Yet like all blanket categorizations, "age" as a generic descriptor fails to capture the subtleties of individual life experiences. Indeed, radical democratic theory, as epitomized by the work of Chantal Mouffe (2005) and Ernesto Laclau (Laclau and Mouffe, 2001; Laclau, 2005), is concerned with exploring the radical agent as a wholly corporeal entity: we are all immanent radicals, retaining multiple identities and multiple capacities to act, both inhibited and enabled by the bodies that frame us. The radical agent is embodied – perceives, senses, considers, acts through the body; we cannot separate mind and body. That mind and body ages over time consequently reshapes how the radical subject may act. This concept of the corporeal is laboured here, because the reality of the ageing body as a fundamental aspect of political processes, constructing and determining the efficacy of the radical agent, appears overlooked in most literature.

As embodied selves we all age differently; this process is responsive to our environment. Not everyone has the luxury of ageing well; the global North enjoys asymmetrical opportunities, and even within this categorization there are stark differences of health and well-being strongly associated with income (Dorling, 2015) and class. Ageing is a process that does not sit outside of power regimes and power discourses. How we age reflects our socio-economic context. Further, neoliberal societies embed the notion that ageing well reflects a positive contribution to society; we use one another as gauges for normative evaluations of "success" or "failure". Increasingly, those with poor health or with no financial resources in retirement are viewed as negligent; they have failed to live well, to prepare themselves for later life.

As Lynne Segal (2013) has pointed out in her recent work on age and ageing, as an ageing feminist herself she is able to critically review how our elders become shoe-horned into participating in civic and economic life in particular ways. Simone de Beauvoir (2006) first noted how "age" was not viewed as a suitable academic subject area more than 40 years ago and persuaded to change her research's title from "old age" to "the coming of age".

Our current generation of elders are the ones who supported radical politics in the 1960s and 1970s: the ones that helped usher in, on the whole, more tolerance within democratic societies.

Some of the most radical environmentalists of our time are now elders, still writing, still campaigning, still fighting to raise awareness of our ecological precarity, including Wangari Maathai (2010), James Lovelock (1995), Jonathan Porritt (1986), Gro Harlem Brundtland (1987), Vandana Shiva (2016) and Gary Synder (1995, 2004) among others. Within the literature there seems to be little place for radical environmental elders who have a lifetime's worth of experience with which to assess the scale and speed of change within our economies, to social cohesion, to social justice, gendered lives – to our degraded environments. Elder environmental activists are shoe-horned into positions of knowing sages rather than the liberating position of angry campaigners.

It seems that in front of our eyes, although not recognized in academic research, in community outreach, in the media, are a cohort of elders who care very deeply about the environmental issues they view as catastrophic. The origins of the empirical work discussed below reveals the way that age is rendered invisible, as the participants who were involved in the study only emerged as radical elders as the data collection stage progressed. They were not a target group for this research – they rather emerged through the various pieces of activism that they were engaged with, but that had not been previously identified.

Making themselves known: the undercover activists

During 2015 I undertook a piece of empirical research along the River Adur valley in West Sussex in the UK. The overall objective of the research was to understand in what ways the dissemination of scientific research about climate science has been successful in communicating the scale and scope of the emergent environmental impacts to non-scientific communities. To enable this, the research sought to interrogate at a micro level what environmental changes are perceived by non-scientists, and if these experiences are framed within the discourse of climate change. To do this the research focused on changes to local water environments and rainfall patterns, incidences of flooding or drought events, alterations in water quality and how all these factors may positively or negatively alter local biodiversity. One river catchment was selected, the River Adur, and interviews with people living and working in three waterside villages were undertaken. Through qualitative fieldwork interviews, participant observation and "walking and talking" ethnographic practise the research sought to capture the range of practices, opinions and behaviours expressed by respondents within the study site when asked to reflect on "changing local water environments" however they chose to frame their response. Understanding how local residents perceived changes to their local water assets – the ponds, streams, ditches, springs and sewers that form their waterscapes – and what actions these changes prompted, would indicate what types of technologies, policies and other interventions local residents may be willing to accept to protect the integrity of their water environments. Further, their responses also indicated what they felt was prompting or enabling change – which also indicated whether climate change science research was informing these responses. By encouraging the local residents to define the specific issues regarding changes in their local water environments that they wanted to discuss, the respondents lead the topic range of discussions, not the researcher. If people were concerned about flooding, then this became the central topic of the interview. As a result, a wide range of issues were discussed alongside flooding – including environmentl biodiversity, water costs for local businesses, water quality for livestock or agriculture and the potential future impacts of climate change.

Participants were recruited through purposive sampling, which was undertaken to access respondents who were deemed likely to have insights into water resources management due to their professional, recreational or civic water related interests, or those whose domestic residences situated them close to local water resources. To structure the conversations respondents were invited to talk widely about their memories, responses and actions towards changing local water environments in whatever context appealed to them.

The results were fascinating and took the research into a completely new direction, highlighting how the politics of austerity have adversely impacted on elders, and the activism they have undertaken as a response. Although the research did not actively set out to engage mainly with elders, and despite approaching a wide age range of potential respondents at the recruitment stage, it was mainly an older cohort that agreed to participate, with three-quarters of respondents over retirement age. This work, ethnographic in approach, reveals how the elders that I spoke to framed their activism both in terms of storytelling and through relationships of affect; their actions had a physical and emotional imprint on the world around them.

Through exploring both the range of local knowledges evident within a specific geography of place connected with water resources, together with experiences of lived time, memories and future prospects, it was possible to establish respondents' narrative sense of their world (Newton and Parfitt, 2011). Within the UK some work has been undertaken to explore the connectivity between people and their local waterscapes (Strang, 2004), although this is generally framed within a specific context such as flooding (Lane et al., 2011; McEwan et al., 2017), drought (Dessai and Simms, 2010) or water quality (Faulkner et al., 2001). To capture the intimacy of the stories of people who live and reside alongside their local water resources the research approach was to select three interconnected riparian villages, all sharing one riverside, but with their own distinct array of springs, ponds, sewers, drains, streams, ditches and brooks that collectively make up their local water resources.

The following section of the chapter outlines three respondent stories that are emblematic of the range of insights regarding water resources sustainability in the face of austerity, shared with the author. The stories, and an interrogation of their usefulness in exploring the concept of "gerontocracies of affect", is offered in the next section.

It's a house; but it isn't a home

Talking to people who have experienced flooding in their homes is always painful. Even years after experiencing flooding, although the trauma may subside, it never leaves. Jan and David had built their home in 1987, on the grounds of a property they had moved into in 1976. With their children now having left home, the new property was designed to be future-proofed – to still be accessible as they aged. In other words, a home for life. Yet in winter 2000/2001 a period of heavy rainfall within the region led to the water table rising quickly, but unseen, under the ground. Over the two decades in which they had lived on their property they had never experienced any flooding of their home until the night of 18 January 2001. In just a few short hours their entire downstairs floor was flooded – but not from a burst river bank or the stream, but from a rising water table that leads to the water "bubbling" up through the ground and into their home.

When they called the emergency services they were told that no help was coming on the basis that "there's nowhere to pump the water to". They asked what they should do and were told to go and stay with friends, wait for the water to recede and then call their home insurers. In other words, the state is no longer there to assist. As a homeowner you should have the requisite provisions in place to protect yourself. As Jan and David put it, this was the first moment they realized that they were "on their own". This feeling grew as they pursued both recovery of losses from their insurance company and as their next premium arrived. Their insurance company dragged their heels, did not employ reputable builders and then quadrupled the couple's insurance. This is financially difficult for those on a fixed income. Months of hard negotiations, faulty repairs and sleepless nights followed.

This is the sharp end of neoliberalism. In many ways this couple are quintessential middle Englanders. They have run their local business together, raised three children, remained self-sufficient in terms of contributing to the welfare state system but never taking benefits, building their own home to use as financial collateral for later years. Yet the flood, and the realization that there was no state to support them created a rupture in their personal and political vision. They realized that the mantra of the "resilient" subject was nothing more than a call to be self-sufficient, even when the scale of response needed was beyond that of the individual.

Jan and David's response was to get political. They joined the local Flood Action Defence Group (FADG), which monitors river, drain and water levels in the local area, as well as trains residents to respond to flood events; they now network with local community members to petition the next tier of local governance, the District Council, to undertake infrastructural works to keep water flowing off the land to lessen the risk of flooding; and they both participate in their local parish council to discuss widely changes in local building development in their community and further along the catchment to prevent exacerbating potential flooding. They have also begun to think widely about climate change and how the ways that they, and their children, live impacts on the environment.

Although in their early 70s, Jan and David's experience has lead them to view life very differently. There is some regret that their community engagement activities had to wait until they had retired. Their house has lost significant value since the flood and they question what the hard work "was all for". They are angry that the current political landscape is immune to the different needs of the elderly, particularly the rural elderly. But rather than feel vulnerable, this recognition has enabled them to take action – to use their time to argue against the "resilience" agenda so beloved of neoliberal perspectives. Instead, they are more engaged with their neighbours – knocking on doors as part of the FADG has led them to mix with neighbours from different social classes they would never have otherwise met, and to have a different outlook regarding other lifestyles and approaches. The "eco-warriors" that they felt hallmarked the 1980s as trouble makers are now viewed as prescient scryers of things to come.

What's clear is the importance of home, of building an identity in a locality, and how easily that can be shaken. The austerity politics that have removed the support structures for householders in the UK, and left them reliant on profit-seeking insurance companies and their own self-reliance has, at least for some, sparked the genesis of activism. Even the introduction of a government-backed flood insurance scheme, named "Flood Re", initiated in April 2016, is only partially helpful for householders, such as Jan and David, as there are strict criteria concerning which properties are defined as being at a "high risk" of flooding. Jan and David are now networked with other FADG volunteers across the region; they are now embedded within the fabric of their local community and their political awareness is burgeoning as they begin to connect their life choices with wider environmental changes.

This elder radicalism is rooted in an appreciation of time: present time, making the best of good health and a sound financial retirement provision, and past time – reflecting back on what makes a "good life". There is also the issue of legacy – of not so much handing on to your own family, but to future generations, your role in what Jason Moore has described as "the web of life" (2015, p. 178). It is possible to say that this deliberation on time refines our understanding of the ways in which neoliberalism impacts on the natural world and on our own lives, as we reflect on human life spans and ecological life cycles working independently and together, in relationships of co-construction.

Jan and David are just one couple who have re-orientated their perspectives towards environmental activism. I met others too during the fieldwork who have become involved with local politics because of changes in their local environment, and an acute sense of how modern lives have pushed them away from themselves, their families and their communities. This next story builds upon this critique of the impacts of neoliberalism on local communities – and their fight back.

We won't stop until they listen to us

Cary and Philip moved to Trinton Lane seven years ago when they retired and wanted to downsize to a pretty cottage nestled under the chalklands of the South Downs National Park. They looked forward to dog walking and gardening during their retirement in their new home. Not any more. They are now the leading part of a resident's campaigning group, involved in petitions and direct action, crowd-funding to raise money to pay for engineering reports and to create signage on their local highways.

Cary and Philip moved to the lane in part because of its natural spring, running downhill alongside the road. Traditionally, village children would sail home-made paper boats here. Over the last few years, however, during autumn and winter the spring morphs into a debris-laden cascade, heavy with soil sediments and loose road surface aggregate. Local residents blame the changes on local government spending cuts. Now, there is less money to pay for highways maintenance and drainage clearance, leading to water billowing across the road and deteriorating the lower grade, ageing tarmac. Added to this, residents claim that it is poor land management by the farming estate at the top of the lane that also contributes to soil run off during rainy periods. Local homeowners also assert that large delivery vehicles servicing the estate use the lane as a "rat run" further compounding road surface deterioration, leading to tarmac chippings smashing car windows and pools of water washing away the mortar in garden walls. The 6000-acre farming estate is owned by one ancestral landowner who denies singular responsibility for the lane's decrepitude. Postal workers refuse to deliver mail here and other service providers refuse to service the lane's residents while stagnant water remains on the lane.

The lane's residents are angry. They pay their taxes, they support local business yet no-one is helping them pay for their broken car windows and their falling garden walls or helping them with the noise and worry of large trucks ploughing along this quiet country road. Having banded together to petition the local council, the residents have recognized the need to unite and take action among themselves. They invited local newspapers to document the debris they sweep up in huge piles on the roadside and to photograph the damage caused by the pooling water and heavy machinery traffic. They presented talks and information campaigns at local events to persuade other residents to take action about the ways their own domestic lives are impacted by government cuts. Reflecting on their own experiences they have helped the residents to broaden their own understanding of the structural nature of their issues. For many this has led to a late onset political awakening. Their experiences highlight that government funding cuts impacts rural spaces differentially. They now perceive an asymmetry between rural and urban economies. Rural spaces receive less investment than their urban counterparts – and this is explained

by residents as happening due to ageing rural populations being deemed economically unproductive and, hence, politically unimportant.

The water becomes a metaphor for things drifting apart – all the assurances they
worked and paid their taxes for, no longer reflect their lived reality. These elder
residents, the majority of whom from the campaign group who I met were in their
mid to late 60s and early 70s, have seen at close hand the way the environment
has been devalued. These insights have crystallized for many the problems that the
younger generation now inherits. Rather than an acceptance there is anger. The
environmental campaign that brought the residents together is now also a political
campaign. Cary and Philip now connect financial austerity with a wider "politics
of austerity" whereby the state is retracting responsibility for a range of tasks, using
public spending cuts to justify the implementation of neoliberal policies.

"Think local, act global" could summarize their approach. I was struck by
the multiple ways they were trying to galvanize support – blog writing, crowd-
funding, presenting and petitioning the parish and local councils – to change land-
management practices and return the lane to a quiet country path leading up to the
downland. A reminder of the longstanding character of the lane, and the range of
biodiversity it used to hold, is captured half way up the lane, within a poem inscribed
on a stone tablet embedded in the wall (Figure 20.1). The poem was written by
a British soldier, John Stanley Parvis, in the trenches during the First World War.

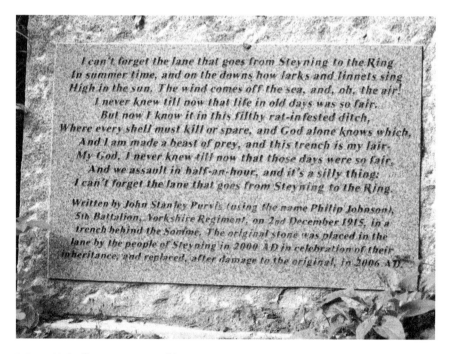

FIGURE 20.1 Poem on stone tablet

Author: Mary Geary

If you get it right for the fish, you get it right for everything else

The final story developed from unexpected sources. In this case study three disparate community groups – conservationists, anglers and a social food growing network – have collaborated even though they are not usually cohorts. Their collaboration is directed towards protecting fish species. The three usually work not so much in opposition but with some discordance. Conservationists wish to protect ecosystems, and the biodiversity within, and see angling as oppositional to this aim. Anglers want open access to river courses and adjacent land; the community orchard scheme desires regulated access to their site and specific planting schemes. Conservationists opt for indigenous planting and forms of re-wilding, antithetical to some types of food production.

Normally these three organizations would work in separate spheres, often with antagonistic interaction. Yet in this case study developing trout-breeding sites is the unifying factor as all three groups have been persuaded that we need to protect biodiversity over the long term. This radical affiliation was seeded by the local rivers trust who mediated between the three community groups. As one conservationist stated: "if you get it right for the fish you get it right for everything else".

As a result, all three have worked together – physically by adding aggregate to the river and planting trees for shade, financially by collaborative fundraising initiatives and politically by uniting for a long-term goal. Importantly, the key players in all organizations have been group elders.

While the activity of river restoration was motivated from various sustainability perspectives around enhancing natural environments, the communal outcome was to create a thriving river, with enhanced water quality, improved conditions for spawning fish and strengthened riverbanks to slow water progress and deter flooding events. Of great interest is that these community groups do not publicize their work: their stories need to remain secret. This invisibility is linked to poaching, and in particular to the action of renegade anglers.

From a community perspective the three groups, over the course of the restoration work, have developed mutual respect. Their "story" of affect is orientated around the fish, and this enables a side stepping of difficult conversations about group motivation and goals. But there is more to it than this. Each interlocutor talked of the importance of the riverside as a special place. This returns us to the importance of time, of temporality, when we consider elder environmental radicalism. Within this research site many respondents had moved to the area upon retirement. Interactions with their new environments have a dual function: first, to enable them to embed themselves within their new locale through making social contacts and being physically and mentally active, and second, these landscapes have a symbolic resonance – they represent care for all environments, past, present and future. To a great extent the work undertaken by these community elders is a legacy for future generations and a re-affirmation of the value of their own lives in the present.

Gerontocracies of affect

Each of these stories reveals in its own way how the "politics of austerity" (see Kitson et al., 2011, p. 292) have impacted on rural elders. For many it has led to an abrupt change in their personal politics, the way they relate to others in their community from different life paths, worldviews and approaches. This stage of their lives has changed dramatically, away from the idealized idle indolence of retirement to a vigorous, engaged and vocal participation with others in their community to demand their rights as citizens and protect their local environment.

It would be too simplistic to see their actions as merely self-seeking protectionism. For that to be the case there would have been no self-development, no wider awareness of the impacts of a neoliberal framing of the world that they have seen, through lived experiences, divides and degraded communities and environments. Theirs is a righteous anger, forged with a desire to change things, even if that change is small, incremental and local.

I end this chapter by considering how these gerontocracies of affect can contribute to wider struggles for the "right to nature". These relationships of affect, of the way our concerns for our local environments are an extension of care for ourselves, stem from our embodied identities and are closely linked with the landscapes in which we live (Ingold, 1993; Massey, 2013) directly impacting on the creation of radical responses. Many of the elder respondents whose stories are detailed here, have found that the rights they presumed were sacrosanct – in fact, have evaporated as neoliberalism has embedded itself within the fabric of life. As incremental and creeping as the root ball of a plant, over time the democratic civic structures that these elders have paid for over their working lifetime have withered. These elders' stories presented in this chapter may seem, at some level, almost whimsical – no Amazonian forest saving, or campaigns for universal access to water and sanitation or clean air: these pressing issues quite rightly demand to be elevated in order to support dignified lives and social justice issues.

I would also like to emphasize that we must pay attention to the fieldwork findings. Even in this relatively affluent research site, citizens are experiencing the impacts of financial austerity on their immediate and everyday lives. Given the breadth of their life experiences, these community elders are able to contextualize these negative environmental consequences of public spending cuts not as a short-term UK policy response to budget deficits but within a broader context of transnational neoliberal strategies that privilege economic development over environmental sustainability. The radical actions of the elders in these communities are necessary acts to begin to connect the global activities that demand a "right to nature" that is socially and environmentally just, which elevates the dignity of all lives and life forms to equal status and that affirms that we all play a part in creating alternative sustainable futures.

Bibliography

Bauman, Z. (2000) *Liquid Modernity*. Cambridge: Polity.
de Beauvoir, S. (2006) The Coming of Age. *Aging: Concepts and Controversies*, 119–124.

Brundtland, G.H. (1987) Our Common Future – Call for Action. *Environmental Conservation* 14 (4), 291–294.

Dessai, S. and Sims, C. (2010) Public Perception of Drought and Climate Change in Southeast England. *Environmental Hazards* 9 (4), 340–357.

Dorling, D. (2015) *Injustice: Why Social Inequality Still Persists.* Bristol: Policy Press.

European Commission (EC) (2007) Promoting Solidarity between the Generations. COM (2007) 244.

Faulkner, H., Green, A., Pellaumail, K. and Weaver, T. (2001) Residents' Perceptions of Water Quality Improvements Following Remediation Work in the Pymme's Brook Catchment, North London, UK. *Journal of Environmental Management* 62 (3), pp. 239–254.

Goerres, A. (2009) *The Political Participation of Older People in Europe. The Greying of our Democracies.* London: Palgrave Macmillan.

Heller, P.S. (2003) *Who Will Pay? Coping with Aging Societies, Climate Change, and Other Long-term Fiscal Challenges.* Washington, D.C.: International Monetary Fund.

Ingold, T. (1993) The Temporality of the Landscape. *World Archaeology* 25 (2), pp. 152–174.

Kitson, M., Martin, R. and Tyler, P. (2011) The Geographies of Austerity. *Cambridge Journal of Regions, Economy and Society* 4 (3), pp. 289–302.

Laclau, E. (2005) *On Populist Reason.* London: Verso.

Laclau, E. and Mouffe, C. (2001) *Hegemony and Socialist Strategy: Towards a Radical Democratic Politics.* London: Verso.

Lane, S.N., Landström, C. and Whatmore, S.J. (2011) Imagining Flood Futures: Risk Assessment and Management in Practice. *Philosophical Transactions of the Royal Society of London A: Mathematical, Physical and Engineering Sciences* 369 (1942), 1784–1806.

Lovelock, J. (1995) *The Ages of Gaia: A Biography of Our Living Earth.* USA: Oxford University Press.

Maathai, W. (2010) *Replenishing the Earth: Spiritual Values for Healing Ourselves and the World.* New York: Doubleday Image.

Massey, D. (2013) *Space, Place and Gender.* Cambridge: John Wiley & Sons.

McEwen, L., Garde-Hansen, J., Holmes, A., Jones, O. and Krause, F. (2017) Sustainable Flood Memories, Lay Knowledges and the Development of Community Resilience to Future Flood Risk. *Transactions of the Institute of British Geographers* 42 (1), 14–28.

Mies, M. and Shiva, V. (1993) *Ecofeminism.* London: Zed Books.

Moore, J.W. (2015) Capitalism in the Web of Life. *Ecology and the Accumulation of Capital,* 172–181.

Mouffe, C. (2005) *The Return of the Political* (Vol. 8). London: Verso.

Newton, J. and Parfitt, A. (2011) Striving for Mutuality in Research Relationships: The Value of Participatory Action Research Principles. *Researching Sustainability: A Guide to Social Science, Methods, Practice and Engagement,* 71–88.

Porritt, J. (1986) *Seeing Green: The Politics of Ecology Explained.* Oxford: Blackwell.

Segal, L. (2013) *Out of Time: The Pleasures and the Perils of Ageing.* London: Verso Books.

Shiva, V. (2016) *Earth Democracy: Justice, Sustainability and Peace.* London: Zed Books Ltd.

Snyder, G. (1995) Ecology, Place, and the Awakening of Compassion. *The Deep Ecology Movement: An Introductory Anthology.* Berkeley: North Atlantic Books.

Snyder, G. (2004) Ecology, Literature and the New World Disorder. *Irish Pages* 2 (2), 19–31.

Strang, V. (2004) *The Meaning of Water.* Berg: Oxford.

Whatmore, S. (2006) Materialist Returns: Practising Cultural Geography in and for a More-than-human World. *Cultural Geographies* 13 (4), 600–609.

Whelehan, I. and Gwynne, J. (2014) Introduction: Popular Culture's "Silver Tsunami". In *Ageing, Popular Culture and Contemporary Feminism.* UK: Palgrave Macmillan UK. Pp. 1–13.

21

HUMANS IN THE LANDSCAPE

Low-impact development as a response to the neoliberal environmental agenda

Julyan Levy

Introduction

We continue to live under the misguided doctrine that economic growth can continue indefinitely. Some of the world's wealthy are simply avaricious; others hold tightly to the dogmatic belief that profit can "resolve almost all social, economic and political problems" (Monbiot, 2014). The blurring of lines between corporations and the nation-state (Fergason and Gupta, 2002) incarnates neoliberal ideologies and agendas (Harvey, 2007) and facilitates the irrepressible capitalist growth economy. These agendas, enacted through the wholesale privatization of land and resources, are resulting in both the systematic destruction of socio-ecological environments (see, for example, Shiva, 1991; Jenson, 2006; Odeoemene, 2011; Hudgins and Poole 2014; Mercer, de Rijke and Dressler 2014; Willow and Wylie, 2014) and a profound sense of alienation (see, for example, Seeman, 1959; Kalekin-Fishman, 1996; Neal and Collas, 2000) among many across the globe. Our species may already be past tipping point; if we have any chance of survival we must first recognize that "[w]e are beings within ecological webs not outside them" (Tsing, 2015a, p. 5). This seems like an obvious statement and yet we continue to view ourselves as somehow separate from nature.

Nature itself is a contested concept (see, for example, Castree, 2005). Is it something out there, independent of human culture, there purely for our exploitation? Is it somewhere we visit for recreation? Or do nature and society co-produce one another (Hinchcliffe, 2007, pp. 7–9)? If we travel through an agricultural heartland of the type found in Mid Devon, for example, we could be excused for thinking that it is the first. If we then travelled down a small lane and arrived at a beauty spot, then perhaps it would be closer to the second. For the purpose of this essay I want to think of nature as a complex interplay between human activity and non-human activity, and thus closer to the third explanation.

However, this is not the current idea of nature in the West and this is evident when one looks at the rural landscape in the UK, which is largely composed of agricultural monocultures. Monoculture begins as ideology. As Shiva (1993, p. 5) so succinctly states, "[m]onocultures of the mind make diversity disappear from perception, and consequently from the world. The disappearance of diversity is also the disappearance of alternatives – and gives rise to the TINA (There Is No Alternative) syndrome." However, "if we care about livability . . . we are going to have to figure out how to make landscapes lively protagonists of our stories" (Tsing, 2015b). In order to cultivate a biodiverse culture, it is vital that we seek out the "cracks and contradictions" (Hall et al., 2015, p. 21) that arise from within the neoliberal monolith and highlight them as both "partial connections" (Strathern, 2004) and "viable alternatives" (Graeber, 2004, p. 12). Viable alternatives emerge from spaces "that differ from dominant models" (Firth 2012.68). Low-impact living is a case in point.

The activities that manifest in alternative spaces seek to interrupt the "culture of capitalism" (MacFarlane, 1987; Robbins, 2008) and "must take place at many levels simultaneously" (Clark, 2008, p. 17) if we are to create vibrant post-capitalist (Gibson-Graham, 2006) landscapes. These activities include, "worker co-operatives, consumer co-operatives, land trusts, co-operative housing [. . .] other non-capitalist initiatives – in short, an emerging solidarity economy" (Clark 2008, p. 17). The Low-impact Community (Bunker et al., 2014) or Low-impact Development (LID),[1] which by virtue has a "low or benign environmental impact" (Fairlie, 2009a, p. 2), offers radical solutions to the overlapping crises of housing, food and energy production in the UK (Pickerill, 2012, p. 181). The LID situates humans and their dwellings as mutual agents and as part of "nature". Low-impact living is part of a burgeoning, global back-to-the-land movement kicking back against neoliberalism; the global organization La Via Campesina (2017) and the UK's own Landworkers Alliance (2017) exemplify this movement. Further examples of LIDs in the UK can be found in a recent publication called "Settlements" by the photographer David Spero (2017). Spero has been photographing the progress of some of these communities for the past decade, showing how they integrate themselves into the natural landscape. In this essay, I will draw on my own ethnographic research and explore the spaces created by two low-impact communities in the UK, Diggerville and Woodville. But first, I want to make the land a little more visible.

Land

> They simply seized it by force, afterwards hiring lawyers to provide them with title-deeds. In the case of the enclosure of the common lands, which was going on from about 1600 to 1850, the land-grabbers did not even have the excuse of being foreign conquerors; they were quite frankly taking the heritage of their own countrymen, upon no sort of pretext except that they had the power to do so.
>
> *(Orwell, 1944)*

Plainly, a space is required for a community to emerge from the imagination into the material world. This is the first and most obvious obstacle to overcome. Access to land is notoriously difficult due mainly to its cost. The cost is also reflected in what kind of land it is classed as, that is, agricultural, recreational, woodland and so forth.[2] An acre of *woodland* in Somerset will be a lot more affordable than an acre of *strategic* land in the home counties. Furthermore, there is an obvious scarcity in urban environments, add to this the actual logistics of low-impact living (for example, sanitary considerations), and the options open to a group looking to form a community are limited. It is important to remember that land was, and continues to be, the major protagonist in "accumulation by dispossession" (Harvey, 2004), a process essential for the Industrial Revolution, leading to the strengthening of the modern nation-state and the eventual neoliberal globalization we are currently experiencing. Accumulation by dispossession, put simply, is a modern form of enclosures, the privatization of land, on an industrial scale. Essentially, communities and ecological systems are dispensible in the exploitation of "nature" by hegemonic powers. In the 21st century the hegemony emerges from neoliberalism, the marriage of corporation/nation-state/global organizations (for example, the World Health Organization (WHO) and the International Monetary Fund (IMF)) with neoliberal enclosures enacted through a number of processes. In the case of developing countries (but not only) this has mostly happened through structural adjustment programmes (SAPs). When a country is undergoing an economic crisis the World Bank and the International Monetary Fund loan money to the struggling country. In return the country may be required to sell off its natural resources. In the UK the transfer of publicly owned assets into private ownership occurred on mass when Margaret Thatcher sold a large percentage of council houses in the 1980s whereas in the last decade we have seen the gradual selling of the NHS to companies like Virgin. These economic policies provide a means for private capital to accumulate a nation's assets – and enclosures at an industrial scale often causes devastating impacts on local communities (Sparr, 1994).

If we take a cursory glance at the phenomenon of enclosures in the UK over the past 1000 years we can see how the human population of peasants were displaced. First, by Duke William of Normandy who divided and distributed the land between 180 barons (Wyler, 2004, p. 4), when he colonized the kingdoms of what would become England in the years following 1066. Land enclosures were becoming prevalent in the 13th century and from the late 14th century they claimed increasingly more communally worked land, to facilitate a growing mercantile class.[3] From1600 to 1850 enclosures became enshrined in law through the legitimacy of Parliamentary Acts, "the legal device used to include common lands in landed estates and to exclude the peasantry who lived off the common land from an economic existence" (Cahill, 2002, p. 25). Despite a catalogue of political movements aimed at resisting enclosures, most notably the Diggers[4] and the Levellers in the mid-1650s (see Kennedy, 2008)[5] the open field system and the communally grazed land, that provided livelihoods to peasant communities, eventually disappeared. Moreover, this wasn't just a matter of economics for these communities; as Silvia Federici (2014, p. 71) highlights, "[b]eside encouraging collective decision-making and work cooperation, the commons were the material foundation upon which peasant solidarity and sociality could thrive", the very elements required to address alienation. Enclosures are often framed within the flawed yet persistent myth of *the tragedy of the commons* (Hardin, 1968). This is essentially the belief that communities cannot be trusted to manage the land, but as Cox (1985, p. 60) states:

> [W]hat existed in fact was not a "tragedy of the commons" but rather a triumph: that for hundreds of years – and perhaps thousands, although written records do not exist to prove the longer era – land was managed successfully by communities.

There are many contemporary examples of groups who have occupied land illegally in a bid to reclaim the commons. The road protests of the 1990s in the UK is a prime example (*Tales of Resistance*, 2017). Two further examples can be found with Yorkley Court Community Farm, who were eventually evicted in 2016 (2016) and Grow Heathrow (2017), a community that emerged to protest the construction of a third runway at Heathrow.

For this chapter I have chosen two case studies, Diggerville and Woodville,[6] who have taken the more conventional route of purchasing the land in the quest for permenance. Their commonality with the relationships peasants used to have with the land is implicit in their ethos and practices.

Case study 1: Diggerville

Diggerville is a permaculture project and a registered co-operative, a legally recognized entity. Its sociogenesis involved 18 founding members from diverse backgrounds, made up of individuals and already existing smaller groups. Through a complex set of circumstances – people dropping out, people dropping in, disagreements over organizational decisions and social boundaries – a core group emerged and people came together navigating one another and their respective expectations. They formed a legally bound co-operative, with each member contributing £3000 for membership. The co-operative model of land ownership ensures that no-one can profit from the land. In 2003, with further funding secured by external sources, the co-operative bought a 42-acre[7] site a few miles outside of a UK National Park.[8] They spent a year familiarizing themselves with the land before moving onto it. This was to get to know the land in each season – to get a feel for the ideal location to place their dwellings, vegetable gardens and other community activities. This is termed "visioning" by permaculturists.

Permaculture, a portmanteau of permanent and (agri) culture, is a practically based, ethical design system originally developed by Bill Mollison and David Holmgren in the 1980s. Holmgren states that permaculture's vision is to develop:

> Consciously designed landscapes which mimic patterns and relationships found in nature, while yielding an abundance of food, fibre, and energy for provision of local need. I see permaculture as the use of systems thinking and design principles that provide the organizing framework for implementing the above vision. It draws together the diverse ideas, skills and ways of living which need to be rediscovered and developed in order to empower

us to move from being dependent consumers to becoming responsible and productive citizens.

(Holmgren, 2002, p. xix)

Mollison explains further:

[permaculture] is about designing sustainable human communities, and preserving and extending natural systems. It covers aspects of designing and maintaining a cultivated ecology in any climate: the principle of design; design methods; understanding patterns in nature; climatic factors; water; soils; earthworks; techniques and strategies in the different climatic types; aquaculture; and the social, legal, and economic design of human settlements . . . Strategies for the necessary changes in social investment policy, politics itself, towards regional or village self-reliance are now desperately needed.

(Mollison, 1988, p. i)

A sign hangs on the gate to the entrance of Diggerville illustrating what permaculture means to the community (see Figure 21.1).

After moving onto the land, they soon got to work building their dwellings and developing community dynamics and decision-making processes. Like in most intentional communities, people wanted to adopt some form of direct democracy (Levy, 2018). Community members live in a variety of dwellings, including yurts, benders,[9] a cob roundhouse (see Figures 21.2 – 21.3 for examples) and a wooden chalet style house built using wood from their land. Diggerville, like all LIDs, is off-grid, generating its electricity from solar PV panels and on-site mini windmills. Drinking water comes from a borehole[10] and all other water from rainwater harvesting. Community members grow a significant percentage of their own food and human faeces are disposed of and transformed into compost using compost toilets.[11]

A herd of six goats, chickens, ducks, geese and honey bees are also essential members of the community. The lived experience of the community can be felt in the words written on a sign nailed to the side of the barn – *Words are not enough* – a quote by the 17th-century Digger, Gerard Winstanley.

Lydia, one of the founding members of Diggerville, spoke of her activist background. In her early 20s, while living in Berlin, she became involved in the burgeoning environmental movement. This was the early nineties, just after the fall of the Berlin Wall, and the environmental movement was fertile ground consisting of more than 200 separate groups (Rucht and Roose, 2001, p. 6). She attended various environmental protests in Berlin before coming to England to find a common ground with the road protest culture that had mobilized around locations like Twyford Down and Newbury (*Tales of Resistance*, 2017). What emerged on these sites were, essentially, proto low-impact communities made up of environmental protesters protecting the natural environment from further development. The conflict that ensued from the protest camps gained a lot of media attention at the time. However, this temporary culture was not enough; as Lydia went on to say, "At some

FIGURE 21.1   Earth rules OK

Author: Julyan Levy, 2015

point after a few years I realized I don't just want to protest against, I want to create the world that I want to see." Albert, another of the founders, had also been part of the same road protest culture:

> I saw benders, and people with protest tree houses, and just total anarchist collective temporal, autonomous zones, and it was really inspiring . . . I came across some yurts before when visiting Samye Ling . . . that was the first time I came across someone living in a yurt . . . I thought wouldn't it be nice if there were little communities of people living like that?

The land had no buildings, no access, the boundaries were derelict and there was little chance of planning permission. Before they moved onto the land they spent a long period becoming intimately acquainted with it and planning how they would design the community. After a year, they moved onto the land and began

FIGURE 21.2 Woodville home under construction

Author: David Spero, 2017

to put their vision of a permaculture community into practice with the intention of applying for retrospective planning permission. After a lengthy legal battle, the community received temporary planning permission in 2007 for eight dwellings, for a three-year period. In 2011, they were given a further five years temporary planning permission and, in 2016, they were finally awarded permanent planning permission. It is often the case that applying for retrospective planning permission once you have established your homes is the best course of action. There are obvious and rational reasons behind why certain areas shouldn't be built on; sanitary conditions being one of the most important considerations involved in the organization of human dwellings. Preserving areas of natural beauty (nature) is also a consideration. However, when we look at how LIDs interact with nature we see that they complement the natural environment and tread lightly in the landscape (Pickerill and Maxey, 2009). This is certainly true of Woodville and Diggerville. Furthermore, LIDs have been recognized on the global stage and the UK government itself committed to Agenda 21 at the 1992 Rio summit. Chapter 7 of Agenda 21, entitled "Promoting Sustainable Human Settlements" (UNEP, n.d.), states the following in sections 7.27 and 7.28,

> [a]ccess to land resources is an essential component to sustainable low impact lifestyles . . . The objective is to provide access to land for all households

FIGURE 21.3   Communal roundhouse

Author: David Spero, 2017

> through environmentally sound physical planning and . . . the encouragement
> of communally and collectively owned and managed land.

Despite the success of Diggerville and the commitment of the UK government to
Agenda 21, people in Woodville have not been so fortunate in their application
for permanence and have been denied permanent planning permission on a legal
technicality.

Case study 2: Woodville

In 1997, a group of committed environmental and social justice activists came
together in a series of meetings to discuss the possibility of setting up a low-impact
community based on permaculture principles. The group spent the next few years
researching the logistics of setting up an intentional community. They formed a
housing co-op to transform the group into a legal structure and then a workers
co-op (see Radical Routes, 2015), issuing zero interest loan stock shares to raise
money to buy a piece of land. In 2000, the co-op purchased 32 acres of plantation
woodland on a steep hillside in a valley within the same National Park as Diggerville, and Woodville was born. Since those early meetings the community has sustained itself and blossomed into a thriving small community that now meets 80%

of their basic needs from living on their land. Community members are extremely industrious, building their own dwellings from reclaimed materials and wood from their woodland and utilizing materials found in the landscape. Like other off-grid communities they have an efficient compost toilet system that requires no complex sewerage infrastructure, virtually no water or chemicals. They compost their own waste and use it for food production.

On my last visit one of the founding members had been working on his two-story roundhouse with reciprocal roof. He had been breaking huge rocks from the land using a sledgehammer and pegs to use as the foundations to his home. As with any building project the roundhouse had been planned and designed using meticulous architectural drawings that were submitted to the National Park Authority (NPA) as part of their planning application. Working with the landscape, Woodville was built on the hillside fascilitating the successful harnessing of the power of gravity in the design of their water system. Their water system includes a bath house running an efficient hot-water system heated via a wood-burning stove using wood from their own sustainable woodland. This produces ample hot water for the community's needs. It is difficult to fully convey what an incredible welcoming space Woodville is; full of warmth and hope, built in harmony with the natural environment. In the words of one community member:

> It may be hard for others to understand, quantify and prove the benefits of living in harmony with our human, animal and plant relations in a world where separation, disconnection and greed are the norm. But having lived this way for the last 12 years, for us and our children this way of life is the only way of life. It allows for the development of skills that enable provision of shelter, fuel, food and water for families without the call for huge financial input. In addition, it creates a deep sense of connection to each other and the natural world, encouraging responsibility and care without the huge and harmful impact that comes with conventional living.

Unfortunately, their way of life is coming to an end and future members of the public will not have the opportunity of experiencing firsthand the innovative life-style this community has developed over time due to a seemingly arbitrary planning decision. A decision that will force the families to dismantle their own homes and their whole way of life. Empiricism, compassion and imagination appear to be absent from the responsible government agency.

Last summer I attended the final public hearing to determine the appeal lodged by Woodville against the NPA for the authority's refusal to accept the co-op's application for full planning permission. The only objection at this hearing came from a very elderly landowner who lives close to the community. He simply did not approve of the community's way of life. He criticized the number of hours the community spent on food growing and home schooling and how little they spent their time in more conventional ways. Hidden in the language the elderly man used was an implicit bigotry, bigotry towards a community working very hard to be truly sustainable. The reality is that community members do have "real" jobs in the wider local community, ranging from care workers to teaching assistants. They have successfully integrated their low-impact lifestyle with their conventional jobs. Community members also tell me that many people they meet in their daily jobs express a sense of solidarity for their way of life. Support for their bid for permanence has come from all sections of society, including the local vicar and the independent national park society. However, despite all the support, their planning application was rejected by the NPA. A decision that can only be perceived as discriminatory and prejudiced against their way of life. There does not appear to be the same level of objection four miles up the road, still within the national park, to a brand-new housing development, built on green belt for those who can afford a house from £450,000 or an apartment from £325,000.

In December 2016, Woodville's High Court challenge to the Planning Inspector's original decision was turned down by a judge and now Woodville have been ordered to dismantle their homes by December 2017. The official stance from the NPA maintains that the community has a damaging impact on the appearance and the biodiversity of the national park, but this is simply untrue. The community is not publicly visible unless you fly over with a helicopter. More importantly, Woodville's whole ethos is built on a foundation of environmental sustainability. I have witnessed firsthand how respectful they are of their immediate environment. They spend much of their time conserving the woodland by removing invasive species, creating habitable environments for wildlife and documenting the variety of birds and other species in the woodland. They use permaculture principles in their food growing, planting companion species that attract important pollinating insects; they run conservation days to involve the local community, providing education and exposure to an alternative way of life that many would otherwise not be aware of; and they limit their car use using communal vehicles. So, while the NPA boast about their sustainability credentials, they reject an exemplary example of a sustainable community right on their doorstep. Woodville are an asset to the national park and the community has always been vocal about how they would be willing to work with the NPA to raise the profile of the park. Not only is it irrational and misguided of the NPA to deny permanence, it is also a missed opportunity that would mutually benefit both parties.

Discussion

While low-impact living communities offer conventional society an invaluable perspective into an alternative way of living it is essential that we understand it as a partial connection (Strathern, 1994), an ontology that resists offering a simplified vision of utopia. These communities have significantly reduced their reliance on fossil fuels through the generation of their own wind and solar energy, also reducing their reliance on the car. They also rely less on the purchasing of food and medicines and have provided a viable solution to their housing needs. While I have not had the space to explore this aspect here, low-impact living communities are proactive in community dynamics, making decisions together democratically, relying more on their immediate community than on conventional spaces. In other words, I think of a partial connection as a glimpse into how humans may adapt their behavior to ameliorate the stresses involved in the potential breakdown of capitalism.

As there are so many variables to account for regarding a transition to a post-capitalist society it would be a folly to suggest that these communities offer any kind of blueprint. They, however, offer some clues as to how small groups of people born into an individualistic Western capitalist society can maintain and promote social cohesion in a communal setting, how they respond effectively and sustainably to the burgeoning housing and energy crises and how they loosen their dependence on monetary economics for food. In this sense, low-impact communities exemplify the realities of economic degrowth. They embody post-capitalist relationships by engaging in communal activities that rely a little less on monetary economics and by providing tantalizing examples of alternative social organization. They are prefiguring relationships with each other and the non-human based on the principles of mutual aid. It is only through direct experience of living low-impact that the reality of "reconnecting" with nature is truly felt. In doing so these communities also break down the often-misguided romanticism that can often be found in primitivist/eco-new-age circles. This is a very challenging way of living that requires the sacrifice of comforts most of us have become accustomed to.

It is also important to understand that this is just a snapshot of two communities and their particular desire to live more sustainably. I want to avoid the concept of a fixed, "arrived at" alternative destination as the struggle for emancipation from capitalism is proving to be highly complex. The destination is increasingly uncertain, polarizing the exigency to co-operatively develop effective processes as opposed to prescribing utopian ends. So, I am not advocating that everyone must stop what they are doing and begin living this way. This is echoed by many community members I have spoken with. They are not pious about their way of life and are more acutely aware than most of the hypocrisies involved in living sustainably in the modern world. They are also aware of how difficult it is to untangle oneself from the neoliberal webs of exploitation. Low-impact community living is not for everyone; many groups simply do not have the means (money and/or access to alternative spaces) to successfully create a small community. However, it is essential that we do not fool ourselves about the challenges that humanity faces. As one of the founders of Diggerville states:

> People who come to visit may look around and say "oh my god this is really, really basic" and they're not that wrong in various respects. Then I say we are still 1.3 planets in our footprint, we are not even one planet according to our last ecological survey. Then they start to get a bit of an idea of what it might actually involve and how big the crisis is that is looming.

With this reality in mind we can place low-impact community living at one end of a spectrum. There are endless ways that a group could design their community; there is even the potential for 21st-century social housing to draw on some of the principles of LIDs, such as communal food growing, localized renewable energies and alternative housing solutions. When we begin to break down the monoculture of our minds (Shiva, 1993) and imagine a society composed of a tapestry of eco-logical livelihoods (Gibson-Graham and Miller, 2015) then we can begin to care and nurture those new shoots that poke through the concrete. As Bookchin (1989) put it, "the assumption that what currently exists must necessarily exist is the acid that corrodes all visionary thinking". It is time that we ask some fundamental ques-tions such as, *is the current system of land ownership and land use socially and ecologically beneficial to the majority of people in the UK* and *why is it acceptable to build expensive housing developments and not acceptable to encourage LIDs?* I am convinced that low-impact communities provide us with examples of the latent human potential that flourishes in a culture of co-operation. It also challenges our expectations of sus-tainability, providing a glimpse into some of the realities involved in a transition to a socially and ecologically, post-capitalist, sustainable culture.

Acknowledgements

Many thanks to Dr Elia Apostolopoulou for her encouragement and invaluable contributions to the final draft; to Dr Andrea Butcher for her guidance on my original dissertation; to the communities who have welcomed me into their homes; and to Hannah.

Notes

1 I will move freely between definitions. The term *development* highlights the material aspects; the term *community* highlights the social aspects. Both are relevant, neither has primacy. Also some low-impact developments may not be communities.
2 There is no official government literature on this as it is appears to be determined by the "market"; see *Land Use, Land Types & Land Usage* (Vantage Land, 2016).
3 See the article "A Short History of Enclosure in Britain" (Fairlie, 2009b) for a compre-hensive overview.
4 In 1999, on its 350th anniversary, a group of land activists can be seen re-creating the "Diggers Occupation" of St Georges Hill, Surrey (Public Enquiry, 2009).
5 See also evidence of a rising sense of injustice among farm labourers across Britain in the 18th and 19 centuries (Hammond and Hammond, 1987).
6 Community names are pseudonyms to protect community members.
7 Consisting of 17 acres of semi-natural woodland and 22 acres of pasture.
8 As with community names I want to keep the identity of the national park anonymous. I do not think it is important which national park I am referring to as the National Park authorities are all essentially extensions of the government whereby a percentage of board members are appointed by local and national government.
9 A bender is a very old traditional low-impact living structure using coppiced Hazel poles to form a frame. This is covered by a water-proof, breathable tarpaulin; animal skins would have been used traditionally. These were commonly used by rural nomadic peasants in the UK, circa. the eighteenth and nineteenth centuries, moving to where the work was, as they were quick and easy to assemble.
10 The bore-hole goes down 40 metres and is pumped up by hand. The community were gifted this experimental model by an NGO.
11 See Anand and Apul (2014) for a review of the literature regarding compost toilets and sustainability. See also lowimpact.org (2017) for a useful introduction.

References

Anand, C. and Apul, D. (2014) Composting Toilets as a Sustainable Alternative to Urban Sanitation – A Review. *Waste Management* 34, 329–343.

Anderson, P. (ed.) (2007) *Orwell in Tribune: As I Please and Other Writings 1943–47*. London: Politico's Publishing.

Bookchin, M. (1989) The Meaning of Confederalism. *Green Perspectives*, No. 20, November. Available at: http://dwardmac.pitzer.edu/anarchist_archives/bookchin/gp/perspectives20.html [Accessed 13 July 2017.]

Bunker, S. et al. (eds) (2014) *Low Impact Living Communities in Britain*. London: D&D Publications.

Cahill, K. (2002) *Who Owns Britain*. Edinburgh: Canongate.

Castree, N. (2005) *Nature*. London. Routledge.

Clark, J. (2008) *Bridging the Unbridgeable Chasm: On Bookchin's Critique of the Anarchist Tradition*. Available at: http://theanarchistlibrary.org/library/john-clark-bridging-the-unbridgeable-chasm-on-bookchin-s-critique-of-the-anarchist-tradition [Accessed 26 September 2018.]

Cox, S.J.B. (1985) No Tragedy of the Commons. *Environmental Ethics* 7 (1), 49–61. DOI: 10.5840/enviroethics1985716

Fairlie, S. (2009a) Foreword. In J. Pickerill and L. Maxey, *Low-Impact Development: The Future in Our Hands*. Available at: www.jennypickerill.info/wp-content/uploads/Low-Impact-Development-Book.pdf

Fairlie, S. (2009b) *A Short History of Enclosure in Britain*. Available at: /www.thelandmagazine.org.uk/articles/short-history-enclosure-britain [Accessed 29 June 2017.]

Federici, S. (2014) *Caliban and the Witch: Women, The Body and Primitive Accumulation*. 2nd edition. Brooklyn: Autonomedia.

Ferguson, J. and Gupta, G. (2002) Spatializing States: Toward an Ethnography of Neoliberal Governmentality. *American Ethnologist* 29 (4) (November), 981–1002.

Firth, R. (2012) *Utopian Politics: Citizenship and Practice*. London: Routledge.

Gibson-Graham, J.K. (2006) *A Postcapitalist Politics*. London: University of Minnesota Press.

Gibson-Graham, J.K. and Miller, E. (2015) Economy as Ecological Livelihood. In K. Gibson, D. Bird Rose and R. Fincher (eds), *Manifesto for the Living in the Anthropocene*. Brooklyn: Puncum Books. Pp. 7–16.

Graeber, D. (2004) *Fragments of an Anarchist Anthropology*. Chicago: Prickly Paradigm Press.

Grow Heathrow (2017) www.transitionheathrow.com/grow-heathrow/ [Accessed 26 July 2017.]

Hall, S. et al. (eds.) (2015) *After Neoliberalism? The Kilburn Manifesto*. London: Lawrence and Wishart.

Hammond, J.L. and Hammond, B. (1987) *The Village Labourer 1760–1832: A Study of the Government of England before the Reform Bill*. Gloucester: Alan Sutton Publishing.

Hardin, G. (1968) The Tragedy of the Commons. *Science* 162, 1243–1248.

Harvey, D. (2004) The "New" Imperialism: Accumulation by Dispossession. *Socialist Register* 40, 63–87.

Harvey, D. (2007) *A Brief History of Neoliberalism*. Oxford: Oxford University Press.

Hinchcliffe, S. (2007) *Geographies of Nature: Societies, Environments, Ecologies*. London: SAGE.

Holmgren, D. (2002) *Permaculture: Principles and Pathways beyond Sustainability*. Hepburn: Holmgren Design Services.

Hudgins, A & Poole, A 2014/ Framing fracking: private property, common resources, and regimes of governance. *Journal of Political Ecology*, 21, 303–319

Jenson, D. (2006) *End Game, Volume 1*. New York. Seven Stories Press.

Kalekin-Fishman, D. (1996) Tracing the Growth of Alienation: Enculturation, Socialization, and Schooling in a Democracy. In F. Geyer (ed.), *Alienation, Ethnicity, and Postmodernity*. Connecticut. Westwood. Pp. 107–120.

Kennedy, G. (2008) *Diggers, Levellers, and Agrarian Capitalism: radical political thought in seventeenth century England*. Plymouth: Lexington Books.

Landworkers Alliance (2017) https://landworkersalliance.org.uk [Accessed 12 August 2017.]

La Vie Campesina (2017) https://viacampesina.org/en/ [Accessed 12 August 2017.]

Levy, J. (2018) *Decision-making Processes in Diggerville*. Available at: https://www.researchgate.net/publication/327895321_Descision-making_Processes_in_Diggerville

Lowimpact.org (2017) *Compost Toilets: Introduction*. www.lowimpact.org/lowimpact-topic/compost-toilets/ [Accessed 12 August 2017.]

Mercer, A., de Rijke, K. and Dressler, W., 2014. Silences in the Boom: Coal Seam Gas, Neoliberalizing Discourse, and the Future of Regional Australia. *Journal of Political Ecology*, 21, 292–302

MacFarlane, A. 1987. *The Culture of Capitalism*. Oxford: Blackwell.

Mollison, B. (1988) *Permaculture: A Designers Manual*. Tylagum: Tagari Publications.

Monbiot, G. (2014) *The Pricing of Everything*. www.monbiot.com/2014/07/24/the-pricing-of-everything/ [Accessed 13 July 2017.]

Neal, A.G. and Collas, S.F. (2000) *Intimacy and Alienation: Forms of Estrangement in Female/Male Relationships*. New York: Garland.

Odeoemene, A. (2011) Social Consequences of Environmental Change in the Niger Delta of Nigeria. *Journal of Sustainable Development* 4 (2) (April). Pp. 123–135

Orwell, G. (1944) As I Please, *Tribune*, 18 August. Reprinted in Anderson, P. (ed). *Orwell in Tribune: As I Please and Other Writings 1943–47*. London: Methuen Publishing. P. 175.

Pickerill, J. (2012) Permaculture in Practice: Low Impact Development in Britain. In J. Lockyer and J. Veteto (eds), *Environmental Anthropology Engaging Ecotopia: Bioregionalism, Permaculture and Ecovillages*. Oxford. Berghahn. Pp. 180–194.

Pickerill, J. and Maxey, L. (2009) Geographies of Sustainability: Low Impact Developments and Radical Spaces of Innovation. *Geography Compass* 3 (4), 1515–1539.

Public Enquiry (2009) *Diggers Occupation April 1999 350th Anniversary St Georges Hill, Surrey* [YouTube]. www.youtube.com/watch?v=EsXb84mUNiw [Accessed 26 July 2017.]

Radical Routes (2015) *How to Set Up a Workers' Co-op*. Fourth Edition. Available at: www.radicalroutes.org.uk/publicdownloads/setupaworkerscoop-lowres.pdf

Robbins, R.H. 2008. *Global Problems and the Culture of Capitalism*. 4th edition. Boston. Pearson

Rucht, D. and Roose, J. (2001) The Transformation of Environmental Activism in Berlin. *Social Science Research Centre. ECPR Joint Sessions, Grenoble, 6–11 April 2001*. Available at: https://ecpr.eu/Filestore/PaperProposal/05262578-28eb-46a6-9c93-8c4da44d2d98.pdf

Seeman, M. (1959) On the Meaning of Alienation. *American Sociological Review* 24 (6) (December), 783–791.

Shiva, V. (1991) *You're listening to a sample of the Audible audio edition. Learn more The Violence of the Green Revolution: Third World Agriculture, Ecology and Politics: Ecological Degradation and Political Conflict*. London: Zed Books.

Shiva, V. (1993) *Monocultures of the Mind: Perspectives on Biodiversity and Biotechnology*. London: Zed Books.

Sparr, P (ed.) (1994) *Mortgaging Women's Lives: Feminist Critiques of Structural Adjustment*. London: Zed Books.

Spero, D. (2017) *Settlements*. London. David Spero.

Strathern, M. (2004) *Partial Connections*. (Updated Edition). Oxford: AltaMira Press.

Tales of Resistance: The Battle of The Newbury Bypass (2017) Dir. Jamie Lowe [Film]. UK: Jamie Lowe.

Tsing, A. (2015a) *The Mushroom at the End of the World: On the Possibility of Life in Capitalist Ruins*. Princeton: Princeton University Press.

Tsing, A. (2015b) *In the Midst of Disturbance: Symbiosis, Coordination, History, Landscape*. ASA Firth Lecture. Available at: www.theasa.org/downloads/publications/firth/firth15.pdf

Vantage Land (2016) *Land Use, Land Types & Land Usage*. Available at: /www.vantageland.co.uk/land-use.asp#woodland [Accessed 23 July 2017.]

Willow, A.J. and Wylie, S. (2014) Energy, Environment, Engagement: Encounters with Hydraulic Fracking. *Journal of Political Ecology* 21, 222–348.

Wyler, S. (2009) *A History of Community Asset Ownership*. London: Development Trusts Association.

Yorkley Court Community Farm (2016) https://yorkleycourt.wordpress.com/2016/03/21/on-footpaths-shut-and-attempts-at-communication-shutdown/ [Accessed 26 July 2017.]

AFTERWORD

The right to nature: lessons learned and future directions

Jose A. Cortes-Vazquez and Elia Apostolopoulou

We envisioned this book as a dialogue and exchange of ideas and experiences between scholars and activists involved in different struggles and social movements against neoliberal environmental agendas. However, the reader will have realized at this stage that the term *dialogue* is just suggestive, rather than descriptive. The book is in fact a fragmented palette of voices and perspectives. By presenting together just a few representatives of the many voices, perspectives and positionalities within the field of environmental activism, our goal is to show the actual diversity of experiences and points of views and encourage comparison, contrast and exchange. As stated in the introduction, we believe that this dialogue must materialize "out there", outside the confined space of this book or the boundaries of academia, in the field of day-to-day political and social struggle. Although the seeds of this book were a conference held in an academic institution, we are aware and strongly advocate that such exchange of ideas and experiences cannot merely take place in conferences, seminars, publications and books – all these are necessary steps, but they are not enough. Furthermore, and relatedly, we strongly believe that it is not enough for radical academics to just claim in conferences or scientific publications that their research is radical – they should also support this through their own political stance and involvement in social-environmental struggles and movements. This is not to disregard that being radical within the confines of academia is important, and, many times, especially in the context of neoliberal academia, quite hard; but we also believe that "academic activism" cannot substitute direct political engagement, active participation in social-environmental struggles and an on-the-ground commitment to social-environmental justice and to the need for a direct, social control of the production of nature (and of production more generally).

Having said that, we would like to conclude this book with a number of reflections that come out of the combined reading of all the chapters included in this edited volume. These reflections aim to build key themes out of the different contributions and chart future directions for research and practice. In other words, they provide just a few examples of the fruitful dialogue that can be established between academics and activists. The diversity of topics and themes covered is enormous and each reader will probably identify a different set of them, but, over-all, we feel that a majority of chapters in this book engage in one way or another with debates about seven key themes: the dialectics of coercion and consent in the relation between state, capital and social movements; environmental justice, recog-nition and participation; the possibilities and impediments of a genuine red-green agenda; the pre-conditions and meanings of successful environmental movements; a critique of the economic valuation of nature; alternatives to the neoliberal pro-duction of nature; and mutual imputs and lessons to be learned from a closer aca-demic–activist dialogue. All these themes speak directly not only to the day-to-day troubles and opportunities of activist practice, but also to academic studies at the intersection between radical geographical and social sciences, environmental justice and political ecology. Let us try to briefly summarize below the main points that we consider of key importance for each of these themes.

Coercion and consent

One of the key subject themes connects with how the relation between the state, capital and social movements in cases of environmental conflicts is usually mediated by the use of coercion and the engineering of consent (in Gramscian terms). This includes cases of violence where protestors have been repressed or even killed by state or private agents as well as direct attacks on free speech and the criminaliza-tion of environmental movements, like in Colombia (Chapter 1), Romania (Chap-ter 6) and Greece (Chapter 4); land expropriations in the USA (Chapter 2); and relocations in Brazil (Chapter 9). It also encompasses forms of "slow violence" that intermingle with strategies for the engineering of consent, including lack of access to information and neglect of demands for Full Prior Informed Consent (FPIC) by different communities; using media to discredit activists or to divide them; some forms of soft harassment; and bribing bureaucrats and policy-makers. We have seen examples of these strategies in the cases of movements against megaprojects in Europe (Chapter 11), mining in Greece (Chapter 4), the Keystone XL Pipeline in Nebraska (Chapter 2) and urban megaprojects in Brazil (Chapter 9). Relatedly, the manipulation of public opinion takes sometimes a more perverse turn when consultations are turned against the interests of local communities and activists, as we have seen in Mozambique (Chapter 5), or even when local groups are paid to defend corporare interests, like in Colombia (Chapter 6). The way that states and big industries may use consensual policies while in practice exercizing the violent repression of access to nature and land, and the control and use of natural resources, is also evident in market-based policies, like biodiversity offsetting, as the case of Rio Tinto in Madagascar clearly shows (Chapter 14). Neoliberal hegemony as con-sent is thus dialectically intertwined with domination by force (including physical, economic and symbolic coercion), as well as by direct and indirect manipulations, exerted both by states and capitalists.

One of the lessons to be extracted from these different accounts of environmental conflicts is that there are different but interconnected ways whereby contestation to the neoliberalization of nature can be tackled and repressed, which should provide grassroot and environmental movements some insights to calibrate and understand the barriers that uneven power relations and class differences place to their actions. Some authors suggest alternative ways of operating that avoid direct confrontations, which may be useful in case of extreme power imbalances. For example, Symons (Chapter 5) and Rodriguez and Loginova (Chapter 3) argue that, in certain circumstances, communities can actually use the state to gain rights against corporate interests by taming laws or even engaging with some progressive legislation in place. However, the way coercion dialectically interwines with consent also shows the limits of reformist change bringing forward the need for radical, anti-capitalistic alternatives.

Environmental justice, recognition and participation

The uses of coercion and consent consolidate and reproduce what many authors in this book describe as three basic forms of injustice. First of all, and more obviously, distributional injustice, where the benefits and burdens of the neoliberalization of rural and urban natures are distributed unevenly, as in the case of gentrification in New York city (Chapter 10), gas extractivism in Mozambique (Chapter 5), mining in Madagascar (Chapter 14) or housing and oil pipeline construction in Canada (Chapter 19). The uneven distribution of environmental bads and goods is a long-standing concern for the environmental movement (Chapter 15), and especially the fact that it is often the marginalized groups (in terms of class, gender and race) and indigenous populations (Chapter 19) who are denied the opportunity to enjoy and experience nature in their everyday lives.

However, advances made in the field of environmental justice demonstrate that the distributional dimension is insufficient if it neglects two other sources of injustice: lack of recognition and participation (Chapter 11). Many of the experiences described in this book provide strong evidence that both forms of injustice must be at the forefront of activism and radical practice for achieving more equitable ways of producing human–nature relations. For example, Christiaens et al. (Chapter 1) describe the neglect of spiritual and cultural values of indigenous communities, and Winter (Chapter 19) the ignorance towards "stolen native land" as forms of invisibilizing these communities. Ordner explains how the oil and gas industry dominates decision making concerning gas extraction in the USA, ignoring, isolating and, thus, disempowering landowners and ranchers (Chapter 2). In fact, as Rodriguez and Loginova argue in Chapter 3, seeking the recognition of affected and usually invisibilized communities and their interests – whether through direct actions or the taming of existing legislation – is a key step towards resisting the neoliberalization of nature successfully.

However, an analysis of recognition can be complex. Wahby (Chapter 7) describes how divided environmental movements in Cairo complicate a genuine recognition of the most vulnerable communities as the state forges alliances with bourguoise environmental movements to co-opt oppositions and invisibilize different forms of environmentalism of the poor. Florea and Rhoades (Chapter 6) go a step further in this sense and describe how corporations can actually bribe representatives of local communities to defend corporate interests as if they were local interests. Therefore, movements for recognition must always be alert of the risks of co-optation.

With regards to participation, Alves (Chapter 9) also points out how contestation and reactions from affected communities are prevented by lack of information. Sometimes this form of procedural injustice, as a form of coercion, connects with the engineering of consent and recognition injustices through media manipulation. Alves defines this as a process of "accumulation by symbolic dispossession" whereby affected communities are invisibilized as a pre-requisite for capital accumulation, particularly when economic stakes are very high, as in the case of Olympic Games. Similar cases of procedural injustices are described, for example, in the USA (Chapter 2). Here, too, the risk of co-optation is a reality that many environmental movements must face. For example, Symons (Chapter 5) describes how consultations can actually be manipulated against the interests of local communities and eventually permit their relocation in cases of gas extraction in Mozambique.

It is important to notice that all of the above aspects of injustice are key to the critique against market environmentalism and neoliberal conservation. As all authors in Section 3 highlight, market-based conservation instruments, by approaching biodiversity, ecosystem services and natural resources as largely separated from local communities, inevitably intensify existing inequalities while also creating new ones. As Re:Common (Chapter 14) point out through the case of Rio Tinto operations in Madagascar, policies like biodiversity offsetting, by favouring a technocratic approach to the calculation of biodiversity losses and gains, often result to the restriction of local access and use of the land with detrimental effects for local people, while reproducing the familiar rhetoric of mainstream conservation according to which traditional users of land and resources are primarily responsible for environmental degradation.

Crucially, in this book, there are also examples of alternative ways of participation organized by communities themselves. For example, Partridge (Chapter 18) discusses how an irrigation community project has been governed and administered by members of the San Isidro community council, in discussion with regular assembly meetings for all participating households, how decisions were made by majority vote after extensive deliberations and how responsibility for decisions ultimately fell to the community as a whole. Winter (Chapter 19) also refers to the willingness of low-impact communities in the UK to base their decisions on direct democracy.

Red–Green agenda

Another key issue described in different chapters as impeding effective contestation and resistance is the division within local communities around red and green agendas.

This can take the form of identity politics, as in Nebraska (Chapter 2), or have a clearer class dimension, as in Cairo (middle class versus poor people, Chapter 7) or even rely on ethnic divisions, as in New York City (Chapter 10). Such divisions never happen naturally; they are created by certain types of policies and interventions. For example, in cases of urban gentrification in New York, ethnic divisions are created by rent and real estate policies that make vulnerable groups compete for scarce resources. In Romania, mining corporate lobbies work to create divisions and split resistence by confronting people advocating jobs and royalties, and people opposing pollution and relocations (Chapter 6). In Cairo, state monopoly in the production of nature also means that it plays the mediator between different classes, effectively dividing and co-opting different environmental movements (Chapter 7).

Contributions to this book not only warn us against such divisions, but also point the way towards bridging the Red–Green gap that they tend to either create or reinforce. Speaking of oppositions to the Keystone XL Pipeline in Nebraska, Ordner (Chapter 2) suggests that efforts must be made to mobilize situated strategies and tactics that reflect the cultural values of different communities so that they all feel represented. Comparing cases in Romania and Colombia, Florea and Rhoades (Chapter 6) also recommend taking social and environmental justice issues together as strongly interconnected. Looking into cases of gentrification in New York City, Beck (Chapter 10) urges the environmental movement to forge alliances and attack the very neoliberal policies that create new divisions or intensify already existent ones. Here it is also relevant to refer to Winter's emphasis on the need to better integrate environmental and social justice agendas and move beyond problematic dichotomies, such as Indigenous/non-Indigenous people and pristine/urban nature if we want environmental struggles to succeed (Chapter 19).

Against the economic valuation of nature

Another key theme is the critique of the economic valuation of nature, a hegemonic discourse and practice in nature conservation, particularly during the last two decades. A first major issue relates to the role of science, and particularly of neoclassical economics. Hernandez–Trejo (Chapter 12) deals with this by unravelling the assumptions that guide market-based conservation, and particularly payments for ecosystem services. He shows how scientific knowledge and policy-making merge into the political project of market environmentalism with the aim to support its key assumption: namely that markets are the appropriate tool to regulate nature–society relationships. In a related analysis, Levidow (Chapter 13) explores the role of financial metaphors in the regulation of natural resources and the related emphasis on market-based instruments, and sheds light on the way biodiversity, ecosystem services and natural resources are seen as stocks and/or proprietary assets, described through universal equivalences and largely separated from local communities.

By placing at the core of his analysis Natural Capital Accounting, Ledivow also shows how market-based instruments have informed corporate strategies for "green-supply chains" within a broader strategy to strengthen and stabilize access to natural resources. By citing several interesting examples, he shows that companies' attempt to "internalize" environmental externalities is often related to their attempt to protect competitiveness. The strategic alliance between corporations and market environmentalism are also discussed by Ito and Montini (Chapter 16) who argue that market-based instruments are often acquired by corporations to offset their overuse, degradation or pollution of the environment, or even to further profit from trading them, and by Re:Common (Chapter 14) who show how biodiversity offsetting can be used by corporations to green-wash controversial projects and gain them a new "social licence to operate".

Finally, Bell and Wulf (Chapter 15) point out a different aspect of the critique of the economic valuation of nature, namely how it can sideline other values of nature. They call for a different way to talk about the value of nature that would move beyond putting a price to nature towards the acknowledgement that nature is a fundamental right for everyone. Ito and Montini (Chapter 16), by focusing on the case of environmental law, further build on the need to move beyond the economic valuation of nature and the paradigm of the "green economy" and take into account the intrinsic value of nature, by recognizing nature as a rights-bearing subject of the law equal to humans and corporations (see also Chapter 18, where Partridge refers to the institutionalization of the "Rights of Nature" in Ecuador).

It is important to point out that all contributions show that market environmentalism and the wider shift towards the economic valuation of nature, despite being hegemonic, nonetheless remains profoundly incoherent, leaving space for challenging the persistence of neoliberalism in political terms and its orchestrated attempt to depoliticize environmental and conservation conflicts. In fact, Lohmann (Chapter 17) picks up on the very subject of this book, the right to nature, and argues that the capitalist rationale -as a violent process of separating humans from nature- reappears even on the arguments of those advocating for the rights to nature. According to Lohmann, the very definition of rights (whether they are 'rights to' or 'rights of') reproduce such violent separation and thus fails to tackle the roots of the material and symbolic way of producing nature under capitalism. In order to stimulate discussions and other actions directed at more mutually-respectful ways of living and being tout court, he not only encourages us to reject the economic valuation of nature, but also the very notion of rights.

The pre-conditions and meanings of success for environmental struggles

Another key theme that appears both implicitly and explicitly in almost all contributions is the idea that environmental movements are, in essence, a process, and their success or failure should, therefore, be understood not in a static but in a dynamic way. For example, Symons (Chapter 5) shows how what may seem a successful strategy to gain recognition and participation against extractive corporate interests in Mozambique may actually involve further embracing of neoliberal and colonial logics that, in the end, facilitate relocations of local communities. Florea and Rhoades (Chapter 6) explain how opposition to extractivism in Romania could end up relying on claims to private property and right-wing nationalism against foreign interests, which distract people from actual economic interests at stake and lead to compromises with the dominant economic system. In both cases, apparently successful strategies end up after some time in failures. Furthermore, Alves (Chapter 9) explains how participatory mechanisms may be demanded and eventually estabished but they may not be actually operative because the necessary human resources (for example, staff to respond to information requests) is not made available or the mechanisms that ensure anonymity of requests may be absent, exposing citizens to forms of coercion.

Looking at success from a wider perspective, the Citizens' Coordinating Committee of Ierissos against gold-copper mining (Chapter 4) argue that, beyond winning or losing, real success of environmental movements should be measured in terms of changing visions of a life of reciprocity with nature, a transformation of the kind of nature that we produce, by whom and for whom, in a world without "sacrifice zones". In different terms, but essentially in the same direction, Christiaens, Mears, Whitmore and Rhoades (Chapter 1) contend that, to be successful, a movement should achieve the return of collective power back to communities in order to allow for greater self-determination of local people.

Contributions also provide a series of detailed recommendations towards success. For example, Christiaens et al. (Chapter 1) advocate going beyond local protests in order to seek international solidarity. They explain how connecting anti-extractivist movements in Colombia with activists in the UK allowed them to organize protests in London to make the voice of local communities be heard at the headquarters of mining multi-national companies. Ordner (Chapter 2) provides a detailed analysis of the financial resources and human capital that successful movements against the Keystone XL Pipeline in Nebraska had to mobilize in order to activate a variegated "repertoire of contention". In this very same direction, Rodriguez and Loginova (Chapter 3) emphasize the need for "fluidity" in environmental movements. This means an enhanced capacity to be flexible and adapt to changing contexts, community perceptions and political environments. In essence, this fluid strategy involves being able to: a) network and build alliances with other social movements, nationally and internationally; b) seek support of authorities, when possible, or enhance the participation of community members; c) engage and tame legal frameworks and strategize with bureaucrats (and avoid the risk of cooptation and demobilization, as shown in Wahby's analysis of Cairo's movements); and d) be flexible to adapt and operate through coexisting multiple identities and agendas. The "repertoire of contention" towards successful movements included in this edited volume range from reactive actions, mobilization and opposition, such as in cases on anti-mining struggles in Greece (Chapter 4), to different forms of pro-active resistance, such as in the case of pressures of agroindustrial and extractivist systems in the countryside and land regularization and real estate speculation in cities in Mozambique (Chapter 8).

Finally, Partridge (Chapter 18) shows the importance of the wider political context for the success of community activism and collective action, but also the role of the latter in the materialization of national political agendas. This is exemplified in the case of Ecuador where "post-neoliberal" political visions at the national level rely for their actualization on the labour, cooperation, commitment and social resources of indigenous and rural communities. Partridge shows how through their collaborative work on the pipeline project, San Isidro residents have realized a number of objectives that the 2008 Constitution aimed to achieve, improving the quality of life not only of those participating in the project but also of those plants and animals that also benefit from more sustainable farming and irrigation practices.

Community activism and alternatives to the capitalist production of nature

The variety of cases and experiences discussed in this book offers a valuable insight into the different strategies, tactics, motivations, objectives, agendas and aspirations of grassroots activism. Winter (Chapter 18) explores the role of "illegal" camping on public land as a form of resistance to state-corporate power, to the privatization of land, to the housing crisis and the neoliberal regulation of public space(s) and nature(s). Gearey (Chapter 20) explores community resistance to austerity politics by paying attention to radical elder activism – an aspect that is often excluded from scholarship concerning environmental activism. By focusing on the River Adur Valley in West Sussex (UK) she sheds light on the inventive, collaborative and unexpected ways that community elders have worked together to challenge public cuts for road maintenance, education, social housing, waterways management and environmental stewardship. These community activists have created what she calls "gerontocracies of affect" – freeform of elder lead consortia based around an ethics of care, in which custodianship for the environment is the central axiom. Importantly, community elders due to the breadth of their life experiences have been able to contextualize the impacts of prolonged austerity within a broader context of transnational neoliberal strategies that privilege economic development over environmental sustainability and thus should be seen as contributors to wider struggles for the "right to nature" in the Global North, as a way to achieve social and environmental justice and reclaim our right to dignified everyday lives and radically alternative sustainable futures.

This book not only reports several cases of grassroots resistance but also of grassroots innovation, such as urban agriculture, edible landscaping at outdoor domestic spaces, community-operated irrigation systems, low-impact living communities, economic degrowth, permaculture, community actions to support biodiversity conservation and examples of alterative social organization and of community ownership of land and resources. A clear example is the analysis of Outdoor Domestic Spaces analysed by Veríssimo and Name (Chapter 8). These initiatives are often a neglected aspect of radical literature despite the fact that such community initiatives have the potential to protect livelihoods, food sovereignty, environmental quality, community empowerment and local and indigenous knowledges and support social processes that generate more socially and environmentally just outcomes.

Such community attempts not only try to respond effectively and sustainably to the various crises of capitalism (ecological, housing, energy crises), but also in some cases openly discuss the transition to post-capitalist societies. Therefore, it is also an issue of environmental justice to recognize their alternative ways of producing nature and human–nature relations and the emancipatory character of these actions.

Another indicative example of an alternative production of nature comes from Partridge's analysis of a collectively managed irrigation system in Ecuador that has transformed agricultural production in a semi-arid Andean climate while boosting community co-ownership, cooperation and commons-based initiatives. Collective control over shared resources has also supported communities in achieving and maintaining territorial autonomy and legal recognition, and pursuing collective interests through interactions with the state and with other communities and organizations. Levy (Chapter 21) transfers us to a different context, to an advanced economy of the Global North where neoliberal policies prevail, by exploring low-impact living in the UK. Without idealizing the two communities analysed and by considering the serious challenges they face in building alternative ways of living and acting within the limits of capitalism, Levy sheds light on the radical solutions that these communities have the potential to offer to the overlapping crises of housing, food and energy production. Occupying land and challenging private property rights can challenge what David Harvey has termed "accumulation by dispossession" of land, as well as enclosures; and set a way to reclaim the commons.

However, Levy focuses on two cases, Diggerville and Woodville, where people have taken the more conventional route of purchasing the land. Their way of living and interacting with nature as well as their efforts to apply direct democracy offer examples of an alternative social organization and production of nature beyond capitalism. Even though this "alternative destination" is not for everyone, mainly because many people do not have the means (money and/or access to alternative spaces) to create such communities, the examples that Levy discusses offer valuable insights on what a 21st-century social housing could look like (for example, communal food growing, localized renewable energies and alternative housing solutions) while prompting us to question and challenge the current system of land ownership. Ultimately, low-impact communities provide us an example of the latent human potential that flourishes in a culture of co-operation and challenges mainstream ideas and hegemonic discourses about sustainability by providing a glimpse into what the transition to a socially and ecologically, post-capitalist, sustainable culture could look like.

A closer academic–activist dialogue and praxis

Although the discussions about these different subject themes emerge from the cross-fertilization of both academics and activists' accounts of different environmental movements, there are some contributors who speak openly and explicitly about the possibilities and limitations of this dialogue. With regards to international networking, while it is broadly acknowledged as a key contribution to the success of environmental movements, some authors like Florea and Rhoades (Chapter 6) warn us about certain risks. They speak particularly of the "distant gaze" that may make well-intentionated scholars and international activists ignore the vulnerabilities of frontline activists. This can generate misunderstandings and even put frontliners at higher risk in cases of violent forms of coercion, like in the cases in Romania and Colombia where they have been involved. To redress these problems, they provide a number of suggestions to take advantage of opportunities and avoid the risk of making things worse.

Another explicit lesson for this dialogue is provided by Burballa-Noria (Chapter 11). Through the comparative analysis of different movements against unnecessary and imposed megaprojects across Europe, the author attempts to conceptualize demands around an environmental justice framework. This analysis is exemplary of the kind of work that academics can do to make sense of different, disconnected local struggles, and identify commonalities so that new networks can be forged. As we have seen in previous sections, this is not only helpful to scale up contestation from the local to the national and international levels, but also to bridge the gaps between divided and fragmented movements, which often impede the consolidation of actual Red–Green agendas.

On the other hand, Hernandez-Trejo (Chapter 12) calls us to rethink the strict division between scholars and activists that may obscure the socio-political implications of theory. He emphasizes that political ecologists should move beyond the – undoubtedly necessary – theoretical critique of market environmentalism, and get directly involved in politics to socialize their research insights (both theoretical and empirical), while also identifying fields of action that would subvert the dominance of neoliberal conservation. For political ecologists based in academia, a first step to bridge the gap between theoretical cognition and practice is to offer an open critique of academic syllabus as well as the role of experts in legitimizing market environmentalism.

Finally, Re:Common (Chapter 14) emphasizes the need for a close collaboration between civil society organizations and groups, grassroots movements and local communities while, simultaneously, addressing a pressing question to environmentalists and engaged academics: which side are they on, and on what basis do they identify their allies? By critically approaching the alliances between conservation organizations and academics in the case of Rio Tinto and the role that these alliances played in granting scientific legitimacy and accuracy to the company's "no net loss" claims, they call non-governmental organizations (NGOs), activists and engaged academics to openly reject policies, like offsetting, that are fundamentally flawed, instead of wasting their time in exploring how they can offer recommendations for improvement.

As the cases discussed in this book clearly show, the intensification of the economic exploitation of urban and rural landscapes across the globe is increasingly creating profound social, economic, cultural and environmental injustices. The impacts of governmental policies across the globe clearly reflect the class character of land use change under capitalism and the way landlords and the different sections of capital govern the uses of space and nature. So, what is the way forward now?

Claiming our right to nature will require putting forward a completely different understanding that approaches the right to nature as something that can be gained through collective struggle for social and environmental justice and for an alternative mode of organizing production and society. Mainstream discourses and neoliberal ideologies move until today from the promise of perpetual Kantian peace to the threat of the "end of history" and "there is no alternative". But many movements have been saying rather clearly that they cannot see themselves (ourselves) in this continuum. It is time to also say that we dare to bring again at the forefront the revolutionary potential as essential for a new production of nature. This will entail – as the law of the "negation of the negation" indicates – a struggle of opposites until the resolution of their contradiction that will be, inter alia expressed in the end of the capitalist alienation of humans from non-human nature. As a song written in 1931 by Florence Reece reminds us, there won't be any neutrals in this battle and we will not be "all in this together", as one of the key EU environmental slogans of the last decade tried to convince us. There are different and oppositional sides. And we are called to decide on which side we are. And, as always, we won't have any chance unless we organize.

INDEX